The Militant Face of Democracy

Democratic peace theory – the argument that democracies very rarely go to war with each other – has come under attack recently for being too naïve and for neglecting the vast amount of wars fought by democracies, especially since the end of the Cold War. This volume offers a fresh perspective by arguing that the same norms that are responsible for the democratic peace can be argued to be responsible for democratic war-proneness. The authors show that democratic norms, which are usually understood to cause peaceful behaviour, are heavily contested when dealing with a non-democratic other. The book thus integrates democratic peace and democratic war into one consistent theoretical perspective, emphasising the impact of national identity. The book concludes by arguing that all democracies have a 'weak spot' where they would be willing to engage militarily.

ANNA GEIS is Professor of International Relations at the University of Magdeburg, Germany.

HARALD MÜLLER is Executive Director of the Peace Research Institute Frankfurt (PRIF) and Professor of International Relations at Goethe University Frankfurt, Germany.

NIKLAS SCHÖRNIG is a senior research fellow at the Peace Research Institute Frankfurt (PRIF), Germany.

The Militant Face of Democracy

Liberal Forces for Good

Edited by

Anna Geis

Harald Müller

Niklas Schörnig

CAMBRIDGE
UNIVERSITY PRESS

CAMBRIDGE
UNIVERSITY PRESS

University Printing House, Cambridge CB2 8BS, United Kingdom

Published in the United States of America by Cambridge University Press, New York

Cambridge University Press is part of the University of Cambridge.

It furthers the University's mission by disseminating knowledge in the pursuit of education, learning and research at the highest international levels of excellence.

www.cambridge.org
Information on this title: www.cambridge.org/9781107037403

© Cambridge University Press 2013

First published 2013

Printed in the United Kingdom by CPI Group Ltd, Croydon CRO 4YY

A catalogue record for this publication is available from the British Library

Library of Congress Cataloguing in Publication data
The militant face of democracy : liberal forces for good / edited by
Anna Geis, Harald Müller and Niklas Schörnig.
    pages   cm
Includes bibliographical references and index.
ISBN 978-1-107-03740-3 (hardback)
1. Military policy.   2. Intervention (International law)   3. Democracy.
4. Liberalism.   5. Liberty.   I. Geis, Anna.
UA11.M4625 2013
355′.0335–dc23   2013012188

ISBN 978-1-107-03740-3 Hardback

Contents

Figures

Tables

Contributors

UNA BECKER-JAKOB is a research associate at the Peace Research Institute Frankfurt (PRIF) and studied Political Science and English in Frankfurt, Germany and Galway, Ireland. Her research interests include social-constructivist approaches to foreign policy, democratic peace and justice in international relations. She also specialises in the theory and practice of arms control and disarmament, in particular biological weapons control and biosecurity, and in the security policies of Ireland and Canada. Her most important publications include 'Democracy and Nuclear Arms Control: Destiny or Ambiguity?', *Security Studies* 17 (4) (2008), co-authored with Harald Müller and Simone Wisotzki, and 'Good International Citizens: Canada, Germany, and Sweden', in Harald Müller and Carmen Wunderlich (eds.) (2013) *Norm Dynamics in Multilateral Arms Control: Interests, Conflicts, and Justice Claims*, co-authored with Gregor Hofmann, Harald Müller and Carmen Wunderlich.

JOHANNA ECKERT studied international politics in Frankfurt and Lyon with a focus on German–French relations and received her Master's degree from the Goethe University Frankfurt, Germany, in 2007. After two years in the private sector, she has been working for the regional government authority since 2009. Currently she is carrying out a mediation project in connection with the expansion of the Frankfurt international airport, including a dialogue process with all stakeholders and public participation.

MARCO FEY is a research associate at the Peace Research Institute Frankfurt (PRIF). He studied International Relations, International Law, Philosophy and History at the Goethe University Frankfurt. He was a visiting researcher at the Royal Military Academy Sandhurst (RMAS) in March 2010 and a visiting scholar at the Institute for Security and Conflict Studies (ISCS) at George Washington University from July to December 2011. His research focuses on British and US foreign and defence policy. His most recent publications include 'The Ideal Type of the Democratic Soldier in Britain', in Sabine Mannitz (ed.) 2012, *Democratic Civil–Military Relations: Soldiering in 21st Century Europe* and *Democracy, the Armed Forces and Military Deployment: The 'Second Social Contract' is on the Line* (PRIF Report No. 108, 2011, Frankfurt, Germany, co-authored with Harald Müller, Sabine Mannitz and Niklas Schörnig).

ANNA GEIS is Professor of International Relations at the University of Magdeburg, Germany. She received her PhD from the University of Hamburg. From 2002 to 2009, she worked as a research fellow and project director at the Peace Research Institute Frankfurt (PRIF); from 2009 to 2012 she was a senior research fellow in the Cluster of Excellence, 'The Formation of Normative Orders', at the Goethe University Frankfurt. She was appointed Acting Professor at the Goethe University Frankfurt and the Ludwig Maximilians University Munich. Her fields of interests are theories of peace and war, critical theory, democratic theory, constructivism, critical governance studies, recognition in international relations and German foreign policy. Her book publications include *Democratic Wars: Looking at the Dark Side of Democratic Peace* (2006, co-edited with Lothar Brock and Harald Müller), *Den Krieg überdenken: Kriegsbegriffe und Kriegstheorien in der Kontroverse* (editor, 2006) and *Schattenseiten des Demokratischen Friedens: Zur Kritik einer Theorie liberaler Außen- und Sicherheitspolitik* (2007, co-edited with Harald Müller and Wolfgang Wagner). Her articles on democratic peace/democratic war have been published in, *inter alia*, *Politische Vierteljahresschrift*, *Zeitschrift für Internationale Beziehungen*, *Leviathan*, *International Relations* and *Review of International Studies*.

HARALD MÜLLER, Executive Director of the Peace Research Institute Frankfurt (PRIF), received his PhD from the Goethe University Frankfurt, where he teaches as Professor of International Relations. He has also been teaching at the Technical University Darmstadt, the Johns Hopkins University Center for International Studies in Bologna, Italy, the Hebrew University of Jerusalem and the Sorbonne, Paris. As one of the few German IR scholars who bridge the gap between academic work and diplomatic practice, he has participated in four Review Conferences of the Nuclear Non-Proliferation Treaty as a member of the German delegation, served seven years in the UN Secretary-General's Advisory Council on Disarmament and was a member of the IAEA Expert Group on Multilateral Nuclear Arrangements in 2004/5. Since 2011, he has been the Vice-President of the EU Consortium on Non-Proliferation and Disarmament, a body advising the EU member states and the European External Action Service. He has written, co-authored, edited and co-edited 14 books on non-proliferation, arms control and disarmament. Besides this specialisation, Dr Müller has contributed to the theory of international security cooperation, communicative action in international negotiations, democratic peace and the role of justice in international politics. His most recent book is *Building a New World Order*, 2009.

NIKLAS SCHÖRNIG is a senior research fellow at the Peace Research Institute Frankfurt (PRIF) and received his PhD from the Goethe University Frankfurt, where he was appointed substitute Professor in Winter 2011/12. In 2012 he received the ZIB-Award from the *Zeitschrift für Internationale Beziehungen* (German Journal of International Relations) for best article 2006–11. His research focuses on, *inter alia*, the transformation of Western armies after the end of the Cold War, US and European defence-industry issues, arms dynamics and arms control, liberal and realist International Relations theory and Australian foreign policy. His most recent publications include 'Killer Drones: The Silver Bullet of Democratic Warfare?', *Security Dialogue* 43 (4) (2012), with Frank Sauer, *Auf dem Weg zu Just Peace Governance: Beiträge zum Auftakt des neuen Forschungsprogramms der HSFK*, 2011, co-edited with Claudia Baumgart-Ochse, Simone Wisotzki and Jonas Wolff and *The Roo and the Dragon: Australia's Foreign Policy towards China during the Rudd Era* (PRIF-Report No. 99, 2010, Frankfurt, Germany).

STEPHANIE SOHNIUS studied Political Science, Psychology and Philosophy and received her MA in Political Science from the University of Frankfurt, Germany. One of her research interests has been the analysis of Palestinian and Israeli environmental NGOs in peacebuilding processes (in cooperation with PRIF/Peace Research Institute in the Middle East). Her recent research focuses on the foreign policy of the United States. Her publications include *Demokratie auf dem Rückzug? Zur Konfrontation zwischen amerikanischem Präsidenten und Kongress über einen Truppenabzug aus dem Irak* (HSFK-Standpunkte, No. 5/2007, Frankfurt, Germany).

CARMEN WUNDERLICH is a research associate at the Peace Research Institute Frankfurt (PRIF). She studied Political Science, Philosophy and German Language and Literature at the University of Frankfurt. She is currently working on theories of international norms and so-called rogue states as counter-hegemonic norm entrepreneurs. Her further research interests include arms control and disarmament, critical constructivist theory and Swedish foreign and security policy. She was a pre-doctoral fellow at the Vienna Center for Disarmament and Non-Proliferation in early 2012. She is co-editor, together with Harald Müller, of *Norm Dynamics in Multilateral Arms Control: Norms, Interests, and Justice*, 2013.

Acknowledgements

Democratic actors fight wars for worthwhile reasons, or so they believe, or at least so they say. This may be so or not, but it does not change the fact that numerous fatalities are claimed, however valuable the reasons may be. This moral dilemma cannot be escaped, certainly not with euphemisms like 'just war' and 'humanitarian intervention' that have become quite fashionable: every decision to take up arms is fraught with hazards and is of enormous weight, which is not always reflected in the ways in which some democracies take this fateful decision. *Some* democracies – for the variance among them is quite strong.

The moral trouble – concern for the victims – and the academic curiosity – the reasons for variance – have been the driving motivations behind the project the results of which are presented in this book. To probe the variance among democracies with regard to the use of force, a rather extensive research design and project organisation was required. Comparative research of that size cannot be done by a single person – no one could combine the in-depth expertise on a sizeable number of countries. In order to make sure that the comparison would arrive at valid results, contributors had to comply strictly with the requirements of the unified research design: this is a monograph that could not be written by a single person. For the admirable discipline with which our collaborators subjected themselves to the straitjacket of the design, the editors owe them immense gratitude.

We are very grateful that the German Research Foundation (*Deutsche Forschungsgemeinschaft*) funded the research project, which enabled us to see the work through. We also thank the Cluster of Excellence 'The Formation of Normative Orders' for additional support and our cluster colleagues for very useful comments. We are much obliged to Lothar Brock for his substantial input into the theoretical development of the project and his enduring support. Several people contributed to the progress of the research design in the first phase and did some empirical work which was useful for its implementation: we thank

Claudia Baumgart-Ochse, Catherine Götze, Fabian Grabbe, Andreas Hasenclever and Daniela Schüngel.

Our research assistants were the workhorses of the project; without them, the empirical work could not have been accomplished. Sebastian Dietrich, Fredrik Doms, Karl Hampel, Nicole Heider and Susanne Hemmerling provided source and document research and participated in the vast coding exercise. Annabel Schmitz, finally, not only participated in the document research and coding but mastered the demanding job of editing the final manuscript with ease and excellence and we are particularly grateful for her assistance.

The theoretical framework and preliminary empirical results of the project have been presented at numerous occasions and we thank the following colleagues for very helpful comments: Sven Chojnacki, Sebastian Harnisch, Cathleen Kantner, John MacMillan, Hanns W. Maull, Matthew Rendall, Thomas Risse, the late Volker Rittberger, Stefanie Sifft, Georg Sørensen, Stephen Watts and Michael Zürn.

The numerous in-house discussions we had at the Peace Research Institute Frankfurt (PRIF) were of great value in refining our design and correcting shortcomings in the empirical work. We cannot enumerate all those who were of help, but wish to address a particular 'thanks' to our former colleague Wolfgang Wagner. Finally, PRIF researchers Anja Jakobi, Dirk Peters and Jonas Wolff scrutinised parts of the manuscript, helping us tremendously in the final refinement of the results of our work. We are also very grateful to the two anonymous reviewers of Cambridge University Press whose highly instructive comments and suggestions were very helpful for improving our first version of the manuscript. The diligence and empathy which guided their – quite critical – comments in the first round and their friendly assistance in completing the manuscript in the second round demonstrated an exemplary professional ethics that deserves highest praise.

Last but not least, we owe a debt of gratitude to all the cooperative people whom we met during our fieldwork in the seven countries analysed in this book. By acting as interviewees or by helping to procure documents, they were indispensable for our work.

As this long list shows, there were many people who contributed to what the readers will find in the following pages. Nevertheless, as usual, it is the editors and the chapter authors who bear the responsibility for the final product.

Anna Geis
Harald Müller
Niklas Schörnig

Abbreviations

ABM	anti-ballistic missile
ADF	Australian Defence Force
AMF-A	Allied Command Europe Mobile Force's Air component
ANZAC	Australian and New Zealand Army Corps
ANZUS	Australia, New Zealand, United States Security Treaty
AP	anti-personnel
BND	Bundesnachrichtendienst (German intelligence service)
BQ	Bloc Québécois
BWC	Biological Weapons Convention
CBW	chemical and biological weapons
CCW	Convention on Certain Conventional Weapons
CD	Conference on Disarmament
CDU/CSU	Christlich Demokratische Union Deutschlands/ Christlich-Soziale Union
CFSP	Common Foreign and Security Policy
CIA	Central Intelligence Agency
CICC	Coalition for the International Criminal Court
CSCE	Commission on Security and Cooperation in Europe
CTBT	Comprehensive Nuclear Test Ban Treaty
CWC	Chemical Weapons Convention
DFAIT	Department of Foreign Affairs and International Trade (Canada)
DFAT	Department of Foreign Affairs and Trade (Australia)
DND	Department of National Defence (Canada)
DP	democratic peace
EC	European Community
ESDP	European Security and Defence Policy
EUFOR	European Union Force
FAZ	*Frankfurter Allgemeine Zeitung*

FCO	Foreign and Commonwealth Office (United Kingdom)
FDP	Freie Demokratische Partei
FMCT	Fissile Material Cut-off Treaty
FN	Front National
FRG	Federal Republic of Germany
IAEA	International Atomic Energy Agency
ICC	International Criminal Court
IFOR	Implementation Force
ILC	International Law Commission
INF	Intermediate-Range Nuclear Forces
INTERFET	International Force for East Timor
ISAF	International Security Assistance Force
JSCOT	Joint Standing Committee on Treaties (Australia)
KFOR	Kosovo Force
KLA	Kosovo Liberation Army
MBT	Mine Ban Treaty
MONUC	United Nations Organization Mission in the Democratic Republic of Congo
MP	Member of Parliament
NAC	New Agenda Coalition
NACD	non-proliferation, arms control and disarmament
NDP	New Democratic Party
NGO	non-governmental organisation
NORAD	North American Aerospace Defense Command
NPT	Nuclear Non-Proliferation Treaty
NSS	National Security Strategy
NWS	nuclear weapon state
NYT	*New York Times*
OPEC	Organization of the Petroleum Exporting Countries
OSCE	Organization for Security and Co-operation in Europe
P5	five permanent members of the United Nations Security Council
PC	Progressive Conservative Party
PCF	Parti Communiste Français
PDS	Partei des Demokratischen Sozialismus
PfP	Partnership for Peace
PM	Prime Minister
PS	Parti Socialiste
R2P	Responsibility to Protect

RMA	Revolution in Military Affairs
RPR	Rassemblement pour la République
SALT	Strategic Arms Limitation Treaty
SDR	Strategic Defence Review
SFOR	Stabilisation Force
SMH	*Sydney Morning Herald*
SPD	Sozialdemokratische Partei Deutschlands
START	Strategic Arms Reduction Treaty
SWERAP	Swedish Rapid Reaction Force
SZ	*Süddeutsche Zeitung*
UDF	Union pour la Démocratie Française
UMP	Union pour un mouvement populaire
UNMOVIC	United Nations Monitoring, Verification and Inspection Commission
UNPROFOR	United Nations Protection Force
UNSC	United Nations Security Council
UNSCR	United Nations Security Council Resolution
WEU	Western European Union
WMD	weapons of mass destruction
WT	*Washington Times*

Part I

Introduction

1 Investigating 'democratic wars' as the flipside of 'democratic peace'

Anna Geis and Harald Müller

1 Introduction

1.1 The aim of this book

This book sets out to tackle two issues that have remained in the shadow of mainstream 'democratic peace' (DP) research: why do democracies fight wars beyond self-defence, and why do they do so with strikingly different frequency? In furthering knowledge about 'democratic wars', we offer a necessary and innovative amendment to DP theory. We also contribute to critical self-reflection about liberal foreign policies by elucidating the dilemmas that result from our liberal convictions and norms. Democratic leaders usually envision their countries to be 'forces for good' in international politics, portraying their foreign policies as serving a higher common good beyond narrow self-interest. In extreme cases, this might pertain to the use of military force. Given that the use of force is the most sensitive issue within democratic polities, involving high costs and risks, it remains a perennial task of peace and conflict studies to increase self-awareness of the pitfalls of our own convictions.

Our volume illuminates 'democratic wars' from a theoretical perspective and provides an empirical analysis of seven liberal democracies, as this introductory chapter will explicate. First of all, we outline the problematic political implications and the neglected fields and lacunae of mainstream DP research that we seek to address with our study. Section 2 introduces the concept of normative ambivalence that is central to our approach. Section 3 discusses the concept of 'democratic wars' and then goes on to elaborate the ambivalence of norms in the field of 'democratic wars' in more detail, considering the liberal purposes, the liberal 'other', the issue of rightful authority and the ambivalences within the democratic actors themselves, including the relationship between norms and interests. Section 4 explains the structure of the book.

1.2   The political hazards of democratic peace theory

Democratic peace is, without doubt, something positive. It frees an increasing number of interstate dyads from the scourge of war and opens up the long-term perspective of a peaceful world. This effect and the prospects that it offers are celebrated by DP research and even more so in their adaptation by the body politic. The 'dark side', the frequent participation of democracies in military operations, is noted but dismissed as a less interesting collateral phenomenon; it has affected the theory of democratic peace very little. This disregard is dangerous: understanding why we go to war and how we justify wars is crucial for a self-critical inspection of democratic polities. Only the combined study of democratic peace and war can prevent us from making all-too-optimistic claims about the civilising force of democracy.

Since the 1990s, mainstream DP scholarship has had practical policy implications: the truncated equation 'democracy is peace' suggested the global promotion of democracy as a Western foreign policy imperative (Ish-Shalom 2006). When democracy promotion is conducted by peaceful means, few people object. However, when members of the George W. Bush administration referred broadly to democratic peace in order to justify forcible democratisation in Iraq, a peace theory was perverted into a legitimisation of war. This brought DP scholarship under heavy attack as being politically naive at best and serving as handmaidens of US imperial power at worst (Smith 2007; Steele 2007; Hobson 2011). The political (mis)use of (positivist) DP research is highly problematic, but should not result in abandoning the study of the relationship between democracy and peace. The present volume is motivated by the idea that analysing 'democratic wars' as the 'dark side' of democratic peace not only enhances our knowledge about the conflict behaviour of democracies, but also counteracts simplified political messages.

1.3   The gaps in mainstream DP research

Liberal DP scholarship has been blossoming for more than 25 years. It has been extended ever more to issues of democratic foreign policies, but domestic decisions on war and peace have remained at the heart of DP research.[1] The core finding of dyadic DP theories states that consolidated democracies do not (or rarely) fight each other, but are nevertheless as war-prone as other regime types (Chan 1997: 62–3). In contrast

---

[1] For overviews of the literature, see Müller and Wolff (2006) and Geis and Wagner (2011); for a detailed discussion of a range of DP hypotheses, see also Rousseau (2005).

to the dominant dyadic approaches, monadic DP theories claim that democracies are in general more peaceful than non-democracies, especially if one takes into account manifold crisis activities preceding the use of force: democracies are slightly less involved in war, initiate wars and militarised disputes less frequently and tend to seek negotiated conflict resolution more often (Russett and Oneal 2001: 95–6, 116, 122; Rousseau 2005: 14, 24). However, the evidence of these findings is weaker than evidence relating to interdemocratic peace. Democracies *do* fight wars against non-democracies, and they *do* initiate wars and other militarised conflicts with them from time to time (Rousseau 2005). As Charles Lipson (2003: 3) states:

[I]t is clear that democracies go to war often. In the twentieth century, for instance, Britain went to war more frequently than Germany. The US has obviously been willing to use force repeatedly, both to defend its material interests and to extend its values. Moreover, democracies do not merely respond to provocations by others. They often seize the initiative and sometimes attack first. We need to understand, then, how norms and beliefs could lead democracies to make war against some states but not against others.

Indeed, the two decades following the end of the Cold War marked a liberal heyday, with Western democracies shaping world politics as never before in history – by peaceful as well as forcible means. During these years, liberal democracies made a substantial contribution to the global transformation of war: via their armament and arms control policies, their risk-sensitive way of warfare, their alignment policies, their normative justifications of war and their interpretations of international law (Shaw 2005; Evangelista *et al.* 2008). Their wars left a strong imprint on the regions concerned and ultimately on international order; their frequent justification using liberal norms and principles warrants the parlance of a specific *liberal* interventionism.

The relationship between democracy and war is thus delicate: Western democracies possess overwhelming material capabilities to fight wars, but the use of force is restrained by numerous legal provisos and by norms and values deeply rooted in their societies. The preference for peaceful conflict resolution, respect for human rights, fear of casualties and high material costs are among the norms inherent in political liberalism. According to normative variants of DP theory, such features help to explain the peace-proneness of liberal democracies. However, increasing liberal interventionism following the end of the Cold War has thrown the militant side of democracies – acknowledged but neglected by mainstream DP research – into sharp relief. Although dyadic DP research is well aware of this Janus face of democracies (Risse-Kappen 1995: 492), its work has been mainly dedicated to explaining the peaceful relations among democracies rather than to investigating the militant side. As a consequence, studies on the separate democratic peace abound and have been celebrated as a rare example of a progressive research programme in International Relations (Chernoff 2004), whereas complementary research on the external use of force by democracies has remained comparatively scarce. '[T]he democratic peace proposition by itself does not deal with the issue of how democracies get into war with nondemocracies' (Moore 2004: 13).

Addressing this lacuna, we pursue a research agenda on 'democratic wars' that is designed to complement DP research, not to dismiss it. Such an approach is overdue. Indeed, liberal interventionism and recent 'liberal wars' have attracted enhanced attention from scholars outside the DP community (e.g. Freedman 2005, 2006; Shaw 2005; Vasquez 2005; Chandler 2006, 2010). The debate on 'liberal wars' should thus be integrated into a contextualised DP theory as it illuminates neglected aspects of democratic violence. Developing the concept of 'democratic war' as the flipside of democratic peace also ties in with accounts of the ambivalence of liberalism throughout its philosophical and political history (e.g. Doyle 1983a, 1983b; Owen 1997; Peceny 1999; Barkawi and Laffey 2001; MacMillan 2004, 2005; Jahn 2005; Desch 2007/8).

Like mainstream DP research, 'liberal war' studies neglect an important fact that adds to the puzzle about the democratic 'Janus face': democracies go to war with significantly different frequency. The formula 'democracies never fight wars with each other but conduct armed conflicts with non-democracies as frequently as autocracies' is thus not sufficiently precise: a small group of democracies such as the United States, the United Kingdom, France, Australia, India and Israel have been involved comparatively often in military conflicts, while some democracies take part rather rarely and others abstain altogether (Müller 2004a: 494–7; Chojnacki 2006: 21). Neither liberal DP research nor the critics of liberalism can consistently explain within their theoretical frameworks why *all* liberal democracies do not behave in the same manner, if the assumption is valid that certain institutional and normative causal mechanisms should take effect in an average democratic polity, or that liberalism should produce an invariable dichotomy of friends (fellow liberals) and enemies (non-liberals) (Müller and Wolff 2006). In order to understand 'democratic war', we also have to understand this variance.

We explore variance in the external use of force from a dyadic DP perspective: we assume that the same domestic preferences, institutions and norms that promote peacefulness in interaction with other democracies can under certain circumstances also permit the legitimisation of violence in interactions with some non-democracies. In that, we draw an analogy to the use of force within democratic polities: using force is not ruled out per se in the domestic sphere of democracies, but its legality and legitimacy are governed by the respective legal order and politico-cultural norms, which vary between democracies. Transferred to the external use of force, decisions on war participation will have to meet certain domestic and international legitimacy standards. First, they must be in accordance with procedural requirements, i.e. fulfil standards of domestic and international lawful decision-making, and, second, they must be justified with substantial reasons acceptable to the domestic public (Müller and Wolff 2006: 61; see also Brock et al. 2006: 197–204).

Both considerations regarding legitimating democratic wars refer back to two basic modes of explaining democratic peace, i.e. normative and institutional explanations, which require differentiation. *Normative-cultural* accounts of democratic peace assume that democratic actors transfer the norms of peaceful conflict resolution, tolerance and fairness, which they have gradually learned and internalised within their domestic communities, to the international realm (Russett 1993: 31–3). We qualify this perspective and consider liberal-democratic norms as being *inherently ambivalent*. Transfer beyond borders does not necessarily engender peaceful consequences: depending on the counterpart, they can legitimate the peaceful settlement of conflicts as well as the use of force; they are thus constraining and enabling at the same time.

Rationalist-institutional explanations rest on the basic assumption that democratic actors are averse to costs and risks (Fearon 1994). Whereas citizens reject the material and human costs that they would have to bear when drawn into a war (beyond self-defence), it is the primary interest of governments to stay in power. Due to various institutional mechanisms that provide for the responsiveness, accountability and control of democratic governments such as elections, parliamentary control and public scrutiny (e.g. Auerswald 2000), war-prone executives will feel restrained by the peaceful preferences of their citizens and weigh the benefits and costs of wars cautiously. These assumptions also require modifications: democratic governments are restrained by parliaments to quite different degrees, since Western parliaments possess differing oversight powers concerning military deployments (Dieterich et al. 2009; Peters and Wagner 2011). What is more important, not even severe institutional constraints would be sufficient to prevent democracies from going to war if the governmental decision was supported by a majority of the public: it may be misleading to assume prior and unchangeable peaceful preferences on the part of the people.

2   The concept of normative ambivalence

Among post-Cold War Western political leaders, the idea of a militant liberal internationalism has been championed most pronouncedly by former British Prime Minister Tony Blair (see Chapter 4). In his seminal Chicago speech of 24 April 1999, during the Kosovo War, Blair outlined a 'new doctrine of international community' and summed up the core ideas of liberal interventionism:

> Our armed forces have been busier than ever – delivering humanitarian aid, deterring attack on defenceless people, backing up UN resolutions and occasionally engaging in major wars as we did in the Gulf in 1991 and are currently doing in the Balkans ... Now our actions are guided by a more subtle blend of mutual self interest and moral purpose in defending the values we cherish. In the end values and interests merge. If we can establish and spread the values of liberty, the rule of law, human rights and an open society, then that is in our national interests too. The spread of our values makes us safer.[2]

When contemporary democracies use force, they often intervene in ongoing conflicts (Chojnacki 2006) and occasionally start armed conflict themselves. Such interventions are directed not towards acquiring territory, but towards enforcing a normative order defined in terms of universal values. In contrast to the rationalist meta-theories underpinning the bulk of DP studies,[3] our inquiry into democratic wars starts from the insight that, as shown in Blair's speech, Western politicians have taken recourse predominantly to *normative* arguments when they have had to legitimate decisions on war and peace to their constituencies. Thus, our study is informed by social-constructivism. The preferences of actors are not considered as fixed and their actions as primarily driven by rational utility maximisation and a 'logic of consequentialism', but as malleable and guided by shared norms and a 'logic of appropriateness' (Risse 2000; Müller 2004b).[4] In a juxtaposition of normative and structural models, DP research has often treated norms

---

[2] Tony Blair, 'Doctrine of the International Community', Address to the Economic Club, Chicago, 24 April 1999.

[3] For a comprehensive treatment of various approaches to democratic peace and war, see Rousseau (2005). For a critique of the dominant ontology and epistemology of (US) DP research, see Steele (2007).

[4] 'The appropriateness of rules includes both cognitive and normative components ... Rules are followed because they are seen as natural, rightful, expected, and legitimate. Actors seek to fulfil the obligations encapsulated in a role, an identity, a membership in a political community or group, and the ethos, practices and expectations of its institutions. Embedded in a social collectivity, they do what they see as appropriate for themselves in a specific type of situation' (March and Olsen 2004: 3).

and institutions as separate phenomena (Rousseau 2005: 7), although norms and institutions are intricately linked. If a norm is defined as a 'standard of appropriate behaviour for actors with a given identity', institutions embody collections of such standards, defining appropriate behaviour for specific actors (Finnemore and Sikkink 1998: 891). From our perspective, it thus makes more sense to focus on the comprehensive role of *norms* in an analysis of the relationship between democracy, peace and war. Constructivist research emphasises the importance of ideational factors in structuring political actions: the material capabilities of a state are not treated as objective pushing and pulling factors, but the focus is on communicative processes within a society that interpret and negotiate how to use (or not use) such capabilities in the light of prevalent norms. Material and ideational structures are not determining, not even in a probabilistic sense, but constraining and enabling certain interpretations and ensuing actions.

This perspective alerts us to the contradictions faced by liberal interventionism in practice: political judgements on the use of force have to cope with enormous complexity, imperfect knowledge and moral/political ambivalences (MacMillan 2005: 7). People are killed in order to save people; the rule of law is disregarded in order to instal it; international security is undermined in order to strengthen it. The controversial public debates within democracies as well as disputes between democracies about the appropriateness and legitimacy of the use of force indicate that democratic publics are quite aware of these problems. The enhanced emphasis on liberal values in justifying the use of force by democracies after the end of the Cold War has intensified these political and moral dilemmas for belligerent democracies:

[I]t is the efforts by democratic states to exercise and/or justify the use of force in terms of higher values – the pursuit of higher goods – than the pursuit of state interests alone that add layers of politically significant complexity and create tensions and dissonance between the proclaimed ends of foreign policy and the means through which these are pursued. (MacMillan 2005: 3)

The hazardous consequences of fighting for the good has informed our key starting proposition: the sources of the contradiction between the normative value of intentions and results are rooted in ambivalences that are already present in the normative setting that leads some to advocate and others to oppose military action in the same situation. To further clarify: this ambivalence, we maintain, does not emerge from contradictory norms, but resides in the ambivalent meaning of each of the norms themselves. This basic concept underpins the approach taken in this volume.

3   Democratic war and its ambivalences

3.1   *Liberal wars and democratic wars*

The normative underpinning of recent wars fought by democracies has been reflected by the scholarly literature on 'liberal wars':[5] Lawrence Freedman (2005: 98) means by 'liberal wars' wars 'conducted in pursuit of a humanitarian agenda ... The ideal type for a liberal war is that it is altruistic in inspiration and execution ... It is liberating and empowering while involving as few casualties as possible.' In a similar vein, John Vasquez considers the Kosovo War as 'the quintessential liberal war of our time' (Vasquez 2005: 311). Liberal wars are, according to Vasquez's definition, 'wars that are based on moral claims to do what is right rather than claims about the national interest. These wars include wars for democracy or humanitarian wars arising out of armed humanitarian interventions' (Vasquez 2005: 307).

The phenomenon of 'liberal wars' as such is not as new as the recent debate might suggest (Doyle 1983a, 1983b; Owen 1997). Liberal justifications of the use of force were submitted, for example, by British politicians as early as in the Crimean War of 1854 (Martin 1963) or by the United States in the late nineteenth century or in the context of both world wars (Peceny 1999). However, liberal interventionism gained new relevance after the end of the Cold War when there was a new wave of democratisation and when the claims by Western democracies of creating a liberal global governance architecture could unfold untrammelled. Since then, there has been no fundamental ideological challenge to the liberal ordering project advanced by powerful other states,[6] and the use of force has become a means of liberal global governance (Duffield 2001).

The concept of 'democratic wars' is related to, but not fully congruent with, that of 'liberal wars'. While Freedman and Vasquez conceive of the latter as wars that interveners justify with humanitarian or moral claims, the former concept is derived from DP research and may encompass three phenomena: first, a war between democracies, hence reversing the term 'democratic peace', which means the absence

---

[5] The term has also been used to describe historical cases of wars fought by liberal democracies; see, for example, Owen (1997). A 'liberal war' can refer to colonial wars and to imperial wars, as well as to seemingly altruistically motivated liberal 'crusades' in the sense of an 'imperialism of good intentions' (ascribed to US President Woodrow Wilson). See Joas (2000: 56–64).

[6] Violent non-state actors such as transnational radical Islamic terrorists attempt to challenge the further extension of liberal norms and values, but they lack the material capacities to make this a challenge comparable to that presented by powerful states or groups of states (such as the former Soviet Union and its affiliated states).

of war among democracies. According to DP research, however, such wars between (consolidated) democracies have not occurred. Second, in a broad understanding, it could simply refer to wars fought by democracies. Third, a more specific conception – which is closer to the understanding of 'liberal wars' and which is employed in this study – signifies wars that are fought for liberal purposes, i.e. wars that are justified by reasons that are compatible with liberal norms. In contrast to Freedman's and Vasquez's ideal-type notion of 'liberal wars', these norms need not be restricted to a humanitarian agenda only.

3.2   War for what? The ambivalence of regulative liberal norms

What are the 'popular, liberal purposes' that, according to Michael Doyle (1983a: 230), provide the reasons other than self-defence for which democracies take up arms? Such 'purposes' can be read as *regulative norms*, which prohibit fighting certain types of war that are incompatible with liberal values (such as conquest or genocide) but permit others (such as preventing genocide). We take Immanuel Kant's essay on *Perpetual Peace* (Kant 1795) as the source of inspiration for differentiating the spectrum of such liberal purposes. Kant is most pertinent here as his approach to liberal internationalism is the most systematic and comprehensive elaboration of the universe of law-oriented, normative liberal thought on international politics. His *Perpetual Peace* was a complex and visionary proposal for establishing a law-based peace that would have to rely on three entwined levels of rights: domestic constitutional law, international law and cosmopolitan law (Eberl 2008). In addition, Kant was highly war-averse and called for non-interference in the domestic affairs of other states out of respect for the autonomous evolution of law-based communities by their own, self-determined efforts. He certainly had no intention of delivering justifications for the use of force. If ambivalences that opened the argumentative space for such justifications appeared in his work, this would underline the proposition of a basic ambivalence in liberal thought towards peace and war.

The first definitive article in *Perpetual Peace* (Kant 1795: 204–8) states that the civil constitution of each state shall be republican. Only republican constitutions ensure the legal division of political powers and prevent the self-authorisation of governments; the will of citizens must be taken into account in such constitutions. Republican constitutions enhance the peace-proneness of states as the citizens who have to bear the costs of war will have great hesitation about consenting to a war. A militant liberal reading of this article, however, might take this logic to an extreme and postulate forcible republican 'regime change' in order to promote peace in the long run.

The second definitive article postulates that the law of nations shall be founded on a federation of free states (Kant 1795: 208–13). It is a command of reason that states exit the lawless 'state of nature' that would lead them into permanent wars with each other and instead restrict their freedom of action and enter lawful contracts with each other. The ultimate goal is not simply to establish peace contracts after a war but to establish a pacific union that would endeavour to end all wars. This article reflects the paramount importance of international law for securing peace, and the idea of the *foedus pacificum* has been read as a precursor to the United Nations Organization (Czempiel 1996: 93–7). Nevertheless, a militant liberal reading of this article could justify 'order wars', which are reactions to grave breaches of international law and which are fought to enforce or to restore a lawful global or regional order.

The third definitive article is devoted to cosmopolitan law (Kant 1795: 213–17). Kant has couched this law in rather minimalist terms – intended as a critique of the colonial practices of his time – as limited to the conditions of universal hospitality. Men, as beings who commonly inhabit the Earth, shall have the right to visit foreign territories, and a visitor who enters foreign territory and behaves peacefully shall not be treated in a hostile manner. Notwithstanding this specification of cosmopolitan law as visitors' law, advocates of a cosmopolitan world order have cited this article as the authoritative source of comprehensive, universally valid human rights (for a critique, see Eberl 2008: 148–83, 222–55). A militant liberal reading could thus construct a case for a 'humanitarian intervention' that legitimates intervention in the internal affairs of a sovereign state responsible for gross violations of human rights (Habermas 1999; Brock 2002).

Hence, three ideal types of 'democratic wars' can be deduced from these considerations: wars for democratic 'regime change', 'order wars' and 'humanitarian interventions' constitute a spectrum of liberal purposes that can motivate democratic wars and supply the respective justifications in political discourse. These justifications, however, cannot stop at elaborating a *purpose*. They must also name the *adversary* against whom the purpose must be enforced by violent means.

3.3   War against whom? The ambivalence of the 'non-democratic other'

Social-constructivist explanations for democratic peace maintain that democratic polities are aware of their politico-ethical and institutional particularity. They identify with other collectives of the same kind. Thomas Risse-Kappen (1995) and John Owen (1997) have argued that this mutual identification leads to community-building and thereby ensures peaceful relations among democracies. As critical security studies on collective identity formation show (e.g. Campbell 1992), the flipside of identity construction is the demarcation of an 'other', who in extreme cases can be perceived as an abhorrent foe. Inquiring into such constructions of self and other can establish whether there are resonant enemy images apt to mobilise citizens in favour of a war and to enhance the perceived legitimacy of military action.

Liberal thought has dealt with its 'others' from the very beginning; a recent rediscovery of Kant's figure of the 'unjust enemy' in his *Metaphysics of Morals* (1797: 487, § 60) exposes these seeds of self-empowerment to interventionism contained within liberalism itself (Müller 2006). Such an enemy is characterised as one 'whose publicly expressed will (whether by word or deed) reveals a maxim by which, if it were made a universal rule, any condition of peace among nations would be impossible and, instead, a state of nature would be perpetuated' (Kant 1797: 487, § 60). Ascribing 'unjust enemy' attributes to non-republican entities is not an a priori feature of Kant's thinking that would lead to an indiscriminate hostile labelling, as Michael Desch (2007/8) suggests, but is a matter of contingent 'practical judgement': there is the alternative image of the non-democratic state as based on rudimentary law with the potential of evolution. This assessment is influenced by the character and behaviour of the respective non-democracy, on the one hand, and the perceptual and evaluative apparatus of the democracy in question, as embedded in its political culture, on the other hand (Müller 2006; Müller and Wolff 2006).

To be sure, Kant's *hostis iniustus* as the foe of humankind is one extreme representation of a liberal's 'other', but the tendency to denigrate non-liberal 'others' has been a notorious trait of liberal imperialism throughout history (Jahn 2005). Counter to Beate Jahn (2005), who maintains that this militant element has been introduced into liberalism only in the post-Kantian period, by John Stuart Mill in particular, we maintain that the figure of the 'unjust enemy' allows for justifying offensive military action (Müller 2004a, 2006). While Kant argued in *Perpetual Peace* that no state shall interfere by force with the constitution and government of another one (1795: 199), the 'unjust enemy' appears to constitute an exception to this postulate since the 'right of a state has no limits' against an 'unjust enemy'.[7]

---

[7] See, for example, Desch (2007/8) for readings of Kant's 'unjust enemy' as fathering liberal interventions, and see, for example, MacMillan (1995), Jahn (2005) and Eberl (2008) for readings of a Kantian self-restraint and a prudent evolutionary approach to non-democracies. By arguing that Kant (rightly) recognised the possibility of an

The 'unjust enemy' is not introduced incidentally in Kant's pertinent writings on peace and war. Given Kant's emphasis on free will, man is expected to follow the guidance of reason, but reason is not determining. People are at liberty to follow their lower desires, that is, greed, lust for power and wealth. In a world of imperfect moral (legal) order, 'unjust enemies' may be rare exceptions, but their existence cannot be excluded with absolute certainty.

Therefore, *all* political strands in democracies that have internalised the heritage of the Enlightenment can, under certain circumstances, turn militant. In contrast to John MacMillan (2004), our study does not distinguish between 'liberal', 'non-liberal' or 'less liberal' actors in democratic polities; we see all relevant strands of political actors as heirs to the values of the Enlightenment (the extremist right and left wings excluded, which play a marginal role), though in different interpretations. In our view, they are exposed to the ambivalence of liberal values that MacMillan emphasises, too (MacMillan 2004: 186–7, 189, 200); in other words, conservatives need a genuinely liberal justification for their own war decisions in the same way as leftists.

3.4   *War by which authority? The ambivalence of procedural norms*

Liberal thought on order (domestic and international) always emphasises the rule of law. Politics regarding war and peace are included herein. However, there are three ways in which law and war-making can be related without violating the basic liberal premise that the relation must be lawful. Developments in international law in the twentieth century, which were largely shaped by democracies, have ended the notion that making war is the free decision of the sovereign state. What emerged is the prohibition to take up arms for reasons other than self-defence. The 'proper authority', in the language of just war theory, is the UN Security Council, acting under Chapter VII of the UN Charter. Consequently, the first liberal approach to decisions on military actions is to accept the singular authority of the UN Security Council for providing the only legally valid mandate for the use of force beyond self-defence.

A second understanding doubts this absolute command deriving from the UN Charter. As the Charter is a compromise between democratic and non-democratic governments, and the application of international law to specific cases under Chapter VII involves non-democratic governments, including those with veto powers, they claim a higher

implacable adversary of order, but did not ascribe this attribute to any non-democratic state, we take a position between these two poles (Müller 2006).

authority for organisations of democratic states, because their legitimacy alone rests on the assent of the people (Daalder and Lindsay 2007). In this view, a 'concert of democracies' could or even should substitute for the Security Council if the latter fails to live up to its duty (as defined by democracies) (e.g. Ikenberry and Slaughter 2006: 7, 26; for a critique, see Clark 2009). This position can refer to a notorious but nevertheless mistaken reading of the Second Definitive Article of *Perpetual Peace* that puts international law into the hands of a *foedus pacificum* of 'free states'. However, in Kant's terminology, 'free state' means states that enjoy sovereignty, not only suzerainty. The *foedus* encompasses democratic and non-democratic states as long as the latter exist (Jahn 2005: 191; Müller 2005; Eberl 2008: 200–4).

Third, there is a liberal-democratic argument based on the notion of the supreme priority of popular sovereignty, which might constitute tensions between national and international law (Brock 2002; Maus 2002): as long as the demos on which democracy is based is enshrined within the borders of the nation-state, national law and decision-making procedures prevail when they are confronted with deviating international law and related procedures. From this follows that only the elected national government and parliament possess the ultimate legitimate authority to decide on war and peace, even if their positions differ from interdemocratic organisations or the UN Security Council.

3.5   *War by whom? The ambivalence of constitutive norms and the role of 'interests'*

War is made by collective actors, in our cases by states. Regulative and procedural norms constrain and enable justifications for going to war. The ambivalence of the ideational structures in which decisions and actions of democratic governments are embedded, as discussed in the preceding paragraph, raises the issue of the role of agency. Because of their ambivalence, their interpretation is contested (Müller 2004a; see also MacMillan 2004, 2005; Brock 2005; Sørensen 2006; Wiener 2008). Contestation is a matter of agency – interpretations do not fight each other by themselves: how the identity or international role of a country is framed, how situations are described in moral terms, what regulatory norms are linked to the image of the 'we' in the light of the framed situation, what moral value is ascribed to the 'other' and how procedural norms are handled in the light of all these interpretations – all this depends on the (individual or collective) agent.[8] They must be

---

[8] It should be noted that we focus on collective agency in this book. Individual agency is briefly discussed where it played an obvious role in specific situations (e.g. Madeleine

interpreted by actors in order to take their permissive or prohibitive effect. The same applies for the assessment of the 'enemy'. Collective actors, however, do not produce these interpretations in a voluntaristic way. They are themselves constrained as well as enabled by constitutive norms. These shape collective actors' identity and international role and define the framework for 'appropriate' behaviour. They include legal and politico-cultural norms. Domestic and international legal norms constitute states and their governments as legitimate actors in international relations. Politico-cultural norms consist of norms constituting national identity or collective identity beyond the state; norms derived from 'lessons learnt' from one's own history; and norms encapsulated in a foreign policy role conception of a polity (Harnisch *et al.* 2011; McCourt 2011; see also Chapter 2 of this volume). As norms exert causal power – formal causality, in Milja Kurki's neo-Aristotelian conceptualisation (Kurki 2008) – by enabling and restraining appropriate policy options available in a given society, it matters considerably which public justifications political decision-makers use in order to legitimise their decision to engage in a military intervention, and which justifications are accepted by the democratic public in this specific polity as legitimate (Risse-Kappen 1995: 511). The social-constructivist focus is thus on reasons that are publicly accessible in political language (Fierke 2007: 176–7).[9]

The notion of 'reason' provokes the question of how stated reasons might be related to 'interests' that are usually taken as informing states' policies and how these 'interests' may relate to the ambivalences discussed above. From a social-constructivist view, it is not useful to speak of generalised 'interests' that compel states to pursue a certain policy option. Rather, one has to analyse in detail which kind of interests, preferences and values and which interpretations of pertinent domestic or international norms are articulated in a certain situation of political choice by a given state in its constitutive normative framework. The DP literature usually treats preferences as exogenous and assumes that citizens have peaceful preferences, while governments might have special interests in wars and need to be restrained by citizens' control

---

Albright and George W. Bush in the Kosovo and Iraq Wars, Gerhard Schröder in the Iraq War), but has not been systematically tackled, as this would have overtaxed our resources. Nevertheless, it might be recommendable to address individual agency in a more in-depth way in future studies on democratic peace/democratic war.

[9] Our analysis is less interested in revealing the 'ultimate truth' of individual motives – why, for example, President George W. Bush decided to invade Iraq – since researchers cannot get inside individual minds, than in asking how the social fact of the invasion became possible. See Chapter 2.

(Kahl 1998: 112). This distinction ignores the fact that both act within the same constitutive framework. Why politicians and citizens, socialised within the same cultural environment, should belong to different species of actors has never been explained convincingly. Politicians may hold deeply cherished moral convictions, from pacifism to liberal militancy, while they strive simultaneously for a successful political career. Citizens' attitudes towards military action can range from enthusiasm to indifference and outright opposition; this will depend on the type of military action and the norms evoked. Interests and preference formation within today's liberal democracies are influenced by high interdependence, disagreements about the 'right' interpretation of international law, controversies about the 'appropriate' relations with 'others', i.e. non-democracies, and so on. Since the end of the Cold War in particular, there is a general uncertainty about the style, scope and content of liberal-democratic foreign policy (Freedman 2005: 94) since it is far from clear what the long-term goal of a 'liberal world order' actually implies (Sørensen 2006). Interests are thus not negated in this volume, but simplistic approaches are rejected that put interests and norms on opposite poles, seek explanations by 'either interests or norms' or assume a priori that norms are (material) interests in moral disguise. Instead, attention is directed to the ways in which 'interests' and norms interact, complement and are dependent on each other, or amalgamate into complexes that render the two categories hardly distinguishable empirically.

Liberal-democratic institutions and political cultures rest on different strands of liberal thought. US political culture, for example, contains normative structures that can accommodate interventionist, missionary orientations as well as a self-restrained, 'isolationist' approach to the outside world, presenting their own country as a shining example, but not attempting to convert others (Desch 2007/8). This pluralisation of political culture is not a singular US feature: several Western political cultures exhibit pluralist normative structures rooted in different liberal traditions and in differing conclusions about 'lessons learnt' from history; inevitably, they also result in different interpretations of what is supposed to be the 'national interest'. Since cultures provide and circumscribe the universe of acceptable justifications for the use of force in a polity, much depends on the interpretations of the ruling political coalitions. Left-liberal, liberal, conservative or socialist parties can cite different 'legacies' of their own culture; they refer to different norms rendering the use of force appropriate or inappropriate (MacMillan 2004, 2005). Hence it is crucial for the conception of democratic war as the flipside of democratic peace to scrutinise the ambivalent norms of a political culture and the legitimating processes that underlie democratic governments' decisions to participate in or abstain from a war.

4   The plan of the book

This volume investigates democratic decision-making processes and public discourses in the run-up to three major wars since 1990, which represent the three types of 'democratic wars' inferred in Section 3.2 above. Focusing on the Gulf War of 1990–1 ('order war'), the Kosovo War of 1998–9 ('humanitarian intervention') and the Iraq War of 2003 ('regime change war'), the study encompasses seven democracies with differing participation records in these wars: the United Kingdom and the United States fought with combat troops in all the wars; Australia, Canada and France took part in two of them; Germany in one; and Sweden in none. The comparison allows a closer look at the institutional and normative factors that enabled or restrained the democratic governments in all of these instances.

The book is divided into three sections. The following Chapter 2 of the first part elaborates on methodological aspects of the study such as case selection, structure of the country chapters and merits and problems of the methods used. Part II encompasses the seven country chapters, which are all organised along the structure described in Chapter 2. The country chapters examine the respective domestic political situation, the institutional constellations providing for accountability, citizens' attitudes, leading newspapers' positions and the parliamentary discourse in the run-up to the Gulf War, the Kosovo War and the Iraq War. The country chapters as well as the comparative chapter present original data of a content analysis of pre-war parliamentary discourses that reveal public justifications for positions pro and contra military action. However, the approach of this book is not confined to the investigation of publicly given reasons, analysed through the method of content analysis; the country chapters seek to examine the motivations of national governments by process tracing and primary sources only when such sources permit drawing reasonably plausible inferences as to why political leaders acted the way they did.[10]

Part III of the volume comprises two chapters. The comparative Chapter 10 discusses the institutional and normative factors that enabled or restrained the democratic governments in our cases and outlines what these findings imply for DP research. The final Chapter 11

[10] On the problematique of verifying 'motivation', see Chapter 2; for the difference between reasoning and motivation, see Fierke (2010).

develops elements of an emerging theory of 'democratic wars' and contextualises this phenomenon within our historical era of liberal hegemony. Finally, we return to liberalism, understood both as International Relations theory and as the ideational underpinning of Western democracies, and discuss how our liberal approach differs from established liberal theorising in International Relations. By emphasising the ambivalence of liberal norms, our study differs from accounts that aim at positivist theorising and clear predictions of cooperation and conflict among states, such as in the preference-based liberal theory advanced by Andrew Moravcsik (1997). In a similar vein, we refute the utopian liberal narrative of 'all good things going together'. Bruce Russett and John Oneal (2001) envisioned in their conceptualisation of a 'Kantian peace' a virtuous circle of democracy, economic interdependence and international organisation as promoting peace. In contrast, our study points out the more contingent as well as ambivalent nature of the conflict behaviour of liberal democracies and refrains from overly optimistic liberal narratives of inexorably progressing global peace (Geis 2006; Hobson 2009). Ultimately, our aim is not to discard democratic peace research but to contextualise its theses and to establish an emerging research field of *democratic war*. The time-honoured liberal creed that democracy equals peace is comfortable but deceptive. The displacement of violence within liberal theories must not blind us from recognising the militant potential of liberal democracies.

REFERENCES

Auerswald, David 2000. *Disarmed Democracies: Domestic Institutions and the Use of Force*. Ann Arbor, MI: University of Michigan Press

Barkawi, Tarak and Laffey, Mark (eds.) 2001. *Democracy, Liberalism, and War: Rethinking the Democratic Peace Debate*. Boulder, CO: Lynne Rienner

Brock, Lothar 2002. '"Staatenrecht" und "Menschenrecht": Schwierigkeiten der Annäherung an eine weltbürgerliche Ordnung', in Matthias Lutz-Bachmann and James Bohman (eds.), *Weltstaat oder Staatenwelt? Für und wider die Idee einer Weltrepublik*. Frankfurt a.M.: Suhrkamp, pp. 201–25

2005. 'The Use of Force in the Post-Cold War Era: From Collective Action Back to Pre-Charter Self Defense?', in Michael Bothe, Mary Ellen O'Connell and Natalino Ronzitti (eds.), *Redefining Sovereignty: The Use of Force after the Cold War*. Ardsley, NY: Transnational Publishers, pp. 21–52

Brock, Lothar, Geis, Anna and Müller, Harald 2006. 'The Case for a New Research Agenda: Explaining Democratic Wars', in Anna Geis, Lothar Brock and Harald Müller (eds.), *Democratic Wars: Looking at the Dark Side of Democratic Peace*. Basingstoke: Palgrave Macmillan, pp. 195–214

Campbell, David 1992. *Writing Security: United States Foreign Policy and the Politics of Identity*. Minneapolis, MN: University of Minnesota Press

Chan, Steve 1997. 'In Search of Democratic Peace: Problems and Promise', *Mershon International Studies Review* 41 (1): 59–91

Chandler, David 2006. *From Kosovo to Kabul and Beyond: Human Rights and International Intervention.* London: Pluto Press

2010. 'Liberal War and Foucaultian Metaphysics', *Journal of International Cooperation Studies* 18 (1): 85–94

Chernoff, Fred 2004. 'The Study of Democratic Peace and Progress in International Relations', *International Studies Review* 6 (1): 49–77

Chojnacki, Sven 2006. 'Democratic Wars and Military Interventions, 1946–2002', in Anna Geis, Lothar Brock and Harald Müller (eds.), *Democratic Wars: Looking at the Dark Side of Democratic Peace.* Basingstoke: Palgrave Macmillan, pp. 13–39

Clark, Ian 2009. 'Democracy in International Society: Promotion or Exclusion', *Millennium* 37 (3): 563–81

Czempiel, Ernst-Otto 1996. 'Kants Theorem: Oder – Warum sind die Demokratien (noch immer) nicht friedlich?', *Zeitschrift für Internationale Beziehungen* 3 (1): 79–101

Daalder, Ivo and Lindsay, James 2007. 'Democracies of the World, Unite', *The American Interest* 2 (3). Online: www.the-american-interest.com/article. cfm?piece=220

Desch, Michael 2007/8. 'America's Liberal Illiberalism: The Ideological Origins of Overreaction in U.S. Foreign Policy', *International Security* 32 (3): 7–43

Dieterich, Sandra, Hummel, Hartwig and Marschall, Stefan 2009. '"Kriegsspielverderber?" Europäische Parlamente und der Irakkrieg 2003', *Zeitschrift für Internationale Beziehungen* 16 (1): 5–38

Doyle, Michael W. 1983a. 'Kant, Liberal Legacies, and Foreign Affairs', *Philosophy and Public Affairs* 12 (3): 205–35

1983b. 'Kant, Liberal Legacies, and Foreign Affairs: Part 2', *Philosophy and Public Affairs* 12 (4): 323–53

Duffield, Mark 2001. *Global Governance and the New Wars: The Merging of Development and Security.* London: Zed Books

Eberl, Oliver 2008. *Demokratie und Frieden: Kants Friedensschrift in den Kontroversen der Gegenwart.* Baden-Baden: Nomos

Evangelista, Matthew, Müller, Harald and Schörnig, Niklas (eds.) 2008. *Democracy and Security: Preferences, Norms and Policy-Making.* London: Routledge

Fearon, James D. 1994. 'Domestic Political Audiences and the Escalation of International Disputes', *American Political Science Review* 88 (3): 577–92

Fierke, Karin M. 2007. 'Constructivism', in Tim Dunne, Milja Kurki and Steve Smith (eds.), *International Relations Theories: Discipline and Diversity.* Oxford University Press, pp. 166–84

2010. 'Wittgenstein and International Relations Theory', in Cerwyn Moore and Chris Farrands (eds.), *International Relations Theory and Philosophy: Interpretive Dialogues.* London: Routledge, pp. 83–94

Finnemore, Martha and Sikkink, Kathryn 1998. 'International Norm Dynamics and Political Change', *International Organization* 52 (4): 887–917

Freedman, Lawrence 2005. 'The Age of Liberal Wars', in David Armstrong, Theo Farrell and Bice Maiguashca (eds.), *Force and Legitimacy in World Politics*. Cambridge University Press, pp. 93–107

　　2006. 'Iraq, Liberal Wars and Illiberal Containment', *Survival* 48 (4): 51–66

Geis, Anna 2006. 'Spotting the "Enemy"? Democracies and the Challenge of the "Other"', in Anna Geis, Lothar Brock and Harald Müller (eds.), *Democratic Wars: Looking at the Dark Side of Democratic Peace*. Basingstoke: Palgrave Macmillan, pp. 142–69

Geis, Anna and Wagner, Wolfgang 2011. 'How Far Is It from Königsberg to Kandahar? Democratic Peace and Democratic Violence in International Relations', *Review of International Studies* 37 (4): 1555–77

Habermas, Jürgen 1999. 'Bestialität und Humanität', *Die Zeit*, 29 April. Online: www.zeit.de/1999/18/199918.krieg_.xml

Harnisch, Sebastian, Frank, Cornelia and Maull, Hanns W. (eds.) 2011. *Role Theory in International Relations: Approaches and Analyses*. London: Routledge

Hobson, Christopher 2009. 'Beyond the End of History: The Need for a "Radical Historicisation" of Democracy in International Relations', *Millennium* 37 (3): 631–57

　　2011. 'Introduction: Roundtable – Between the Theory and Practice of Democratic Peace', *International Relations* 25 (2): 147–50

Ikenberry, G. John and Slaughter, Anne-Marie 2006. *Forging a World of Liberty under Law: U.S. National Security in the 21st Century*. Final Report of the Princeton Project on National Security. Princeton University Press

Ish-Shalom, Piki 2006. 'Theory as a Hermeneutical Mechanism: The Democratic-Peace Thesis and the Politics of Democratization', *European Journal of International Relations* 12 (4): 565–98

Jahn, Beate 2005. 'Kant, Mill, and Illiberal Legacies in International Affairs', *International Organization* 59 (1): 177–207

Joas, Hans 2000. *Kriege und Werte: Studien zur Gewaltgeschichte des 20. Jahrhunderts*. Weilerswist: Velbrück

Kahl, Colin H. 1998. 'Constructing a Separate Peace: Constructivism, Collective Liberal Identity, and Democratic Peace', *Security Studies* 8 (2–3): 94–144

Kant, Immanuel 1795. *Zum ewigen Frieden* (in Weischedel, Wilhelm (ed.) 1977. *Werkausgabe Volume XI*. Frankfurt a.M.: Suhrkamp, pp. 195–254)

　　1797. *The Metaphysics of Morals* (in Gregor, Mary J. (ed.) 1996. *Practical Philosophy: The Cambridge Edition of the Works of Immanuel Kant*. Cambridge University Press, pp. 353–603)

Kurki, Milja 2008. *Causation in International Relations: Reclaiming Causal Analysis*. Cambridge University Press

Lipson, Charles 2003. *Reliable Partners: How Democracies Have Made a Separate Peace*. Princeton University Press

MacMillan, John 1995. 'A Kantian Protest against the Peculiar Discourse of Inter-Liberal State Peace', *Millennium* 24 (3): 549–62

　　2004. 'Liberalism and the Democratic Peace', *Review of International Studies* 30 (2): 179–200

2005. 'Introduction: The Iraq War and Democratic Politics', in John MacMillan and Alex Danchev (eds.), *The Iraq War and Democratic Politics*. London: Routledge, pp. 1–19

March, James G. and Olsen, Johan P. 2004. 'The Logic of Appropriateness', *ARENA Working Papers* No. 9/2004, Oslo

Martin, Kingsley 1963. *The Triumph of Lord Palmerston: A Study of Public Opinion in England before the Crimean War*. New and revised edition of the 1923 edition, London: Hutchinson

Maus, Ingeborg 2002. 'Vom Nationalstaat zum Globalstaat oder: der Niedergang der Demokratie', in Matthias Lutz-Bachmann and James Bohman (eds.), *Weltstaat oder Staatenwelt? Für und wider die Idee einer Weltrepublik*. Frankfurt a.M.: Suhrkamp, pp. 226–59

McCourt, David M. 2011. 'Role-Playing and Identity Affirmation in International Politics: Britain's Reinvasion of the Falklands, 1982', *Review of International Studies* 37 (4): 1599–1621

Moore, John Norton 2004. *Solving the War Puzzle: Beyond the Democratic Peace*. Durham, NC: Carolina Academic Press

Moravcsik, Andrew 1997. 'Taking Preferences Seriously: A Liberal Theory of International Politics', *International Organization* 51 (4): 513–53

Müller, Harald 2004a. 'The Antinomy of Democratic Peace', *International Politics* 41 (4): 494–520

2004b. 'Arguing, Bargaining and All That: Communicative Action, Rationalist Theory and the Logic of Appropriateness in International Relations', *European Journal of International Relations* 10 (3): 395–435

2005. 'Triangulating Kant: You Got It All Wrong', paper presented at the ECPR Conference, 8–10 September, Budapest

2006. 'Kants Schurkenstaat: Der "ungerechte Feind" und die Selbstermächtigung zum Kriege', in Anna Geis (ed.), *Den Krieg über-denken: Kriegsbegriffe und Kriegstheorien in der Kontroverse*. Baden-Baden: Nomos, pp. 229–49

Müller, Harald and Wolff, Jonas 2006. 'Democratic Peace: Many Data, Little Explanation?', in Anna Geis, Lothar Brock and Harald Müller (eds.), *Democratic Wars: Looking at the Dark Side of Democratic Peace*. Basingstoke: Palgrave Macmillan, pp. 41–73

Owen, John M. 1997. *Liberal Peace, Liberal War: American Politics and International Security*. Ithaca, NY: Cornell University Press

Peceny, Mark 1999. *Democracy at the Point of Bayonets*. University Park, PA: Pennsylvania State University Press

Peters, Dirk and Wagner, Wolfgang 2011. 'Between Military Efficiency and Democratic Legitimacy: Mapping Parliamentary War Powers in Contemporary Democracies, 1989–2004', *Parliamentary Affairs* 64 (1): 175–92

Risse, Thomas 2000. '"Let's Argue!": Communicative Action in World Politics', *International Organization* 54 (1): 1–39

Risse-Kappen, Thomas 1995. 'Democratic Peace – Warlike Democracies? A Social Constructivist Interpretation of the Liberal Argument', *European Journal of International Relations* 1 (4): 491–517

Rousseau, David L. 2005. *Democracy and War: Institutions, Norms, and the Evolution of International Conflict*. Stanford University Press

Russett, Bruce 1993. *Grasping the Democratic Peace: Principles for a Post-Cold War World*. Princeton University Press

Russett, Bruce and Oneal, John 2001. *Triangulating Peace: Democracy, Interdependence, and International Organizations*. New York, NY: W. W. Norton

Shaw, Martin 2005. *The New Western Way of War: Risk-Transfer War and Its Crisis in Iraq*. London: Polity Press

Smith, Tony 2007. *A Pact with the Devil: Washington's Bid for World Supremacy and the Betrayal of the American Promise*. New York, NY: Routledge

Sørensen, Georg 2006. 'Liberalism of Restraint and Liberalism of Imposition: Liberal Values and World Order in the New Millennium', *International Relations* 20 (3): 251–72

Steele, Brent J. 2007. 'Liberal-Idealism: A Constructivist Critique', *International Studies Review* 9 (1): 23–52

Vasquez, John A. 2005. 'Ethics, Foreign Policy, and Liberal Wars: The Role of Restraint in Moral Decision Making', *International Studies Perspective* 6 (3): 307–15

Wiener, Antje 2008. *The Invisible Constitution of Politics: Contested Norms and International Encounters*. Cambridge University Press

2   The empirical study of 'democratic wars': methodology and methods

Niklas Schörnig, Harald Müller and Anna Geis

This chapter provides information on the methodology and methods of our study on democratic wars. While the majority of works in the field of democratic peace are still grounded in rationalism, our research on democracy and war is informed by constructivism. As has been discussed widely in epistemological and ontological debates between International Relations positivists and post-positivists during the last decades, adopting a post-positivist approach to research implies differing understandings of causality and explanation, which positivists regard as 'soft'.[1] Nevertheless, the post-positivist approach to 'understanding' is a scientific endeavour (e.g. Wendt 1998: 104) and allows for a broad range of methods for analysing international politics. It should be emphasised that whenever we speak in this study of 'explaining' or 'explanation' for the (non-)participation of democracies in war, this must not be misunderstood as a switch to the strong positivist line of explaining a phenomenon, in the sense of 'efficient cause' (Kurki 2008: 189–241), but is meant as an attempt to trace how certain outcomes have become possible (Wendt 1999: 83; Fierke 2007: 176–7).

The introductory chapter outlined the basic methodological choice in broader terms; this chapter engages in more detail with crucial methodological issues and is structured as follows: Section 1 explicates the selection criteria for the three 'democratic wars' and for the seven liberal democracies under study. Then the structure and purpose of the country chapters are explained in detail (Section 2). As all seven country chapters follow the same design, Section 2 should be read as the universal roadmap through all of the subsequent seven chapters. Following these technical details of the country chapters, an engagement with the two central methods of process tracing and content analysis discusses the merits of these methods for our study, as well as the problem of identifying motivations of actors (Section 3). A separate section then

---

[1] This is not the place to go deeper into details of this 'great debate'; see, for example, Lapid (1989).

24

presents the technical details of our content analysis such as coding scheme and coding procedure (Section 4). A final section summarises the strengths of the methods combined in this study (Section 5).

1   Case selection: 'democratic wars' since 1990 – which wars, which democracies?

1.1   Three kinds of 'democratic wars'

This book focuses on seven Western democracies and their respective behaviour with regard to three particular 'democratic wars'. In Chapter 1, a 'democratic war' was defined as a war fought for liberal purposes and it was argued that Immanuel Kant's three definitive articles in *Perpetual Peace* can be used as a heuristics for differentiating the spectrum of such liberal purposes. The first war type derived from these definitive articles is an 'order war': a *liberal* idea of regional or international order is more than simple hegemony or balance of power, as it contains by definition an element of law. The notion of an 'order war' thus implies that the main purpose is the restoration of international law. The second war type, 'humanitarian intervention', is conducted to protect the basic human rights of a foreign population, while the third type, 'war for regime change', aims at replacing a dictatorship by a more democratic type of rule. These are ideal types; real wars are usually mixed-motive endeavours in which more 'mundane' state interests also play a role. But often, one type of reason to take up arms dominates. In that sense, the three categories of wars are represented by three major interstate wars fought since the end of the Cold War, which have been chosen as the subject of our examination: the 1990–1 Gulf War represents an 'order war'; the 1998–9 Kosovo War represents a 'humanitarian intervention';[2] and the 2003 Iraq War represents a 'war for regime change'.

These three wars make a perfect sample for the purpose of developing democratic peace (DP) research further by including the phenomena of 'democratic wars'. First of all, they were not clear cases

---

[2] We decided to select the Kosovo case as representative of a 'humanitarian intervention' since the former military intervention in Bosnia was – at least in our understanding – the result of so-called 'mission creep' rather than a deliberate decision by the interveners in favour of a large-scale military action. In addition, with troops already in theatre, specific effects, like the 'rally around the flag' effect, might have influenced the decision to escalate militarily. Finally, the Bosnian intervention was conducted on the basis of a UN mandate and thus in terms of international legitimisation not different from the situation of the 1991 Gulf War. As will be stated below, variance in international legitimisation was a selection criterion for our cases.

of self-defence for the participating democracies, i.e. a reaction to an attack on their own or an ally's territory. In this vein, the three wars were 'wars of choice'.[3] In addition, all of these wars were fought not by one democracy on its own but in cooperation with a smaller or larger number of partners. Liberal bellicosity beyond self-defence poses a particular problem for monadic DP theories, and such wars also raise a number of questions from a dyadic DP perspective, namely how exactly the factors promoting peace among democracies have been 'suspended' so as to permit the use of force in such cases, and why not all democracies take part in a particular war. The three cases also varied in a third dimension that is important for our research question: international legitimisation. The Gulf War of 1990–1 was mandated by a UN Security Council resolution. The Kosovo War of 1998–9 was determined by a decision of the NATO Council. The Iraq War of 2003 was agreed only by the small group of participating countries. This case selection permits the examination of the role of multilateralism and international legitimacy in the domestic deliberations of the seven democracies under study.[4]

We excluded the Afghanistan War from our sample as this war is not a clear-cut example of a 'war of choice', nor is it a clear example of one of the three specific 'democratic wars' described above. It was *perceived* by the United States as a case of self-defence after the Taliban regime had refused to extradite the terrorists suspected of being responsible for the attacks of 11 September 2001. On 12 September 2001, in response to the terrorist attacks of the previous day, the UN Security Council confirmed in its Resolution 1368 the inherent right to individual and collective self-defence, thereby legitimising self-defence action under Article 51 of the UN Charter. The NATO allies declared almost simultaneously that they would take collective action according to Article 5 of the Washington Treaty. Australia invoked the Australia, New Zealand, United States Security Treaty (ANZUS) only a few days later. The interpretation of the Afghanistan War as a self-defence action was thus widely shared. In contrast to the other wars under study here, the decision by almost all the democracies in our sample to participate in military action against the Taliban regime was therefore bound by formal treaties, impeding an independent evaluation and decision. As Charles Lipson (2003) has argued, democracies make quite 'reliable

---

[3] We borrow this term from Lawrence Freedman (2006: 52) and Richard Haass (2009).

[4] For reasons of research economy, we had to limit the analysis to three wars as the methods chosen required extensive work and the resources available were not sufficient to deal with additional cases.

partners', who show a strong tendency to honour international treaties and to enter international organisations (Hasenclever and Weiffen 2006: 569, 573). Seen from this institutional perspective on democratic peace, the participation of allies in a war that falls under the specific juridical definition stated in the alliance treaty does not pose a puzzle, but is rather the expected choice.

One might object that the 2003 Iraq War was also regarded as a war of self-defence by the United States – but to the extent that this war had been justified with reference to national security by the belligerents (see the chapters by Fey, Sohnius and Schörnig in this book), it was legitimated by the purpose of *prevention*, which according to the dominant legal opinion cannot be subsumed under a war of self-defence. In addition, contractual obligations like the NATO or ANZUS treaties were not relevant in this case, permitting even close allies to deliberate whether or not to participate unhampered by regulations. As the frank admission by then Deputy Secretary of Defense Paul Wolfowitz revealed (Wolfowitz 2003), the focus on weapons of mass destruction was chosen as the lowest common denominator for those actors participating in US governmental decisions.

The three wars chosen show that the analysis focuses on the period after the end of the Cold War. There are two reasons: first, as far as DP research has generated detailed case studies, these are often dedicated to historical cases of the late nineteenth, early and mid-twentieth centuries or the Cold War period (e.g. Ray 1995; Elman 1997; Owen 1997; Rousseau 2005). While recent literature on 'liberal wars' or liberal interventionism (see Chapter 1) has been dealing with the period since 1990, there is not yet an abundance of such studies in DP research. Second, the end of the Cold War created an unprecedented global constellation in which liberal democracies were largely able to shape international politics according to their visions of a world order; their military activities were no longer 'distorted' by strategic calculations that dominated the bipolar security constellation. These calculations could lead to an *enhanced* propensity to engage militarily (in order to prevent the communist counterpart from making important geopolitical gains) as well as a *reduced* propensity because of the implied risk of nuclear strike.

1.2   Seven democracies under investigation

According to DP research, the pacifying effects of democratic norms and institutions are greatest in mature democracies. We therefore only examined democracies that have scored '9 and higher' in the Polity

IV Project dataset since the 1990s.[5] The sample encompasses democracies that participated in all of the wars, in two of them, in just one, or in none at all, with 'participation' meaning the deployment of combat troops to the war theatre. As the three wars under investigation were preceded by shows of military force or military build-ups months before the actual fighting began ('coercive diplomacy'), this 'participation' could also include the deployment of such troops in order to build up a credible threat of force in the crisis region.

The focus on consolidated Western democracies provided a sample of relatively similar states. However, in selecting the countries, we also considered factors independent of democracy that can influence the cost–benefit calculations of actors or their normative attitudes towards the use of force and that can hence 'suspend' the peace-proneness of democracies: we included democracies with differing power status (superpower, great power, middle power);[6] democracies with memberships of defence alliances and non-allied democracies; and democracies with different norms of political culture, collective identity and foreign policy role conception.

The concept of 'role' requires some explanation here. Roles are understood as 'notions of actors about who they are, what they would like to be with regard to others, and how they therefore should interact in (international) social relationships' (Harnisch *et al.* 2011: 1–2), that is, as 'social positions … that are constituted by ego and alter expectations regarding the purpose of an actor in an organised group' (Harnisch 2011: 8). A role conception is 'an actor's perception of his or her position vis-à-vis others (the ego part of a role) and the perception of the role expectations of others (the alter part of a role) as signalled through language and action' (Harnisch 2011: 8). In an empirical analysis it is often rather difficult to distinguish norms that refer to a collective identity, i.e. self-images of a community, clearly from norms that refer to external role expectations. For the purpose of our research question, we have decided not to distinguish such norms in our coding scheme, but have treated identity/role references as one 'cluster' of norms (see below, Section 4.1). For the purpose of our case selection, we deduced

---

[5] See www.systemicpeace.org/polity/polity4.htm.
[6] We constructed these three groups via a cluster analysis, using the dataset on the national material capabilities index of the 'Correlates of War' (CoW) project and the economic datasets on the per capita income provided by the World Bank in order to determine the power status for democracies scoring 9 and higher in the Polity IV dataset. Among our sample of seven democracies, the CoW index ranked these as follows for our period of study: United States (1), Germany (2), United Kingdom (3), France (4), Canada (5), Sweden (6), Australia (7). See the dataset national material capabilities (v.3.02) online at: www.correlatesofwar.org.

collective identities and role conceptions from secondary literature on the countries' foreign policies and included democracies that lean more towards the ideal type of a 'civilian power' (Harnisch and Maull 2001) and those with features of the opposite ideal type of a 'military power'.

The notion of a 'civilian power' was introduced by François Duchêne in the early 1970s with regard to the special character and international role of the European Community and has resonated within European research ever since (Orbie 2006). A research team at the University of Trier around Hanns W. Maull developed the concept further in the 1990s as an ideal type for comparative foreign policy analysis in the post-Cold War era (e.g. Maull 1990; Harnisch and Maull 2001). Based on a liberal worldview, Maull argued that in an international system shaped by the complex interdependence of states, multiple new challenges would increase the demand for 'soft power' instruments, for enhanced multilateralism and the juridification of international politics. The promotion of democracy, human rights and sustainable development would contribute more to the solution of international problems than military force. In this perspective, a 'civilian power' ideally pursues the civilianisation of international relations and prefers non-military to military means, although it is not necessarily a pacifist power and might use force as a very last resort in order to secure peace or enforce international law when a collective of states agrees on such a use of force for 'worthy' purposes. Goals, means and policy style of a civilian power are geared to ethical values in foreign policy, and such powers are prepared to renounce part of their sovereignty as they prioritise the pursuit of collective goods over the pursuit of narrowly understood national interests (Maull 2000: 65–76). While the opposite concept of a 'civilian power', which might be termed a 'military power', has not been clearly defined by Maull and others, the characteristics of an ideal-type 'military power' might be derived from the opposite values of a 'civilian power': such a country tends to emphasise its autonomy and its narrow national interests, which renders it a rather reluctant multilateralist; the pursuit of power politics ranks highly in its international policy goals and military means are more acceptable for tackling international conflicts than in the case of civilian powers.

Taking the selection criteria of power status, identity/role conception and defence alliance membership, the final sample of democracies was as depicted in Table 2.1.[7]

---

[7] We had to make a preliminary assessment of the value of the respective political culture, which later required corrections and differentiations when the case studies were elaborated. The parameters for assessing a democracy's political culture and foreign policy role type are presented in detail in the country chapters.

Table 2.1 *Case-selection criteria*

Country	War participations	Power status	Political culture/ collective identity/ role conception	Defence alliance membership
United Kingdom	3	Great power	Rather 'military power'	Allied
United States	3	Superpower	Rather 'military power'	Allied
Australia	2	Middle power	Rather 'civilian power'	Allied
Canada	2	Middle power	Rather 'civilian power'	Allied
France	2	Great power	Rather 'military power'	Allied
Germany	1	Great power	Rather 'civilian power'	Allied
Sweden	0	Middle power	Rather 'civilian power'	Non-allied

2   A roadmap for all cases: the structure of the country chapters

The seven country chapters in this book are all based on a similar structure. First of all, the institutional features of decision-making on war and peace are outlined. Security policy is a field dominated by the executive in all democracies, but nevertheless the accountability mechanisms differ: while some executives enjoy wide discretionary powers (e.g. Australia, Canada, France), others are formally constrained by the comparatively far-reaching oversight powers of their parliaments (e.g. Germany and Sweden). Following this, we sketch out the normative guidelines of the country's foreign and security policies. This normative framework signifies constitutive and regulative norms shaping the collective identity and foreign policy role conception of the state, but it also includes (recurring) ambiguities and tensions within several norms. No political culture consists of one coherent, stable set of norms, but instead builds on an incessant dynamic process of producing, reproducing, negotiating and contesting norms (Wiener 2008).

Each author then delineates the country's record in a number of foreign policy fields in order to determine a more precise 'role profile' of this state in international politics, including attitudes towards the International Criminal Court (ICC), international regimes of arms control and disarmament, the United Nations and special interactions with 'significant others' (alliances, regional organisations or bilateral relations; Harnisch 2011: 11–12). The issue areas serve as a check on, and helpful corrective to, the description of the country's 'identity' or 'role' found in the secondary literature. While the attitude to, for example, the ICC is neither clear evidence nor undisputable counter-evidence of a country's more general attitude towards international law, the way the ICC was debated domestically offers an indication of the general role attributed to international law, particularly the country's readiness to submit its own incriminated citizens to international legal scrutiny. Arms control policies denote the willingness to accept constraints on one's freedom of action in security policy; and the policy towards the United Nations is a general indicator of the country's attitude towards multilateralism.

Given that our analysis covers seven different countries, lack of space dictates a condensed description of individual institutional features as well as role profile, which country experts might find broad-brushed. However, as it is safe to assume that not all readers are familiar with both the political system and the foreign policy role conception of all seven countries under scrutiny, these introductory parts of the country chapters should be regarded as a compromise between space constraints and the need to offer background information for the following analysis of the respective (non-)participations in war. The country chapters will show that even this highly condensed approach reveals important differences between the countries concerned. In addition, the sections of the chapters that explore the reasons for a country's (non-)participation in the wars go on to present a fuller account of the individual democracy's attitudes towards international law and multilateralism than the brief 'role profile' could capture. In these sections, each author analyses the domestic decision-making processes and public debates prior to the beginning of the wars under investigation. Given the research question grounded in DP theory – how the assumed reluctance of liberal democracies towards war was overcome – as a rule, the analysis ends with the day the wars actually began, in order to exclude 'rally around the flag' effects, which often enhance public support at the beginning of a war and hence distort the public debate (see below, Section 4.2). In a few cases, however, polls taken after the war had started are quoted, when insufficient data was available for pre-war public opinion, but with the caveat that the distortion of the 'rally' effect must be kept in mind.

The account of each pre-war period in each individual country is based on four individual analytical steps. First, on a reconstruction of the domestic decision-making process via process tracing;[8] second, on a formal content analysis of pertinent parliamentary debates; third, on the analysis of newspaper commentaries; and fourth, on the analysis of available opinion polls. A final section summarises the findings of all four steps against the background of DP theory. The main foci of the analyses, however, lie on process tracing as well as on content analysis, with the other two steps serving to give a more detailed account of the published as well as the public opinion in the respective cases. As DP research assumes that democratic leaders are restrained by public opinion, a closer look at the argumentations of commentaries in leading newspapers and at the polled opinion of citizens about the considered military action is necessary to gain a broader understanding of the public 'mood' in this case. Finally, every individual section on a particular war concludes with an assessment of the most important factors for (non-)participation and the most important reasons for actors.[9] The country chapter itself ends with a broader evaluation of whether the domestic processes and debates were in accordance with 'traditional' DP theory, pointing to areas where significant deviations from theory could be spotted, and considering whether additional factors have been overlooked by DP theory as it stands.

3   Process tracing and content analysis: methodological purposes and pitfalls

3.1   *Process tracing: from the 'chain of events' to the actors' motivation*

Process tracing focuses on relevant actors and their actions as the conflict progresses, resulting in a description of the individual country's path towards or away from war participation. We have drawn on secondary literature, memoirs of political actors, newspaper accounts and expert interviews in the field in order to reconstruct the chronology of events in each individual country, the specific decision-making process and the steps leading to the country's participation or non-participation. The purposes and problems of process tracing are discussed in the following

---

[8] Of course, decisions on war are not exclusively prepared in domestic settings, but to a large extent shaped by international actors and structures. Since our main focus is on the question of how national political elites arrive at such decisions and justify these to their publics, we adopt prima facie a view mainly from *within* the respective democracy. However, national speakers themselves often refer in the public debates to structures or actors beyond their borders. In addition, we also refer to events and actors beyond the national borders in the reconstruction of the decision-making processes.

[9] The problems that occur when trying to identify 'true' motives will be debated below.

pages in order to outline its methodological status in our study, which is informed by social constructivism.

King, Keohane and Verba maintain that process tracing is only useful for identifying all relevant steps in a causal chain connecting independent and dependent variables, and thereby for establishing the assumed relationship between them. In addition, when theory testing is the aim of research, process tracing can increase the number of theoretically relevant observations (King *et al.* 1994: 227). However, this is a rather narrow interpretation. Sidney Tarrow argues that 'the goal of process tracing was not to increase the number of discrete decision stages and aggregate them into a larger number of data points but to connect the phases of the policy process and enable the investigator to identify the reason for the emergence of a particular decision' (Tarrow 2004: 173). Process tracing can – in a broad sense – also be categorised as a 'theoretically oriented narrative' (David Laitin, quoted in George and Bennett 2005: 205). Finally, from a social-constructivist perspective, process tracing has yet a different twist as '[t]hicker constructivists might object that talk of causal "mechanisms" reflects an overly materialist discourse that misunderstands the role of rules and self-understandings in social life' (Wendt 1999: 81). Instead of relying on what might be called a 'domino' understanding of a political process,[10] these constructivists stress the importance of self-understanding, appropriateness, norm-guided behaviour and the contingency of actors' behaviour. 'Causes' will lead to action only if they are taken as 'reasons' to act by the actors themselves: material factors or events must be perceived, evaluated and brought into intentional connection with decisions and actions by them (Kurki 2008: 223–30; Breuning 2011: 18).

It is obvious that process tracing assumes a different shape under this constructivist premise. Instead of reconstructing a clear causal path, our analyses traced how key actors struggled with structural restraints – i.e. the political system of their respective country – as well as with normative constraints and potential conflicting demands derived from different logics of appropriateness on different levels (domestic, international). This approach, however, faces two difficulties: one that can occur in any 'conventional' process tracing, and one that is specific to the constructivist approach. The first problem is that the quality of process tracing as a tool for theory testing is, to a large extent, influenced by the elaborateness of the theory guiding the tracing. An underdeveloped understanding of causal mechanisms makes it difficult for the researcher to trace the intermediate steps of the process as it is not clear

---

[10] For the analogy, see George and Bennett (2005: 206–7).

what he or she is actually looking for. However, case studies using process tracing can still be a valuable device for the development of theories as they might reveal the (or a) yet unknown causal chain or point to hitherto overlooked or underrated factors (George and Bennett 2005: 209). DP theory is a prime example here (George and Bennett 2005: 37–59, 209): being a child of quantitative analysis, democratic peace has more often been discussed as an empirical 'law' rather than a valid theory, with the causal paths 'causing' interdemocratic peace to remain underdeveloped or leading in too many directions (see Chapter 1).

The second problem of process tracing is more specific to the constructivist perspective: as the actors' actions are understood to be contingent rather than following a subtle stimulus–response scheme, the relevance of a normative background for a specific action is far from clear. Actors might pretend to follow (domestic, international) normative constraints while they in fact have a hidden agenda or deviating preferences. To fully understand the empirical relevance of normative constraints in the individual cases, one has to check the consistency between the actor's alleged motives (see the remarks on content analysis below) and what can be assumed to be his 'true' motives.

Deducing the motivations that guided key actors is a tricky business in the absence of access to classified documentation or personal records. From a methodological point of view, it has to be admitted, of course, that genuine motivation cannot be ascertained – at least not until neurosciences have found ways to literally read a decision-maker's mind. However, detailed process tracing based on broad background information can be regarded as a proxy to infer actors' motivations and interests. Depending on the type and quality of sources, such inferences can reach the level of reasonable plausibility. Figure 2.1 depicts this basic idea.

3.2   Content analysis: an inquiry into public justification and community norms

3.2.1   Speech act theory and 'rhetorical action'

The content analysis of parliamentary speeches identifies the arguments used by political elites to legitimate their decisions and also shows the weighing up of the arguments pro and contra war, which offers deeper insights into constraints on the use of force and how to overcome them. It is important to stress that the analysis of speech acts uttered by a political actor to justify a particular action does not provide reliable information about the *motivation* behind the actor's policy choice. It is, of course, possible that a political actor makes fully *sincere* statements

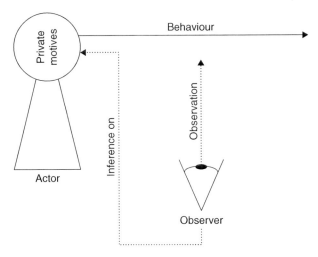

Figure 2.1 The aim of process tracing

about his own motivations when justifying a certain action vis-à-vis the public. But neither researchers nor voters nor any other observers can ever know for sure whether a speaker utters something out of personal conviction or on the basis of strategic considerations: actors can always act *strategically* when stating their motivation for a particular action or justifying their position on a particular issue. They can simply lie about their motives. Analysing speech acts will thus inform us insufficiently about the actors themselves.

However, drawing on speech act theory, it is possible to infer something more reliable about the audience, or, to be more precise, to infer what the speaker thinks his or her audience is going to accept as a valid argument. Speech *act* theory emphasises the *performative* dimension of the utterance (Searle 1969): the speaker intends to achieve a particular purpose. Political speech acts aim at generating specific and diffuse support (Easton 1965). Specific support means assent to the particular political decision in question. Diffuse support includes the appreciation of the speaker beyond the special political action in question.[11] Politicians 'belong to a community whose constitutive values and norms they share' (Schimmelfennig 2001: 62) – or at least are familiar with. Consequently, even if actors have private motives or interests in pursuing a particular course of action, they will at least try to relate their action to an accepted argument within the range defined by the

---

[11] Diffuse support also means general legitimacy for the political system.

constitutive values and norms mentioned above: 'Actors whose self-interested preferences are in line with the community norms have the opportunity to add cheap legitimacy to their position. They will argumentatively back up their selfish goals and delegitimise the position of their opponents. This strategic use of norm-based arguments in pursuit of one's self-interest is rhetorical action' (Schimmelfennig 2001: 63).

From this perspective, it is very likely that democratically elected agents who have to justify their actions or intentions publicly in order to reach consent submit 'resonant' arguments, i.e. arguments that they think will correspond best to the value orientations and interests of their constituents. This applies in particular to parliamentary debates where speakers have to justify their positions to the public and defend them against the opposition. So, instead of collecting evidence about the actor himself, analysing speech acts is a tool for learning something about the target audience as it helps to understand what the speaker considers the best argument to convince a public audience of his course of action – given his *perception* of the audience's understanding of the country's collective identity or foreign policy role conception. Therefore, even under the auspices of the rationalist concept of 'rhetorical action', content analysis of political speech acts is a useful tool for answering our research questions. Figure 2.2 depicts this indirect inference.

The underlying assumption is that the speaker has a quite accurate perception of the constitutive values, norms and identity of his electorate, but we cannot rule out the possibility that an individual politician might have a distorted view or is simply wrong. However, analysing a large number of public justifications for a particular course of action will allow the deduction of what can – in a broader sense – be understood as a country's particular identity and as the reasons for action or inaction that are appropriate in the framework of this identity. As Karin Fierke has put it succinctly in her discussion of Wittgenstein's speech act theory and international relations: 'A focus on the reasons for action provides a much clearer empirical connection (present in public texts) between an argument about the need for the invasion and majority acceptance of the decision ... which provided the legitimacy to move ahead and, in this respect, made the invasion possible' (Fierke 2010: 86).

3.2.2   *Justifications and motivations*

What is the relationship between speech acts and motivations? While relying on rhetorical action might appear as 'cheap talk' to rationalists, it is not without consequences. Speakers who put forward an argument in public, be it with a strategic or 'sincere' intention, have to reckon with the effect that audiences will take this seriously and hold the 'sender'

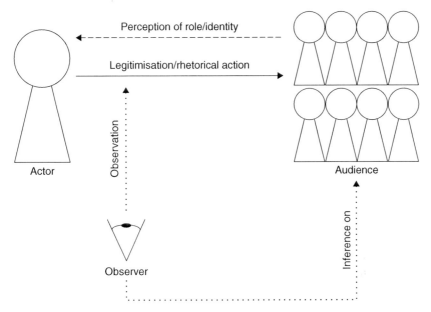

Figure 2.2 The aim of the content analysis

accountable for his arguments in public. The 'sender' is then compelled for reasons of credibility to behave as if he had made the arguments sincerely ('argumentative self-entrapment'; Risse 2000: 32). When a speaker's statements thus diverge from his internal thoughts, he runs the risk of later being caught up in inconsistencies that would cause loss of reputation and impact negatively on the public's diffuse support for his political status. Rationalist rhetorical action theory thus, unexpectedly, creates a weak assumption that public utterances carry a certain probability of authenticity for strategic reasons: the specific support required for a particular political action should weigh less in the calculations of a politician than the diffuse support that extends over a longer period of time and that constitutes a crucial political capital for any politician.

This reasoning is supported by more sociological considerations: as politicians are part of the community that they represent, they are likely to share this community's values (Breuning 2011: 24). Utterances that resonate with the value orientations and attitudes of the public have thus a certain probability of authenticity. Neither of the two arguments, nor their combination, gives sufficient certainty about motivations. However, when they are corroborated by additional sources from process tracing – consistency across time, investigations by journalists or scholars, memoirs that were written after the political career is over – inferences on motivations have considerable plausibility, although certainty can never be completely assured. When we occasionally speak about actors' motivations in this volume, it will be the result of this combination of content analysis and insights from the process tracing analyses.

4   The content analysis of parliamentary speeches in our study

As described above, it can be assumed that political actors are familiar with the constitutive values and norms of their electorate. Critics might, however, object that especially in the realm of international politics it is almost impossible to establish what the public's preferences are. Indeed, early research on public opinion in the United States suggested that public opinion on foreign policy was inconsistent, unstable and susceptible to elite manipulation (Sobel 2001: 12–13; Aldrich *et al.* 2006: 478–9). This early consensus was challenged during the 1970s due to the application of more sophisticated methods. Studies subsequently came to the conclusion that public attitudes towards foreign policy were far stronger and more stable than formerly assumed (Sobel 2001: 13). Richard Sobel concludes that '[s]pecific policy views derive from more general policy orientations, which in turn are related to value preferences. Foreign policy opinions can be structured and maintained even in the face of little information' (Sobel 2001: 14). In other words: even if the general public lacks exact information on a particular foreign policy issue, it will resort to basic beliefs and values to evaluate the problem at hand – a mechanism that the political decision-maker has to bear in mind when framing his justification for a particular action. As framing an issue in a way that does not connect with basic and stable foreign policy beliefs is risky and entails the hazard of significant political costs, even someone considered an opinion leader has to remain within the boundaries of the permissible interpretation of an issue (Aldrich *et al.* 2006: 492).

This proposition appears particularly appropriate in the case of decisions on war. Such decisions are more salient than routine politics and involve tangible risks and costs, which even an ill-informed public can sense. Public interest and involvement in the issue can thus be assumed to be high. It is, of course, possible that opinion leaders do misread the public and misjudge what is accepted as a valid or legitimate framing of their concern. In order to mitigate this problem, our content analysis focused on the legislative, i.e. parliamentary debates where the pros and cons of military participation by one's own country were debated by a – depending on the country and war – larger number of politicians. Focusing on representatives provides not only a larger 'n' than relying on speeches by members of the executive,[12] but also a more reliable match between the beliefs of the representatives and those of the public. Analysing parliamentary debates therefore offers the opportunity to infer what a broad base of representatives considers to be the constitutive values and norms of their electorate. Following these preliminary considerations on the purpose of our content analysis, the following two sections describe the design of our coding scheme as well as the coding procedure in order to enhance transparency and comprehensibility.

4.1 The coding scheme

The basis for the content analysis is a coding scheme of 45 arguments (see the scheme depicted in Table 2.2), which was developed in a two-tiered process. First, arguments with which democratic actors might legitimate or reject going to war were deduced from different theories and approaches of International Relations. Second, this line-up of deduced arguments was then complemented by further arguments that had been identified inductively in the pre-test and subsequently developed in discussions within the group of researchers.[13] The 45 arguments were assigned to seven *frames* that capture the central logic and argumentative reference. The seven frames refer to 'power', 'alliance membership', 'national identity/foreign policy role conception', 'international law', 'universal values', references to 'democratic norms/procedures' and to 'enemy image'.[14]

The *first frame* contains arguments related to power, including arguments based on national interest or national security, military capabilities or the (regional) balance of power. The *second frame* is based

---

[12] It should be noted that in the five parliamentary democracies in our sample, governmental actors were also included in the parliamentary speeches as they are often members of parliament and/or regularly speak to parliament. In the cases of the semi-presidential democracy France and the presidential democracy the United States, where legislative and executive are more clearly separated, a few pertinent speeches by the executive were additionally included for the content analysis.

[13] The description of all arguments and more information on the coding process can be found in the code book, which is available (in German only) online at: www.hsfk.de/Ursachen-der-wechselnden-Beteiligung-demokratisch.140.0.html?&L=1.

[14] It later turned out that two arguments, the reference to a military show of force (assigned to the 'power' frame) and the reference to peaceful means (not) exhausted (assigned to the 'international law' frame), play a special role and should rather be considered as two discrete frames. The particular role of these two arguments is discussed in the comparative chapter of this book.

Table 2.2 *Coding scheme*

Type of argument/ argumentative frames	Arguments justifying war (participation)	Arguments supporting war (participation)	Arguments rejecting war (participation)
Power	**1101**: national interest **1102**: keep/improve power position in international system **1103**: (regional) stability **1104**: show of force **1105**: national security	**1201**: military superiority **1202**: clear military (and exit) strategy exists	**1301**: not in the national interest (NI)/ NI not at stake **1302**: loss of power through war **1303**: regional instability/escalation caused by war **1304**: increasing insecurity through war **1305**: lacking power capabilities **1306**: lacking military (or exit) strategy **1307**: national security not concerned
Alliances	**2101**: internal dimensions of alliance (pro): material and normative commitments of members **2102**: external dimensions of alliance (pro): international credibility; expectations by others	**2201**: consensus within the alliance	**2301**: internal dimensions of alliance (contra): membership commitments not concerned/ inappropriate **2302**: external dimensions of alliance (contra): negative consequences for third parties; loss of reputation through war
National identity/role conception	**3101**: national identity norms; self-image **3102**: expectations by others; role conception	**3201**: in accordance with national identity norms/ role conception	**3301**: restraining norms of national identity/role **3302**: rejection of ascribed identity/role conception **3303**: restraining expectations by others

Table 2.2 (*cont.*)

Type of argument/ argumentative frames	Arguments justifying war (participation)	Arguments supporting war (participation)	Arguments rejecting war (participation)
International law	**4101**: enforcement of international law; support of the UN	**4201**: covered by international law **4202**: appropriateness of means: peaceful means are exhausted	**4301**: lack of UN mandate/weakening of UN through war **4302**: appropriateness of means: peaceful means are not exhausted
Universal values	**5101**: humanitarian catastrophe **5102**: existing political or economic world order threatened	**5201**: multilateral consensus/ support for war	**5301**: political or economic world order not threatened **5302**: pacifism; war damages basic global norms **5303**: concern for civilian casualties **5304**: multilateral rejection of war
Explicit references to democratic norms/ procedures	**6101**: regime change/ democratisation	**6201**: war decision taken in accordance with democratic norms and procedures **6202**: cost reduction by swift action	**6301**: democratic norms/procedures preclude war **6302**: casualty aversion (own soldiers) **6303**: prohibitive material costs
Enemy image	**7101**: 'enemy character' of the adversary (e.g. war criminal; Hitler comparison; WMD)	N/A	**7301**: 'enemy character' of the adversary questioned or no sufficient justification for war

on the effect of institutions and alliances. Being a member of an alliance might put pressure on a state to participate in a military mission either because the state in question is under internal pressure to provide unique military capabilities or because there are external expectations putting the whole alliance or institution under pressure ('NATO is expected to ...'). The *third frame* contains arguments related to norms of collective identity and the foreign policy role conception of a speaker's country. According to constructivist approaches to identity and role, a state possesses a unique cultural identity from which certain normative standards, obligations and international commitments are inferred by speakers, including lessons from one's own history (key phrases here are 'we as ... should ...'). While identity arguments refer to a self-image within a broader role conception of a state, the role conception in the international realm is also made up of external expectations. Governments anticipate or reflect in their speeches and actions what other important actors might expect of them as appropriate in a given situation.

The *fourth frame* consists of arguments related to international law; national governments and publics can be expected to frequently refer to legal issues since decisions on interstate war/no war are crucially structured by international law and the UN Security Council. The *fifth frame* focuses on arguments rooted in values that are understood as being universal or as embodying basic notions of a global order in liberal thought. It is obvious that arguments of the fourth and fifth frame are closely related, but we intended to reserve the 'international law' frame for more specific legal references, while arguments within the fifth frame usually refer to broader notions of order and justice. The *sixth frame* contains arguments that should be specific for democracies such as, for example, democratic regime change as a war aim, or the insistence on democratic procedures and consideration for the majority opinions of the people. The *seventh frame* is closely connected to the third frame as collective identity conceptions are dependent on the demarcation between 'me'/'us' and 'them' or 'others'. In pre-war situations, the adversary is often described in pejorative terms; specific images of a brute 'enemy' are created in order to mobilise national consensus in favour of a military fight.

These seven frames capture nearly all arguments brought forward in the public debates both for and against military participation in war. Each frame was divided into three subcategories. The first category comprises arguments that offer a valid or plausible reason for going to war and that do not require further justification. These arguments can be understood to offer a *sufficient rationale* for national participation in a military mission (e.g. 'we must prevent a humanitarian disaster'). The second category encompasses arguments that are neither sufficient without further explanation nor necessary, but that *support* arguments of the first category against possible objections. To claim, for example, that a military engagement is covered by international law or facilitated by military superiority does not offer a substantial reason for this course of action, but does strengthen the speaker's position against objections. The third category subsumes arguments *against* war. While some of these arguments are simple negations of causative arguments ('The national security is *not* at stake'), others have a unique quality: for example, references to pacifism or to casualty aversion.

4.2   The coding process

For every country and conflict we conducted a content analysis of up to 50 parliamentary speeches with the individual speech being the unit of analysis. In *parliamentary* democracies, debates in parliaments include speakers from the government; in the (semi-)*presidential* systems of France and the United States, where the president does not speak before parliament, additional speeches of the executive were randomly selected and included in the sample. For all countries, we defined the same time span of investigation within which substantial debates on the international crisis had to be identified.[15] In a first step, a list was established of all possible speeches related to the participation of the speakers' own country in the conflict. In a second step, a random sample of 50 speeches was drawn, depending on the number of relevant speeches available. The sample size of 50 was chosen because it appeared to be the highest realistic number to be gathered in all countries for every conflict.

All speeches were checked for an *explicit conclusion* regarding participation of one's own troops in a war. As it was the aim of the project to analyse the specific decision to go to war or to refuse to do so, it was imperative to identify an undisputed conclusion regarding the speakers' position. If it was not possible to decide whether the speaker was a proponent or opponent of military participation (which occurred more often than anticipated), the text was not included in the sample but replaced. Focusing on speeches with a clear-cut conclusion reduced the number of eligible units in some countries enormously. Finally, the speeches had to be of a certain length to offer room for a more sophisticated argumentation, reducing the number even more. In some cases, like the United States, the total number eligible was still very extensive and drawing a sample was not problematic, while for other states, such as Sweden, Germany and France, selecting 50 speeches that met the requirements

---

[15] This period ended – as stated above – with the day the war actually began, in order to exclude a 'rally around the flag' effect. In the case of the 1990–1 Gulf War, the period of investigation was from 2 August 1990 to 17 January 1991; in the case of the Kosovo War it extended from 23 September 1998 to 24 March 1999; and in the case of the recent Iraq War from 8 July 2002 to 20 March 2003.

for coding proved impossible. There are several reasons for this comparatively low number of eligible speeches in some cases: the low perceived
affectedness of one's own country, specific cultures of parliamentary
debates, limited participation of parliaments in deployment issues or the
reluctance of some members of parliament to commit themselves to a
clear-cut position. In such cases, we coded all eligible speeches.

All arguments were dummy-coded as being either present or absent
in a speech.[16] To maximise the reliability of the coding,[17] all relevant
texts were coded by two researchers separately and disagreements
were finally solved with the help of a third person or within the whole
research group.[18] As a result, we obtained the frequency of a particular argument as a percentage in relation to the number of speakers in a
particular country and with regard to a particular conflict (for example:
if 10 out of 20 speakers in country C refer to argument A during the
Kosovo debates, the frequency of the argument is 50 per cent).

5   The interplay of process tracing and content analysis

It has been explained in the previous sections that the content analysis
of political actors' speech acts aims at mapping public legitimisation as
a proxy for the assumed self-attribution of the national foreign policy
role conception or identity. Whereas content analysis produces, as a
side effect, weak assumptions about motivations, process tracing, on
the other hand, allows (among other things) plausible, but still fallible,
conclusions about the actors' motivations. In other words: process tracing uncovers the reasoning of democratically elected decision-makers
concerning military engagements, while content analysis captures what
a particular polity accepts as legitimate reasons for engaging in war.

But how do these two methods interplay in the analysis beyond the
'motivation' question discussed above? First, while process tracing is a
qualitative endeavour, formal content analysis opens up the possibility
of quantitative analyses, thus providing a complement to the qualitative
analyses by revealing broad *patterns* of reasoning. Second, the results
of the process tracing analysis are particularly important for identifying congruence or discrepancies between the public justifications, as

---

[16] We did not qualify or quantify the use of the argument within the unit of analysis. If
a speaker used one particular argument repeatedly and another one only once, then
the argument was counted as equally present.

[17] The individual reliability level of the pre-test was 0.64.

[18] The dataset of 781 parliamentary speeches coded in all seven countries is available online as an SPSS file. See: www.hsfk.de/Causes-of-the-Differences-in-War-
Involvement-of-De.140.0.html?&L=1.

revealed by the content analysis, and the probable reasons, motivations and objectives that induced the executive leadership to participate in, or abstain from, military intervention. If, for example, process tracing indicates that decision-makers had a particular motive for engaging in war that was not addressed in the public justification, this suggests that war was waged for a reason that would not pass public scrutiny as it was not compatible with the basic beliefs of the public.

Of course, public discourses do not only consist of parliamentary debates but are also constituted by other actors and arenas. Democratically elected governments have to justify their decisions not only vis-à-vis members of parliament but also to the public at large. Newspaper commentaries and opinion polls are useful indicators of published and public opinion in a political crisis. Comparing them with the arguments given by politicians makes it possible to identify congruence (indicating that politicians are drawing on shared knowledge in their community) or divergence (pointing to a disconnection between politicians and their community). Therefore, the analysis also included newspaper commentaries and editorials from a left-liberal and a right-of-centre/conservative quality newspaper dealing with the military action under consideration. Since many editorials had no clear-cut position on the question of whether or not their country should or should not participate in war, but often pondered more broadly on the crisis, the government's policies or the appropriateness of the use of force, it was decided to abstain from submitting the editorials to a systematic content analysis (which rested upon a coding scheme that was tailored for discernible yes/no positions on participation with own troops). Instead, the researchers summarised the main argumentative lines and, as far as possible, opinion tendencies presented in the newspapers.[19]

Citizens' attitudes towards military deployment issues are usually measured by national or cross-national opinion polls. Most of these polls survey the assent or opposition of the public to the use of force and national participation in such military operations. To the extent that pertinent polls were conducted in the respective country prior to a war, summaries of these data are presented in the chapters. Given the crucial importance of citizens' attitudes for DP theses, the purpose is to establish whether a majority of citizens can be counted as supporting the participation of the country's combat troops in the potential military action.

We hope that this chapter has explained the overall design of our study and the structure of the following country chapters adequately.

---

[19] For more details, see Appendix, Section 2.

The engagement with the methodological issues should have shown that there are pitfalls of our applied methods but that the merits hopefully far outweigh the disadvantages.

REFERENCES

Aldrich, John H., Gelpi, Christopher, Feaver, Peter, Reifler, Jason and Sharp, Kristin T. 2006. 'Foreign Policy and the Electoral Connection', *Annual Review of Political Sciences* 9: 477–502

Breuning, Marijke 2011. 'Role Theory Research in International Relations: State of the Art and Blind Spots', in Sebastian Harnisch, Cornelia Frank and Hanns W. Maull (eds.), *Role Theory in International Relations: Approaches and Analyses*. London: Routledge, pp. 16–35

Easton, David 1965. *A Systems Analysis of Political Life*. New York, NY: Wiley

Elman, Miriam Fendius 1997. 'Introduction', in Miriam Fendius Elman (ed.), *Paths to Peace: Is Democracy the Answer?* Cambridge, MA: MIT Press, pp. 1–57

Fierke, Karin M. 2007. 'Constructivism', in Tim Dunne, Milja Kurki and Steve Smith (eds.), *International Relations Theories: Discipline and Diversity*. Oxford University Press, pp. 166–84

2010. 'Wittgenstein and International Relations Theory', in Cerwyn Moore and Chris Farrands (eds.), *International Relations Theory and Philosophy: Interpretive Dialogues*. London: Routledge, pp. 83–94

Freedman, Lawrence 2006. 'Iraq, Liberal Wars and Illiberal Containment', *Survival* 48 (4): 51–66

George, Alexander L. and Bennett, Andrew 2005. *Case Studies and Theory Development in the Social Sciences*. Cambridge, MA: MIT Press

Haass, Richard N. 2009. *War of Necessity – War of Choice: A Memoir of Two Iraq Wars*. New York, NY: Simon & Schuster

Harnisch, Sebastian 2011. 'Role Theory: Operationalization of Key Concepts', in Sebastian Harnisch, Cornelia Frank and Hanns W. Maull (eds.), *Role Theory in International Relations: Approaches and Analyses*. London: Routledge, pp. 7–15

Harnisch, Sebastian and Maull, Hanns W. (eds.) 2001. *Germany as a Civilian Power: The Foreign Policy of the Berlin Republic*. Manchester University Press

Harnisch, Sebastian, Frank, Cornelia and Maull, Hanns W. 2011. 'Introduction', in Sebastian Harnisch, Cornelia Frank and Hanns W. Maull (eds.), *Role Theory in International Relations: Approaches and Analyses*. London: Routledge, pp. 1–4

Hasenclever, Andreas and Weiffen, Brigitte 2006. 'International Institutions Are the Key: A New Perspective on the Democratic Peace', *Review of International Studies* 32 (4): 563–85

King, Gary, Keohane, Robert O. and Verba, Sydney 1994. *Designing Social Inquiry: Scientific Inference in Qualitative Research*. Princeton University Press

Kurki, Milja 2008. *Causation in International Relations: Reclaiming Causal Analysis*. Cambridge University Press

Lapid, Yosef 1989. 'The Third Debate: On the Prospects of International Theory in a Post-Positivist Era', *International Studies Quarterly* 33 (3): 235–54

Lipson, Charles 2003. *Reliable Partners: How Democracies Have Made a Separate Peace*. Princeton University Press

Maull, Hanns W. 1990. 'Germany and Japan: The New Civilian Powers', *Foreign Affairs* 69 (5): 91–106

  2000. 'Zivilmacht Deutschland: Vierzehn Thesen für eine neue deutsche Außenpolitik', in Dieter Senghaas (ed.), *Frieden machen*. Frankfurt a.M.: Suhrkamp, pp. 63–76

Orbie, Jan 2006. 'Civilian Power Europe: Review of the Original and Current Debates', *Cooperation and Conflict* 41 (1): 123–8

Owen, John M. 1997. *Liberal Peace, Liberal War: American Politics and International Security*. Ithaca, NY: Cornell University Press

Ray, James Lee 1995. *Democracy and International Conflict: An Evaluation of the Democratic Peace Proposition*. Columbia, SC: University of South Carolina Press

Risse, Thomas 2000. '"Let's Argue!" – Communicative Action in World Politics', *International Organization* 54 (1): 1–39

Rousseau, David L. 2005. *Democracy and War: Institutions, Norms, and the Evolution of International Conflict*. Stanford University Press

Schimmelfennig, Frank 2001. 'The Community Trap: Liberal Norms, Rhetorical Action, and the Eastern Enlargement of the European Union', *International Organization* 55 (1): 47–80

Searle, John R. 1969. *Speech Acts: An Essay in the Philosophy of Language*. Cambridge University Press

Sobel, Richard 2001. *The Impact of Public Opinion on U.S. Foreign Policy Since Vietnam*. Oxford University Press

Tarrow, Sidney 2004. 'Bridging the Quantitative–Qualitative Divide', in Henry Brady and David Collier (eds.), *Rethinking Social Inquiry: Diverse Tools, Shared Standards*. Lanham, MD: Rowman & Littlefield, pp. 171–80

Wendt, Alexander 1998. 'On Constitution and Causation in International Relations', *Review of International Studies* 24 (5): 101–17

  1999. *Social Theory of International Politics*. Cambridge University Press

Wiener, Antje 2008. *The Invisible Constitution of Politics: Contested Norms and International Encounters*. Cambridge University Press

Wolfowitz, Paul 2003. 'Deputy Secretary Wolfowitz Interview with Sam Tanenhaus, Vanity Fair', News Transcript. Online: www.defense.gov/transcripts/transcript.aspx?transcriptid=2594

Part II

Opting in, opting out: liberal democracies and war

3 The United States: the American way of leading the world into democratic wars

Stephanie Sohnius

The United States (US) led the warring forces in the 1990–1 Gulf War, the 1998–9 Kosovo War and the 2003 intervention in Iraq and dominated the international pre-war proceedings. None of the wars took place close to US borders, none of the opponents represented an immediate threat to US national security and in none of the three crises did circumstances dictate taking up arms. Yet, the US government decided to do so, and was supported, or at least not determinedly opposed, by Congress and the public. US power made military action possible without determining it. The decisions to go to war were rooted in a particular interpretation of US exceptionalism and the role of world leadership, as well as the mission to defeat evil, to provide order and to promote democracy and human rights.

1 Institutional and ideational factors of US foreign and security policy

1.1 Regime-type features and decision-making in American security policy

The founding fathers of the US created a system of checks and balances in order to avoid a concentration of power such as in European monarchies. However, a great deal of power in foreign and security policy lies in the hands of the president. As head of government *and* of state, as chief diplomat and commander-in-chief of the armed forces, the president occupies the dominant position in foreign policy. He is entitled to conclude 'executive agreements' that take effect unless both houses of Congress vote against within a prescribed period. Treaties, on the other hand, become binding on the US only when two-thirds of the Senate consent to ratification. In turn, the president is entitled to veto laws enacted by Congress; only a two-thirds majority in both houses can overrule a veto. The national security advisor, the secretaries of state and defense, the director of the Central Intelligence Agency (CIA) and – in military matters – the chairman of the Joint Chiefs of Staff also exert influence on external policy. They are the core members of the National Security Council, which deliberates all important security issues concerning US security.

The members of the House of Representatives are elected every two years. The term of the 100 Senators lasts six years, one-third of the 'upper house' is elected every second year. The majority voting system has led to a two-party system: only the Republicans and the Democrats have ever won an election. The decentralised and fragmented structure of the parties, the lack of caucus discipline in parliament and the weight of the interests of electoral districts and states allow only a loose connection between the president and the members of his party in Congress, though partisanship has grown over the last two decades (Fisher 2004; Jentleson 2004: 10–74). Many access points in the system encourage interaction between state and societal actors and lobbyism, and accord some influence to non-governmental organisations and the media (McCombs 2006).

The US constitution contains some twilight zones concerning the division of authority between president and Congress. Accordingly, phases of stronger congressional control alternate with phases of executive dominance. The latter alternative prevails when the same party controls the presidency and both houses of Congress, or when the American people perceive an existential threat. The twilight zone also applies to war powers. Article I, 8 of the constitution transfers 'the power to declare war' to Congress. Article II renders the president commander-in-chief of the US military. Since independence, *Presidentialists* ascribe exclusive authority for declaring and fighting wars to the president, whereas *Congressionalists* ascribe this right to Congress, and accept related congressional influence through the power of the purse and oversight rights (Fisher 2004).

In reaction to the defeat in Vietnam and the excesses of the 'imperial presidency' (Schlesinger 1974), Congress tried to curb presidential authority to deploy US military abroad in the War Powers Resolution of 1973: the president may send troops into combat for no more than 60–90 days without the consent of Congress (Grimmett 2010: 4, 6). However, every single president since Richard Nixon has contested the resolution's constitutional validity. Only five of the more than 200 military interventions in the history of the US, and none since 1945, have been launched pursuant to a formal declaration of war. Presidents ask Congress to approve military action just to garner public support and avoid deep rifts in Congress (Fisher 2004).

1.2 America's role conception and role profile in foreign and security policy

1.2.1 Foreign policy traditions, guidelines and role conception

Foreign policy conceptions: American identity, worldview, and the ensuing understanding of the US global role in all varieties start from US exceptionalism, the founding fathers' belief that Americans are 'the chosen people' with a 'manifest destiny' and a society and system of rule of a higher moral order. This attitude can assume religious or even apocalyptic traits and supports a manichaean worldview with strong enemy images. It is mixed with, and bolstered by, a deep belief in liberal values: democracy, liberty, sovereignty, human rights, equality and the rule of law (Lipset 1997: 60–7; Mead 2001: 56).

After the demise of isolationism, US policy was guided by the combination of, or compromise between, two distinct translations of self-image and worldview into foreign and security policy guidance, liberal internationalism and conservative realpolitik (Schweigler 2004). The first approach starts from the idea that it is the US mission to promote American values in the world. Spreading democracy, the rule of law and the market economy is viewed as the best for both the world *and* the US. In the tradition of President Woodrow Wilson, international organisations are considered crucial to achieving these goals. *In extremis*, these objectives might even be pursued by military means in a 'crusade for the good'.

The conservative alternative believes that America's uniqueness and values must be protected by a consistent realpolitik. Advocates of this view want to shape the world with a view to fostering US security and economic interests. The striving for a favourable balance of power is justified by the belief that geo-strategic and/or geo-economic hegemony is the only reliable guarantor for US security and welfare. This political orientation requires heavy investments in defence and tends towards militarising foreign policy. Proponents are also concerned about US sovereignty and are thus inclined towards unilateralism, but may utilise international institutions and law for the pursuit of national interests if it fits their cost–benefit analysis.

From the 1970s onwards, an ultra-conservative ideology emerged on the right edge of the political spectrum. It endorses strong manichaean interpretations of both domestic politics and foreign policy, conceived of as the enduring fight against evil that can only be overcome if American values prevail: 'Victory or holocaust' (Frum and Perle 2003: 9). Enemy images are exceptionally strong here; the spectre of a 'new Hitler' has been repeatedly invoked. Ultra-conservatives (of whom the neoconservatives are an important part) prefer a neo-liberal market economy, a security state and a militant foreign policy that relies on strength and is averse to the constraining forces of multilateralism and international law (Kristol 1995; Halper and Clarke 2004). Pierre Hassner (2002) has labelled this worldview succinctly as 'Wilsonianism in boots'. Neoconservative writers (e.g. Boot 2003) embraced 'liberal imperialism', while liberal internationalists condemned imperialism as a deviation from the genuine role of the US as a benevolent hegemon, working through multilateralism and soft power (Ikenberry 2004).

Foreign policy developments: The US emerged from the Second World War as the strongest global power. It shaped the world order according to its own vision, and initiated and promoted international institutions that make up the institutional fabric of world politics today.

After 1945, the 'Munich Syndrome' inclined the US against appeasement. Containment thus provided the template for US foreign policy throughout the Cold War, uniting idealist and realist components (Gaddis 1982). In a manichaean division of the world into good and evil, communism was the enemy. The containment of communism motivated military action in the Korean War (1950–3) and interventions involving covert action, the most fateful example being in Iran (1953). The Vietnam War, which was also fought for reasons of containment, damaged the US's image around the world. 'No more Vietnams' emerged as the leitmotif of a whole generation of Americans. The increased need (and difficulty) to justify military interventions before the American people significantly influenced US military doctrine (Powell 1995).

After the Cold War, there was no longer a consensual foreign policy paradigm or confrontation with an undisputed enemy. While the administration of George H. W. Bush (1988–92) pursued a pragmatic policy of cooperative leadership, the overwhelming victory in the Gulf War (1991) brought home to Americans their singular position as the only superpower. *How* to shape *which* order became a central subject for the US foreign policy discourse.

The team around President George H. W. Bush was dominated by realist-pragmatic Republican centrists. Only the Pentagon hosted some neoconservatives, such as Paul Wolfowitz. Bush's team conceived US leadership as creating and presenting the 'new world order', which was in some respects framed in terms of liberal internationalism: under the leadership of the US, order, peace, free trade and democracy were to be spread around the world. The United Nations (UN), whose significance was revived in the course of the Gulf War of 1991, was accorded an important function. Notwithstanding the moral-legalistic rhetoric of the Bush administration, the 'new world order', as a corollary, was to secure and enlarge US hegemony, a realpolitik consideration. International organisations were used for US purposes. The Bush Sr administration was willing to defend the 'new world order' and the US hegemony within it against aggressive challengers, if necessary with military force (Tucker and Hendrickson 1992; Bowen and Dunn 1996: 8–14).

While a majority of Americans endorsed an active leadership after 1990, many expected a tangible 'peace dividend'. Turning to the domestic economy, the Democrats promoted an enlargement of the welfare state in the successful election campaign of 1992. The Clinton administration (1993–2000) followed an internationalist foreign policy conception. The 'National Security Strategy of Engagement and Enlargement' (The White House 1995) declared the spread of democracy, human rights and free markets as the principles of security policy and the precondition for continued US world leadership. Assertive multilateralism was the instrument for realising these objectives; this included humanitarian interventions within the framework of the UN in Somalia, Haiti and Bosnia.

The costs and doubtful successes, if not outright failures, of 'humanitarian interventions', however, divided the Democrats into 'idealists' and 'pragmatists' who grew increasingly sceptical. In addition, the conservative revolution of 1994 resulted in strong pressure for foreign policy change and narrowed the executive's freedom of action. Towards the end of the 1990s, the US pursued only a highly selective multilateralism (Bowen and Dunn 1996: 22–4, 96–107; Hyland 1999). During these years, the enemy image of the 'rogue state' became dominant (Klare 1995; Litwak 2000). The Clinton administration employed this template increasingly in its dealings with Saddam Hussein and with Iran, while the neoconservatives integrated it into their narrative of the fight against evil.

The conservative revolution reached the White House with the presidency of George W. Bush (2001–9). After the terrorist attacks of 11 September 2001 and the declaration of the 'global war on terror', the security imperative under the state of emergency led to a compromising of liberal-democratic principles: Bush's new imperial presidency became more independent of congressional control and civil society. The grand design for foreign policy, which the neoconservatives had envisioned for a long time, was finally adopted by the government (Mann 2004): 'rogue states' and terrorists were amalgamated in the overarching threat perception.

Fighting these enemies was a central theme in the National Security Strategy (NSS) documents of 2002 and 2006, combined with promoting democracy, human rights and free markets. The Middle East became the geo-strategic focus; institutionalist approaches remained subordinate to principled unilateralism. Neoconservative ideology focused on using military prevention to eliminate future threats emerging from 'rogues' and terrorists.[1] The military budget rose significantly under Bush's war presidency with its quasi-imperialist worldview. The US government relied on its own strength and dealt with international law in an opportunistic way, using it when it seemed to support its own positions and ignoring it when it did not (Greenstein 2003; Roß 2005).

The foreign policy role conception followed by US governments since the end of the Cold War has thus undergone several metamorphoses: from a mainstream internationalism through particularly committed internationalism to a much more cautious pragmatism and finally to a determined unilateralism with imperial overtones – with the US all the while claiming leadership as a matter of course, including in wartime.

1.2.2 *The US approach to international law: the example of the ICC*

The perceived US mission in the world includes strengthening international law. Beginning with the Nuremberg Court, the US supported the creation of ad hoc international criminal courts. However, the sense of exceptionalism and ensuing global responsibilities frames US attitudes to these types of courts in a particular way: their adjudication is applicable to wrongdoers – by definition *others* but not to the US itself. Indeed, self-subordination to international law has always been problematic in the US political and legal discourse (Henkin 1972). This ambivalence was revealed in the debates on the creation of the International Criminal Court (ICC). Sovereignty concerns, especially subjecting US soldiers to foreign jurisdiction, were seen as unacceptable by leading Republicans, notably in the light of US responsibility as the guarantor of world order. While President Clinton initially supported the establishment of an ICC, he had to retreat in the face of conservative pressure, and eventually voted against the Rome Statute in 1998. Clinton finally signed the statute, committing the US to the objectives of the ICC, just before leaving office. The US position documented that '[r]ealising individual liberty through the sovereign state and the

---

[1] Pre-emption is anticipating defence against an imminent attack and covered by the right to self-defence. Prevention aims at eliminating apparent risks before they grow into real threats. It is generally seen as incompatible with international law. The Bush administration declared what in fact was a doctrine of prevention in the 'war on terror' to be one of pre-emption (Mantho 2004: 13).

law of nations continues to appeal to Americans because it allows them to square the universalist and nationalist goals in their political culture' (Ralph 2005: 43).

The Republican-dominated Congress never ratified the statute, and George W. Bush withdrew the US signature, thereby claiming the right to work actively against the statute's objectives. Under the Bush government, the US only participated in UN missions on the conditions secured by two UN Security Council (UNSC) resolutions that exempted soldiers from non-parties to the Rome Statute from the ICC's jurisdiction. Bush concluded numerous bilateral agreements to the same effect for other deployments (Jentleson 2004: 435–7; Deitelhoff 2006).

1.2.3   *The US approach to international regimes: arms control and disarmament*

Despite its continued effort to maintain its nuclear deterrent, the US initiated agreements like the Strategic Arms Limitation Treaty (SALT), the Anti-Ballistic Missile Treaty (ABM Treaty), Intermediate-Range Nuclear Forces Treaty (INF) and the Nuclear Non-proliferation Treaty (NPT) during the Cold War. Neither George H. W. Bush nor Bill Clinton took advantage of the end of the Soviet Union to pursue nuclear disarmament. However, Bush did conclude the Strategic Arms Reduction Treaty (START) I and Clinton START II. The numbers of deployed nuclear weapons were reduced, but at the same time new missions for nuclear weapons were developed for fighting wars against 'rogue states'.

The Clinton administration strove to ensure the indefinite extension of the NPT at the 1995 Review and Extension Conference and a consensus document at the 2000 NPT Review Conference, both of which included American concessions on nuclear disarmament. However, the Senate blocked the Comprehensive Test Ban Treaty (CTBT) in 1999, one of the promises of 1995 that Clinton had signed. Moreover, the Senate added conditions to its resolution on ratifying the Chemical Weapons Convention that were incompatible with this Convention, as they established constraints on what the Organisation for the Prohibition of Chemical Weapons could do to verify US chemical activities. The US also expressed reservations on the desirability of the Additional Protocol to the Biological Weapons Convention, and terminated its participation in the 2001 negotiations under the Bush administration, breaking off these talks for good. Finally, Congress forced the National Missile Defense Act of 1998 upon the Clinton administration. This obliged the government to build a ballistic missile defence system and foreshadowed the end of the ABM Treaty, which had maintained a stable deterrence system for 30 years.

For George W. Bush, counter-proliferation dominated multilateral non-proliferation as part of national security policy. Bush's nuclear strategy envisaged first-use nuclear options in a number of possible contingencies. Multilateral instruments, including the NPT, were devalued and instrumentalised for specific US interests; the 2005 Review Conference failed because of this attitude. The US negotiated the Moscow Treaty on Russia's insistence; this treaty prescribed further reductions of deployed strategic nuclear weapons but lacked any verification system. Bush put a brake on the nuclear disarmament process by withdrawing from the ABM Treaty, provoking fears, and ensuing countermeasures, from Moscow and Beijing that their nuclear deterrents might become ineffective (Müller and Sohnius 2006).

US policy was ambivalent towards the effort to ban anti-personnel landmines. The Clinton administration engaged in landmine removal, supported the idea of banning 'dumb mines' (i.e. devices without a self-destruction system), and committed in 1996 to not using these in future. However, the US delegation to the Ottawa negotiations requested an exemption for the possible use of anti-personnel mines along the inter-Korean border and, when this effort failed, refused to sign the Ottawa Convention, again under congressional pressure. Clinton opened the prospect of joining the treaty in 2006 if technical progress would then permit US participation. Bush rejected this plan and instead promoted the development of new mines with a short operational lifetime, which would allegedly render them harmless to civilians after conflict (Jentleson 2004: 459–60).

1.2.4   The US approach to the United Nations

It is fair to say that the US 'invented' the United Nations and has acted as leader of the Security Council ever since it was founded in 1945. At the same time, Washington has often ignored resolutions (rarely of the Security Council, regularly of the General Assembly) when the content of these documents seemed to run counter to US interests. The US displays a selective-pragmatic, utilitarian use of its veto, requests special rules for itself and has a record of repeatedly delaying or refusing to pay its membership dues.

Following the Cold War, President George H. W. Bush attempted to reactivate the UN system after decades of superpower stalemate. The Gulf War of 1990–1, which was mandated by the Security Council, put new emphasis on the UN's importance. Later, however, many US politicians, notably Republicans, blamed the UN for failed interventions in Somalia and Haiti, counter to the continued sympathy of the US public for the world organisation. This was the prelude to the complete devaluation of the UN by Bush's son: George W. Bush used the UN for the 'war on terror' (Jentleson 2004: 428–43) but otherwise accorded it no attention.

1.2.5   Relations with significant others

NATO: The US power position and its largely inward-looking society limit the influence of external expectations on US policy. Within these limits, NATO and its members remain the most important collective '*alter*'. This was the case after the Cold War, with the proviso of the diminished importance of Europe in the global US outlook. From 1991 onwards, presidents have striven to strengthen NATO vis-à-vis its competitors in the transatlantic area, the EU and the OSCE. NATO enlargement was the key strategy for achieving this goal. With the growing emphasis on 'out of area' operations, the US worked towards changing NATO's strategy and posture in order to make it a useful instrument in such endeavours. This ever more utilitarian attitude towards the Alliance became obvious after 9/11 and the war in Afghanistan: while the Alliance invoked Article V on mutual support after an attack, the US insisted on leading the operations in a national capacity and was highly selective in involving a few allies. Within NATO and beyond, the United Kingdom enjoyed a 'privileged partnership' with Washington and demonstrated this frequently by supporting US positions in NATO, the UN or the EU (Czempiel 2003: 138–45; Jentleson 2004: 382–7).

Significant bilateral relationships: Israel is the most significant 'other' for the US in the Middle East, where two of the three wars studied in this book were fought. The end of the Cold War placed the US in the dominant position in the Middle East. Securing stable access to crude oil, fostering peace between Israel and the Arabs and containing the 'rogue states' of Iraq and Iran constituted strategic goals; after 9/11, the 'war on terror' was the hegemonic template for national security policy in which all other aspects were to be integrated. When balancing its interest in access to oil and its protector role towards conservative non-democratic Arab countries, on the one hand, and its commitment to Israel, on the other hand, this latter commitment has often proved stronger than what unbiased observers would believe to be US realpolitik interests (Spiegel 1997: 295–316), not least because of the strong position of pro-Israel groups in US domestic politics.[2]

---

[2] See the – highly contested – study by Mearsheimer and Walt (2007).

On the global stage, relations with Russia and China as (potential) rivals for primacy are important for the way the US defines itself. The contrast between the US as a democracy, Russia as a defect democracy and China as an autocracy plays an increasingly prominent role in the US political discourse, as does the need to stay ahead of them, notably in military matters (e.g. Kagan 2008).

1.3   Conclusion: the US foreign policy role conception

American exceptionalism as a source of national identity is immersed in all variations of the worldview and self-image of the US. America's power, which was overwhelming after 1990, as well as the lack of a new grand strategy such as containment, opened a variety of possibilities for translating these cultural traits into policy concepts and related strategies. The balance in the mixture of internationalism, realism and unilateral nationalism changed as the polarisation of the US polity sharpened. From the mid 1990s onwards, the US showed ambivalence towards, and a trend away from, multilateralism and international law. Unilateralist, ultraconservative concepts, with neoconservative missionarism at the fore, prevailed first in Congress and later, under George W. Bush, also in the executive. Bush relegated multilateralism to the margins. This move from a pragmatic internationalism to unilateral missionarism was mirrored in US warmaking.

2   Decision-making and public debates on three wars

2.1   The 1990–1991 Gulf War

2.1.1   The road to war
Together with the British government, the US administration was the leading advocate for repelling the Iraqi occupation of Kuwait, reversing previous American support for Baghdad's war against Iran. President George H. W. Bush, whose government had ignored Iraqi preparations for aggression, interpreted the invasion and the taking of international hostages (including Americans) as being not just an ordinary interstate conflict. For him, it was an assault on the 'new world order' that he had announced the same day. From the beginning, Bush pursued an uncompromising policy and rejected attempts towards a regional solution as well as all Iraqi concessions. With moralistic rhetoric he personalised the conflict, calling Saddam Hussein 'Hitler revisited' (e.g.

Bush 1991: 1411, 1449, 1455, 1541),[3] which sounded rather atypical for this 'realist' president; a critic called Bush's ostensibly moralistic approach a 'crusade' (Atkinson 1993). His hard line was supported by Secretary of Defense Cheney and National Security Advisor Scowcroft, whereas Secretary of State Baker pleaded for more diplomatic efforts and the Chairman of the Joint Chiefs of Staff Powell counselled military caution.

In the eyes of the hawks in the government, economic sanctions were not sufficient to force Saddam Hussein to retreat. From 8 August 1990 onwards, the US deployed about 200,000 soldiers to Saudi Arabia in *Operation Desert Shield* to protect the kingdom against an expected Iraqi attack. At the same time, Bush tasked his generals with drafting an offensive strategy for liberating Kuwait. He deemed a UN mandate unnecessary, but Baker convinced him of its usefulness for legitimising military action at home and abroad, as well as for cost-sharing. The US government engaged in intense and eventually successful negotiations in the UN Security Council. In the view of the US administration, the clock was now ticking as it was not possible to keep such a large number of troops in the desert forever (Baker 1995: 277–99; Bennett 1997: 38–68).

During the run-up to the war, the administration mounted an intense media campaign. Sanctions and military deployment enjoyed public and congressional support. However, Congress wanted to avoid voting on a war before the November mid-term elections. Bush decided on preparing offensive military operations (*Desert Storm*) on 30 October 1990, but heeded the congressional wish by postponing the announcement until after the November elections. Congress was thus faced with a fait accompli without previous consultations and without being called on to vote, and a critical chorus grew louder among the media and experts, within the military and among the general public and Congress itself. Critics noted that the administration's justifications for a military offensive shifted continuously. In order to force the president to ask for congressional consent, some Democrats requested the application of the War Powers Resolution; 53 Democrats filed a suit with a District Court but failed (Smith 1992: 214–301).

As thousands of additional soldiers moved towards the Gulf, support for Bush's policy increased among Republicans and conservative and pro-Israeli lobby organisations, while elsewhere criticism was more

---

[3] On several occasions, Bush judged Saddam Hussein as even worse than Hitler (e.g. Bush 1991: 1509, 1513).

pronounced than before. Convincing the opponents of war proved difficult (Bush and Scowcroft 1998: 420–7). Bush reportedly finally decided at the end of December to launch *Operation Desert Storm*, the reconquest of Kuwait. His military planners advised him to begin combat operations in mid-January 1991, when the troops would be ready and the weather not too hot (Powell 1995: 484–5). The Geneva meeting between Baker and his Iraqi counterpart Tariq Aziz on 9 January thus served primarily to enhance domestic and international support (Baker 1995: 370–8).

Bush now consulted with Congress, rightly expecting that many members of Congress would not want to appear unpatriotic shortly before US soldiers were to be sent into action. On 11 and 12 January 1991, after heated debates, the House of Representatives (250:183) and the Senate (52:47) voted largely along party lines to authorise military action and reject proposals for continued economic sanctions. Thus, the almost unanimous support for eliciting Iraqi withdrawal without military action shifted to a more controversial discourse when action became imminent, with partisan considerations becoming stronger. After the failed ultimatum of 15 January, Bush led the coalition under US command into war on 17 January 1991 (Smith 1992: 230–51; Bush and Scowcroft 1998: 436–9).

2.1.2   Content analysis of congressional debates[4]

Among the 50 coded speeches by members of Congress and the executive prior to the Gulf War, there were 28 proponents of the war (26 Republicans, 2 Democrats; shown in Table 3.1) and 22 opponents (Democrats only; depicted in Table 3.2).

The personalised enemy image dominated the arguments in favour of the war. Forcing the dictator back into compliance with international law through a show of force followed in second place; next a bloc of arguments emphasising normative objectives (protection of the world order, multilateral support and international law) indicated a strong commitment to multilateralism. However, only half of the pro-war speakers noted the legality of the action on the basis of the UNSC mandate. National interests were only discussed with lower priority; national security and the power position even ranked at the bottom of Table 3.1. References to elements of role or identity as well as humanitarian issues

---

[4] Members of the executive do not speak in parliamentary debates in the US system. Thus, ten speeches by representatives of the executive (president, secretaries of state and defense, vice-president, national security advisor) have been randomly selected for each of the three wars under scrutiny.

Table 3.1 *Frequencies of arguments, Gulf War, United States, supporters only (n = 28); extracts of results[a]*

Code	Argument	Number of speakers	Percentage of speakers
7101	Enemy image of adversary	21	75
1104	Show of force	21	75
5102	Threat to world order	20	71.4
5201	Multilateral consensus pro	20	71.4
4101	Enforce international law/support UN	18	64.3
1101	National interest	17	60.7
1103	Regional stability	16	57.1
6302	Casualty aversion (own soldiers)	15	53.6
4202	Peaceful means exhausted	15	53.6
6202	Cost reduction by swift action	14	50
4201	Covered by international law	14	50
3101	Identity norms	11	39.3
5101	Humanitarian catastrophe	9	32.1
1102	Keep/improve power position	8	28.6
6201	Democratic norms/procedures respected	7	25
5301	World order not threatened	7	25
1105	National security	6	21.4

[a] Full lists of results for this and all following tables are available from the author.

Table 3.2 *Frequencies of arguments, Gulf War, United States, opponents only (n = 22); extracts of results*

Code	Argument	Number of speakers	Percentage of speakers
4302	Peaceful means not exhausted	22	100
6302	Casualty aversion (own soldiers)	18	81.8
1303	Regional instability	12	54.5
6303	Prohibitive material costs	10	45.5
1103	Regional stability	6	27.3
1301	National interest contra	6	27.3
1306	Lacking military strategy	6	27.3
6301	Democratic norms/procedures contra war	6	27.3
7101	Enemy image of adversary	6	27.3
1104	Show of force	5	22.7

were made in more than a third of the speeches. More than half of the war supporters expressed concerns about potential casualties.

All 22 war opponents denied that peaceful means to solve the crisis had been exhausted – a classical international law argument (see Table 3.2). Some 81 per cent emphasised the risks for US soldiers in the first large US-led war since Vietnam. More than half of the speakers feared regional instability due to a war, and 45 per cent complained about the prohibitive material costs of a war. These main objections are followed by a bloc of realist arguments on stability, national interests and exit strategy. Even among the opponents, however, six speakers acknowledged pro-war arguments such as restoring regional stability and fighting the vicious enemy Saddam Hussein, and five the need for a credible military threat to force the dictator into compliance.

2.1.3   Newspaper debates[5]

The random sample of newspapers contains 50 editorials, 25 each from the conservative *Washington Times* (WT) and the liberal *New York Times* (NYT). In the 25 articles drawn from the WT, 13 supported and 12 opposed the war, while the numbers for the NYT are 8 and 17 respectively. Proponents of the war highlighted the enemy image presented by the Iraqi dictator. Concerns about regional stability and the conviction that relying on peaceful means only was not sufficient were also frequently mentioned. The conservative columnist William Safire and the moderate former executive-editor Abraham M. Rosenthal of the NYT condemned Saddam Hussein vehemently, warned repeatedly against a nuclear war or Iraqi nuclear attacks on the US and Israel and criticised Bush's policy as being too appeasing, using stronger language than many Republican politicians.[6,7]

War proponents frequently mentioned the necessity to demonstrate military resolve and protect regional stability. National interests gained greater prominence than in the politicians' discourse. In contrast, normative concerns such as world order or Iraq's violation of international law attracted less attention. Only a few journalists discussed the possibility of American casualties, the fiscal burden of a war or the possible loss of Iraqi civilian life.

---

[5] Because of the large number of relevant articles, the 25 editorials from each newspaper were selected randomly.

[6] E.g. Safire, William 1990. 'Now or Later?', *New York Times*, 7 August, p. 19; Safire 1991. 'The Letter', *New York Times*, 7 January, p. 17.

[7] E.g. Rosenthal, Abraham M. 1990. 'The Iraqi Nightmare', *New York Times*, 6 November, p. 23; Rosenthal 1990. 'The President's Mistake', *New York Times*, 13 November, p. 31.

War opponents in the NYT warned against Bush's strategy of escalation from the very beginning of the conflict and pleaded for the use of non-violent means such as sanctions.[8] In contrast, opponents in the WT were more concerned about the negative impact of a war on US national interests, particularly on the economy. The NYT mentioned the breakdown of the anti-Iraq coalition and the ensuing loss of US influence in the Middle East as dominant 'realist' factors. Regional instability figured less prominently. War opponents in both newspapers pointed to insufficient public and congressional support, but uttered only a few concerns about the victims and costs of a war.

2.1.4   Public opinion polls

From August 1990 (with the exception of October), a majority of Americans viewed the Gulf crisis as the most important political issue. A first 'rally around the flag' effect emerged following Iraq's aggression, the taking of hostages by Iraq and the *Desert Shield* deployment of US forces: a large majority supported a military response. In most polls, support for using force declined between October 1990 and January 1991, sometimes to below 50 per cent. A stronger rally 'around the flag' effect set in immediately before the fighting started. During the fighting, war support rose to above 80 per cent in some polls. For months, Bush was one of the most popular presidents of the US. However, no pro-interventionist pressure emerged from public opinion. Support for the war frequently fell significantly when sanctions were mentioned as the alternative to military action.

Stable majorities predicted a quick and decisive US victory with 'only' a few thousand US casualties. The war readiness of the population was enhanced by positive cost–benefit expectations, by the UN mandate and by the failure of Baker's meeting with Aziz on 9 January. Polls conducted between November and January showed that a majority thought that the goal of preventing Iraq from obtaining nuclear weapons and the inhumane treatment of Kuwaitis justified going to war. Securing oil supplies, preventing an attack on Israel, ensuring regime change in Iraq or restoring the Emir of Kuwait attracted less support. On the other hand, many respondents suspected that oil was the true motive for the US government's determination to go to war. This was also a key issue in the largest anti-war demonstrations the US had seen since Vietnam (Mueller 1994: 24–77, 179–311).

[8] E.g. Wicker, Tom 1990. 'The War Option', *New York Times*, 31 October, p. 25; Wicker 1990. 'The Wrong Strategy', *New York Times*, 14 November, p. 29; Lewis, Anthony 1990. 'No Thanks', *New York Times*, 23 November, p. 37; Lewis 1990. 'Happy New Year?', *New York Times*, 31 December, p. 23.

2.1.5   Conclusion: the Gulf War

The Bush administration acted as a determined leader of a large coalition to prepare and wage war against Iraq. The US government's considerations were guided by the aim of preserving international order in general, and preventing the dangerous hegemony of a potentially hostile force in the strategically crucial oil region of the Persian Gulf in particular. As the president said: 'Out of these troubled times, our fifth objective – a new world order – can emerge: a new era – freer from the threat of terror, stronger in the pursuit of justice, and more secure in the quest for peace.'[9] A mixture of power/security arguments, international law aspects and moral concerns prevailed in the congressional debate. The strong, personalised enemy image of Saddam Hussein as an evil and dangerous (weapons of mass destruction) leader bolstered the justifications for attack. Multilateral backing was taken as welcome support. Opponents argued that peaceful means were not exhausted – a prohibitive international law argument – and emphasised the risk to US soldiers and the costs of war. The media mirrored the arguments found among parliamentarians; however, there were strong anti-war voices in the NYT. The fact that the US had support from important allies was hardly noted in the public discourse. As the accounts by US leaders indicate, the efforts to obtain a UN mandate were largely aimed at gaining domestic support and less the expression of a principled stance. A massive 'rally around the flag' mood emerged just before fighting started. Solid public support and the eventual consent of both houses of Congress meant that the president was acting in line with democratic requirements.

2.2   The US and the 1998–1999 Kosovo War

2.2.1   The road to war

When violence escalated in Serbia's southern province of Kosovo in spring 1998, the US Congress adopted a resolution condemning the violation of human rights, demanding the end of violence and supporting sanctions. The US government was united in its resolve to prevent a 'second Bosnia' – another humanitarian disaster – but there was much disagreement about the appropriate means. Secretary of State Madeleine Albright, who had escaped from the Nazi regime, used the historical analogy of a 'second Munich 1938', the appeasement of a

---

[9] George Bush, 'Address Before a Joint Session of the Congress on the Persian Gulf Crisis and the Federal Budget Deficit', 11 September 1990, Washington, DC. Online: http://bushlibrary.tamu.edu/research/public_papers.php?id=2217&year=1990&month=9.

ruthless dictator. She demanded uncompromising US leadership in the crisis (Albright 2003: 378–92). She could count on the support of a majority of Democrats in Congress, liberal human rights groups and the liberal media. President Clinton was more reluctant, as he was pre-occupied with the domestic Lewinsky and Whitewater scandals. Some observers suspected that Clinton applied a 'wag the dog' strategy of diversionary war.[10] However, Clinton's memoirs (2004: ch. 49) suggest that he wanted to protect himself against the accusation of going to war for personal reasons and wanted to avoid an unpopular war dur-ing the impeachment process. Against the wish of his secretary of state, Clinton was not willing to indicate as a 'warning' to Slobodan Milošević American readiness to act should Serbia escalate violence in Kosovo. Most cabinet members, including Defense Secretary Cohen, a Republican, and the Joint Chiefs of Staff opposed another 'humani-tarian intervention'. The broader public was also relatively averse to yet another involvement in the Balkans. In the year of congressional elections, most of the Republicans in Congress and some Democrats shared this position.

When it became obvious that Russia would not agree to anything more than sanctions in the Balkan Contact Group, Albright concen-trated on NATO, and at the end of May 1998 succeeded in persuad-ing the allies to start military planning (Daalder and O'Hanlon 2000: 22–36; Clark 2001: 106–11). The situation in Kosovo deteriorated over the summer; the mediation efforts of Ambassadors Richard Holbrooke and Christopher Hill failed. In the light of these developments, Clinton was persuaded that more forceful action was needed. Now, NATO threatened air attacks against Serbia. The US agreed, reluctantly, to French and German requests to negotiate UNSC Resolution 1199. This document, which was adopted on 23 September 1998, declared that the situation in Kosovo represented a threat to peace and inter-national security, but contained only vague operational language ('fur-ther action and additional measures'). China and Russia opposed a more specific text. The US government did not want to concede that NATO could only take military action on the basis of a UN mandate, as this would set a precedent that might narrow future freedom of action (Daalder and O'Hanlon 2000: 36–43).

Early October 1998 saw the Holbrooke–Milošević agreement on ter-minating violence in Kosovo. Albright urged the NATO Council to change its 'activation warning' into an 'activation order' in order to

---

[10] E.g. Philip Coppens, 'Wag the Dog'. Online: www.philipcoppens.com/wagthedog.html.

increase pressure on Serbia. Fearing a humanitarian disaster during the winter, NATO complied on 13 October. The order was suspended at the end of October when Serbia expressed its readiness to cooperate. Throughout the summer and autumn of 1998, Congress devoted only sporadic attention to the issue; when NATO started to act just before the mid-term elections in November, Congress once again avoided adopting a position. The government felt comfortable with this passive attitude as it was not certain that it could gain a majority for eventual military action.

Following the resurgence of violence, the US media focused on the 'Račak massacre' of 15 January 1999. This publicity effect was largely the result of the handling of the Račak incident by the head of the OSCE mission in Kosovo, US diplomat William Walker, who owed his position to the personal engagement of Madeleine Albright; she had virtually imposed her choice on the OSCE. Like Albright and Holbrooke, Walker was imputed with an anti-Serbian attitude (Loquai 2003: 60–1, ch. 8). The sudden media attention impressed hesitant members of the US administration; Albright prevailed with her hawkish policy (Albright 2003: 390–7). The National Security Council agreed that NATO should start air attacks if Milošević did not comply with an ultimatum to stop ethnic cleansing. However, European concerns led to a modification of this course: the Balkan Contact Group called Serbia to negotiations in Rambouillet, while NATO, again under pressure from Albright, renewed its activation order on 30 January. It was hard for the Serbs to accept the military implementation part of the agreement with NATO, rather than the UN, as the force on the ground. NATO's request to march troops through Serbia into Kosovo was predictably unacceptable to Belgrade. These stipulations were only revealed to the Serbs at Rambouillet on the last day of the negotiations, and to Congress and the US public only after the war had ended (Judah 2000: ch. 7; Bellamy 2001). Meanwhile, the allies requested a US commitment to participation in a future Kosovo peacekeeping mission. Clinton accepted, and published this change of position on 13 February 1999 after the impeachment effort had failed in Congress.

Opposition to sending any US ground forces or marine units was strong in Congress and in the Pentagon. Clinton insisted that any NATO action would be conducted from the air to minimise own casualties. Meanwhile, Congress was increasingly occupied with the conflict; the House voted against US participation in peacekeeping forces in mid-March. Clinton consulted Congress just a few hours before the war started. The Senate supported the government's policy with a majority of 58:42 on 23 March 1999, with Democrats contributing 42 votes to that majority. In the House, the vote was delayed until 28

Table 3.3 *Frequencies of arguments, Kosovo War, United States, supporters only (n = 30); extracts of results*

Code	Argument	Number of speakers	Percentage of speakers
5101	Humanitarian catastrophe	30	100
1104	Show of force	23	76.7
1103	Regional stability	21	70
3101	Identity norms	16	53.3
2201	Alliance consensus	11	36.7
7101	Enemy image of adversary	11	36.7
4101	Enforce international law/support UN	10	33.3
2101	Alliance pro (internal aspects)	9	30
1101	National interest	7	23.3
2102	Alliance pro (external aspects)	7	23.3
4201	Covered by international law	7	23.3

Table 3.4 *Frequencies of arguments, Kosovo War, United States, opponents only (n = 20); extracts of results*

Code	Argument	Number of speakers	Percentage of speakers
6302	Casualty aversion (own soldiers)	15	75
1306	Lacking military strategy	12	60
1301	National interest contra	9	45
6301	Democratic norms/procedures contra war	9	45
5101	Humanitarian catastrophe	7	35
6303	Prohibitive material costs	7	35
1302	Loss of power	6	30
1307	National security not concerned	4	20
3302	Rejection of role ascription	4	20

April and ended in a tie (213:213), largely along party lines (Hils and Wilzewski 2006: 54–64).

2.2.2 Content analysis of congressional debates

Among the 50 coded speeches, 30 speakers supported the war (18 Democrats, 12 Republicans; depicted in Table 3.3) and 20 opposed it (Republicans only; shown in Table 3.4).

The humanitarian disaster in Kosovo was the key justification for military action put forward by every single supporter. However, humanitarian arguments were mixed with references to the necessity of demonstrating military strength to force Milošević into compliance (76.7 per cent). The danger that non-intervention might lead to regional instability ranked comparatively high (70 per cent). But only 23.3 per cent described the Kosovo crisis as a matter of US national interest. Some 53.3 per cent referred to America's national identity or its international role as a force for good; many regarded Kosovo as a chance to implement the 'lessons learned' from Bosnia.

Alliance issues were also on the agenda of war supporters: 36.7 per cent pointed to the NATO consensus on a military operation and 30 per cent to the US obligation to show leadership in the Alliance; 23.3 per cent were concerned about NATO's credibility and the protection of allies in South East Europe. Given the lack of a UN mandate, it is noteworthy that one in five speakers claimed that an intervention would be covered by international law and that a third of all proponents maintained that military action would *enforce* international law.

In contrast to war supporters, 75 per cent of opponents rejected military action because it could claim the lives of US soldiers and 35 per cent opposed high budgetary costs. The fear of high costs prevailed, although more than a third of the war opponents conceded that the humanitarian situation in Kosovo was highly problematic. The rejection of military intervention was often also justified by realist arguments: the assessment that neither the national interest (45 per cent) nor national security (20 per cent) were at stake and that the US might face a loss of power through a stalemate (30 per cent), notably in the absence of a convincing exit strategy (60 per cent). After all, the US should not assume the role of the world's policeman (20 per cent). Some 45 per cent of opponents were concerned about the doubtful observation of domestic democratic procedures before going to war; many of them mentioned the lack of authorisation by Congress, but only a few expressed concern about the absence of broad support from the American public. The lack of a UN mandate did not play a prominent role.

2.2.3   *Newspaper debates*
The newspapers as well as Congress were preoccupied with the Clinton scandals and, with the exception of the Račak episode, did not pay much attention to the Kosovo crisis before the war. Of 25 articles in the NYT, only one expressed explicit opposition to air strikes. In the WT, 18 articles supported and 7 opposed war on Serbia. Among war proponents, the reference to the humanitarian catastrophe dominated. The enemy image was given higher priority than in the congressional

debates.[11] Power politics, in contrast, were subordinate, and arguments about international law were as insignificant as in Congress. Alliance arguments or the US foreign policy role did not rank highly either. Opponents such as Abraham M. Rosenthal in the NYT and a variety of WT writers noted the lack of US national interests in Kosovo and the risk of undermining rather than strengthening regional stability.[12] Some opponents also pointed to the absence of public support and the risk of US casualties.[13]

2.2.4 Public opinion polls

The US public was not very interested in the Kosovo crisis; only a few polls were conducted. This indifference was not changed even by the intense reporting on the Račak event. Kosovo never ranked highly in surveys. In the polls of October 1998 and February 1999, support for and opposition to air attacks drew about 40 per cent each (Hils and Wilzewski 2006: 52–3). However, the fear of casualties was relatively low as a short war was expected. Although most respondents believed that the Europeans shouldered the bulk of the costs, they doubted the chances of achieving US objectives through air strikes alone. Majorities (55–37 per cent in February 1999, 50–43 per cent in March 1999, according to Gallup/CNN/*USA Today* polls) rejected the notion that the US had to be involved due to national interests.[14] Surveys conducted during the war showed that the humanitarian catastrophe was the most frequently mentioned reason for war; a majority of respondents believed in the US's moral duty to help build peace in the region. In contrast to the two Iraq wars, aversion to the war was slightly higher among Republicans than Democrats (Larson and Savych 2005: 74–87).

2.2.5 Conclusion: US participation in the Kosovo War

It was Secretary of State Albright, not the president, who exerted leadership in the Kosovo crisis. She prevailed against other cabinet members and sceptics in the Pentagon and in Congress and despite indifferent public opinion. The route through the UN was initially taken not for legal reasons, but to help convince Congress and the public at home

---

[11] E.g. Geyer, Georgie Anne 1999. 'Counterproductive … or Virtuous?', *Washington Times*, 28 March, p. B1; Safire, William 1996. 'Woodrow Wilson Lives', *New York Times*, 28 September, p. 17.

[12] Rosenthal, A. M. 1999. 'On Killing Serbs', *New York Times*, 26 March, p. 23.

[13] E.g. *ibid.*, p. 23; Roberts, Paul Craig 1998. 'Clinton's Commissars … and His Body Language', *Washington Times*, 15 October, p. A15; Roberts 1999. 'Unheeded Warnings on Kosovo Intentions', *Washington Times*, 19 February, p. A19.

[14] 'Gallup/CNN/*USA Today* Poll, 10 June, 1999'. Online: www.pollingreport.com/serb9906.htm.

and after France and Germany had asked for a related mandate. Parliamentary and public support before and during the war was limited and ambivalent. The public and the media were more concerned with President Clinton's domestic scandals than with NATO's first actual war. Stopping a humanitarian disaster was the dominant argument of the war proponents. Probably, the commitment not to put 'boots on the ground' but to stick to air operations prevented concerns about casualties and contributed to the relative public and congressional indifference. Newspaper articles devoted to Kosovo basically mirrored the arguments put forward by both political camps in Congress. However, the press was more eager to describe Milošević (the peacemaker for the Dayton agreement) in harsh terms, while members of Congress restrained themselves, perhaps in order to allow for the possibility of a last-minute diplomatic solution.

Since the war was fought by and through NATO, the Alliance argument played a more important role in justifying this war than in 1991 and 2003. Some proponents sought to frame the conflict as being in the national interest – to maintain NATO's credibility; even Albright, according to her memoirs (Albright 2003: 378–428), largely driven by moral motivations, used this argument to play to the concerns of 'realist' opponents. The public, however, remained sceptical. Overall, references to the Alliance did not figure among the most prominent justifications. Opponents hardly referred to the lack of a UN mandate, but focused on the lack of authorisation from Congress. This might be because many opponents of the 'humanitarian intervention' in Kosovo were affiliated with the more anti-UN Republicans (though some neoconservatives such as Paul Wolfowitz and future president George W. Bush supported the war; see e.g. Wolfowitz 2003).

Weak domestic support did not prevent the Clinton government from acting, since opposition was equally weak. The executive thus had ample freedom to conduct NATO's air attacks without broader domestic consent or a UN mandate. Faced with a liberally framed justification for the war, a public that was not convinced that military action was needed still remained compliant as the prospective costs – both in terms of money and casualties – seemed negligible.

2.3   The US and the 2003 Iraq War

2.3.1   The road to war

Toppling the Iraqi dictator had been a priority for neoconservatives since the Gulf War of 1991 (Kristol and Kaplan 2003). The most succinct formulation of this request was in a 1998 letter to President

Clinton, to which many neoconservatives subscribed who would later enter the Bush administration.[15] Secretary of Defense Rumsfeld and his deputy Wolfowitz proposed tackling Saddam Hussein immediately after the terror attacks of 11 September 2001, but President Bush decided to focus on Afghanistan first. Nevertheless, 9/11 had convinced the president that just containing Saddam was not sufficient. Adopting the neoconservatives' conclusion (Plesch 2005), he asked the Pentagon for detailed military planning against Iraq just 15 days after the attacks of 9/11 (Rumsfeld 2011: 425). The president's 2002 State of the Union address on 29 January introduced the infamous phrase 'axis of evil'. This, as well as later speeches, indicated that Iraq could be the first target of the new pre-emptive military strategy (Woodward 2004: 21–95; McClellan 2008: 126–37). In June 2002, at West Point, President Bush suggested in a speech with Manichaean connotations – comparing the war on terror with the fight against Hitler – that the US preferred a regime change in Iraq, without mentioning the country by name.[16] One month later, in a speech that was not cleared with the secretary of state, Vice-President Cheney declared a pre-emptive strike inevitable as protection against an otherwise certain attack by Iraq using weapons of mass destruction (WMD) (O'Sullivan 2009: 164).

As Wolfowitz revealed later, there were many motivations in the administration for overthrowing Saddam Hussein. The one on which everyone could agree was the need to deprive him of WMD. Consequently, this became the central argument in the administration's public pronouncements (Wolfowitz 2003). At the same time, it was clear that making war meant inevitably establishing democracy once the enemy was defeated (Feith 2008: 283–9, 392; Cheney 2011: 387–8).

The 'White House Iraq Group', supported by influential neoconservative and conservative think tanks and pressure groups and parts of the media (in particular Fox News), launched a public relations campaign in August 2002, describing military action against Iraq as an inevitable necessity (Cheney 2011: 389–90). US and British intelligence played a crucial role. While this campaign made the case for a direct (unilateral) path to war, in August Secretary of State Powell prevailed over Cheney by winning Bush's support for seeking a UNSC

---

[15] 'Letter to President Clinton on Iraq', 26 January 1998. Online: www.newamericancentury.org/iraqclintonletter.htm.
[16] 'Text of Bush's Speech at West Point', 1 June 2002. Online: http://nytimes.com/2002/06/01/international/02PTEX-WEB.html. See also, 'President Says Saddam Hussein Must Leave Iraq within 48 Hours', Remarks by the President in Address to the Nation, The Cross Hall, 17 March 2003. Online: http://georgewbushwhitehouse.archives.gov/news/releases/2003/03/20030317-7.html.

resolution in order to foster popular backing at home and abroad. The European allies, in particular British Prime Minister Blair, demanded a UN mandate (Woodward 2004: 130–85; Tenet 2007: 459–738; Bush 2010: 232, 237–8).

President Bush requested the UNSC to act in his speech to the UN General Assembly on 12 September 2002. He gave several reasons for threatening military action, ranging from the global security threat that Iraq posed, over numerous breaches of UN resolutions, to the beneficial impact of the democratisation of Iraq on the region. Afterwards, Congress became subject to intensive lobbying by the administration, which delivered intelligence reports on Iraq's WMD and terror links that subsequently turned out to be false. Intelligence information was distorted to make the case; this does not mean, however, that the administration was intentionally 'lying'. Paradoxically, proponents of the war were probably distorting information because they believed it was true (Woodward 2004: ch. 27, 28). As Rumsfeld wrote frankly: 'The President did not lie. The Vice President did not lie. Tenet did not lie. Rice did not lie. I did not lie … The far less dramatic truth is that we were wrong' (Rumsfeld 2011: 449).

Congress had already legislated the Iraq Liberation Act in 1998 in order 'to support efforts to remove the regime headed by Saddam Hussein from power in Iraq and to promote the emergence of a democratic government'.[17] So, shortly before the November 2002 mid-term elections, few members of Congress wanted to appear unpatriotic or soft on security in the eyes of a US public still haunted by the memory of 9/11. In early October, strong majorities (77:23 in the Senate; 296:133 in the House) granted sweeping authority to the president to use the military, with many Democrats joining almost all Republicans. Leading Democrat figures such as Senators Biden, Clinton and Kerry supported Bush's policy (Rumsfeld 2011: 436–7). As the crisis escalated, debates continued in Congress and became slightly more critical. However, authority and therefore power had already been surrendered for good (Fisher 2004: 211–35; Woodward 2004: 185–219).

With domestic support ensured, the administration intensified its efforts to establish its case in the international community. In contrast to other UNSC members such as Russia, China or France, the US declared that the 'serious consequences' language of UNSC Resolution 1441, adopted on 8 November 2002, contained implicit authorisation to use force. The US government perceived a second resolution as unnecessary. Bush reportedly decided to go to war at the end of December 2002.

---

[17] www.gpo.gov/fdsys/pkg/PLAW-105publ338/pdf/PLAW-105publ338.pdf.

His military planners advised him to start in March 2003 at the latest, before the hot weather period (Woodward 2004: 223–5, 254).

Although the weapons inspectors' reports indicated the absence of WMD and some improvement in Iraq's cooperation, Bush's legitimisation strategy now concentrated on proving Iraq's non-compliance with UNSC Resolution 1441 and the resulting necessity of a military response. To make its case, the administration attacked the UN Monitoring, Verification and Inspection Commission and the International Atomic Energy Agency (IAEA): American officials expressed doubts about the skills and the integrity of the inspectors and their organisations, implying that they were naively submitting to Iraq's deceptive manoeuvres and lies (Blix 2004).

Prime Minister Blair begged Bush to obtain a second UNSC resolution; he was facing strong opposition to war in his own party and among the British public (Murphy 2004: 169–77; Bush 2010: 244). Therefore, Washington put pressure on countries around the world and split the European allies into willing 'new Europe' aides and 'old Europe' deniers. Bush's State of the Union address on 28 January 2003 and Powell's televised presentation to the UNSC on 5 February 2003 marked the peaks of the campaign to influence public opinion. Powell was perceived by many allies and Americans as the only 'dovish' and thus credible member of the administration; this was the reason the administration chose him for this mission, and he agreed out of loyalty to the president. His speech seemed to address the international community, but was as much directed at the US public. Powell had struggled to eliminate the worst spin from the intelligence reports that provided the basis for his speech; his presentation nevertheless contained a couple of allegations that later proved false (O'Sullivan 2009: 175–8; Rumsfeld 2011: 446).

The majority of UNSC members still opposed an attack on Iraq (Woodward 2004: 239–356). By means of pressure, promises and persuasion, the US government secured the support of some dozens of countries, forming a 'coalition of the willing'. Following Saddam Hussein's disregard for Bush's ultimatum of 18 March to leave the country, the US-led coalition started war against Iraq on 20 March 2003, without a second UNSC resolution (Woodward 2004: 356–82).

2.3.2   Content analysis of congressional debates

Among the 50 speeches analysed, there were 26 war supporters (22 Republicans, 4 Democrats, depicted in Table 3.5) and 24 war opponents (Democrats only; depicted in Table 3.6).

Table 3.5 *Frequencies of arguments, Iraq War, United States, supporters only (n = 26); extracts of results*

Code	Argument	Number of speakers	Percentage of speakers
1105	National security	24	92.3
7101	Enemy image of adversary	24	92.3
3101	Identity norms	15	57.7
4202	Peaceful means exhausted	13	50
6101	Regime change/democratisation	13	50
5102	Threat to world order	13	50
1103	Regional stability	12	46.2
5201	Multilateral consensus pro	11	42.3
4101	Enforce international law/support UN	10	38.5
4201	Covered by international law	8	30.8
1104	Show of force	8	30.8
6201	Democratic norms/procedures respected	7	26.9
5301	World order not threatened	5	19.2

Two arguments dominated among war supporters (see Table 3.5): the benefits for US national security of removing Saddam Hussein from office and the latter's brute character, combined with his WMD and links to terrorism. References to the duty to extinguish the sources of the 9/11 attacks underlined these two arguments. The attacks of 9/11 were framed as the attempt to destroy the US as a beacon of freedom, democracy and Western civilisation, and the American reaction as fulfilling the country's role as leader of the free world. Both frames entangled US identity in the justification for taking military action. These references were followed by a bloc of arguments related to international law, moral aspects and democracy-specific topics, such as the argument that peaceful means promised no further progress, world order was threatened by Iraq and a democratic regime was needed in the Gulf region. A number of politicians mentioned that there was enough backing from other countries, and that military action should enforce, or was covered by, international law. Regional stability, a realpolitik argument, was mentioned by about half the speakers.

As shown in Table 3.6, on the other hand, 19 out of 24 war opponents put forward the argument that peaceful means should have been pursued further. Next, there was a strong group of *realist* counter-arguments against the war: national security or the national interest was not at risk; the war would aggravate, rather than diminish, security

Table 3.6 *Frequencies of arguments, Iraq War, United States, opponents only (n = 24); extracts of results*

Code	Argument	Number of speakers	Percentage of speakers
4302	Peaceful means not exhausted	19	79.2
1307	National security not concerned	16	66.7
1304	Increasing insecurity	16	66.7
1302	Loss of power	13	54.2
6301	Democratic norms/procedures contra war	11	45.8
6303	Prohibitive material costs	11	45.8
5302	Pacifism/war damages global norms	10	41.7
6302	Casualty aversion (own soldiers)	10	41.7
7101	Enemy image of adversary	10	41.7
3301	Restraining identity/role norms	10	41.7
4301	No UN mandate/damage to UN	9	37.5
5304	Multilateral war rejection	9	37.5
1301	National interest contra	8	33.3
1306	Lacking military strategy	8	33.3

problems; the US power position would suffer; and there was no exit strategy in sight.[18] More than 40 per cent of the opponents feared the material costs and the casualties that a war would incur. Insufficient public support and the moral duty of keeping peace were mentioned by a strong minority. Only 29 per cent challenged the majority view of the enemy image, whereas more than 40 per cent of opponents conceded that Saddam Hussein was a dangerous enemy; but they regarded war as the wrong approach. The lack of a UN mandate was mentioned by more than a third of the speakers.

2.3.3 Newspaper debates

Among the random sample of 25 NYT articles, just 6 supported the war. Of 25 WT articles, only 5 were opposed to it. As in the political speeches, the main argument of the proponents in both the NYT and the WT articles was the brute character of the enemy, combined with the dictator's alleged WMD and his links to terrorism.[19] Regional

[18] This mirrors the strong criticism of academic realists against the war and its neoconservative proponents (Schmidt and Williams 2008).
[19] E.g. Safire, William 2002. 'Saddam and Terror', *New York Times*, 22 August, p. 23; Safire 2003. 'Irrefutable and Undeniable', *New York Times*, 5 February, p. 39; Lambro, Donald 2003. 'With Clarity ... and Linkage Forthcoming', *Washington Times*, 30 January, p. A16.

stability and the violation of international law by Iraq were regularly mentioned.[20] Democratic regime change was the subject of only a few articles.[21] After the war, the mainstream liberal media came under harsh criticism for neglecting their watchdog function. The NYT apologised for painting an inaccurate picture of the Iraqi threat, and prominent journalist Judith Miller left the paper because of her misleading statements in front-page stories (Massing 2004).

The position of continuing to pursue peaceful means was dominant in the 19 NYT and 5 WT articles that were opposed to the war. In both papers, the debates focused on national security and national interest issues. The security threat from Iraq, they argued, was not serious enough to merit a military response. But frank doubts about the dictator's WMD and terror links only persisted in a few articles. In addition, the fear was widespread that a war would aggravate rather than diminish the terrorist threat against the US, would shatter regional stability and would undermine the power position of the US.[22] About half of the opponents in each paper referred to the lack of multilateral backing, but only a few were concerned about the *legal* issue of the lack of a UN mandate. The financial or human costs of a war attracted little attention.

2.3.4   Public opinion polls

Throughout the 1990s and into 2002, there had always been some public support for military action against Iraq. Support for the war peaked after the terror attacks of September 2001, but diminished slightly even while the executive's public relations campaign gained momentum. After the summer of 2002, the Iraq crisis was perceived as the most important current foreign policy issue (Larson and Savych 2005: 132–6). The average support for the war ranged between 57 and 65 per cent from August 2002 to March 2003 (Larson and Savych 2005: 150–2). In a number of polls, a majority of respondents gave credence to the allegations of Saddam Hussein's WMD and connections with Al-Qaeda. When asked this question, a majority interpreted the Iraq War as part of the 'war on terror'. Regime change also played a prominent

---

[20] E.g. Anonymous 2003. 'Blix Documents Iraqi Violations', 28 January, p. A28.

[21] E.g. Friedman, Thomas L. 2003. 'Thinking About Iraq', *New York Times*, 22 January, p. 21; Gaffney, Frank Jr. 2002. 'Defining "Regime Change"', *Washington Times*, 3 December, p. A17.

[22] E.g. Herbert, Bob 2003. 'With Ears and Eyes Closed', *New York Times*, 17 March, p. 23; Krugman, Paul 2003. 'Games of Nations', *New York Times*; 3 January, p. 21; de Borchgrave, Arnaud 2002. 'Across the Rubicon ... to the State of War', *Washington Times*, 6 February, p. A17; Roberts, Paul Craig 2003. 'GOP's Last Hurrah?', *Washington Times*, 2 February, p. B03.

role in some polls. The lack of Alliance consensus and the absence of a UN mandate, if mentioned, reduced support for the war. In some surveys, more inspections and/or a diplomatic solution were favoured; in other surveys, a quick military intervention was preferred. In some polls, majorities approved military action even without UN agreement from January 2003 onwards. This support might have resulted from Americans expecting a short war with few costs and casualties (Larson and Savych 2005: 129–211). Despite majority public support, the largest anti-war demonstrations since the 1991 Gulf War took place in the US in 2003 (Larson and Savych 2005: 129, 184, 193).[23]

2.3.5   Conclusion: US participation in the Iraq War

The Bush administration comprised many leading members who had entered office convinced that democratic regime change was needed in Iraq. The reasons for this were manifold, but the solution to all the problems that the US had with Saddam Hussein, and in the broader region, was seen in replacing the dangerous tyrant by a democracy.[24] The security threats were closely interwoven with the type of regime and ruler (Feith 2008: 283, 288). In his memoirs, the ultimate decision-maker, President George W. Bush, gives no less than 15 reasons for going to war (Bush 2010: ch. 8). Six refer to US interests, two to regional interests, four to universal (including UN) security aspects and three to human rights and democracy. Probably, this mixture reflects very well the range of concerns that the American leadership harboured. As for the president himself, there are two instances where he presumably revealed his genuine priorities. When he gave the order to attack, he vowed that he was doing it 'for the peace of the world and the benefit and freedom of the Iraqi people' (Bush 2010: 223–4). The same day, he reports, he wrote a letter to his father; there he emphasised the goal 'to liberate Iraq and rid the country of WMD'; 'Iraq will be free', he stated, 'the world will be safer' (Bush 2010: 223–4). Here American interests astonishingly disappear in the face of universal benefits and the liberation of a people.

The administration enjoyed remarkable room for manoeuvre in leading the country into the war: Congress, the mainstream media and the public were still in shock from 9/11 and seized by a surge of patriotism. For the sake of the 'global war on terror', even people critical of the

---

[23] See also, 'Public Opinion on the War with Iraq', *AEI Public Opinion Studies*, March 2009. Online:www.aei.org/files/2012/01/23/-aeipublicopinioniraq2009_133351682593. pdf., p. 5.

[24] For the mix of justifications for regime change, see Rumsfeld (2011: 436) and Feith (2008: ch. 6, 246).

Bush administration accepted calls to strengthen US national security, were taken in by false information and exaggerations and embraced manichaean descriptions of the enemy. References by the war opponents to international law, multilateralism, the lack of a UN mandate, the different opinion of allies or doubts about the truth of executive allegations about WMD and terror links gained no ground against the US-focused positions of the war proponents. Some war opponents tried to join the debate by referring to the lack of US interests in the matter, and occasionally played the international law card, but to no avail. Congress was out of the game after having granted the president a carte blanche in October 2002.

The US administration's walk through UN corridors was primarily aimed at influencing the domestic audience. It was also aimed at assembling a 'coalition of the willing' and serving the needs of the closest ally, Tony Blair. Still, the preferred course remained one of US action, accompanied by some minor combatants, with the US president in command, no UN secretary-general interfering and no UNSC involved.

Despite all the criticisms about false information, bad planning and lack of progress on the ground, which set in soon after the initial fighting had ceased, Bush managed to frame the war as an US success story. He was re-elected in 2004, and it was only in the elections of 2006 and 2008 that the Democrat Party was able to capitalise on the disastrous post-war planning of the Bush administration.

3   Conclusion: explaining US participation in all three wars

3.1   *Moral and realist justifications*

All three post-Cold War US foreign policy approaches – George H. W. Bush's 'New World Order', Clinton's 'Strategy of Engagement and Enlargement', and George W. Bush's 'National Security Strategy' of 2002 – included enemy images and realist as well as liberal-idealist elements of foreign policy orientations, albeit in different combinations (see Bowen and Dunn 1996; Hyland 1999; Daalder and Lindsay 2003). Even the George W. Bush administration employed realist arguments, the protestations of academic realists notwithstanding (Schmidt and Williams 2008): far too salient is the 'national interest' in US foreign policy thinking to leave out this basic tenet of realist thinking when it comes to justifying the use of the US military abroad. Similar combinations appeared in the arguments of war advocates.

The Gulf War of 1990–1 was a defining event in the transition towards a new foreign policy paradigm following containment. Iraq's aggression against Kuwait influenced the construction of a new enemy image, the 'rogue state', personified by the dictator Saddam Hussein. The perceived pivotal threat by that enemy to the evolving 'new world order' made the war a 'world order war'. A brutal autocratic style, flagrant violations of human rights and the illegal acquisition of WMD became common features of enemies of the world order such as Saddam Hussein (Klare 1995; Litwak 2000). While the legal and moral framing of the war was more the result of the executive's cost–benefit calculus than of normative considerations, it resonated well with the strategy of a law-based 'new world order'.

The justificatory narrative for the air attacks against Serbia was primarily framed by moral arguments. At the same time, the influence of the Clinton administration's shift towards a more pragmatic foreign policy (Hyland 1999) was mirrored in this discourse. It reinforced the effect of ill-conceived 'humanitarian interventions' and strengthened the reservations of many members of the administration and the military elite before the decision to use force was taken. This is why war supporters repeatedly framed the war as conforming to US national interests in order to broaden their basis of support. In addition, compared to Saddam Hussein, Milošević, peacemaker of Dayton, projected only a pale 'rogue' image, as he was lacking two important attributes of a 'rogue': WMD and a connection with terrorism. In contrast to both wars against Iraq, the NATO-led intervention in Kosovo gave some credit to Alliance arguments and, consequently, to the duty of the US to lead and to ensure the credibility of NATO. While a few politicians maintained that the intervention served to enforce international law, the lack of a valid UN mandate pointed to increasing unilateralism in US foreign policy. The discourse about the war in Kosovo suggests that – after the disaster in Somalia – the defence of liberal norms alone might be an insufficient justification for sending American soldiers into harm's way.

The transition to a permanent war posture in the 'global war on terror' after 9/11 marked the victory of the 'rogue state' paradigm. The way Saddam Hussein was portrayed by George W. Bush's administration combined the features of a cruel, inhumane dictator with the security threat embedded in his WMD and his support for terrorism (Greenstein 2003). This image was linked to the framing of the 9/11 attack as an assault on the US role of the standard-bearer of civilising progress, and to the US need and duty to lead in the fight against the terrorist evil (Frum and Perle 2003). The neoconservatives in the administration also stressed the benefits of democratic regime change. Moral arguments, some legal reflections and the neoconservative vision of spreading democracy by force were combined in the pre-war discourse.

The impact of casualty aversion on the argumentation of both war proponents and war opponents confirms findings from earlier research: the public tolerates the expectation of higher casualties the more the war is perceived as reflecting core US national interests and is believed to be winnable (Mueller 1994; Larson and Savych 2005). The administration's framing of the 2003 war was more successful in that regard than the other two cases in our sample.

Liberal-internationalist opponents to the two Iraq wars referred to international law. However, the fact that both the Kosovo War and the 2003 Iraq War were conducted without legal authority played a surprisingly small role even in the opponents' critiques. For the – mostly Republican – critics of the Kosovo operation, this is rooted in their general scepticism towards multilateralism and international law. But generally, this finding indicates that international law has a less constraining effect on US external policy than for other states in our sample. This dismissive attitude also applies to alliance politics: references to NATO are absent from the debates, with Kosovo being a moderate exception.

The two Presidents Bush as well as Secretary of State Albright used strong manichaean rhetoric against Saddam Hussein and, in a significantly lower tone, Milošević, comparing them to Hitler and citing the 'Munich Syndrome'. This created a difficulty for war opponents as they sought to deconstruct, ignore or adapt the enemy image in their speeches and columns, and it proved hard work to balance this strong image with counter-arguments.

3.2   *American democracy and war decisions*

Democratic checks and balances functioned only within limits in the run-up to the three wars. The three presidents defended a 'presidentialist' position. It was not for legal reasons but for reasons of political expediency that all three administrations asked Congress to agree to the use of force. But George H. W. Bush and Clinton only did so after the decision to go to war had already been taken by the executive, that is, at the last minute, when the emerging 'rally around the flag' effect persuaded sceptics to cast a positive vote in order to avoid being denounced as 'unpatriotic'. George W. Bush sought and obtained a blank cheque six months in advance. In no case did either house of Congress oppose the administration, though Congress approved the first Gulf War and the Kosovo War with slim majorities and one tie (the House in 1999). All votes were perceived as 'conscientious votes', but were de facto decided along party lines. Members of Congress remained on the whole too passive to apply effective checks and balances on the executive. This is remarkable since all the presidents had to run a divided government at that time.

Compared to the congressional elections, presidential elections (1992, 2000, 2004) did not have an obvious effect here. Congress was at times reluctant to debate sensitive issues of war shortly before elections and consequently postponed related votes. In 1990 and 1998, they postponed votes on the war until after the elections – not convincing proof of a willingness to 'check and balance'. In contrast, in 2002, they were eager to show their solidarity with the popular commander-in-chief over the 'war on terror', when Americans were highly concerned about national security.

Many journalists of the newspapers analysed did not fulfil their role as critical, attentive watchdogs. Media comments largely mirrored those of the political elite, particularly before the 2003 Iraq War. The false allegations concerning Iraq's terror links and WMD before the war of 2003 as well as human rights abuses in Kosovo and by Saddam Hussein in Iraq were often received uncritically by the mainstream media.

Support for the two wars against Iraq in civil society organisations and the media resided largely in conservative/neoconservative milieus and among supporters of Israel (Mearsheimer and Walt 2007).[25] Liberals and their civil society organisations tended – with the limitations mentioned above – to be more opposed to the wars against Iraq. On the subject of Kosovo, however, many former liberal doves became hawks and attempted to mobilise public and congressional support in order to move the Clinton administration to action (Daalder and O'Hanlon 2000).

As the polling results indicate, the general public exerted no pressure on the political elite to employ military force in any of the three cases. The majorities in favour of war in many polls were not very large before both Iraq wars; only slightly more than 40 per cent supported air attacks against Serbia. Nevertheless, support being large or small, the majority always condoned the government's war-fighting preference. With the 'rally around the flag' effect, which has been observed as a regular feature of US war involvement, significant majorities supported the wars once fighting began in 1991 and 2003, and a smaller majority did so in 1999. The executive benefited from the traditional patriotism and the loyalty of Americans towards troops in action and the commander-in-

---

[25] The authors of this book, both well-positioned realists, counted among the most outspoken critics of the war.

chief; even when the public was not convinced, it was still accommodating. In all cases, the American public preferred low casualty numbers and cheap, brief, successful, multilateral and UN-mandated wars.

Congress, media and public opinion did not substantially shape decisions by the presidents and their closest advisors. The presidents enjoyed a predominant position on security policy and privileged access to (intelligence) information (Fisher 2004). This characteristic of the US political system was an important reason why the executive managed to control the domestic debates.

3.3   *US role and identity and its impact on war*

There is broad agreement that the US has to lead international military interventions. And the US did lead: the UN in 1991, NATO in 1999 and the 'coalition of the willing' in 2003. With some effort, the US administrations succeeded in gaining allies who helped to share the burdens and gave military operations (some degree of) legitimacy in order to garner support for the war at home. The most important ally in all cases was the United Kingdom, but that forced Washington to accept some constraints (like turning to the UN). Except for some concessions, the US in general dominated the international proceedings, and acted independently whenever it seemed beneficial.

This behaviour matches the self-image of the US, which is inspired by exceptionalism and to which national sovereignty is very important: the US political elite locates the legitimacy of decisions in domestic procedures. Whether multilateralism, international law and the UN are disregarded or appreciated, they do not appear to be a constraining factor once the US government deems right what the international community deems wrong or international law prohibits. The trend towards unilateralism in Washington was evident to different degrees in all three cases, even though there was a continued preference for multilateralism among public opinion.

American exceptionalism can be an important source of the expansive imperial ambitions of the US superpower. The liberal mission of spreading values and the realist ambition of shaping the world in favour of US security and economic interests offer war proponents an opportunity structure to associate their justification with supporting elements of national identity.

The content analyses of parliamentary discourses demonstrated that in all discourses realist and liberal-inspired reasons for war were present in a similar mixture and focus as in the foreign policy doctrines of the time. All three presidents framed the imminent military operation as the war they preferred to fight: George H. W. Bush, who favoured real-politik internationalism, fought a war for international order that was identical to the US national interest; liberal-internationalist Clinton fought for humanitarian reasons – and to lead an alliance; George W. Bush and his neoconservatives fought for regime change against an 'evil' threat. Hence, the pre-war discourses could also be interpreted as efforts to adapt and flesh out a preferred foreign policy role conception of the US as the only superpower following the end of the Cold War. This conception apparently appealed to a majority of Americans.

In conclusion, the US power position in the international system and the pre-eminent role of the executive in foreign policy formation enabled the US government to dominate discourses on war domestically, to act with considerable independence and to prevail with its political preferences. The American way of leading the world into the three 'democratic wars' was characterised by the use of the country's power preponderance after 1990 to combine its orientation towards liberal values with its perceived economic and strategic national interests and to pursue the resulting policy with determination, unilaterally if necessary, and without serious leanings towards international law. The amalgam of liberal ideology, enemy images, a foreign policy role conception that emphasises the duty to lead, and perceived national interests delivered important justifications for US governments to pursue and to spearhead three 'democratic wars' following the end of the Cold War.

REFERENCES

Albright, Madeleine (with Bill Woodward) 2003. *Madam Secretary: A Memoir.* New York, NY: Miramax Books

Atkinson, Rick 1993. *Crusade: The Untold Story of the Persian Gulf War.* Boston, MA: Houghton Mifflin

Baker, James A. 1995. *The Politics of Diplomacy: Revolution, War and Peace 1989–1992.* New York, NY: Putnam

Bellamy, Alex J. 2001. 'Reconsidering Rambouillet', *Contemporary Security Policy* 22 (1): 31–56

Bennett, Andrew 1997. *Friends in Need: Burden-Sharing in the Gulf War.* Basingstoke: Macmillan

Blix, Hans 2004. *Disarming Iraq: The Search for Weapons of Mass Destruction.* New York, NY: Pantheon

Boot, Max 2003. 'Neither New Nor Nefarious: The Liberal Empire Strikes Back', *Current History* 102 (667): 361–6

Bowen, Wyn Q. and Dunn, David 1996. *American Security Policy in the 1990s: Beyond Containment.* Aldershot: Dartmouth

Bush, George H. W. 1991. *Public Papers of the Presidents of the United States: George H. W. Bush. 1990, Book II.* Washington, DC: US Government Printing Office

Bush, George H. W. and Scowcroft, Brent 1998. *A World Transformed.* New York, NY: Knopf

Bush, George W. 2010. *Decision Points.* New York, NY: Crown

Cheney, Dick 2011. *In My Time: A Personal and Political Memoir.* New York, NY: Simon & Schuster

Clark, Wesley K. 2001. *Waging Modern War: Bosnia, Kosovo and the Future of Combat.* New York, NY: Public Affairs

Clinton, William J. 2004. *My Life.* New York, NY: Knopf

Czempiel, Ernst-Otto 2003. *Weltpolitik im Umbruch: Die Pax Americana, der Terrorismus und die Zukunft der internationalen Beziehungen.* Munich: C. H. Beck

Daalder, Ivo H. and Lindsay, James M. 2003. *America Unbound: The Bush Revolution in Foreign Policy.* Washington, DC: Brookings Institution Press

Daalder, Ivo H. and O'Hanlon, Michael E. 2000. *Winning Ugly: NATO's War to Save Kosovo.* Washington, DC: Brookings Institution Press

Deitelhoff, Nicole 2006. *Überzeugung in der Politik: Grundzüge einer Diskurstheorie Internationalen Regierens.* Frankfurt a.M.: Suhrkamp

Feith, Douglas J. 2008. *War and Decision, Inside the Pentagon at the Dawn of the War on Terrorism.* New York, NY: Harper

Fisher, Louis 2004. *Presidential War Power.* Lawrence, KS: University Press of Kansas

Frum, David and Perle, Richard 2003. *An End to Evil: How to Win the War on Terror.* New York, NY: Random House

Gaddis, John Lewis 1982. *Strategies of Containment: A Critical Appraisal of Postwar American National Security Policy.* New York, NY: Oxford University Press

Greenstein, Fred I. 2003. 'The Leadership Style of George W. Bush', in Fred I. Greenstein (ed.), *The George W. Bush Presidency: An Early Assessment.* Baltimore, MD: Johns Hopkins University Press, pp. 138–72

Grimmett, Richard F. 2010. 'The War Powers Resolution: After Thirty-Six Years', *CRS Report for Congress* RL41199, 22 April, Washington, DC

Halper, Stefan and Clarke, Jonathan 2004. *America Alone: The Neo-Conservatives and the Global Order.* Cambridge University Press

Hassner, Pierre 2002. 'The United States: The Empire of Force or the Force of Empire?', *Chaillot Paper* No. 54, Paris

Henkin, Louis 1972. *Foreign Affairs and the Constitution.* Mineola, NY: The Foundation Press

Hils, Jochen and Wilzewski, Jürgen 2006. 'Second Image Reconsidered: Die parlamentarische Kontrolle von Militärinterventionen der USA in den 1990er Jahren', *Occasional Papers in Political Science* No. 1/2006, Kaiserslautern

Hyland, William G. 1999. *Clinton's World: Remaking American Foreign Policy.* Westport, CT: Praeger

Ikenberry, G. John 2004. 'Liberalism and Empire: Logics of Order in the American Unipolar Age', *Review of International Studies* 30 (4): 609–30

Jentleson, Bruce W. 2004. *American Foreign Policy: The Dynamics of Choice in the 21st Century.* New York, NY: W. W. Norton & Company

Judah, Tim 2000. *Kosovo: War and Revenge.* New Haven, CT: Yale University Press

Kagan, Robert 2008. *The Return of History and the End of Dreams.* London: Atlantic Books

Klare, Michael T. 1995. *Rogue States and Nuclear Outlaws: America's Search for a New Foreign Policy.* New York, NY: Hill and Wang

Kristol, Irving 1995. *Neoconservatism: The Autobiography of an Idea.* New York, NY: The Free Press

Kristol, William and Kaplan, Lawrence F. 2003. *The War over Iraq: Saddam's Tyranny and America's Mission.* San Francisco, CA: Encounter Books

Larson, Eric V. and Savych, Bogdan 2005. *American Public Support for U.S. Military Operations from Mogadishu to Baghdad.* Santa Monica, CA: RAND Corporation

Lipset, Seymour M. 1997. *American Exceptionalism, A Double-Edged Sword.* New York, NY: W. W. Norton & Company

Litwak, Robert S. 2000. *Rogue States and U.S. Foreign Policy: Containment after the Cold War.* Washington, DC: Woodrow Wilson Center Press

Loquai, Heinz 2003. *Weichenstellung für einen Krieg: Internationales Krisenmanagement im Kosovo-Konflikt.* Baden-Baden: Nomos

McClellan, Scott 2008. *What Happened: Inside the Bush White House and Washington's Culture of Deception.* New York, NY: Public Affairs

McCombs, Maxwell E. 2006. *Setting the Agenda: The Mass Media and Public Opinion.* Cambridge: Polity

Mann, James 2004. *Rise of the Vulcans: The History of Bush's War Cabinet.* New York, NY: Viking Press

Mantho, Mark G. 2004. 'The Bush Doctrine: Origins, Evolution, Alternatives'. Online: www.comw.org/pda/fulltext/0404mantho.pdf

Massing, Michael 2004. *Now They Tell Us: The American Press and Iraq.* New York, NY: New York Review Books

Mead, Walter Russell 2001. *Special Providence: American Foreign Policy and How it Changed the World.* New York, NY: Knopf

Mearsheimer, John J. and Walt, Stephen M. 2007. *The Israel Lobby and US Foreign Policy.* New York, NY: Farrar, Straus, and Giroux

Mueller, John E. 1994. *Policy and Opinion in the Gulf War.* University of Chicago Press

Müller, Harald and Sohnius, Stephanie 2006. 'Intervention und Kernwaffen: Zur neuen Nukleardoktrin der USA', *HSFK-Report* No. 1/2006, Frankfurt a.M.

Murphy, John F. 2004. *The United States and the Rule of Law in International Affairs.* Cambridge University Press

O'Sullivan, Christopher D. 2009. *Colin Powell: American Power and Intervention from Vietnam to Iraq.* Lanham, MD: Rowman & Littlefield

Plesch, Dan 2005. 'The Neo-Cons: Neo-Conservative Thinking Since the Onset of the Iraq War', in Alex Danchev and John MacMillan (eds.), *The Iraq War and Democratic Politics*. London: Routledge, pp. 47–58

Powell, Colin L. 1995. *My American Journey*. New York, NY: Ballantine Books

Ralph, Jason 2005. 'International Society, the International Criminal Court and American Foreign Policy', *Review of International Studies* 31 (1): 27–44

Roß, Ingrid 2005. 'Hijacking of the President? Der Einfluss der Neokonservativen auf die Entscheidung zum Irakkrieg 2003', *John F. Kennedy-Institut Working Paper* No. 134, Berlin

Rumsfeld, Donald 2011. *Known and Unknown: A Memoir*. New York, NY: Sentinel

Schlesinger, Arthur M., Jr. 1974. *The Imperial Presidency*. London: André Deutsch Verlag

Schmidt, Brian C. and Williams, Michael C. 2008. 'The Bush Doctrine and the Iraq War: Neoconservatives versus Realists', *Security Studies* 17 (2): 191–220

Schweigler, Gebhard 2004. 'Außenpolitik', in Peter Lösche and Hans D. von Loeffelholz (eds.), *Länderbericht USA*. Bonn: BpB, pp. 410–95

Smith, Jean Edward 1992. *George Bush's War*. New York, NY: Henry Holt and Company

Spiegel, Steven L. 1997. 'Eagle in the Middle East', in Robert J. Lieber (ed.), *Eagle Adrift: American Foreign Policy at the End of the Century*. New York, NY: Longman, pp. 295–317

Tenet, George 2007. *At the Center of the Storm: My Years at the CIA*. New York, NY: Harper Collins

Tucker, Robert W. and Hendrickson, David C. 1992. *The Imperial Temptation: The New World Order and America's Purpose*. New York, NY: Council on Foreign Relations

The White House 1995. *A National Security Strategy of Engagement and Enlargement*. Washington, DC

Wolfowitz, Paul 2003. 'Deputy Secretary Wolfowitz Interview with Sam Tanenhaus, Vanity Fair', News Transcript. Online: www.defense.gov/transcripts/transcript.aspx?transcriptid=2594

Woodward, Bob 2004. *Plan of Attack*. New York, NY: Simon & Schuster

4 'The right thing to do'? British interventionism after the Cold War

Marco Fey

The United Kingdom (UK) is one of those democracies that are particularly often involved in military conflicts. Britain went to war five times in the first six years of Tony Blair's premiership alone: 'No British Prime Minister and few world leaders come close' (Kampfner 2003: ix). John Kampfner goes on to say that British interventionism in the post-Cold War era is no longer defined by traditional concepts of national interest. As I intend to illustrate in this chapter, it is rather the idea of standing up for certain values and being firm against aggressors, both notions stemming from a strong liberal tradition in Britain, as well as the desire to play an active role in shaping international relations – all integral parts of Britain's foreign policy role conception – that help us to understand its military engagement in the world.

1 Institutional and ideational determinants of Britain's foreign and security policy

1.1 *Regime-type features and decision-making in British security policy*

The UK is a parliamentary democracy and constitutional monarchy. Although it has no written constitution, it does have a material one. With statute law, common law and conventions, the constitution derives from a multitude of sources and has developed over the centuries. It is an indicator of parliamentary sovereignty that every constitutional norm can be changed by a simple majority vote and no court is authorised to scrutinise parliamentary legislation.

The British government, headed by the prime minister, holds a strong position. Checks and balances are poorly developed and scarcely institutionalised. Most notably, the executive's predominance culminates in the area of foreign and security policy; the Royal Prerogative includes the power to go to war. Although the government can deploy the armed forces at will, it usually submits the question of war to a procedural parliamentary vote by introducing a motion for the 'adjournment of the

House'. This enables a debate without granting Parliament a substantial say in the matter. Instead of making use of the prerogative, the government may also introduce a substantive motion. With a majority in favour, this would not only mean that the armed forces are committed by an Act of Parliament, but would also allow for amendments. While a defeat in such a substantive motion would not prevent the government from deploying troops, observers agree that the political pressure not to do so would be immense (Taylor 2005: 8).

Yet, there are also formal as well as informal checks and balances. Ministers are accountable to Parliament in two ways. They are responsible for their own departments and they also have to resign collectively from office in case the government no longer finds a majority for its policy in the lower house of Parliament, the Commons. The principle of collective responsibility functions as an additional mechanism of accountability within the executive. In addition to plenary debates and question time, since 1979 Parliament has had another instrument for holding the government accountable through its select committees. Finally, because of the Commons' power of the purse, the government needs Parliament's approval for funding military missions. Its room for manoeuvre is thus not infinite. However, a number of developments have led to the marginalisation of most of Parliament's means of scrutiny; party discipline, bipartisanship as well as a palpably decreasing interest in foreign affairs on the part of most Members of Parliament (MPs) work against the already weak checks and balances (Gaskarth 2006). The same is also true of the executive, particularly since the premiership of Margaret Thatcher, where a strong tendency away from collective decision-making and towards a 'prime-ministerial government' can be observed (Foley 2000).

1.2   Britain's role conception and role profile in foreign and security policy

1.2.1   Foreign policy traditions, guidelines and role conception

Pragmatism is a central characteristic in terms of the traditions, ideologies and maxims at the root of British foreign and security policy in the second half of the twentieth century. A pragmatic foreign policy is not based on grand designs, ideologies or principles, but focuses on flexibility and the realisation of short-term interests (Vital 1968: 98–103). While British politics have indeed manifested a certain flexibility since the end of the Second World War, they are, however, by no means free of ideational factors. A whole string of traditions and principles can be identified that act as normative structures shaping national identity and that have thus become elements of the foreign and security role profile. The most formative of these are status-orientation, liberal values and anti-appeasement.

Status-orientation: The former global power's continued decline is a recurrent topic in the twentieth-century discourse on British foreign policy (Aggestam 2004: 115). It has always been accompanied by the – at least implicit – bipartisan promise to reverse this trend and to help the UK back to the kind of status that would befit the country (Williams 2005: 2–3): 'while the great power label may no longer be in vogue, successive British leaderships have formulated foreign policies conscious of the fact that the country is a global power with a global responsibility' (Morris 2011: 342). This line of thought among the elites can be explained not only by Britain's past as a world power at the time of Queen Victoria's empire, but also by the long and uninterrupted tradition of democracy, freedom and wealth. The Second World War is another important point of reference for British identity. The image of Britain as one of the victorious allies and a military heavyweight, combined with a determination to oppose totalitarian enemies, has become a source of national pride and status-consciousness (Wallace 1991: 73–4).

After the Second World War, Britain's global influence could no longer be accounted for by hard-power capabilities. But this in no way diminished the country's pursuit of prestige and status. The 1956 Suez crisis highlighted the decline. Britain's striving for recognition underwent a transformation with the country now adopting a more realistic perception of itself as no longer a *global* but a *major* power, but still with global influence and responsibilities. Nonetheless, the elites in London still asserted their claim to a high-profile status (Aggestam 2004: 130).

In this context, the military performed an important function within the social system. In the years of decline, particularly in the 1960s and 1970s, it was one of the few institutions that society could esteem: 'When Britain's international status declined and economic growth faltered the belief in its military professionalism often served to compensate for dented prestige' (Ellner 2000: 20). Indeed, the British armed forces are among the most highly regarded in the world. For the former colonial and sea power, the regular deployment of its troops outside its own territories was nothing unusual. Rather, it was always considered to be an important and legitimate means of achieving its foreign and security policy aims (Edmunds 2010: 382). Even today, Britain aims at being proactively involved in shaping international relations and at exerting a disproportionate global influence (Macleod 1997: 183–4). Both New Labour under Tony Blair and Gordon Brown – although it distanced its foreign policy explicitly from that of previous governments – and Conservative leaders of the Cameron government repeatedly claimed 'a seat at the top table of international politics' (Morris 2011: 327; see also Williams 2005: 1–2).

Liberal values: When Labour came to power in 1997, the new Foreign Secretary Robin Cook announced that the new government would support the demands of other peoples for democratic rights and put human rights at the heart of Britain's foreign policy, thereby adding an 'ethical dimension' to it. This new direction of the Foreign and Commonwealth Office (FCO) was to differ notably from the supposed pragmatism of the preceding Conservative governments and their more traditional view of national interests. The spread of liberal values such as human rights, civil liberties, the rule of law, democracy and good governance was meant to be a constitutive element (Wickham-Jones 2000: 3). All this was, of course, not as new as Labour pronounced it to be. The declaratory politics of the Blair government followed rather the party's tradition of liberal internationalism (Williams 2005: 23–4) and gave new emphasis to long-established values that the Tories too, especially under Thatcher, promoted in their foreign policy.

The bipartisan commitment to the spread of liberal values and, equally important, free markets and a liberal economic order has a long tradition. The Magna Carta as an entrenched set of liberties, an uninterrupted tradition of parliamentary sovereignty and the common law were all sources of the myth of English exceptionalism. The idea of Britain as a bastion of liberal values was consolidated in the nineteenth century. Not only were these values evoked in the fight against external enemies, they were also exported to the British colonies. Moreover, the importance for identity formation of a vague but shared understanding of freedom and democracy cannot be underestimated in the light of a missing definition of 'Britishness' (Noakes 1998: 143). The Second World War further reinforced Britain's self-perception as a champion of freedom and democracy in the world. Liberal values remained important identity elements, for the defence of which Britain would even go to war. The 1998 *Strategic Defence Review* (SDR) declared that British armed forces should not only defend the UK and its interests but also act as a 'force for good' by defending and advocating human rights and democracy in the world (MoD 1998). While this notion did not make it into the *Strategic Defence and Security Review* (SDSR) of the new Conservative government in 2010, the country's global responsibilities and 'proud history of standing up for the values we believe in' figure prominently in the prime minister's foreword (HM Government 2010).

Anti-appeasement: standing firm against aggressors: A considerable part of the British elites of the 1930s considered the appeasement of Hitler to be a rational and even 'noble' policy. The catastrophic failure and the subsequent horrors of the Second World War unmasked this policy as an immoral backing-down. In terms of lessons learnt, tyrants and despots have emerged as particularly strong enemy images that need to be fought, if necessary, with the use of force. A 1940 poem by Dorothy L. Sayers that ends with 'Please God give us English peace / But if another tyrant comes / Then we shall fight again' summarises this important identity trait quite well (Bartlett 1977: 30; Noakes 1998: 134–45).

In the post-Second World War era, these enemy images have exerted a particularly strong influence on the members of all British governments, even those who were too young to have experienced the days leading to the war. Tony Blair's famous speech to the Economic Club in Chicago in April 1999 also stands in this tradition. At the height of the Kosovo crisis and against the background of gross human rights violations and ethnic cleansing in the Balkans and in Africa in the 1990s, Blair outlined a 'doctrine of international community' that called for a qualification, and thus a softening, of the principle of national sovereignty. This concept of liberal interventionism indicated a rather creative and pragmatic approach towards international law that is also reflected in Britain's attitude towards the International Criminal Court (ICC) and international regimes, as the next sections will show.

1.2.2 Britain's approach to international law: the example of the ICC

The country's foreign policy elites have always stressed the importance of an international order based on international law. Yet, Britain adopted a hesitant initial stance on the establishment of a new independent permanent court that tries persons accused of the most serious crimes of international concern, the ICC. During the preliminary negotiations on the Rome Statute, the UK, like the other permanent members of the UN Security Council (P5), supported the conservative draft introduced by the International Law Commission (ILC), which proposed not touching the principle of state sovereignty and making the ICC directly subordinate to the Security Council. In 1997, however, following Labour's election victory, Britain joined the 'like-minded group', which called for a strong court and in doing so destroyed the solidarity among the P5. This was seen as an extremely important step in the establishment of an independent ICC (Ralph 2007: 154). Britain eventually ratified the Rome Statute on 3 October 2001.

But even the Blair government dealt with controversies related to the ICC in a non-dogmatic manner when it reacted to the US threat to withdraw from peacekeeping missions should the Security Council not exclude personnel from countries not party to the protocol from the ICC's jurisdiction (which it ultimately did in S/RES/1422 and 1487). Britain voted in favour of both resolutions, thus putting the United States (US) in a position to further contribute to UN peacekeeping and hoping at the same time to get them to change their policy in the medium term by showing a willingness to compromise. This was not well received by the European partners. London was accused of having violated both its obligations under the Rome Statute and the European Union's (EU) Common Position of 16 June 2003. The British attitude to an independent ICC can therefore be described as initially reserved and from 1997 on as proactive, even if at all times pragmatic.

1.2.3   *Britain's approach to international regimes: arms control and disarmament*

Though the level of activity in the area of nuclear arms control and disarmament fluctuated, it was weak until immediately after the change of government in 1997. The Non-Proliferation Treaty (NPT) recognises the UK as a Nuclear Weapon State (NWS). Britain traditionally closely follows the US in questions of nuclear arms control. Although considerably weaker than some NWSs, it is intent on preserving the nuclear status quo.

After the Cold War, Britain embarked on a nuclear strategy of credible minimum deterrence. Britain had already given up its nuclear artillery and short-range missiles under John Major and taken its Tornado GR1/1A bomber squadrons out of service. The number of warheads on each submarine was reduced to a maximum of 96. The Blair government implemented further unilateral reductions and, in addition, reduced the readiness and heightened the transparency of its nuclear arsenal (Clarke 2004a: 51). The 1998 SDR for the first time proclaimed the ultimate aim of a world without nuclear weapons. New Labour was noticeably more strongly committed to promoting new multilateral agreements such as the Comprehensive Test Ban Treaty (CTBT) and the Fissile Material Cut-off Treaty (FMCT). This boost in British nuclear arms control policy did not hold for long, however. Following the 9/11 terrorist attacks, closer security cooperation with the US brought the British approach to multilateral nuclear arms control closer to the rather uncompromising position of the Bush administration.

Britain showed high to very high levels of activity in the biological and chemical weapons regimes. It was, for example, particularly committed to strengthening the Chemical Weapons Convention (CWC) with regard to implementation and verification. The British position in the controversy about strengthening the Biological Weapons Convention (BWC) through the creation of a verification mechanism was closer to the European position and differed considerably from the US position of rejection. Yet, London deemed the regime best served if the US were on board and thus, as of 1998, moved away from maximum demands with regard to the verification protocol.[1]

In the area of land mines, Britain was initially among those sceptical of the Ottawa Process. This, once again, changed after the election in 1997. The new government was willing to agree to a comprehensive ban and work towards this ban at the Conference on Disarmament (Lloyd 1999: 24). The UK signed the Ottawa Agreement on 3 December 1997 and ratified it on 31 July 1998.

On the whole, Britain has a mixed record of contributing to international (arms control) regimes. While its policy towards the regulation of biological and chemical weapons as well as landmines was overall beneficial to the respective regimes, its nuclear weapons policy can hardly be considered constructive, even though it is moderate compared to that of other NWSs. As discussed earlier with regard to the ICC, for the most part, Labour's 1997 election victory had a positive impact on Britain's willingness to proactively support international cooperation and regulation.

1.2.4   Britain's approach to the United Nations

Another indication of the importance of international organisations and multilateralism for British foreign policy is the high and undisputed standing that the UN family enjoys across the whole political spectrum. Britain has an outstanding and some would say anachronistic position in the UN, which manifests itself in Britain's permanent seat on the Security Council. Of the five veto powers, the UK is the most fervent supporter of the International Court of Justice, as well as the largest voluntary donor to several UN special programmes. Many member states value the technical skills of British diplomats in committee work and regularly rely on British drafts and position papers. In the Security Council, Britain pursues a modest veto policy with a total of 32 vetoes and not a single veto used since 1996.[2] While all this documents Britain's willingness to take on responsibility in the international

---

[1] Kelle, Alexander, 'Britische BW-Rüstungskontrollpolitik, 1990–2002', and 'Die Chemiewaffen-Rüstungskontrollpolitik Großbritanniens, 1990–2002', unpublished manuscripts, 2006, Belfast.

[2] As of July 2011, in comparison: China 6, France 18, United States 83, USSR/Russia 125. See 'Subjects of UN Security Council Vetoes', online: www.globalpolicy.org/component/content/article/102/40069.html.

system as well as the high value that it attributes to international law and regulation, the permanent seat on the Security Council, of course, also serves to enhance the country's status. Without the UN, the influence of British diplomacy in the world would be considerably weaker (Groom and Taylor 1995: 371).

1.2.5   *Relations with significant others*
In his famous speech to the 1948 Conservative Party Conference, Winston Churchill saw the UK at the intersection of three circles: the English-speaking alliance, Europe and the Empire. On the one hand, this was an expression of the country's perception of itself as a major power with global influence and, on the other, of the desire to assume a leading role in all three arenas without getting entangled in one at the expense of the others. Churchill's doctrine became the main foreign policy concept of the post-war cra (White 2001: 120). The colonial past and the modern Commonwealth were constitutive parts of the country's view of itself as a global player. Although the international significance of the Commonwealth has declined over the decades, London continues to maintain close and stable relations with its former colonies and has a special sense of responsibility for their fate. Probably even more at the centre of British foreign policy, however, is the constant balancing act between 'Atlanticism' and 'Europeanism'.

NATO: NATO has always played the main role in Britain's defence following the Second World War. The Alliance became the most important factor in bilateral relations with the US and was also seen as an institution that brought together Europe and North America, as such being at the intersection of two of Churchill's three circles. Both the Conservatives and Labour saw NATO as the primary instrument for global crisis management after the end of the Cold War. Even prior to September 11, 2001, London was one of the initiators of a transformation of the Alliance aimed at swift power projection capabilities beyond Europe's borders. Following 9/11, British opinion came to see NATO as the undisputed and primary tool in the fight against international terrorism (Williams 2005: 127).

Europe: Its patently instrumental treatment of Europe quickly gave Britain the reputation of being an awkward partner. The reason for the difficult relationship with Europe is primarily to be found in two elements of British identity. On the one hand, increasing integration has always been seen as a danger for the doctrine of parliamentary sovereignty (Wallace 1991: 76) and, on the other, the British viewed any decision in favour of stronger integration in Europe as harmful to Britain's own influence within the transatlantic circle. This changed under Labour; the Blair government no longer regarded 'Atlanticism' and 'Europeanism' as a zero-sum game. Blair tried to assume a leading role in Europe and shake off the traditionally reactionary attitude towards the EU (Duff 1998: 45).

For 50 years, Europe's leading military power rejected a genuine European security and defence policy. Although Britain favoured the establishment of a European identity *within* NATO following the Cold War, it vehemently fought against the extension of the Common Foreign and Security Policy (CFSP) to include defence. Therefore, the perceived paradigm change that paved the way for the European Security and Defence Policy (ESDP) at the Franco-British summit in St Malo in December 1998 came as a surprise to everyone. There has been speculation as to the motivation for this initiative. It seems plausible that with this step the Blair government intended to alleviate Europe's significant weakness in defence matters, which was becoming apparent in the Balkans in particular, *thereby* ensuring the future of NATO. Following this argument, the British ESDP initiative was based rather on a change of tactics, not on a fundamental change in the traditional transatlantic strategy. After 9/11, the necessity of the ESDP was not questioned, but its priority very much was. Blair's focus turned away from Europe to a more global context. It soon became clear that Britain saw the responsibility for fighting international terrorism not with the EU, but with NATO (Williams 2005: ch. 3).

'Special relationship': The US has been Britain's most important partner since the Second World War. This 'special relationship' is based primarily on privileged cooperation in the fields of defence, nuclear weapons and intelligence. Both sides also frequently refer to historical, cultural and emotional connections as well as to the common language (Dumbrell 2004). A certain asymmetry characterised the relations from the outset. Britain was both the more dependent partner as well as the one who benefited most. The proximity to the US provided not only access to military know-how; it also strengthened British influence in international relations. For the UK, a strong, permanent junior partnership helped to slow down the advancing decline. Britain is often cynically referred to as 'Washington's poodle', which is, however, a far too one-sided description. Britain at no time aligned its foreign policy entirely to the other side of the Atlantic or lost sight of Europe. It saw itself rather as a transatlantic bridge (Aggestam 2004: 141).

1.3   Conclusion: Britain's foreign policy role conception

The combination of the three role segments of status, liberal values and anti-appeasement culminates in a foreign policy role that can best be described as 'promoter of a liberal order'. This role conception has not been free from tensions. The repeatedly visible lack of harmony between European and transatlantic identity elements put pressure on the transatlantic bridge, especially since the end of the Cold War and with integration on the continent increasingly gathering pace during the 1990s.

The strong anti-appeasement element within the foreign policy role consists of a pronounced enemy image. Decision-makers have commonly referred to adversaries in a Manichaean way: Anthony Eden called for action against evil dictators; Thatcher once explained that she was in politics 'because of the conflict between good and evil' and stated in the House of Commons that 'when good has to be upheld and when evil has to be overcome, Britain will take up arms';[3] and Blair also introduced a dichotomy of good versus evil into his doctrine of liberal interventionism. However, British governments time and again have had to face criticism for their rather pragmatic treatment of regimes that violate human rights. Although Labour's foreign policy proved to be more consistent with the foreign policy role conception compared with Conservative predecessor governments, the Blair government, for example, lost a lot of credibility due to a number of arms exports to conflict zones (Cooper 2000). Thus, Britain's activities at the international level definitely reflect a combination of both pragmatic and more principled approaches to foreign policy.

2   Decision-making and public debates on the Gulf War, Kosovo War and Iraq War

2.1   The UK and the 1990–1991 Gulf War

2.1.1   The road to war

With over 40,000 soldiers, *Operation Granby*, the British code name for *Desert Shield* and *Desert Storm*, was the biggest deployment of British troops since the Second World War. From the outset, the US dominated the political and military decision-making processes, and it is unclear to what extent Britain influenced the Bush administration at the time. Prime Minister Margaret Thatcher and her successor

---

[3] House of Commons, 22 November 1990.

John Major favoured a resolute approach towards Saddam Hussein. Thatcher in particular pushed for a military solution to the conflict early on (Dumbrell 2006: 207).

Thatcher was visiting the US when Iraq invaded Kuwait in August 1990. She immediately sent two warships to the Gulf before meeting President Bush. Reports of this meeting differ as regards the prime minister's influence on the American handling of the conflict. Various sources, in particular British, assume that she forced a hesitant president to respond decisively and assume a leadership role (e.g. Lepgold 1997: 69; Hurd 2003: 391). There is no doubt that Thatcher was already intent on an utmost resolute stance against Iraq and assured Bush of Britain's full support.

Whereas US Secretary of State James Baker considered a Security Council resolution indispensable for any measures against Saddam Hussein, the prime minister wanted to avoid the risk of restricting the coalition's freedom of action through a weak resolution or even a Russian or Chinese veto. She argued instead that Article 51 of the Charter, in conjunction with Resolution 660, was sufficient to legitimise the use of force (Thatcher 1993: ch. 27). Foreign Secretary Douglas Hurd, on the other hand, considered a resolution explicitly sanctioning the use of force to be necessary in order to also get the opposition at home on board. After a meeting in London on 9 November, Hurd and Baker together succeeded in convincing the reluctant prime minister to agree to the later Resolution 678 (Fawcett and O'Neill 1992: 145).

In the meantime, there was increasing evidence that Western nationals in Kuwait and Iraq were being held hostage and used as human shields at strategically important locations. Thatcher refused to negotiate with Iraq as long as British citizens were being held. The prime minister was also resolute with regard to the sea blockade. Bush had informed her that in deference to the Soviets there was no intention of intercepting two Iraqi tankers that were threatening to break through the sea blockade. Thatcher, however, wanted to stop the ships in order to avoid a precedent. She advised the president, 'This is no time to go wobbly' (Campbell 2003: 666).

London rejected Russian and French initiatives suggesting negotiations with Saddam Hussein and sharply criticised its European partners for their lack of willingness to provide troops. At the Commission on Security and Cooperation in Europe meeting in Paris on 19 November, Thatcher argued that the taking of hostages in itself was reason enough for using military force. Three days later she presided over her very last cabinet meeting, at which the decision was made to deploy a further brigade and increase the number of British troops in Saudi Arabia. At 30,000 soldiers, the British contingent was now three times bigger than during its last major campaign, the Falklands War.

Contrary to American fears, Major's assumption of office on 28 November did not soften the uncompromising British position (Dumbrell 2006: 207–8). Unlike Thatcher, who had been certain that war was inevitable as early as in September (Thatcher 1993: 824–7), Major was initially convinced that ultimately Saddam Hussein would bow to pressure.[4]

British Defence Minister Tom King and US Secretary of Defense Richard Cheney were openly questioning the effectiveness of sanctions at that time. Shortly before Christmas, Major made it clear while visiting the US in support of President Bush, who was facing both a reluctant Congress and public opinion, that only an immediate and complete Iraqi withdrawal could avoid further consequences. He emphasised on 10 January 1991, one day after a meeting between Baker and the Iraqi Foreign Minister Aziz failed to produce any results, that there was no weakening of the UN ultimatum. Hurd declared the policy of sanctions as failed and said Britain was preparing for war. The British government had now made its decision and was concerned that Saddam Hussein could succeed in weakening the determination of the coalition through a last-minute initiative, as proposed by France.

Throughout the crisis, there was hardly any opposition in Britain to the uncompromising policy being pursued. By and large, the government was confident of support from its parliamentary party and the opposition, civil society, the media and the general public. While the peace movement was able to draw some attention to itself, the protests were relatively low-key compared to those in other European countries or the US.[5]

Until the war started on 17 January 1991, Parliament exercised its (weak) controlling function through extensive debates (White 2003: 312). However, it was never actually granted a substantive vote on the deployment of troops and it was not until four weeks after Iraq's invasion of Kuwait that the government recalled Parliament from its recess for a two-day emergency session on 6 and 7 September 1990. At this time, British troops were already deployed in the Gulf region. In a motion to adjourn, Parliament expressed its overwhelming support with 437 votes to 31; in a further motion to adjourn immediately before the outbreak

---

[4] Frankel, Glenn 1991. 'Britain Reclaiming Role as Top U.S. Ally', *Washington Post*, 18 January, p. A23.

[5] White, Michael 1990. 'British Groups Rally against Build-up', *The Guardian*, 29 August; White, Michael 1991. 'No Rocking the Warship', *The Guardian*, 12 January.

Table 4.1 *Frequencies of arguments, Gulf War, United Kingdom, supporters only (n = 34); extracts of results*[a]

Code	Argument	Number of speakers	Percentage of speakers
5102	Threat to world order	28	82.4
4101	Enforce international law/support UN	26	76.5
4201	Covered by international law	21	61.8
5201	Multilateral consensus pro	15	44.1
1103	Regional stability	14	41.2
1104	Show of force	14	41.2
4202	Peaceful means exhausted	11	32.4
5101	Humanitarian catastrophe	11	32.4

[a] Full lists of results for this and all following tables are available from the author.

of war, Parliament voted by 534 to 57 in favour of the government's decision (Fawcett and O'Neill 1992). One of the few differences that emerged between the government and opposition centred on the question of the need for a Security Council resolution explicitly legitimising the use of force.

2.1.2 Content analysis of parliamentary debates

The debate about the first military intervention in the post-Cold War era was relatively clear-cut. In the 50 speeches selected from parliamentary debates, 34 (68 per cent) argued in favour of and 16 (32 per cent) against the use of force. Eight of the ten most frequent arguments featured references to liberal values, international law and power.

As Table 4.1 reveals, over 80 per cent of those favouring the use of force stressed a perceived danger to the world order. Three-quarters (76.5 per cent) feared that the UN and international law would be damaged if Saddam Hussein were not driven out of Kuwait, and three out of five speakers (61.8 per cent) pointed out that the use of force was covered by international law. Fifteen speakers (44.1 per cent) highlighted the consensus with the Arab states. Among the ten most frequently mentioned arguments, six made reference to universal values and international law, among them the four most frequently used.

Opponents of a war also made reference in particular to universal values and international law as can be seen in Table 4.2. In almost every speech (93.8 per cent) there was a demand for more time for the sanctions to work. Frequent mention was made of the negative consequences for stability in the region (62.5 per cent) in case of intervention.

Table 4.2 *Frequencies of arguments, Gulf War, United Kingdom, opponents only (n = 16); extracts of results*

Code	Argument	Number of speakers	Percentage of speakers
4302	Peaceful means not exhausted	15	93.8
1303	Regional instability	10	62.5
5303	Civilian casualties	8	50
5302	Pacifism/war damages global norms	7	43.8
6302	Casualty aversion (own soldiers)	7	43.8
4301	No UN mandate/damage to UN	6	37.5

One in two speakers who argued against the use of force warned of the civilian casualties that could be expected, and 7 out of 16 (43.8 per cent) referred to the negative consequences for global goods, in particular to the economic and ecological implications of an intervention. Just as many opponents pointed out the risk for British troops.

2.1.3   Newspaper debates

On 13 January 1991, the *Sunday Times* wrote: 'If Britain does go to war, it will be with the united support of the 21 national newspapers.'[6] This was certainly true for the conservative *Times*. The left-wing *Guardian*, however, had pleaded against the use of force and instead for exhausting all peaceful means ever since the beginning of the crisis.

The *Guardian* had as little doubt about Saddam Hussein's highly problematic character ('war criminal', 'murderous thug', 'monster') as it had about the fact that he was mainly responsible for the crisis.[7] The leading articles also saw a danger for the world order in the invasion; Iraq's aggression needed to be countered decisively. Yet, their tenor was that the economic sanctions imposed by the Security Council were the only promising way, and that they had to be given sufficient time. The *Guardian* criticised the massive increase in the number of allied forces deployed and their transformation from purely defensive to offensive troops. It saw in this a weakening of the sanctions policy and feared that a momentum could emerge for sending the troops into action swiftly.[8]

[6] MacArthur, Brian 1991. 'Tabloids Lead a United Press into the Battle', *Sunday Times*, 13 January.
[7] E.g. Anonymous 1990. 'A Cause for the World, Not Just for the West', *The Guardian*, 9 August; Anonymous 1990. 'The Hitler League', *The Guardian*, 17 October.
[8] See Anonymous 1990. 'Choosing the Best Option', *The Guardian*, 6 August; Anonymous 1990. 'The Success of Sanctions', *The Guardian*, 17 December.

The incalculable risks in the form of loss of troops and civilian casualties spoke against the use of force; the ecological consequences and political implications for the world order were also mentioned frequently. At the beginning of the conflict, the leading articles opposed the prime minister's view that no explicit authorisation from the Security Council was necessary for an intervention.[9] Furthermore, until the very last, *The Guardian* criticised the fact that there had never been a debate in Parliament.[10]

Although immediately after the occupation of Kuwait, *The Times*, for its part, had lent careful support to an embargo in conjunction with a credible threat of force, it subsequently soon came to doubt the prudence of this strategy. Sanctions alone, the leading articles explained, would not function and as such were wholly unsuitable for driving Saddam Hussein out of Kuwait.[11] The newspaper then accused all those who wanted to solve the conflict by peaceful means of lacking courage, claiming that they were using sanctions as a fig leaf to conceal their diffidence and thus almost capitulating in the face of Iraqi aggression; it dismissed the various peace initiatives by the French and others as appeasement.[12] *The Times* saw the forceful removal of the Iraqi dictator from power as the only key to defusing the crisis. In addition to the danger to the world order and the integrity of the UN, which had resulted from the Iraqi invasion, the leading articles saw in particular stability in the region and Western (primarily economic) interests under threat. The re-establishment of the status quo ante through an Iraqi retreat from Kuwait was not an acceptable solution. This would only postpone a future war instigated by Saddam Hussein, which would be considerably more expensive, not only in terms of human life. *The Times* repeatedly referred to the dictator's problematic character ('Iraq's Hitler', 'evil', 'ruthless barbarian') as well as his intolerable striving for weapons of mass destruction.[13]

---

[9] Anonymous 1990. 'Breakfast with Saddam Hussein', *The Guardian*, 27 August; Anonymous 1990. 'The Narrow Options on a Broad Front', *The Guardian*, 8 September.

[10] Anonymous 1991. 'While Britain Still Slumbers', *The Guardian*, 3 January; Anonymous 1991. 'Debate at Deadline', *The Guardian*, 16 January.

[11] Anonymous 1990. 'Uniting for Peace', *The Times*, 7 August; Anonymous 1991. 'No Choice But War', *The Times*, 16 January.

[12] Anonymous 1990. 'Withdraw or Fight', *The Times*, 1 December; Anonymous 1991. 'Labour Didn't Say Yes, and It Won't Say No', *The Sunday Times*, 13 January.

[13] Anonymous 1990. 'The Peace Party', *The Sunday Times*, 2 September; Anonymous 1990. 'America, Bush and Munich', *The Sunday Times*, 9 December.

2.1.4 Public opinion polls

As long as the Gulf conflict lasted, the government had public opinion behind it. The British public even emerged as the 'most hawkish' of all the anti-Iraq coalition.[14] A Gallup poll in mid-August identified an overwhelming approval of 83 per cent for sending British troops to Saudi Arabia, while 89 per cent were in favour of a blockade of Iraq.[15] This figure remained relatively stable for a long time. MPs from the major parties were also in agreement that the small amount of protest mail was an expression of broad-based approval of the government's course.[16] Another Gallup poll in early October revealed that 86 per cent of the population supported the liberation by force of both Kuwait and the hostages.[17] According to several polls in late December and early January, the number of those in favour of an uncompromising stance was the same as those who wanted to give sanctions more time.[18] Following the expiry of the ultimatum, a majority emerged in favour of the immediate use of force.[19]

2.1.5 Conclusion: explaining Britain's participation in the Gulf War

Britain persistently attempted to narrow the road to war in the run-up to the Gulf War. The government, in particular under Thatcher in the initial phase of the conflict, displayed a remarkable level of determination to use force. Britain generally accepted the American leading role, but attempted to exert influence with regard to the overall political strategy and the timing of an attack.

The content analysis of the parliamentary debates shows that there was little reference to the national interest. The crisis was discussed rather as a matter of international law and world order. Britain's historical links to the Gulf made the risk for the region an issue for both supporters and opponents alike (e.g. Fawcett and O'Neill 1992: 156). The leading articles and editorials in *The Guardian* and *The Times* as well as the parliamentary debate display similar patterns of argument. Interestingly, both papers, even more than MPs, framed Saddam Hussein as an unjust enemy.

---

[14] Wintour, Patrick 1990. 'Britons Head the Hawks as Heath Flies to Baghdad', *The Guardian*, 19 October.
[15] Wintour, Patrick 1990. 'Polls Give Strong Support to Thatcher's Military Action', *The Guardian*, 13 August.
[16] Ford, Richard 1990. 'Stand-off in Gulf Brings Crop of Letters to No 10', *The Times*, 24 August.
[17] Wintour 1990. 'Britons Head the Hawks'.
[18] Simmons, Michael 1991. 'Majority Back Use of Force', *The Guardian*, 8 January.
[19] Brown, Paul 1991. 'Opinion Hardens for Quick Attack', *The Guardian*, 15 January.

The aggression of the Iraqi dictator was the first major challenge for the emerging post-Cold War order. It addressed both the liberal values as well as the anti-appeasement segment of the British foreign policy role, thereby triggering a special identity feat: standing firm against aggressors.

2.2   The UK and the 1998–1999 Kosovo War

2.2.1   The road to war

Whereas Britain remained reluctant during the Balkan wars in the early 1990s, in the Kosovo conflict it not only vehemently supported a diplomatic approach to the crisis from the outset but in the course of the crisis also turned out to be the 'leading hawk in the West' (Richardson 2000: 145). Thanks to Britain's initiative, the situation in Kosovo was on the Balkan Contact Group's agenda with effect from September 1997 (House of Commons 2001). Britain, which held the presidency of the European Council in the first six months of 1998 and also chaired the G8, assumed a leading role in the EU, the Contact Group, the UN and NATO (Duke *et al.* 2000: 136).

In early June, Blair warned the Serbian President Slobodan Milošević that neither NATO nor the EU would tolerate an escalation of the conflict.[20] Parallel to demonstrating power through two NATO manoeuvres, Britain tried to bring about a peaceful solution to the conflict at a bilateral level between March and September (Duke *et al.* 2000: 137). It also played a leading role in drafting the Chapter VII Resolution 1199, which the Security Council adopted on 23 September 1998.

Following the publication of UN Secretary-General Annan's pessimistic report about the situation in Kosovo, the Cabinet Committee on Defence, at a meeting chaired by Blair on 5 October, decided to put British aircraft and troops on stand-by for possible participation in combat operations. Now prepared even to deploy ground troops, Britain criticised the US administration's indecisiveness.[21] The FCO sent a memorandum to the NATO allies stating that, in its opinion, military intervention was legal even without a Security Council resolution, given the humanitarian necessity. There had been higher hopes in London regarding the Holbrooke mission in October; off the record, disappointment was expressed that the American mediator had been

---

[20] Webster, Philip and Bremner, Charles 1998. 'Blair Warns Milosevic of NATO Intervention', *The Times*, 4 June; see also Richardson (2000: 149).

[21] Evans, Michael 1998. 'Blair Summons Cabinet to Agree on Military Force', *The Times*, 3 October; Beaumont, Paul and Wintour, Patrick 1999. 'Kosovo: The Untold Story', *The Observer*, 18 July.

unable to push through the deployment of a robust international peace-keeping force (Woollacott 2000: 422–3). In Resolution 1203 of 24 October 1998, the Security Council welcomed the Holbrooke agreement and set up an OSCE observer mission. The draft for the resolution, which was drawn up by British diplomats, was considerably harsher, as it threatened the use of force if the Serbs did not adhere to the agreement (House of Commons 2000). The wording had to be weakened, however, due to Russian and Chinese resistance.

The 'massacre of Račak' on 15 January 1999 marked the turning point. The Balkan Contact Group decided to summon both parties to talks in Rambouillet. On 30 January, the British foreign minister met Milošević in Belgrade and leaders of the Kosovo Albanians in Skopje and informed them of the resolutions and the Contact Group's ultimatum. In London, plans were drawn up for the deployment of 8,000 soldiers as well as tanks and artillery, which in the case of an agreement were intended to help enforce the peace accord. The negotiations, conducted jointly by the foreign ministers of Britain and France, Cook and Védrine, failed on 18 March due to the Serbs' refusal to agree to the deployment of NATO peacekeeping troops. British officials were of the opinion that the Americans had continually undermined a strong joint position against Milošević. Whereas the British government had been working on an invasion plan since the summer of 1998, from a British point of view the US government had made the mistake of ruling out a ground offensive (Richardson 2000: 146–7).

On 24 March 1999, NATO started air strikes against Serbian military targets. Although the attorney general in his capacity as the government's legal advisor expressed strong concerns about the legality of *Operation Allied Force*, Britain to a greater extent than most NATO partners argued that there was indeed a legal basis for the air strikes under international law – even without explicit Security Council authorisation. The Security Council in its Chapter VII Resolutions 1199 and 1203 had deemed the situation in Kosovo to be a threat to peace and security in the region and Serbian aggression towards the civilian population to be causing a serious humanitarian disaster. The government argued that, in the event of the failure of the Security Council to implement its resolutions, it had to be possible for individual states to put an end to humanitarian disasters through the use of force (Wheeler and Owen 2007: 86–7).

Similarly to the situation during the Gulf conflict in 1990–1, the cabinet's determined stance against Milošević enjoyed a high level of support in Parliament and society. Humanitarian NGOs attempted to increase pressure on the government and, given the massacres and the catastrophic situation of the refugees in Kosovo, even called for an intervention.[22] In the run-up to the war, the Conservatives supported air strikes as well as the deployment of ground troops for the purpose of monitoring a peace agreement (Richardson 2000: 157). Blair demanded and received enormous discipline from his parliamentary party – one heard almost no objections to the prime minister's resolute stance from the Labour back benches. Labour's left wing itself was divided: Tony Benn was the leader of the war opponents, whereas other prominent MPs supported Tony Blair. Parliament did not play an important role in the decision-making process prior to the air strikes, and was only informed of developments with delay (White 2003: 314).

2.2.2   Content analysis of parliamentary debates

The random sample of parliamentary speeches reflects the consensus among the three major parties. The analysis covered 37 MPs and government representatives (74 per cent) in favour of an intervention as well as 13 MPs (26 per cent) against one.

As Table 4.3 indicates, by far the most important argument put forward by those in favour of air strikes and the use of ground troops was the precarious humanitarian situation (70.3 per cent). Massacres of the civilian population were cited as well as the large numbers of refugees, whose situation was threatening to deteriorate further with winter coming. Half of those in favour wanted the deployment of troops on the Macedonian and Albanian border as a deterrent and wanted to force Milošević to cooperate by threatening air strikes. These are the two arguments primarily used. The danger to the region's stability (21.6 per cent) and the credibility of NATO (18.9 per cent) were of minor importance. The high risk to British soldiers was a concern to five supporters (13.5 per cent), although the humanitarian consequences for the Kosovo Albanians that would have arisen if no action were taken weighed more heavily for them.

Roughly half of the speakers (46.2 per cent) among the relatively few opponents to the war criticised the lack of UN authorisation for military intervention (Table 4.4). Air strikes or the use of ground troops would violate Serbia's sovereignty and be a breach of international law. The same number feared that air strikes would only strengthen Milošević, as the Serbs would close ranks and fight more fiercely. Some opponents of the war (38.5 per cent) argued against air strikes, as they believed

---

[22] Author's interview with Edmund Cairns, Senior Policy Advisor Research, Oxfam UK, on 15 October 2007.

Table 4.3 *Frequencies of arguments, Kosovo War, United Kingdom, supporters only (n = 37); extracts of results*

Code	Argument	Number of speakers	Percentage of speakers
5101	Humanitarian catastrophe	26	70.3
1104	Show of force	19	51.4
1103	Regional stability	8	21.6
2102	Alliance pro (external aspects)	7	18.9
6302	Casualty aversion (own soldiers)	5	13.5

Table 4.4 *Frequencies of arguments, Kosovo War, United Kingdom, opponents only (n = 13); extracts of results*

Code	Argument	Number of speakers	Percentage of speakers
4301	No UN mandate/damage to UN	6	46.2
1302	Loss of power	6	46.2
1306	Lacking military strategy	5	38.5
5303	Civilian casualties	4	30.8

this type of intervention would not produce the desired results; or criticised the lack of an exit strategy, if ground troops were sent into action after all. Almost a third (30.8 per cent) were against bombing, as the humanitarian situation on the ground would only deteriorate and cause even more casualties.

2.2.3   Newspaper debates

Early on in the Kosovo conflict the large majority of leading articles and editorials in *The Guardian* and *The Times* spoke in favour of NATO using force. *The Guardian* already considered the situation in Kosovo to be a serious danger to world peace in January 1998 and demanded that Milošević be stopped.[23] Though two commentaries argued in favour of a military intervention as early as June,[24] the majority of articles initially

[23] See Anonymous 1998. 'The New Balkan Flashpoint', *The Guardian*, 16 January, p. 16.

[24] Woollacott, Martin 1998. 'The Final Evil', *The Guardian*, 6 June, p. 22; Steele, Jonathon 1998. 'We Must Rescue the Oppressed of Kosovo', *The Guardian*, 19 June, p. 20.

pleaded for all peaceful means to be exhausted through the tightening of sanctions in conjunction with the deployment of troops on the Macedonian and Albanian border. From October on, the articles were united in their call for the use of ground troops; it was argued that air strikes were not sufficient and would, moreover, endanger the population. Although it was aware of the risks that an intervention entailed for Kosovars and Serbs as well as for British soldiers, *The Guardian* saw no alternative if an end were to be put to the massacres of the civilian population and the catastrophic situation of the large number of refugees. Milošević, painted as a 'demon king', 'murderous and untrustworthy thug' and 'war criminal', could not be part of the solution.[25]

Overall, *The Times* offered a broader spectrum of opinion, as it also printed articles against the war.[26] Nonetheless, the majority of articles spoke out in favour of an intervention. Unlike *The Guardian*, alongside the humanitarian reasons *The Times* also cited as reasons primarily the danger to stability in the region and the credibility of NATO. As of March 1998, the articles argued that displaying a determination to use force was the best way to end the conflict; diplomacy alone would not influence Milošević.[27] Like *The Guardian*, *The Times* judged Western diplomacy and in particular the Holbrooke agreement extremely critically. It did not regard the unarmed OSCE observers as a solution to the conflict.

2.2.4   Public opinion polls

No opinion polls were conducted in the lead-up to the Kosovo War.[28] However, observers assume that there was broad-based approval for a tough stance against Milošević and ultimately for the use of force (Richardson 2000: 157; Dunne 2009: 111). One indication of this, albeit weak, is the high level of approval shortly after the bombing had started. According to a Marplan poll of 26–27 March 1999, over two-thirds of the British population were in favour of air strikes and 31 per cent against. On 2 April, approval of the continuing air strikes rose to

---

[25] Woollacott 1998. 'The Final Evil'; Anonymous 1998. 'Wheen's World: Why Slobodan Needs a Slap', *The Guardian*, 7 October, p. 5.

[26] Jenkins, Simon 1998. 'Too Many Cooks', *The Times*, 11 March; Jenkins 1998. 'Oh, What a Silly War', *The Times*, 9 October; Jenkins 1999. 'The Real Catastrophe', *The Times*, 24 March.

[27] Anonymous 1998. 'Bloodshed in Illyria', *The Times*, 4 March; Anonymous 1998. 'Against Milosevic', *The Times*, 9 June; Anonymous 1998. 'Poker in Kosovo', *The Times*, 28 October; Anonymous 1999. 'Bombing the Balkans', *The Sunday Times*, 21 February.

[28] Norton, Richard 1998. 'Tough Talk Masks Lack of Debate', *The Guardian*, 9 October.

75 per cent. There was even 66 per cent approval for the deployment of British ground troops as part of a NATO mission, with only 27 per cent disapproving.[29]

2.2.5   Conclusion: explaining Britain's participation in the Kosovo War

Britain was very much involved in the efforts to settle the Kosovo conflict from an early stage. To this end, the government pursued a two-pronged strategy. On the one hand, it assumed a leading role in diplomatic initiatives and, on the other, it was the most resolute of all those involved in backing up demands to Serbia with the threat of force. Throughout the entire conflict, the UK worked on getting the various measures drawn up by different institutions authorised by the UN, but ultimately did not shy away from a pragmatic handling of the stalemate in the Security Council. As in 1991, the population was behind the government's decision to go to war.

The massacres of the civilian population and the catastrophic situation of the refugees strengthened the British government's determination. This was also the dominant argument in the parliamentary debates as well as in the newspapers, which for the most part called for the use of military means at a very early stage. In contrast, the lack of UN legitimisation for an intervention proved to be an enormous problem for supporters of the war. Britain, unlike most other NATO partners, argued that there was a solid base for an intervention under international law deriving from previous resolutions and the spirit of the UN Charter. In the same way as during the Gulf crisis, hardly any argument was based on Alliance-related questions. This is quite remarkable in view of NATO's crucial role throughout the conflict.

2.3   The UK and the 2003 Iraq War

2.3.1   The road to war

Britain's contribution to the 2003 Iraq campaign has been its most controversial participation in a war since the 1956 Suez War. Even before the crisis unfolded, Blair was convinced that in the medium term an enforced regime change had to replace what he considered the failed containment policy of the 1990s. From the outset, he stood by President Bush in the international controversy over Iraq. The country became the focal point of British cabinet meetings following Bush's State of the Union address in January 2002 (Campbell 2007: 607–8). From spring

---

[29] Smith, David 1999. 'Britain Backs Land Assault', *The Sunday Times*, 4 April.

2002, the entire British decision-making process regarding the policy on Iraq lay with Blair and a small circle of advisors, key ministers, civil servants and the military.

On 6 April 2002, the prime minister met President Bush in Crawford, Texas. Blair wanted to be included in the decision-making process to as great an extent as possible. This way he was hoping to convince the Americans to invade 'only in the right circumstances' (Seldon 2004: 572). The meeting ultimately made it clear to the British just how determined the Americans were to remove Saddam Hussein from power; if necessary, by the use of force. Observers assume that in Crawford Blair assured Bush of Britain's support – 'come what may' (Kampfner 2003: 168; Kettell 2006: 61). While Blair himself later told the Chilcot Inquiry that nothing was decided at that meeting, he confirmed that he made it clear to Bush that if there had to be military action, Britain would unconditionally be at America's side.[30]

The prime minister and his advisors came to realise at an early stage that large sections of the population, and indeed the Labour Party, were strongly against unilateral action. Blair's strategy was to multilateralise the looming conflict and convince the US administration to take the 'UN route'. From now on, the focus was no longer to be on regime change but on Iraq's breaches of its disarmament obligations. During the summer, the British repeatedly emphasised to the Americans how important a UN resolution was for support at home. On 7 September, Blair wrenched a deal from Bush: the Americans would choose the UN route and exhaust all peaceful means. In return, Blair would ensure the support of the Europeans and – in case the process failed – go to war at the side of the US anyway (e.g. Kampfner 2003: 196–7; Bluth 2004: 879).

A 'big sell' phase was initiated in Britain during the subsequent drafting process in the Security Council, with the publication of various controversial dossiers in order to boost the poor approval rating among the population. For example, the 'Iraq's Weapons of Mass Destruction' dossier, published on 24 September, in which intelligence material about the Iraqi arsenal of WMD and plans for developing long-range missiles had been processed, came to the conclusion that these weapons posed a serious *immediate* threat. Fifty-six Labour MPs rebelled at the end of the debate on the dossier in an emergency meeting of Parliament. Neither the British public nor the EU partners or Russia were particularly impressed by the dossier (Seldon 2004: 582).

---

[30] Tony Blair, Oral Evidence before the Iraq Inquiry, 29 January 2010, London. Online: www.iraqinquiry.org.uk/transcripts/oralevidence-bydate/100129.aspx.

On 8 November, the Security Council eventually unanimously passed Resolution 1441. Britain put a lot of effort into persuading the other council members to vote in favour and, at the same time, opposed attempts by the 'hawks' in the US administration to push through a tougher formulation. Whereas on 8 November Foreign Minister Jack Straw still considered that Resolution 1441 legitimised the use of force even without a second resolution were Iraq not to honour its obligations, he backtracked two weeks later following vehement protests from Labour's parliamentary party and spoke out in favour of a second resolution. Furthermore, the government held out to MPs the prospect of putting the deployment of British troops to a substantive vote rather than relying on its prerogative power (Riddell 2004: 222–3). While such a move would have been unique in the recent history of deployment decisions, it was not particularly risky for the government, as it was sure of the support of the Conservatives.

The road to war narrowed when in December 2002 the US and British governments judged the report that Iraq presented to the UN weapons inspectors to be so incomplete, imprecise and flawed that they saw in it a material breach of the country's obligations under Resolution 1441. At this point, many in Blair's closer circle saw war as inevitable, but wanted to avoid giving the public the impression that the decision was definite. Blair needed a second resolution and, above all, more time for the inspections (Clarke 2004b: 43–4). In early January 2003, he decided on implementing a two-pronged strategy: while still pursuing the UN route, massive contingents of troops were to be deployed in the region (Campbell 2007: 656). Defence Minister Geoff Hoon told Parliament on 20 January that he was sending 26,000 troops and over 100 fighter jets to the Gulf.

At a meeting between Blair and Bush in Camp David on 31 January, agreement was reached on refraining from attack for at least the next six weeks in order to win over public opinion. At home, however, the sloppily prepared dossier, 'Iraq: Its Infrastructure of Concealment, Deception and Intimidation', by no means produced a higher level of public approval; rather, it now looked as if the government was desperately trying to convince its critics with facts for which it was unable to provide any proof (Clarke 2004b: 45). Blair's policy came under increasing pressure. The mass demonstration by over one million people in London on 15 February was an impressive show of the population's negative response. Moreover, on 26 February, the government experienced an unusual rebellion in Parliament: 121 Labour MPs voted against the government in a motion on Iraq.

As a reaction, London intensified the pressure on Washington, stressing the importance of a second resolution. On 7 March, Jack Straw presented a draft. Blair attempted to win over the French President Chirac and other so far undecided members of the Security Council, but failed. Blair and Straw waited for the weekend summit with Bush on the Azores before they too officially abandoned the UN route and then withdrew the draft resolution on 17 March. The die was finally cast with the 24-hour ultimatum set at the Azores summit. The domestic controversy surrounding Blair's Iraq policy intensified; Robin Cook and other members of the government announced their resignation.[31] In addition to the Liberal Democrat parliamentary party, several Labour MPs, numerous high-profile Conservatives, the minor parliamentary parties as well as a number of spokesmen for Muslim associations and church representatives spoke out against participating in an intervention (Sharp 2004: 65; Keohane 2005: 68).

The British government, however, used Chirac's veto threat to put the blame for the 'failure' of the UN process on the French. The attorney general, Lord Goldsmith, for a long time of the opinion that a further Security Council resolution was needed, now concluded that the use of force based on Resolution 1441 and all previous Iraq resolutions was covered by international law.[32] With these two trumps in its hand, the government, following a debate on 18 March, gave Parliament an opportunity to give the go-ahead for the use of British troops. It was able to land a victory due to the Conservatives – 85 per cent of whose MPs voted for the government – but was once again forced to endure a large number of dissenters in its own ranks: 139 Labour MPs, over a third of the parliamentary party, rejected the proposal.

2.3.2   *Content analysis of parliamentary debates*
The analysis of the 50 randomly drawn parliamentary speeches prior to the Iraq War reveals just how controversial the debate was. Eighteen MPs and the ten government representatives (56 per cent) supported intervention, 22 MPs (44 per cent) rejected it. By way of contrast with the two debates previously analysed, no single argument was considered

---

[31] BBC 2003. 'Blair Loses Third Minister over Iraq', 18 March. Online: http://news.bbc.co.uk/2/hi/uk_news/politics/2859189.stm.
[32] Norton-Taylor, Richard 2010. 'Chilcot Inquiry: Iraq Papers Show Lord Goldsmith's Warning to Tony Blair', *The Guardian*, 30 June; Norton-Taylor 2011. 'Chilcot Inquiry: Blair Shut Me Out, Says Former Legal Chief Lord Goldsmith', *The Guardian*, 17 January.

Table 4.5 *Frequencies of arguments, Iraq War, United Kingdom, supporters only (n = 28); extracts of results*

Code	Argument	Number of speakers	Percentage of speakers
7101	Enemy image of adversary	22	78.6
5102	Threat to world order	16	57.1
4101	Enforce international law/support UN	15	53.6
1105	National security	13	46.4
1104	Show of force	12	42.9
4202	Peaceful means exhausted	9	32.1
1103	Regional stability	8	28.6
1102	Keep/improve power position	7	25
6101	Regime change/democratisation	7	25
5101	Humanitarian catastrophe	6	21.4

convincing by at least half of the speakers. Rather, there is evidence of a wide range of opinions.

As Table 4.5 reveals, the character of the Iraqi regime was by far the most important argument for supporters of the war. The image of the enemy consisted of its brutality, its lack of compliance with disarmament obligations in the 1990s and its new weapons programmes. The assumed WMD and Scud missile systems were cited as a reason for war in 22 speeches (78.6 per cent). This was placed in the context of the Iraqi dictator's extraordinary perniciousness, the previous use of chemical weapons in the first Gulf War, the past decade of lies and deceit and the continuing disregard for binding UN resolutions. The alleged Iraqi support for terrorists or even links to Al-Qaeda added to this enemy image.

Another important argument (57.1 per cent) was the threat that Iraq posed for world peace and order: directly through the WMD and indirectly by becoming a precedent that showed other dictators the indecisiveness of the international community in dealing with states striving for such weapons. About half of those in favour (53.6 per cent) justified intervention with the necessity of upholding the authority, credibility and future influence of the UN. They reminded those against that Iraq had been in constant non-compliance with Security Council resolutions since 1991. Resolution 1441 had now to be implemented – if necessary through the use of force – in order to prevent the UN from degenerating into a 'talking shop'. In nine speeches (32.1 per cent) this went hand in hand with the argument that all peaceful means had been exhausted over recent years. References to power were also among the arguments used most frequently by those in favour of war: the speakers saw national security and the Western way of life threatened, called

Table 4.6 *Frequencies of arguments, Iraq War, United Kingdom, opponents only (n = 22); extracts of results*

Code	Argument	Number of speakers	Percentage of speakers
6301	Democratic norms/procedures contra war	11	50
4302	Peaceful means not exhausted	11	50
5302	Pacifism/war damages global norms	10	45.5
4301	No UN mandate/damage to UN	9	40.9
1304	Increasing insecurity	9	40.9
1307	National security not concerned	9	40.9
7301	Enemy image questioned	7	31.8

for a credible threat of force, pointed out the danger to stability in the region and to Israel in particular and deemed an intervention necessary to prevent the completion of the nuclear weapons programme.

As indicated in Table 4.6, those opposed to war referred primarily (50 per cent) to the strong opposition in the population, which manifested itself in polls, letters and protest marches. It was argued that the government must not send troops before it had convinced the people that this was necessary. Some speakers emphasised the irony of helping Iraq to democracy through the use of force while disregarding Britain's own democratic procedures. There were also calls for Parliament to have a substantial say in the decision-making process.

Half of the speakers called for the weapons inspectors to be given more time. An intervention prior to expiry of the period demanded by the UN weapons inspectors was seen as totally inappropriate. Ten speakers (45.5 per cent) saw global norms weakened in the case of a unilateral use of force. They argued that the stability and order of the international system were at stake. Arms control regimes would be damaged, as more and more states would strive for WMD in order to protect themselves from intervention by the US and its allies. Nine speakers (40.9 per cent) put this in the context of a weakening of the UN and international law; they rejected a war without a second resolution explicitly legitimising force. The fact that seven speakers (31.8 per cent) explicitly rejected the strongest argument of those in favour is interesting; the Iraqi regime might well be gruesome and possess WMD, but this did not legitimise intervention in their view.

2.3.3 Newspaper debates
The Guardian steadfastly opposed the campaign from its first leading article in the run-up to the Iraq War on 19 March 2002. The most

important arguments were the same as those in the parliamentary debate: large sections of the population were against intervention; there was no basis for it under international law; it weakened the UN and set a dangerous precedent for future conflict resolution.[33] Furthermore, the weapons inspectors deserved more time. After all, the peaceful means for disarming Iraq were not yet exhausted. Also, the leading articles frequently used arguments referring to the power dimension: participation in an invasion was not in the national interest; it endangered national security through a possible increase in terrorist attacks; and further destabilised what was already a fragile situation in the Middle East.[34] Frequent reference was made to the humanitarian consequences – if anything, a war would worsen rather than solve the problems of the Iraqi population. As far as the commentaries were concerned, Saddam Hussein alone was not a legitimate reason for intervention. Though they had no doubt that this was a particularly vicious and inhumane regime, they asked, 'Why now?'[35] *The Guardian* made it quite clear that it mistrusted Blair's public justifications and repeatedly demanded a broad parliamentary debate, at the end of which there ought to be a substantive vote on whether to send British soldiers to war.[36]

The tone in *The Times* was quite different. As early as February 2002, the newspaper encouraged the prime minister to stick to the path he had chosen in spite of opposition in the population, Parliament and even cabinet. The articles focused primarily on the subject of WMD, frequently in conjunction with the vicious character of the regime. Furthermore, given the years of non-compliance with Security Council resolutions, they called for the UN's authority to be restored with force – legitimisation under international law could be deduced from Resolutions 687 and 1441.[37] Unlike *The Guardian*, *The Times* praised Tony Blair for his efforts: as far as possible, he had taken the diplomatic path and it was due to him that President Bush had taken the UN detour at all.[38]

---

[33] Anonymous 2002. 'No Mandate: No War', The Guardian, 30 June, p. 15; Anonymous 2003. 'Speak for This Nation', *The Guardian*, 30 January, p. 23; Anonymous 2003. 'New World Order', *The Guardian*, 11 March, p. 23.

[34] Anonymous 2002. 'The Message for Blair', *The Guardian*, 19 March, p. 19; Anonymous 2002. 'Surviving Saddam', *The Guardian*, 17 September, p. 19.

[35] Anonymous 2002. 'Saddam in His Sights', *The Guardian*, 13 September, p. 19; Anonymous 2002. 'Surviving Saddam', p. 19; Anonymous 2003. 'Powell Shoots to Kill', *The Guardian*, 6 February, p. 23.

[36] Anonymous 2002. 'Recall the Commons', *The Guardian*, 6 September, p. 19; Anonymous 2002. 'All Change on Iraq', *The Guardian*, 3 December, p. 21.

[37] Anonymous 2002. 'To Free Iraq', *The Times*, 15 February; Anonymous 2002. 'Unanimous Resolution', *The Times*, 9 November, p. 29; Anonymous 2003. 'This Is a Just War', *The Sunday Times*, 16 February, p. 20.

[38] Anonymous 2003. 'The Deal', The Times, 26 February, p. 21; Anonymous 2003. 'Air of Resignation', *The Times*, 18 March, p. 21.

2.3.4 Public opinion polls

At all points in the crisis, the opinion polls revealed a clear majority against British participation in an intervention. In MORI and ICM polls conducted in March 2002, only about a third of Britons were in favour, but more than half the population surveyed were against.[39] In January 2003, *The Times* reported that over the last months between 40 and 44 per cent were against intervention, with only 33 to 39 per cent of those polled stating their approval. More sophisticated polls, however, revealed more distinct differences.[40] In September 2002, MORI polled opinion on attitudes to an intervention with a UN mandate and one with no authorisation: whereas only 22 per cent of Britons said they approved of using force (together with the US) without a Security Council mandate, 71 per cent said they approved if international law was respected.[41] These figures vary only slightly until a week before the outbreak of the war. According to MORI polls on 15–16 March, only 30 per cent approved of Blair's approach to dealing with the crisis. Directly before the war, only 26 per cent of the population were in favour of a war without a UN mandate, while 63 per cent were opposed. A Security Council resolution and proof of a secret weapons programme, on the other hand, would have turned these results upside down: under these conditions, 74 per cent would have been in favour of a US-led war.[42]

2.3.5 Conclusion: explaining Britain's participation in the Iraq War

In contrast to the two previously analysed conflicts, the UK was not a driving force towards military intervention prior to the 2003 Iraq War. But it was indeed the closest ally of the US and was also prepared to support it by military means from an early stage. During the crisis, cynics saw in Tony Blair nothing more than the US president's 'poodle'. There can be no doubt that the British were the junior partner and their influence in Washington may well also have been minor. Nevertheless, various indicators, such as Blair's personal conviction that he was 'doing the right thing', show that the lap dog metaphor is

---

[39] MORI poll 2002. 'Going to Iraq and Ruin', 28 March. Online: www.ipsos-mori. com/newsevents/ca/310/Going-to-Iraq-and-Ruin.aspx; see also Travis, Allan 2002. 'Voters Say No to Iraq Attack', *The Guardian*, 19 March.

[40] Riddell, Peter 2003. 'Public Remains Sceptical about Need for War', *The Times*, 14 January.

[41] MORI poll, 'Possible War with Iraq: The Public's View', 26 September 2002. Online: www.ipsos-mori.com/researchpublications/researcharchive/1029/Possible-War-With-Iraq-the-Publics-View.aspx.

[42] MORI poll, 'War with Iraq: The Ides of March Poll', 17 March 2003: Online: www. ipsos-mori.com/researchpublications/researcharchive/831/War-With-Iraq-8212-The-Ides-Of-March-Poll.

inappropriate (Freedman 2006: 14; Campbell 2007). The prime minister was definitely sympathetic to regime change.[43] However, in contrast to the conflicts previously analysed, there was strong opposition from the public, his own party and considerable parts of Europe at a very early stage. Opinion polls as well as mass demonstrations revealed that it was impossible to sell voters a war without a UN mandate. Thus, Blair was forced to publicly replace his original motive for a determined stance vis-à-vis Saddam Hussein – a regime change [44]– with arguments about Iraq's WMD and the long phase of non-compliance with UN resolutions. In addition, the British government had successfully convinced the US government to take the UN route, the 'failure' of which eventually put the government in great difficulties.

Nonetheless, the prime minister persevered in ultimately supporting the US by military means, even though in so doing he went against the preferences of his own constituents. Both Blair's personal conviction that the removal of Saddam Hussein from power was 'the right thing to do' as well as the desire to be included in the US decision-making process emerged as driving factors for shaping British strategy. An enabling factor was the support of the Conservatives, which Blair could be sure of at an early stage. Henceforth, the most important thing for the prime minister was to have as few dissenters as possible on his own side.[45] To this end, he and his advisers as well as MPs, and conservative leading articles constructed a 'necessary war of choice' narrative, in which demonising Saddam Hussein and insisting upon the danger that Iraq posed to world order, to the authority of the United Nations and to Britain's security played a decisive and legitimising role.

3   Conclusion: explaining Britain's participation in all three wars

Britain is one of those democracies that were involved particularly often in military disputes after the Second World War. Monadic democratic peace theory assigns democratic states two characteristics that render them less war-prone than non-democracies: institutional constraints and a normative order in which non-violent modes of conflict-resolution dominate. The British case, however, raises doubts as to the validity of

---

[43] Tony Blair, Oral Evidence before the Iraq Inquiry, 29 January 2010, London. Online: www.iraqinquiry.org.uk/transcripts/oralevidence-bydate/100129.aspx.

[44] There is overwhelming agreement in the literature on that motivation. It is also corroborated by Blair's memoirs (Blair 2010: 371–479).

[45] Overall, in all the conflicts examined there was cross-party consensus with regard to the basic strategy; the dividing lines between supporters and opponents of war ran primarily in the parliamentary parties.

this conception. First, the Westminster system, one of the ideal types in the study of democracy, gives the prime minister unusual leeway with regard to foreign policy decision-making. Through the Royal Prerogative, the British government can send troops into war without granting Parliament a say in the matter. The checks and balances are comparatively weak, and the executive thus faces hardly any structural constraints with regard to foreign and security policy. Second, the United Kingdom perceives itself as a promoter of a liberal world order. This role conception embraces the use of military force as an appropriate and at times necessary means for the solution of international conflicts. Parliament, the media and the public are by no means averse to war per se, and the prime minister can usually count on broad support, unless there is reason for doubt in terms of the legality or legitimacy of an operation. Finally, instead of being a constraining factor, Britain's liberal tradition rather encourages it to stand up against aggression and gross violations of human rights and fight 'democratic wars'.

Britain participated in all of the three conflicts investigated. The British government pushed for the use of force in particular in the run-up to the 1991 Gulf War but also to the 1999 Kosovo War, and in this respect even outdid the determination of the US. Although it was not quite as determined to pursue a policy that would eventually lead to the use of force prior to the Iraq War in 2003, it was still the United States' most loyal ally. In all three conflicts, the British government supported the US course of action at all times and tried to be involved in the decision-making process to as great an extent as possible. It is thus striking that the 'special relationship' was not presented in the respective parliamentary debates as a significant influence on their own position.

Justifications for the use of force in the public discourse prior to each of the interventions focused on arguments derived from the country's foreign policy role conception. The Iraqi occupation of Kuwait in 1990 was seen as the first challenge to the liberal world order that was emerging after the Cold War. It was perceived as an act of aggression from a tyrant regime that must be countered with force, especially when taking into account the lessons learnt from the 1938 Munich Agreement and the failed appeasement policy that led to the Second World War. At the time, Prime Minister Thatcher even had to convince a hesitant US president of the need for a decisive stance vis-à-vis Saddam Hussein. In the case of the Kosovo War, the humanitarian disaster and serious violations of human rights by the vicious Milošević regime were presented as the most important justifications. Once again, Britain seemed more determined than its American allies to opt for an early use of force – and, remarkably, for not ruling out ground operations. Finally, Tony Blair was convinced that in the medium term an enforced regime change had to replace the failed containment policy of the 1990s long before the US plan to disarm and topple Saddam Hussein became known. The British government considered a continuation of the sanctions to be no longer justifiable given the negative impact on the Iraqi population. Once again, the illiberal character of the regime in conjunction with it striving for WMD was seen as an imminent danger for world order. Thus, impetus for action derived from liberal norms and values in each conflict.

Regarding national interests and national security, there was concern about regional stability in all three conflicts, about British hostages being used as human shields by Saddam Hussein during the 1990–1 Gulf crisis, and especially about Iraq's WMD capabilities prior to the 2003 war. However, with the exception of the latter issue, there is only little indication that such power-related factors were among the important determinants in the respective British government's decision-making processes or public discourses.

Thus, British military interventionism follows a logic of appropriate behaviour stemming from its foreign policy role conception. The promotion of a liberal world order and the defence of individual rights and lives abroad are perceived as 'enlightened self-interest'. In conjunction with the claim to being a major power in the international system, this requires the type of activism that is best characterised by what Douglas Hurd once called 'punching above its weight'. The solid liberal tradition in Britain also accounts for a strong affinity with international law and the high esteem in which the country holds the United Nations. While this may modify British interventionism and obviously sets it apart from that of the US, the trauma of appeasement as a core element of its own identity often leads British politics to adopt an uncompromising stance towards tyrants and aggression. In such cases, decision-makers in the UK perceive resorting to the use of force not only as the *necessary* but also the *right* thing to do.

REFERENCES

Aggestam, Lisbeth 2004. *A European Foreign Policy? Role Conceptions and the Politics of Identity in Britain, France and Germany*. Stockholm: Stockholm University

Bartlett, C. J. 1977. 'The Military Instrument in British Foreign Policy', in John Baylis (ed.), *British Defence Policy in a Changing World*. London: Croom Helm, pp. 30–51

Blair, Tony 2010. *A Journey*. London: Hutchinson

Bluth, Christoph 2004. 'The British Road to War: Blair, Bush and the Decision to Invade Iraq', *International Affairs* 80 (5): 871–92

Campbell, Alastair 2007. *The Blair Years: Extracts from the Alastair Campbell Diaries*. New York, NY: A. A. Knopf

Campbell, John 2003. *Margaret Thatcher*. London: Cape

Clarke, Michael 2004a. 'Does My Bomb Look Big in This? Britain's Nuclear Choices after Trident', *International Affairs* 80 (1): 49–62

  2004b. 'The Diplomacy That Led to War in Iraq', in Paul Cornish (ed.), *The Conflict in Iraq 2003*. Basingstoke: Palgrave Macmillan, pp. 27–58

Cooper, Neil 2000. 'The Pariah Agenda and New Labour's Ethical Arms Sales Policy', in Richard Little and Mark Wickham-Jones (eds.), *New Labour's Foreign Policy: A New Moral Crusade?* Manchester University Press, pp. 147–67

Duff, Andrew 1998. 'Britain and Europe: The Different Relationship', in Martin Westlake (ed.), *The European Union Beyond Amsterdam: New Concepts of European Integration*. London: Routledge, pp. 34–46

Duke, Simon, Ehrhart, Hans-Georg and Karádi, Matthias 2000. 'The Major European Allies: France, Germany, and the United Kingdom', in Albrecht Schnabel and Ramesh Thakur (eds.), *Kosovo and the Challenge of Humanitarian Intervention: Selective Indignation, Collective Action and International Citizenship*. Tokyo: UN University Press, pp. 128–48

Dumbrell, John 2004. 'The US–UK "Special Relationship" in a World Twice Transformed', *Cambridge Review of International Affairs* 17 (3): 437–50

  2006. *A Special Relationship: Anglo-American Relations from the Cold War to Iraq*. Basingstoke: Palgrave Macmillan

Dunne, Tim 2009. 'Liberalism, International Terrorism, and Democratic Wars', *International Relations* 23 (1): 107–14

Edmunds, Timothy 2010. 'The Defence Dilemma in Britain', *International Affairs* 86 (2): 377–94

Ellner, Andrea 2000. *Role Images and the Royal Navy: British Naval Policy 1970–1990*. Dissertation, Freie Universität Berlin

Fawcett, Louise and O'Neill, Robert 1992. 'Britain, the Gulf Crisis and European Security', in Nicole Gnesotto and John Roper (eds.), *Western Europe and the Gulf: A Study of Western European Reactions to the Gulf War*. Paris: Institute for Security Studies of WEU, pp. 141–57

Foley, Michael 2000. *The British Presidency: Tony Blair and the Politics of Public Leadership*. Manchester University Press

Freedman, Lawrence 2006. 'Britain at War: From the Falklands to Iraq', *RUSI Journal* 151 (1)

Gaskarth, Jamie 2006. 'Discourses and Ethics: The Social Construction of British Foreign Policy', *Foreign Policy Analysis* 2 (4): 325–41

Groom, A. J. R. and Taylor, Paul 1995. 'The United Kingdom and the United Nations', in Chadwick F. Alger, Gene M. Lyons and John E. Trent (eds.), *The United Nations System: The Policies of Member States*. Tokyo: UN University Press, pp. 367–409

HM Government 2010. *Securing Britain in an Age of Uncertainty: The Strategic Defence and Security Review*. London: The Stationery Office Limited

House of Commons 2000. 'Lessons of Kosovo', Defence Select Committee Fourteenth Report of 2000–01, HC 347-I, London: The Stationery Office Limited

2001. 'Government Policy Towards the Federal Republic of Yugoslavia and the Wider Region Following the Fall of Milosevic', Foreign Affairs Select Committee Fourth Report of 2000–01, HC 246, London: The Stationery Office Limited

Hurd, Douglas 2003. *Memoirs.* London: Little, Brown

Kampfner, John 2003. *Blair's Wars.* London: Free Press

Keohane, Dan 2005. 'The United Kingdom', in Alex Danchev and John Macmillan (eds.), *The Iraq War and Democratic Politics.* London: Routledge, pp. 59–76

Kettell, Steven 2006. *Dirty Politics? New Labour, British Democracy and the Invasion of Iraq.* London: Zed Books

Lepgold, Joseph 1997. 'Britain in Desert Storm: The Most Enthusiastic Junior Partner', in Andrew Bennett, Joseph Lepgold and Danny Unger (eds.), *Friends in Need: Burden Sharing in the Persian Gulf War.* Basingstoke: Macmillan, pp. 69–89

Lloyd, Richard 1999. *Turning Words into Action? The UK and Landmines.* London: The UK Working Group on Landmines

Macleod, Alex 1997. 'Great Britain: Still Searching for Status?', in Philippe G. Le Prestre (ed.), *Role Quests in the Post-Cold War Era: Foreign Policies in Transition.* Montreal: McGill-Queen's University Press, pp. 161–86

MoD (Ministry of Defence) 1998. *Strategic Defence Review: Modern Forces for the Modern World.* London: MoD

Morris, Justin 2011. 'How Great Is Britain? Power, Responsibility and Britain's Future Global Role', *British Journal of Politics & International Relations* 13 (3): 326–47

Noakes, Lucy 1998. *War and the British: Gender, Memory and National Identity.* London: Tauris

Ralph, Jason 2007. *Defending the Society of States: Why America Opposes the International Criminal Court and Its Vision of World Society.* Oxford University Press

Richardson, Louise 2000. 'A Force for Good in the World? Britain's Role in the Kosovo Crisis', in Pierre Martin and Mark R. Brawley (eds.), *Alliance Politics, Kosovo, and NATO's War: Allied Force or Forced Allies?* Basingstoke: Palgrave, pp. 145–64

Riddell, Peter 2004. *Hug Them Close: Blair, Clinton, Bush and the 'Special Relationship'.* London: Politico's

Seldon, Anthony 2004. *Blair.* London: Free Press

Sharp, Jane 2004. 'The US–UK "Special Relationship" after Iraq', in Paul Cornish (ed.), *The Conflict in Iraq 2003.* Basingstoke: Palgrave Macmillan, pp. 59–75

Taylor, Claire 2005. 'Armed Forces (Parliamentary Approval for Participation in Armed Conflict) Bill', *House of Commons Library Research Paper* No. 05/56, London

Thatcher, Margaret 1993. *The Downing Street Years.* New York, NY: Harper Collins

Vital, David 1968. *The Making of British Foreign Policy.* London: Allen & Unwin

Wallace, William 1991. 'Foreign Policy and National Identity in the United Kingdom', *International Affairs* 67 (1): 65–80

Wheeler, Nicholas J. and Owen, Rachel J. 2007. 'Liberal Interventionism versus International Law: Blair's Wars Against Kosovo and Iraq', in David B. MacDonald, Robert G. Patman and Betty Mason-Parker (eds.), *The Ethics of Foreign Policy*. Aldershot: Ashgate, pp. 83–98

White, Brian 2001. *Understanding European Foreign Policy*. Basingstoke: Palgrave

White, Nigel D. 2003. 'The United Kingdom: Increasing Commitment Requires Greater Parliamentary Involvement', in Charlotte Ku and Harold K. Jacobsen (eds.), *Democratic Accountability and the Use of Force in International Law*. Cambridge University Press, pp. 300–22

Wickham-Jones, Mark 2000. 'Labour's Trajectory in Foreign Affairs: The Moral Crusade of a Pivotal Power?', in Richard Little and Mark Wickham-Jones (eds.), *New Labour's Foreign Policy: A New Moral Crusade?* Manchester University Press, pp. 3–32

Williams, Paul D. 2005. *British Foreign Policy under New Labour, 1997–2005*. Basingstoke: Palgrave Macmillan

Woollacott, Martin 2000. 'Großbritannien und die Kosovo-Krise', in Jens Reuter and Konrad Clewing (eds.), *Der Kosovo-Konflikt: Ursachen – Verlauf – Perspektiven*. Klagenfurt: Wieser, pp. 417–28

5 'O ally, stand by me': Australia's ongoing balancing act between geography and history

Niklas Schörnig

Australia prides itself on being a 'warrior nation',[1] and hardly any other country has such a military record as the continent 'down under' has. Australia has been a willing coalition partner with the West in wars led by 'important' allies even far away from its home territory. As US President Barack Obama stressed in his speech to the Australian Parliament on 16 November 2011, 'Aussies and Americans have stood together, fought together and given their lives together in every single major conflict of the past hundred years. Every single one.'[2] Australia participated in both wars against Iraq in 1991 and in 2003, but interestingly enough kept out of the Kosovo War in 1999. To understand these decisions fully, one has to look at the formal policy-making process as well as soft factors like the way Australia sees itself and its national identity, shaped by historical experience and geographical location.

1 How Canberra works: the Australian foreign policy-making process

1.1 The formal side: Capital Hill

Australia gained independence as a commonwealth of six states in 1901, and the Parliament of Australia inherited a two-chamber system, modelled on the Westminster prototype but with a strong American influence. The first chamber, the House of Representatives, is elected by a preferential voting system that favours the major parties – usually the Australian Labor Party, the Liberal Party of Australia and the National Party of Australia (with the second two usually forming a coalition). By contrast, the second chamber, the Senate, is elected through

---

[1] Sheridan, Greg 2011. 'Too Much for Too Few in the Defence Con Job', *The Australian*, 9 July, p. 24.

[2] US President Barack Obama's Speech to Parliament, 17 November 2011, Canberra, reprinted in *The Australian*. Online: www.theaustralian.com.au/national-affairs/obama-in-australia/obamas-speech-to-parliament/story-fnb0o39u-1226197973237.

proportional representation, giving smaller parties a greater chance of getting a representative elected. As under the British system, the prime minister (PM) has the final say in most areas of policy, but 'the fetters are nowhere looser than in foreign policy', and he or she is 'the most influential individual in Australian foreign policy' (Gyngell and Wesley 2003: 97). However, the extent to which the PM gets involved in foreign affairs 'is subject to the role the Prime Minister himself chooses to play' (Evans and Grant 1991: 47). Chief responsibility for external affairs is usually delegated to the minister for foreign affairs.

When it comes to foreign affairs the Australian Parliament has virtually no formal power. Its most important formal power is the power of the purse and public debate. But, '[p]arliamentary debates on foreign policy are relatively rare, and often scheduled around the discussion of domestic matters' (Gyngell and Wesley 2003: 174). The Australian PM has the sole right to send the Australian Defence Force (ADF) into war and to declare war. In sharp contrast to the American constitution, the Australian counterpart 'was founded upon *trust* rather than the *mistrust* of governmental power' (Lindell 2003: 23; emphasis in original), giving the Australian Parliament no effective power of veto whatsoever. This lack of parliamentary power is not widely regarded as a democratic failing by Australia's political elites. Representatives of the Liberal/National Coalition argue for example that parliamentary scrutiny would inhibit the PM's ability to act in times of crisis.[3] Only the smaller parties, the Greens and the Democrats, have been expressly arguing in favour of parliamentary control of the ADF.[4] Furthermore, important foreign policy decisions are made by the PM on a regular basis without consulting the whole cabinet, an attitude adopted by almost all prime ministers since independence. Following his election in 1996, PM John Howard formalised the process and established the National Security Committee of Cabinet, including only a few key ministers and the Attorney General (Firth 2005: 76ff.). Its decisions are binding without further consultation.

Australia has a long history of essentially bipartisanism in the realm of foreign policy, at least between the two major parties, and dramatic shifts in foreign policy are rare, with the Howard era being an exception. When it comes to public scrutiny, matters of foreign policy do not usually create many waves with the Australian public. In general,

---

[3] Author interview with a Liberal MP, Canberra, 1 November 2006.
[4] Author interview with Senator Kerry Nettle (Greens), Canberra 6 November 2006. Author interview with Senator Andrew Bartlett (Democrats), Canberra 7 November 2006.

Australians view the federal government with detachment. In the realm of foreign policy only very serious matters, such as the decision to send the ADF into combat, provoke a public reaction.

1.2   Traditions, national identity and role conceptions in Australian foreign policy

1.2.1   Becoming 'Australian'

When Australia gained independence from Britain in 1901, the State of Australia was created by an act of the British Parliament rather than through a war of independence or at least an act of civil revolt (Firth 2005: 23) and the Australian citizenship was not born out of a particularly strong sense of nationalism. However, many Australians do nowadays have strong feelings when it comes to their 'Australianness'. One of the defining moments of Australia as a nation was the defeat of the Australian and New Zealand Army Corps (ANZAC) at Gallipoli in 1915, the first major military action of Australian troops as *Australians*. Some refer to this as the 'baptism of fire', as Australia suffered an extremely high casualty rate of more than 50 per cent. The 'Anzac Myth' is still important in the Australian collective memory (McDonald 2010: 291–3): it was at Gallipoli that the slang term 'digger' was coined in reference to the extraordinarily tough and modest Australian soldiers, who were, in their self-assessment, physically and mentally superior to their British comrades, which continues to influence Australian views of the ADF today (Smith 2001: 86). Gallipoli was the birthplace of another quintessentially Australian cultural concept, that of *mateship*. An Australian soldier individually, or the country of Australia collectively, never lets a 'mate' down or gives him away. When a 'mate' is in trouble, an Australian – or Australia for that matter – is under an obligation to help. Even more remarkably, all personnel who fought in the Great War did so as volunteers, since legislation at that time did not allow soldiers to be conscripted for overseas service. While this changed during the Second World War, the ADF returned to be a volunteer army in 1972 and has been ever since.

Since 1914, Australians have fought in most of the major conflicts in which the West has been involved (e.g. the Second World War, Korea, Malaysia, Vietnam, Afghanistan and twice in Iraq). The ADF has a high reputation and – with the exception of the Vietnam experience, where Australian troops returning from Vietnam were subject to the same rejection as their American counterparts – has always been held in high esteem. It is seen as an admissible and sometimes necessary political tool, enhancing the options of the political leadership in Canberra.

Thus official documents published by government agencies come to the conclusion that 'the successes and failures of military campaigns involving Australian troops have had a strong influence ... on the way Australians think about themselves' (Department of Defence 2002: 1). Academic scholars support this conclusion: 'War has been central to the development of the Australian identity' (Gyngell and Wesley 2003: 10).

All in all, modern Australian national identity is still influenced by the warrior ethos born on the battlefields of the First World War and reinforced on battlefields around the world ever since. This ideological component is reflected in Australia's military budget of roughly US$23 billion (SIPRI figure for 2011, in 2010 prices),[5] the highest in the region. It is the explicit aim of the ADF, as well as of the political leadership in Canberra, to ensure that the ADF remains the most technologically advanced force in South East Asia (with the possible exception of Singapore), understanding high-tech as a substitute for its limited human resources, especially to protect its long and often only sparsely populated coastline.

Being aware of her limitations, Australia has no 'great power' ambitions. The term commonly associated with Australia is that of 'middle power' (Ungerer 2007). However, there has been disagreement about the scope and applicability of the term, since most scholars use the term in an ambiguous way. The first meaning refers to Australia's position in the international system in terms of capability and power, while the second meaning focuses on the expected behaviour of a 'middle power'.

According to many scholars, the set of behaviours of a typical middle power 'includes a preference for working through multilateral institutions and processes, a commitment to promoting international legal norms and a pro-active use of diplomatic, military and economic measures to achieve selected political outcomes' (Ungerer 2007: 539), as most prominently demonstrated by the Labor governments of Bob Hawke (1983–91) and Paul Keating (1991–6). Both Kevin Rudd, elected PM in 2007, and Julia Gillard, who succeeded Rudd in 2010, making Rudd minister for foreign affairs, have taken up this particular self-description as well.[6] In their view, working with and reinforcing the UN system, multilateralism and international law was in Australia's self-interest in that only international order under UN scrutiny could

---

[5] The SIPRI Military Expenditure Database, Stockholm International Peace Research Institute. Online: http://milexdata.sipri.org.

[6] See Australia and the United Nations, Department of Foreign Affairs and Trade, undated. Online: www.dfat.gov.au/un.

guarantee the security of the fifth continent and offered Australia the chance to exert an influence that it would not otherwise have. From this perspective, Australia should act as a 'good international citizen' (Scott 1998a: 559; Scott 1998b: 226).[7] There has been considerable debate as to whether the idea of the typical behaviour of a middle power as a 'good international citizen' was typical of a specific Labor foreign policy (Firth 2005: 50) or whether the concept was in broader use. According to Carl Ungerer, almost all post-Second World War governments followed this particular middle power approach to different extents. 'As a result, the middle power concept is perhaps the closest that Australia has ever come to articulating a self-conscious theory of foreign policy' (Ungerer 2007: 550).

When John Howard came into office in 1996, however, his government tried to distinguish itself from its predecessors and rejected the 'middle power' rhetoric. His Foreign Minister Alexander Downer, for example, insisted that Australia was 'not just a "middle power"' but 'a considerable power'.[8] The conservative Coalition advocated an 'interest based' approach to foreign policy rather than an 'idealistic' one, and heralded a 'selective approach to the multilateral agenda' (DFAT 1997: iii) in its first foreign policy white paper (see also Schreer 2008). But during the first years of his government at least, even Howard and Downer acted according to the 'good international citizen' doctrine, although they carefully avoided the label. Only after 9/11 and the Bali bombings in 2002 did the 'government's departure from international law' (Baldino 2005: 194) became more apparent. But even after the substantial official turning away from multilateralism, the UN system was still understood to be of significance to Australia and unilateral behaviour or a complete rejection of the UN system was never a viable option for the conservative Coalition as the following sections on international law will show.

1.2.2 Australia and the International Criminal Court: a bumpy relationship

Early in the negotiation process of the International Criminal Court (ICC), Howard's foreign minister, Alexander Downer, was 'one of the most enthusiastic proponents of the ICC at the Rome conference in 1998' (Bellamy and Hanson 2002: 418) and aligned with the 'like-

---

[7] See also 'A Good International Citizen, Australian Labor Party', undated. Online: www.alp.org.au/agenda/more – -policies/good-international-citizens.

[8] Downer, Alexander, 'The Myth Of "Little" Australia', Speech to the National Press Club, 26 November 2003. Online: http://australianpolitics.com/news/2003/11/03–11–26.shtml.

minded group' of the most committed proponents of an ICC, i.e. Canada, Germany and New Zealand. He proposed several important modifications and 'got everything he wanted in Rome' (Bellamy and Hanson 2002: 418). With the backing of the PM, other high-ranking cabinet members and senior military commanders, the foreign minister proposed that Australia be among the first to ratify the treaty. He even went so far as to criticise the obstructive American position in unmistakable terms, and the Liberal Party even gave the explicit election pledge in 2001 to ratify the ICC. The government's positive attitude was endorsed in 2002 by the Australian Parliament's Joint Standing Committee on Treaties (JSCOT) that recommended the ratification of the statute (Bellamy and Hanson 2002: 420).

Despite the backing of both the government and the JSCOT, Coalition backbenchers as well as conservative press commentators started attacking the ICC in 2002 for the very same reasons that Downer had dismissed in Rome four years earlier: the loss of Australian sovereignty in particular and the nature of the United Nations (UN) in general. In addition, shortly before the ratification bill was presented to parliament, the PM visited the United States (US) and '[t]he President took the opportunity to warn Howard about the alleged perils of the ICC' (Bellamy and Hanson 2002: 421). Howard began to waver and Downer finally proposed a compromise acceptable to both the PM and the ICC critics: a series of reservations were added to the ratification, for example, the reaffirmation of the primacy of Australian criminal jurisdiction, among others. The last-minute criticism of the ICC and US President Bush's intervention, which both led to Howard's doubts, nearly stalled the ratification process and made Australia 'a reluctant ratifier' (Bellamy and Hanson 2002: 431) rather than an exemplar.

1.2.3 *Australia's attitude towards international regimes: the case of arms control and disarmament*

When it comes to international arms control, Australia has been very active in many types of regimes, acting exactly as the 'good international citizen' should: 'Australia enjoys a tradition of highly successful input into the negotiations of multilateral arms control treaties' (Scott 1998a: 559).

In the realm of chemical and biological weapons, Australia has a significant international record. In 1972, Australia signed the Biological Weapons Convention on the very day that it was opened for signature. In 1985, Canberra was the initiator of the 'Australia Group' and 'lobbied for a chemical weapons ban in South East Asian and South Pacific Countries' (Firth 2005: 65) in the same decade. In 1992

Australia produced the final treaty draft text for the Chemical Weapons Convention, thereby helping to overcome diplomatic obstacles obstructing the negotiations.

The same degree of activism can be observed in the field of nuclear arms control, at least since Australia abolished her plans for nuclear armament in the early 1970s.[9] Australia is a founding member of the G-10, a group of extra-active supporters of the Non-Proliferation Treaty (NPT), and was an important protagonist in the Comprehensive Nuclear Test Ban Treaty (CTBT) process.

With regard to landmines, Australia was one of the early supporters of a total ban from 1996 onwards, and was one of the original signatories to the Convention on 19 December 1997. Australia's efforts in this field have focused particularly on its immediate region, the South Pacific and South East Asia. In late 1999, the Australian Army destroyed their remaining stockpiles of landmines. These examples seem to illustrate that, when it comes to arms control issues, for 30 years or more Australia has acted as the 'good international citizen', irrespective of the government in power. But one should still be aware of the *motivational* differences between Labor and the Coalition with regard to taking an active role in international arms control regimes. Labor traditionally has close ties with the peace movement and 'presented itself as the "true disarmament party"' (Firth 2005: 64), especially during the 1970s and 1980s.

In contrast to other multilateral issues, arms control usually enjoys bipartisan support across the whole political spectrum in Australia. Labor's motives for fostering international arms control are a mixture of interest and conviction, but even the Howard government 'continued this tradition [of activism in arms control matters] when it announced ... a package of initiatives designed to generate greater international commitment to, and to fast-track negotiations for the conclusion of, a verification protocol to the Biological Weapons Convention' (Scott 1998a: 559). So, while many Australian arms control initiatives emerged under a Labor government in the 1980s or 1990s, the conservative Coalition largely continued the respective policies.

The most likely explanation for the continuity in Australian arms control policy is that Howard perceived the relevant regimes as (at least) unproblematic or not a danger to Australian security, so Australia could only benefit from international regulations while a more critical stance might have caused a loss of international reputation without any payoff.

---

[9] For a detailed overview of Australia's nuclear ambitions, see Walsh (1997).

1.2.4   Australia's alliances: the need for 'strong friends'

Australia has a strong alliance with the US, which has been one of the central pillars of Australian foreign policy for every administration since the Second World War (Kelton 2008). The alliance serves several purposes: Australian security, access to privileged intelligence and regional status. To understand the relevance of the Australian–US alliance, it is necessary to look again into Australia's history. As a former British colony, Australia has considered itself (and does still) to be of European heritage in the wrong environment. From the very early days of the settlement, Australians felt themselves to be vastly outnumbered by the surrounding populations of Asian countries. Paired with a latent tendency towards xenophobia inherited from British colonialism,[10] a feeling of insecurity and fear developed in the collective Australian psyche that is still present. The feeling of insecurity and being outnumbered, coupled with a sometimes high-handed approach towards Asia, fed the conviction that Australia was in need, in PM Robert Menzies' words, of 'great and powerful friends' since Australia was scarcely in a position to be able to defend itself alone. Securing the help of allies has been one of the most important issues in Australian foreign policy-making ever since 1901, while the question of 'at what price' has been the subject of great controversy.

Understanding Britain to be Australia's natural ally at first, Australia had to turn to the US when British forces retreated from Asia in the wake of the fall of Singapore on 15 February 1942. After the war, 'having had its fears of Japanese – and, in a more general sense, Asian – aggression confirmed in the Second World War' (Hubbard 2005: 10) with the bombing of Darwin only four days after the surrender of Singapore, Australia felt more insecure than ever before. When it became clear that there was to be a formal peace treaty between the US and Japan, Australia actively strove for a close and formal security cooperation with the US, the so-called 'lifeline' (Hubbard 2005: 15) of Australian security, resulting in the ANZUS Treaty between America, Australia and New Zealand in 1951. ANZUS has been the central pillar of Australian security policy ever since. No post-Second World War government has seriously questioned the necessity of close ties to the US and, '[e]xcept for the Vietnam War, the US–Australia alliance received overwhelming support in opinion polls in Australia' (Dibb 2007: 33).

---

[10] This xenophobic feeling of Western superiority found its formal expression in the so-called 'White Australian Policy' of restricted immigration of non-white people, which was officially maintained until the 1970s.

Nowadays, the close alliance with the US serves many Australian interests: first and foremost, America is understood to provide security to the Australian homeland in the event that Australian troops are not able to handle a potential threat alone. Second, America has become the most important source of both intelligence and military technology (Dibb 2007: 35), with the latter being the *conditio sine qua non* for the ADF's high-tech posture (Schreer 2006). Third, a close alliance is thought to keep America's presence, influence and interest in the region, which Canberra understands to be vital for the region's stability. Finally, 'Australia's closeness to America and its influence with Washington transforms Australia's regional status: it allows Australia to punch above its weight in regional and, indeed, international security organizations' (Dibb 2007: 33). However, even with such a 'strong friend' as the US in the background, Australia usually refrains from unilateral action (Abdiel 2011: 573).

While no Australian government questions the relationship with the US, the practical handling of the alliance has differed, however. For Hawke and Keating, as well as Rudd and Gillard, the American alliance was of major importance, but did not preclude active engagement with Asia.[11]

Prime Minister Howard, on the other hand, attributed paramount importance to the alliance once again. While relations with Asian states cooled significantly, the connection to Washington grew stronger and more personal, especially given the close friendship between John Howard and George W. Bush (Sheridan 2006: 33). Furthermore, the Coalition readjusted the ADF's priorities again in favour of 'out of area' missions and closer interoperability with US forces, while Labor had focused more on regional threats rather than enabling military engagements of the ADF worldwide as in Korea, Malaya or Vietnam. In effect, under Howard Australia moved closer to the US than in previous decades, leading critics to claim that Australia was on track to become the '51st state of America' (Altman 2006).

1.3   Conclusion: Australia's self-perception as a middle power

In summary, Australian foreign policy seems to be torn between both idealist and realist concepts of foreign policy. From the Australian perspective, however, upholding international law or promoting arms control measures is not only a normative goal but also a means of pursuing

---

[11] See for example, Rudd, Kevin 2008. 'It's Time to Build an Asia Pacific Community', Address to the Asia Society AustralAsia Centre, 4 June, Sydney.

its national interest. Pragmatism, rather than ideology, is the most important feature of Australian foreign policy. Almost every action is evaluated according to how far it serves Australian security as the feeling of insecurity is still present in the collective Australian psyche. Many Australians still feel uneasy with regard to their Asian neighbours, and security concerns take up a huge proportion of the foreign policy debate. Consequently, the close liaison with their powerful friend America is of paramount importance and can be forgone by neither a Labor nor a Coalition government. But Australia is aware that sheer military power might not be enough to protect it. Only an international system based on fundamental rules and laws offers a middle power the protection it needs, and Australians have fought and suffered to protect the normative fabric of the international system in the past.

Interestingly enough, from the Australian perspective, it is the close company of strong international allies that grants the fifth continent more freedom of action than its capabilities alone would allow. Obviously the close affinity with a strong ally has enabled Australia to be the influential middle power it is, especially in the realm of arms control. But everything comes with a price tag, as the close affinity to its strong and powerful allies has resulted in Australia's military involvement in several conflicts of rather limited importance for its national security. But this did not cause it to reconsider its role as a military power, since waging war is considered by a vast majority of the Australian public to be a legitimate means of conducting politics, which plays an important part in Australia's national identity. The engagement and sacrifices during the Great War are understood to have served a higher moral purpose than sheer survival or cynical power politics. The Gallipoli myth of the self-sacrifice of the Australian 'diggers' to serve a greater good is an important part of Australia's self-image, and is becoming increasingly so. This means that Australians are open to the suggestion of military solutions at the international level, especially when its strong ally is involved. Fundamental pacifism or a genuine distrust in the military is restricted to a small minority on the left of the political spectrum, including the Greens, a small fraction of Labor and non-parliamentary groups like the peace movement.[12]

This notion clearly distinguishes Australia from the classical understanding of a *civilian power*. To characterise Australia as a *good international citizen* without further qualification would also miss the point, since such a characterisation understates the pragmatic character of Australian foreign policy. Even under the Labor governments of Hawke

---

[12] Author interview with Rick Kuhn, Canberra, 6 November 2006.

and Keating, supporting international regimes and international law was understood not only to be an end in itself, justified only by moral conviction or an internalisation of norms, but also to be a means of enhancing both Australia's security and its relevance at the international level as well. Under Howard, reservations about the UN as a functioning international organisation grew, to some extent mirroring the American neoconservative critique, but only after the terror attacks of 9/11.

2   Decision-making and public debates on the Gulf War, Kosovo War and Iraq War

2.1   *Australia and the Gulf War 1990–1991: Hawke's war?*

2.1.1   *The road to war: 1990–1991*

Australia's active participation in the Gulf conflict of 1990–1 started only four days after the Iraqi invasion of Kuwait on 2 August 1990. The government announced a package of sanctions, including oil imports and the freezing of Iraqi financial assets, but was reluctant to apply a trade embargo straight away, fearing 'the loss of the lucrative wheat market in Iraq' (Camilleri 1991a: 192). On 10 August, PM Hawke announced the dispatch of two guided-missile frigates and a replenishment tanker to support an international naval blockade of Iraq. Hawke's decision was a lonely one for several reasons: first, he had only consulted with his international advisor Hugh White and a minority of his cabinet members, including Defence Minister Ray and Foreign Minister Evans (Hawke 1994: 512). Second, he had not consulted with Australia's neighbouring countries (Malik 1991). Third, and most important, Hawke had not even waited for an American or Kuwaiti troop request, let alone UN Security Council approval (Powell and Bolt 1992: 30). As late as early 10 August, he had a telephone conversation with President Bush, only hours before informing the Australian public of the deployment of the ADF to the Gulf (Hawke 1994: 513). While from the outside it looked as if Hawke had reacted to Bush's request, Hawke had in fact instructed the Australian ambassador in Washington to indicate Australian willingness to participate in a blockade, actually requesting a telephone call with Bush.[13] Initially, Hawke had considered the naval detachment as an unproblematic and 'safe' military option. After being advised by White about the potential mine threat in the Gulf waters and the considerable

---

[13] Ramsey, Alan 1990. 'President Bob Rolls Over for a Tickle', *Sydney Morning Herald*, 11 August, p. 25.

risk to the Australian crews, Hawke reconsidered for a night, but finally accepted the risk (see also Hawke 1994: 518).[14]

The participation of ADF forces in the allied blockade enjoyed bipartisan support within Parliament, but support was significantly stronger on the conservative side than within the ruling Labor ranks. Among Labor MPs, there was a 'widely held view ... that Australia should avoid active military involvement in the crisis' (Camilleri 1991a: 193). In addition, Labor MPs demanded that 'any involvement should proceed under United Nations command and only after adequate consultation within the structures of the party' (Camilleri 1991a: 193). Not even his cabinet was united behind Hawke: Treasurer Paul Keating and the Minister for Industry and Commerce John Button took a critical stance (Hawke 1994: 517). Due to this pressure from within his own ranks Hawke gave in and ruled out any ADF involvement of ground troops or even naval reinforcement. In addition, Hawke agreed to closer consultations. On 21 August, the House of Representatives passed a motion supporting the government's actions, but the motion was 'carefully couched in terms of support for the UN Charter and for UN initiatives and resolutions' (Hawke 1994: 517), stressing Labor's affinity and historical support for the UN. In the following month, the government repeatedly issued statements that the Australian deployment had acted and would act under the terms of the UN charter.

After arriving in the Gulf, the rules of engagement changed for the Australian frigates from monitoring to active interception of suspicious freighters with a minimum use of force. But it was only four days after the adoption of Security Council Resolution 678 of 29 November 1990 with its 15 January 1991 deadline that the cabinet formally allowed the Australian warships to participate in the looming war. Nonetheless, even up to a week before the end of the deadline, Hawke as well as Foreign Minister Evans were still officially playing down the possibility of war (Camilleri 1991b: 375). In his memoirs, however, Hawke stresses the fact that very early in the build-up to war, 'I feared there was a real likelihood that the world would have to fight to get Iraq out of Kuwait' (Hawke 1994: 514), putting his own pre-war rhetoric into perspective.

For Australia, however, Hawke's decisions paid off: it both increased Australia's standing in Washington and 'left the Australian people more in favor of the United States, the ANZUS alliance and joint facilities than they were before it began' (Firth 1992: 97).

---

[14] Author interview with Hugh White, Canberra, 3 November 2006.

Table 5.1 *Frequencies of arguments, Gulf War, Australia, supporters only* *(n = 41); extracts of results*[a]

Code	Argument	Number of speakers	Percentage of speakers
1104	Show of force	30	73.2
4101	Enforce international law/ support UN	25	61.0
5201	Multilateral consensus pro	20	48.8
4201	Covered by international law	18	43.9
1101	National interest	17	41.5
5102	Threat to world order	16	39.0
1103	Regional stability	15	36.6
6302	Casualty aversion (own soldiers)	15	36.6
7101	Enemy image of adversary	15	36.6
3101	Identity norms	13	31.7
4302	Peaceful means not exhausted	10	24.4

[a] Full lists of results for this and all following tables are available from the author.

2.1.2   Content analysis of the parliamentary debates

The debates in both the House and the Senate display the bipartisan nature of support for Hawke's decision, as 41 out of 48 speakers coded supported the government's decision. Despite the fact that all debates took place after the decision to send the troops had been taken, there was an intensive discussion in Parliament, although a critical voice was raised only by the Greens and Democrats in the Senate. Table 5.1 presents the arguments raised by the proponents of Australian participation in the international alliance to free Kuwait.

Among the strong group of supporters, most speakers argued that a show of force was necessary to coerce Iraq into complying with international law, an argumentation shared by the government. In addition, the broad multilateral nature of the coalition and the clear UN mandate made Australian military participation acceptable to a wide majority of the representatives. This shows that arguments relating to international law and the lawfulness of the dispatch of troops played an important role in legitimising Australian participation. While this supports the general notion of the relative importance attributed to the UN by the Labor Party, it is important to understand that the UN argument was used by both Labor and conservative MPs to support military engagement.

Four out of ten speakers referred to the more rational argument of Australia's national interest, which referred to oil supply and fear of economic repercussions. Interestingly enough, more than 30 per cent of all supporters derived an Australian obligation to stand against Saddam

Hussein's occupation of Kuwait from their understanding of Australia's national identity, especially of Australia's historical fight against the evil forces of history. Finally, roughly a third of all supporters depicted Iraq, or more specifically Saddam Hussein, as a brutal enemy. While this seems quite a large proportion, this number is rather low compared to the dominance of this argument in the 2002/3 debate (see below). This shows that representatives felt that other arguments, i.e. UN-related ones, were more convincing to the electorate than creating a sinister image of the adversary.

Among the supporters of a military engagement in the Gulf it was not very common to weigh arguments for or against war, and only a few arguments against a war were deliberated. The most prominent one was casualty aversion, mentioned by roughly 37 per cent, probably influenced by the fact that the last time the ADF had been sent to battle it had been in Vietnam, but also reflecting genuine fear for the military personnel. Interestingly enough, roughly 15 per cent of the supporters raised doubts about the potential capabilities of the ADF to get involved in the conflict, but supported the deployment nevertheless (probably counting on effective US protection). Only a handful accepted a missing exit strategy or the danger of civilian deaths (both 4.9 per cent) as counter-arguments worth considering.

These results contrast nicely with the arguments used by the opponents of war, shown in Table 5.2. The results for the opponents, however, have to be interpreted with caution, given the total of only seven. Interestingly enough, six out of the seven refer to precluding democratic procedures and values (i.e. they perceived the majority opinion of the Australian people to be against war; see below). Five referred to the UN again. Four of these five claimed the lack of a UN mandate on which the mission or an actual war would rest, while one speaker (not depicted in Table 5.2) conceded that the mission was in line with international law. Arguments in favour of war were virtually absent from the opponents' speeches. Only two arguments related to the role conception can be found in addition to the acceptance of the legitimacy of the mission mentioned before. But from the opponents' perspective, these arguments were not enough to legitimise any Australian participation in a potential war.

Looking at the debate as a whole, both opponents and supporters of the mission did not reflect the arguments of their counterparts in great depth and accepted at least some arguments questioning their own position. One notable exception was the casualty argument. Despite the Australian 'warrior ethos', casualty aversion played an important role in the debate. More than one-third of *all* speakers referred to the potential

Table 5.2 *Frequencies of arguments, Gulf War, Australia, opponents only*
(n = 7); extracts of results

Code	Argument	Number of speakers	Percentage of speakers
4302	Peaceful means not exhausted	6	85.7
6301	Democratic norms/procedures contra war	6	85.7
1303	Regional instability	5	71.4
4301	No UN mandate/damage to UN	4	57.1
5303	Civilian casualties	4	57.1
5304	Multilateral war rejection	4	57.1
5302	Pacifism/war damages global norms	3	42.9

peril to the ADF forces. On the other hand, roughly one-fifth of all speakers – but only supporters of the war – conceded Australia to be militarily superior to Iraq, putting the dangers to the ADF soldiers into perspective. The other relevant argument shared by both groups was the hope that peaceful means were not exhausted, raised by one out of three speakers in the total population.

A final fact worth mentioning is that, notwithstanding the major importance attributed to the alliance with the US in Australian politics, the close ties to the US were only mentioned by 8 out of 48 speakers explicitly as a supportive argument – definitely below what could be expected given its high relevance in Australian foreign and security policy. This shows that politicians felt that an Australian participation to support the US without any material underpinning (UN, national interest, etc.) would not be well received by the Australian electorate.

2.1.3   Newspaper debates[15]

When Prime Minister Menzies decided to send Australian combat forces to Vietnam, the decision barely made the news and was not subjected to critical comment in most Australian newspapers (Tiffen 1992: 115). Some 25 years later, there was a stronger reaction, as the Australian naval deployment to the Gulf was the first major dispatch of Australian forces since Vietnam. Consequently, a huge proportion of the commentaries were concerned with the question of whether or not the naval

[15] The analysis rests on articles systematically taken from the *Sydney Morning Herald* (centre-left; available via LexisNexis). Unfortunately, articles from *The Australian* (conservative) were not available electronically, so the analysis of an additional newspaper for the relevant time span rests on secondary literature as available.

blockade and build-up of troops would necessarily lead to a full-scale war. It was also concerned with whether sanctions should be given time and what costs the West (not particularly Australia) was willing to incur in the event of a war. This led some newspapers to comment on the government's responsibility towards the ADF's soldiers.[16] In general, many articles addressed the Australian soldiers, usually declaring support for 'our boys'.[17] However, there was no really serious fear of large numbers of body bags returning to Australia, probably due to the naval character of the Australian deployment and the government's firm stance not to send ground reinforcements to the Gulf, where the heavy fighting was expected.[18] In this context, a few commentators raised the issue of Iraqi civilian deaths in the event of a war.[19]

Another hot issue in Australian war coverage in the early phase of the build-up was the fact that Saddam Hussein had decided to take Western citizens in Iraq hostage as human shields, including 150 Australians. Questions arose as to whether non-participation in the alliance would have spared these Australians their fate but, as an anonymous commentator in the *Sydney Morning Herald* (SMH) argued, 'that seems highly improbable'.[20] Commentators in general were not critical that Hawke had invoked sanctions and decided to deploy troops so early in the process. Looking back on Australian policy prior to war, a commentary in the *Australian Financial Review* summarised the reasons for the general sympathy for the government's policy as follows: 'Nobody likes a bully. Nobody wants to see an oil dictatorship. And the US is Australia's most important ally.'[21] But some editorials questioned the way the decision was made. On 11 August 1990, a commentator of the SMH accused Hawke of responding to 'the request of an old and powerful friend' and claimed that '[he] did so in formal response to a phone call from Washington at 7 o'clock in the morning. He did so without the approval of his Cabinet, his ministry, or his parliamentary party'.[22]

---

[16] E.g. Robinson, Peter 1990. 'Tall Order Is Under Fire', *The Sun Herald*, 2 September, p. 31.

[17] E.g. Fitzgerald, Sally 1990. 'Prayers as the Frigates Prepare to Sail', *The Sun Herald*, 12 August, p. 2.

[18] Hartcher, Peter 1990. 'Rosy View of War from Hawke's Advisors', *Sydney Morning Herald*, 3 December, p. 1.

[19] E.g. Toohey, Brian 1990. 'Evans Fails to Count the Human Costs of War', *The Sun Herald*, 2 December, p. 32.

[20] Anonymous 1990a. 'Australians and the Gulf Crisis', *Sydney Morning Herald*, 24 August, p. 12.

[21] Byrnes, Michael 1991. 'Inconsistency in Middle East Approach', *Australian Financial Review*, 18 January, p. 17.

[22] Ramsey 1990. 'President Bob Rolls Over For A Tickle'. For a more modest critique, see Anonymous 1990a. 'Australians and the Gulf Crisis'.

All in all, despite the Vietnam experience, the question as to *why* Australia actually joined the coalition was scarcely debated at all in the press. Despite the government's official optimism, however, commentators very early on debated the possibility of war and of Western (to a lesser extent Australian) casualties. What is striking, however, is not what can be *found* within the newspaper comments, but what is *missing* compared to the debates in parliament: newspapers commented only sporadically on the role of the United Nations and Australia's specific obligation towards the UN.[23]

2.1.4   Public opinion polls

With regard to Australian public opinion about the Gulf War in 1991, national polling started as late as 24 August (published on 1 September) and was only sporadic (Goot 1993: 141–2). Reasons for this were Australia's 'modest contribution to the allied force' as well as the bipartisan support the engagement enjoyed in Parliament, which reduced 'the pressure to poll ... even further' (Goot 1993: 142). Several aspects are worth noting. Early in the confrontation, Australian support for UN action, i.e. a military blockade against Iraq, was significantly higher (84 to 89 per cent) than support for an active Australian participation in the blockade (55 per cent).[24] Only a week later, support for Australian participation had increased to 67 per cent with a significant rise among both Labor and Liberal supporters, reflecting the bipartisan nature of the political debate. And in early December, as many as 80 per cent of respondents supported Australian involvement and Hawke's decision.[25] Furthermore, from 3 September, when the question was asked for the first time, the use of force to remove Iraq from Kuwait had a stable majority of 57 per cent or more (Goot 1993: 158). In December, a majority of Australians (again 57 per cent) was anticipating an actual war, despite the government's verbal downplaying.[26]

The strength of the support for the government's actions was reflected in the difficulties that the peace movement faced in mobilising their supporters. During the Cold War, Australia had had an active and critical peace movement; however, this time it lacked both a coherent

---

[23] For an exception, see Anonymous 1990b. 'Deeper into the Gulf', *Sydney Morning Herald*, 5 December, p. 14.

[24] Newspoll for the *Weekend Australian*, 1–2 September 1990, conducted 24–26 August 1990, cited in Goot (1993: 152).

[25] Poll by Irvin Saulwick and Associates for the *Sydney Morning Herald*, conducted 5–6 December 1990, replicated in Muller, Denis 1990. 'Gulf Role: Australians a Hawkish Lot', *Sydney Morning Herald*, 8 December, p. 12.

[26] *Ibid.*

position vis-à-vis the government's action and the sheer numbers to make a significant impression. Divergent factions, ranging from religious groups to the Marxist left, disagreed about the aim of the movement. All agreed that ships had to be repatriated (Firth 1992: 103), but the more moderate wing supported the sanctions and the Iraqi withdrawal from Kuwait but not the military means to enforce these sanctions (Manne 1991: 2), while the radical wing rejected any kind of pressure on Saddam Hussein (Glanz 1991). Again, both groups were united in the assessment that Hawke's anticipatory obedience was primarily motivated by the desire to please the US. But the numbers of critics were few and they admitted that 'the initial wave of opposition to the war was small' (Glanz 1991: 129). Only once the war had started could rally participation be counted in tens of thousands – only a fraction of those who took to the streets against Vietnam (or the Gulf War of 2003; see below).

2.1.5   Conclusion: explaining Australia's participation in the Gulf War

The situation that led to Australian participation in the Gulf War of 1991 was perceived to be a clear-cut case by both the Hawke government and the vast majority of the Australian public. A sovereign nation had been invaded in an act of aggression – an act that clearly violated international customs and law as the UN Security Council was not slow to assert. In accordance with international public opinion, both the Australian elites and most of the critical public were united behind the government's decision to send Australian forces to the Gulf. By deciding so promptly, Hawke was able to kill two birds with one rather cheap stone, acting like the perfect middle power: first, his resolve was understood to be a reinforcement of an international system based on UN principles, principles that the Australian Labor Party had held in very high esteem, depicting Australia as the 'good international citizen'. This matched Australia's self-image as a force for good in the world, not shying away from using military means as a last resort even in the face of potential casualties. Furthermore, Hawke's early decision to support the multilateral coalition led by the US strengthened the Australian–American alliance, a valuable side benefit to any Australian government.

The only issue that gave rise to any serious public concern was that Hawke had taken the decision in a very small inner circle without consulting his party in Parliament, and even before a formal request by Kuwait, America or even the UN had been issued. However, this behaviour was both constitutional and consistent with the practices of former prime ministers. In addition, it had undeniable positive side effects: by offering a naval detachment so early in the process, Hawke was able to confine Australia's participation to a very limited contribution while gaining maximum political benefit both in Washington and with the Australian public. So when pressure from within his own Labor ranks mounted, he was able to stick to the original deployment without losing international credibility or having to face external pressure. Given Hawke's personal concern over potential ADF casualties, he may well have been glad about the limitation imposed on him by his parliamentary group.

From the perspective of a pragmatic middle power, acting in accordance with its own conception of its role was rather easy in this case.

2.2   *Australia and the 1998–1999 Kosovo War*

When the conflict between NATO and the Federal Republic of Yugoslavia escalated in 1998–9, the Australian government monitored the situation closely and implemented the UN arms embargo against Yugoslavia in April 1998. Australia gave NATO its full diplomatic support but according to all unclassified information available, the Howard government never considered a direct Australian participation in the conflict.

In February 1999, Foreign Minister Downer declared in front of Parliament that Australia was 'concerned about the humanitarian consequences of the political disaster of Kosovo' and that the government had provided '$100,000 to help with the problem there'.[27] In response to a direct question by a fellow Liberal Party MP on 24 March 1999 as to whether any Australians would be directly involved in the 'looming confrontation',[28] Downer gave a clear-cut answer: 'On 20 March Australians were advised to leave the Federal Republic of Yugoslavia. The government authorised departure of all Australia-based staff and dependents ... As far as any further Australian involvement is concerned ... the Australian Defence Force will not be involved.'[29] Downer qualified his statement, however, admitting that 'a small number of Australian Defence Force personnel' were on exchange with British and American units in the region and that they 'could be deployed

---

[27] Answer by Mr Downer to a question by Mr Andrews, Hansard of the Parliament of Australia, Canberra, Questions without notice: Kosovo, 8 February 1999.

[28] Question by Mr Nugent to Mr Downer, Hansard of the Parliament of Australia, Canberra, Questions without notice: Federal Republic of Yugoslavia, 24 March 1999.

[29] Answer by Mr Downer to a question by Mr Nugent, Hansard of the Parliament of Australia, Canberra, Questions without notice: Federal Republic of Yugoslavia, 24 March 1999.

with their units';[30] experts estimate the relevant numbers of ADF personnel in Kosovo during the war to be 25 at most.[31] Interestingly enough, however, this participation of Australian soldiers in an actual war required no formal decision by the PM. In the past the withdrawal of exchange officers had provoked severe discord, for example during the Falklands War, undermining the officers' position in their unit. Now there is general consent that Australian soldiers on long-term exchange postings automatically deploy with their respective units and a specific governmental decision is needed to overrule this procedure.[32] Consequently, this minor participation was not considered an official Australian participation in the war by the Australian government.

For the Australian government, Downer's declaration ended any debate about a formal Australian participation in the war. While some individual MPs addressed the Kosovo issue in Parliament (especially after the NATO bombardment began), no MP questioned the government's decision to stay out of the conflict. The general impression across the political spectrum was that engagement was necessary, but all parties agreed that it was a NATO operation and that there was no need for Australia to participate.[33] The operation was not a UN mission, actually lacking a UN Security Council mandate, nor was the most important Australian ally, the US, considered an overly eager promoter of the intervention. Australia had turned down American and British requests to send Australian units to the Balkans on a regular basis during the 1990s, as neither Washington nor London pushed these requests very hard. Consequently, Australia had refused compliance without damaging relations with either ally, and there was no expectation on the American or British side in the run-up to the Kosovo War that Australia would now participate. In other words, 'the US never chose to make an ADF contribution to Kosovo or elsewhere in the Balkans a major test of the relationship'.[34]

However, other factors might also have played a role. Given the combined forces of the participating NATO states and the likely aerial character of the war, Australia had no military niche capabilities to offer anyway, and NATO seemed quite capable of handling a war on its own. Moreover, a mission in Kosovo was not in the Australian national interest whatsoever, and serious issues closer to the fifth continent demanded Canberra's attention. So, despite the fact that Australians were in fact unsettled by the humanitarian catastrophe, military support was out of

---

[30] *Ibid.*
[31] Author's email correspondence with Hugh White, November 2008.
[32] *Ibid.*   [33] *Ibid.*   [34] *Ibid.*

the question, as the costs far outweighed the nearly non-existent gains. Consequently, all parties were able to agree on providing humanitarian assistance without difficulty. Interestingly enough, however, even after the bombing began, the legality of the NATO air strikes was not debated in Parliament. From the PM's position, '[t]he NATO action ... became a regrettable necessity when President Milošević refused to respect the rights of ethnic Albanians in Kosovo'.[35]

One might speculate as to whether a potential Labor government might have acted differently from Howard in 1999, being more sensitive to the humanitarian catastrophe. The most likely answer, however, is that Labor would have declined to participate as well. First, the Kosovo War of 1999 lacked a UN mandate, making it rather difficult for the very pro-UN Labor party. In addition, under the governments of Hawke and Keating the ADF had changed its attitude from 'forward defence' to 'continental defence', voluntarily limiting the ability of the ADF to participate in worldwide military missions (Stephens 2007). From this viewpoint, any potential participation in an air war over Kosovo was in contravention of Labor's defence policy and would have meant a doctrinal U-turn.

2.3   *Australia and the Iraq War 2003: Howard's war*

2.3.1   *The road to war: 2001–2003*

It is virtually impossible to understand Australia's participation in the Iraq War of 2003 without taking the terror attacks of 11 September 2001 in the US into account. When Al-Qaeda terrorists struck the Twin Towers and the Pentagon, John Howard was on an official state visit to Washington, having been to the Pentagon only a day earlier. Howard immediately offered Australian support, both in diplomatic as well as military terms 'within its capabilities', before an American request for military help had even reached Canberra.[36] Seeing the smoke above the Pentagon with his own eyes strengthened the already 'deep and genuine' (Garran 2004: 187) bond between the Australian PM and the US president. In the following month, Australian Special Forces were deployed in Afghanistan in the 'global war on terror', virtually without public debate or dissent as '[t]he Afghan war of 2001–02 was a popular

---

[35] Media release by the US Embassy to Australia, Comments by Prime Minister John Howard, 28 March 1999. Online: http://canberra.usembassy.gov/irc/us-oz/1999/03/28/pm1.html.

[36] Quoted in Shanahan, Dennis and Garran, Robert 2001. 'Cabinet Considers Nation's Role in Retaliation', *The Australian*, 14 September, p. 7.

war' (Firth 2005: 90). In unison with the Bush administration, Howard understood the 'war against terror' to be more far-reaching than just Afghanistan.

As early as 31 January 2002, Howard publicly backed Bush's criticism of Iran, Iraq and North Korea and 'promised to consider any request for further support for a wider US-led military campaign'.[37] In the following months, the Australian government focused attention on Iraq and '[supported] the United States' policy of overthrowing Saddam Hussein's leadership' (Mason 2002: 529). In April 2002 Australia was 'the only government regarded as fully behind regime change through a [US] pre-emptive strike' (Huisken 2003: 42). The same month the opposition released a 'carefully worded' statement (Huisken 2003: 41), not ruling out Australian participation in a war against Iraq in principle but naming criteria and stipulations – for example, a clear UN mandate. Until very late in the day, Labor – except for a minority on the far left – stuck to its caveats (Latham 2005: 210–11) and avoided taking a clear anti-war stance.

Confronted with the ever more pressing question of whether or not to deploy the ADF in an impending war without any clear UN mandate, Howard also refused to make any clearcut statement, rejecting the question as 'hypothetical' and 'speculative' (Gurry 2003: 228). He insisted that no formal decision had been taken about participation in a potential war. Australian vessels had periodically been part of the Multinational Interception Force enforcing sanctions against Iraq on a regular basis in Gulf waters since 1991. Nonetheless, the debate never focused on these ships but instead turned to participation of Australian ground forces very early on.[38]

Howard did, however, put Bush under pressure to seek undisputed UN support while public pressure on him rose.[39] On 26 September 2002, an open letter signed by three former prime ministers, a former leader of the opposition, a former governor general as well as several retired high-ranking military officers was published, appealing to the government not to go to war without an additional specific UN resolution. Despite Howard's non-committal attitude in 2002, his cabinet's National Security Committee had approved the involvement of senior ADF personnel in 'US Central Command deliberations on

---

[37] Henderson, Ian 2002. 'Howard Backs New US fight', *The Australian*, 1 February, p. 2.

[38] Kelly, Paul 2002b. 'Terror on Our Doorstep Limits Iraq Commitment', *The Australian*, 26 October, p. 1.

[39] Wilkinson, Marian and Metherell, Mark 2002. 'Bush Will Call on Australian Troops', *Sydney Morning Herald*, 9 September, p. 1.

detailed operational planning for military action against Iraq' (O'Neil 2003: 541) as early as in July 2002, and the government's rhetoric became more intent during the year while stopping short of any formal commitment.

The Bali bombing of 12 October 2002, which claimed 202 victims including 88 Australian tourists, was perceived as an 'Australian 9/11' and 'the sense of shock felt by many Australians ... is difficult to over-state' (Gurry 2003: 228). Consequently, the debate about the 'war on terror' in general and the potential war with Iraq became yet more emo-tional and controversial. While for Howard fears of militant Islamic ter-rorism seemed to have come true, critical commentators viewed Bali as a retaliation for Australia's support of the US. Howard and his cabinet did not seek official advice in November 2002 from senior public serv-ants on the issue of whether Australia should join the US in a war against Iraq. The policy direction was strongly influenced by the personal con-viction of the PM that war was necessary – however, there seemed to be no opposition in the bureaucracy anyway (Kelly 2009: 261).

On 22 January 2003, Defence Minister Hill announced the pre-deployment of ADF forces to the Gulf, all the time without any for-mal request from Washington. He insisted that Australia was still interested in a peaceful solution, and that the pre-deployment did not imply any decision about participation in the war. He declared that it was necessary due to both in-theatre preparations and the additional pressure on Iraq (O'Neil 2003: 542).[40] For the Labor opposition and other critics, including even the Indonesian and Malay governments, the decision was premature and on 5 February 2003 the Senate passed an unprecedented 'no confidence' motion against the government, but to no avail.[41]

The contingent sent to the Gulf consisted of three naval vessels, a Special Air Service detachment and FA/18 fighters, involving a total of 2,000 ADF personnel, but details remained classified.[42] Australia's participation was minor compared to British and American numbers and provided 'niche capabilities' rather than massive firepower. In early March 2003, Howard, who had still hoped for a second UN resolution

---

[40] An allegedly leaked Foreign Ministry document dating from October 2002 suggested, however, that the ships enforcing sanctions against Iraq could not be pulled back in the case of a US unilateral strike without UN backing; Kitney, Geoff 2003c. 'Your Nation Needs You, John ... to Fess Up', *Sydney Morning Herald*, 5 February, p. 1.

[41] Lewis, Steve 2003. 'PM Loses Support of Senate over Iraq', *The Australian*, 6 February, p. 6.

[42] Allard, Tom 2003. 'Just Quietly, They're Ready for the Heavy Lifting', *Sydney Morning Herald*, 15 March, p. 15.

in February, changed course. Backed up by a legal assessment by the attorney general's office and the Foreign Ministry, Howard now argued that a second resolution was not necessary for legal action and that he had pursued it for political reasons only.[43]

Finally, on 18 March he announced in Parliament that the Australian contingent had been authorised to participate in coalition military operations following a formal request from the White House. Furthermore, he declared that the troops would only stay in theatre for the duration of the actual conflict and that no additional troops would be sent to the Gulf, presenting a clear exit strategy (O'Neil 2003: 543).

2.3.2 Content analysis of the parliamentary debates

By 2003, bipartisan support for Australian participation in another war in the Gulf had vanished, as can be seen in our sample: from a total of 50 speakers sampled, only 52 per cent supported the war (all members of the Liberal/National coalition) while 48 per cent opposed it (Labor, Greens, Democrats). The sample indicates the deep rift in Australia's political landscape with regard to the Iraq War issue, leading to an intensive and sometimes even fierce debate. In consequence, there is a sharp division in the use of arguments, as neither side was willing to grant the other side any argumentative slack. Given this sharp division between the two camps, it is imperative to look at the arguments put forward by proponents and opponents. Table 5.3 shows the arguments used by the supporters of war in detail.

For those supporting the sending of the ADF, the fact that the political world order was at stake was the most important argument (76.9 per cent). This argument had already applied in 1991, but to a lesser extent. Given the government's emphasis on Iraq's alleged nuclear weapons programme, roughly three-quarters of the Coalition MPs made references to Saddam Hussein's brutal character and his weapons of mass destruction (WMD) programme. In other words: a nuclear-armed Iraq was seen as a major and intolerable threat to the post-Cold War world order. More than six out of ten supporters of war were convinced that Iraq had had enough time to disarm and that peaceful means had been exhausted during the debates. This, of course, meant an argumentative 'lock in' towards war, despite the government's rhetoric aimed at keeping all options open.

References to national security were less frequent, but still half of all supporters claimed Iraq to be a direct threat to Australia. A strong

---

[43] Walters, Patrick 2003. 'Diggers May Be Fighting Within Days', *The Australian*, 7 March, p. 7.

Table 5.3 *Frequencies of arguments, Iraq War, Australia, supporters only (n = 26); extracts of results*

Code	Argument	Number of speakers	Percentage of speakers
5102	Threat to world order	20	76.9
7101	Enemy image of adversary	19	73.1
4202	Peaceful means exhausted	16	61.5
1104	Show of force	15	57.7
1105	National security	13	50
4101	Enforce international law/support UN	12	46.2
6202	Cost reduction by swift action	10	38.5
1103	Regional stability	9	34.6
4201	Covered by international law	9	34.6
4302	Peaceful means not exhausted	9	34.6

minority of all supporters (46.2 per cent) saw a potential war as a means to enforce international law and one-third saw no need for a second UN Security Council resolution as they understood the war to be covered by international law without it. This shows that many supporters of military action tried to rationalise a military engagement in UN terms, despite the openly critical stance of the Coalition towards the UN.

Regime change as well as the prevention of a humanitarian catastrophe were used by roughly one-quarter of speakers (23.1 and 26.9 per cent) as an argument in favour of war, while only 11.5 per cent (that is, 3 out of 26) referred to the US alliance as a reason for possible Australian participation. Interestingly enough, the most relevant counter-arguments adopted by supporters were that peaceful means were not yet exhausted (especially in the early phase of the debates) as a caveat (34.6 per cent), and potential civilian as well as Australian casualties (both 19.2 per cent).

Looking at the opponents to war depicted in Table 5.4, more than four out of five complained about the lack of a UN mandate. This is not surprising, as many observers believed that Labor would have supported the war if there had been a clear second resolution by the UN (see below). More than 70 per cent of all opponents refer to precluding democratic values, i.e. the alleged majority opinion of the Australian people against war – at least without a UN mandate (see below). More than half anticipated the danger of civilian casualties (58.3 per cent), and every second opponent feared casualties among Australian troops.

Table 5.4 *Frequencies of arguments, Iraq War, Australia, opponents only (n = 24); extracts of results*

Code	Argument	Number of speakers	Percentage of speakers
4301	No UN mandate/damage to UN	20	83.3
6301	Democratic norms/procedures contra war	17	70.8
4302	Peaceful means not exhausted	15	62.5
5303	Civilian casualties	14	58.3
1301	National interest contra war	13	54.2
6302	Casualty aversion (own soldiers)	12	50
1304	Increasing insecurity	11	45.8
5301	World order not threatened	8	33.3
5304	Multilateral war rejection	8	33.3
7301	Enemy image questioned	8	33.3
2301	Alliance contra (internal aspects)	7	29.2
3303	Restraining expectations by others	7	29.2
7101	Enemy image of adversary	5	20.8

Some 54.2 per cent rejected the notion that a war would be in Australia's national interest, usually with the qualification that a war *without UN mandate* would not serve Australia's national interest, while 45.8 per cent were concerned about increased insecurity, i.e. becoming a target for terrorism. Roughly three out of ten referred to the alliance, usually arguing that the close alliance with the US was dragging Australia into an unnecessary war while a third pointed out that other states were opposing military action as well.

The analysis of the debates shows clearly that only a minority of the opponents accepted the brutal 'enemy character' of Saddam Hussein or his alleged WMD programme as a potential reason for war (20.8 per cent). On the other hand, however, only a third of all opponents actively claimed that Saddam Hussein did *not* possess WMD or actively denied him being more ruthless than other dictators.

The question of whether engagement in Iraq enjoyed UN support or not was a pivotal element in the Australian debate. A UN mandate was a *conditio sine qua non* for most MPs and a significant number of supporters of the war were at pains to argue that the war was either promoting international law or at least covered by UN resolutions, while the opponents' strongest argument was the lack of a UN mandate. On the other hand, many opponents to war would have been happy to support military pressure and military action sanctioned by the UN.

2.3.3   *Newspaper debates*[44]

Looking at the newspaper commentaries and opinion pieces, both the more conservative *Australian* and the centre-left *Sydney Morning Herald* (SMH) focused on certain key issues. In the SMH many commentators agreed very early in the showdown that the Australian government had already made up its mind but could not say so due to divergent public opinion and potential public pressure. Howard's official position of non-commitment did not receive a warm welcome and commentators speculated about a firm commitment to Washington. The general tenor was that the government was delaying a clear statement on what to expect in the hope of a peaceful resolution or a second UN resolution. If a second resolution had come up before an actual war, so the argumentation continues, Howard could have avoided creating the impression that he was willing to wage war without UN support.[45]

In addition, it was argued that the (alleged) early commitment to the US war plans had locked Australia in and had taken away the liberty of independent policy making.[46] In this context, the question of legitimacy was raised and was one of the recurring theses in the SMH commentaries. Almost all commentators at the SMH agreed that the legal status of a potential war against Iraq was highly problematic, to say the least, if there was no new and clear second resolution. As the government had made a case for a second resolution but decided to go forward without one after the end of February 2003, commentators questioned the legal status of ADF participation and mourned the critical stance of the Howard government towards the UN in more general terms.[47, 48]

A final theme raised by some observers was whether or not any participation in a war against Iraq was a waste of resources, as the Bali bombing had shown that Australia ought to keep watch in its own backyard rather than in far-off Iraq. All in all, with only a few exceptions, the SMH commentaries rejected any participation in the war against Iraq, basically because of legal reasons and the fact that the government's case for war based on regime change and WMD had not been a convincing one.[49]

---

[44] The analysis rests on articles systematically taken from the *Sydney Morning Herald* (centre-left) and *The Australian* (conservative) via LexisNexis.

[45] E.g. Riley, Mark 2003. 'PM's Path to War Is a battlefield', *Sydney Morning Herald*, 5 February, p. 1.

[46] Anonymous 2003a. 'Australia in a War That Should Not Have Been', *Sydney Morning Herald*, 19 March, p. 16.

[47] Kitney, Geoff 2003a. 'Evidence Is, We're Going Without It', *Sydney Morning Herald*, 14 March, p. 15.

[48] Anonymous 2003a. 'Australia in a War That Should Not Have Been'.

[49] E.g. *ibid.*

The conservative *Australian* took a less clear stance. While, for example, foreign affairs columnist Greg Sheridan staunchly defended the government's cause, other regular commentators like Paul Kelly took a more reflective position. Furthermore, a variety of external commentators covered a broad argumentative spectrum. As early as August 2002, Kelly raised the question of legitimacy of a war and argued '[b]eneath Australia's pro-US pitch lurks a serious legitimacy problem'. He continued that it 'would be hard for any Australian government not to be involved in a US operation against Iraq'.[50] Commentators at the *Australian* agreed with those at the SMH that Howard had, in fact, committed the ADF to combat and expected direct Australian participation in the war.[51] In addition, the government was again criticised for not answering the 'key question of whether it would join a US-led attack without clear UN backing'.[52]

However, some commentators accepted Bush's perspective on the UN resolution and argued that war was necessary to disarm Iraq and enforce UN resolutions.[53] A week before the actual war, Greg Sheridan once again argued in favour of war, emphasising WMD (potentially in terrorists' hands), humanitarianism and democratisation as the main reasons, and arguing that 'UN power play cannot affect war's morality'.[54] But such strong backing of the government was rare, even in the *Australian*. In total, the *Australian* was 'hawkish, albeit couching its stance in milder language',[55] probably to address the general public mood. On the eve of war, the newspaper again backed the government:

THROUGHOUT [*sic*] the current international crisis, The Australian has argued that if there comes a time when the US and Britain are left with no realistic option but to disarm Iraq by force, Australia should consider joining them. That time has now arrived ... the Howard Government has made the right decision, both in terms of morality and in terms of Australia's national interest.[56]

---

[50] Kelly, Paul 2002a. 'Tangled up in Washington's War Scheme', *The Australian*, 21 August, p. 13.

[51] Walters, Patrick 2002. 'Will Australia Fight Hussein?', *The Australian*, 7 September, p. S15.

[52] Stewart, Cameron 2003. 'World at War', *The Australian*, 25 January, p. 17.

[53] Anonymous 2003b. 'Deployment to Iraq Is in Our Interest', *The Australian*, 24 January, p. 10.

[54] Sheridan, Greg 2003. 'UN Power Play Can Not Affect War's Morality', *The Australian*, 13 March, p. 11.

[55] Jackson, Sally and Doman, Matthew 2003. 'Point Scoring: Pushing Their Opinions', *The Australian*, 27 February, p. B01.

[56] Anonymous 2003c. 'Time Has Now Arrived for Disarming Iraq', *The Australian*, 19 March, p. 12.

2.3.4   Public opinion polls

Public opinion polls started from July 2002 onwards, when the government had already indicated a general willingness to participate in a US-led military mission against Saddam Hussein (see above).[57] The polling results reflected the broken bipartisan consensus on the Iraq issue. A Newspoll survey conducted between 9 and 11 August 2002 revealed that 50 per cent of adults were either somewhat or strongly against Australian participation in any US led military action against Iraq with the objective of deposing Saddam Hussein, while 39 per cent were in favour.[58]

A Morgan poll published on 17 September 2002 showed a similar picture: 54 per cent of Australians disapproved of Australian participation while only 40 per cent approved of it.[59] When it came to voting preferences, only people with an affiliation to the Liberal Party approved of an ADF mission in the majority (55 per cent), while those with other voting intentions disapproved of any engagement. Unsurprisingly, voters for the Greens were the most significant opponents of the war (82 per cent disapproval), followed by supporters of the Democrats (74 per cent). Labor voters were also against war in the majority, but the lower overall level of disapproval (63 per cent) reflects Labor's own reservations and caveats.

When asked about the role of the UN, the Australian population took a clear stance: in a survey published on 15 September, 74 per cent were against Australian involvement in military action if the United Nations had not given approval and only 19 per cent favoured an ADF mission under this condition.[60] Another interesting finding of the 15 September 2002 poll was that even before the Bali bombing, 82 per cent of respondents agreed that Australian participation in military action would increase the risk of a future terrorist attack.

In December 2002, public opinion remained divided, with 52 per cent of Australians still disapproving of Australian military action in Iraq, 2 per cent less than in September.[61] In addition, approval rates

[57] For a complete overview of all relevant polls, see O'Connor and Vucetic (2010: 535–6).

[58] Newspoll survey, 'Thinking Now about Australia's Involvement ...', 14 August 2002. Online: www.newspoll.com.au/image_uploads/cgi-lib.17274.1.0802_iraqI_military.pdf.

[59] Roy Morgan Research poll, 'Majority of Australians Disapprove of Australia Being Involved in U.S. Conflict with Iraq to Depose Hussein', Finding No. 3556, 17 September 2002. Online: www.roymorgan.com/news/polls/2002/3556.

[60] Newspoll and *The Sunday Telegraph* survey, 'Iraq Poll', 15 September 2002. Online: www.newspoll.com.au/image_uploads/cgi-lib.16527.1.0912iraq_poll.pdf.

[61] Newspoll survey, 'Howard Leadership and Iraq Issues Poll', 29 December 2002. Online: www.newspoll.com.au/cgi-bin/polling/display_poll_data.pl.

had gone up from 40 to 45 per cent, probably under the impact of the Bali bombing. There was still a clear division along party affiliation lines. In March 2003, 56 per cent of Australians were in favour of war with UN support, but 71 per cent rejected Australian participation in military engagement without UN backing.[62] UN backing seemed to be the *conditio sine qua non* for the public support of the war. The questions raised by the surveys, however, did not establish whether or not the government made a convincing case that UN backing was already provided by previous resolutions.

Looking at the streets, the peace movement was significantly stronger than 12 years previously and at the height of the protests in February 2003, more than 250,000 people demonstrated in the streets of Melbourne and Sydney each. In addition, those protesting were clear about their aim: they rejected war, with or without a UN resolution.[63] For the peace movement, Labor's caveat against a war seemed hypocritical and inconsistent. Labor leader Simon Crean was booed off the stage in Brisbane at his only public appearance at a protest rally (Latham 2005: 215). But given the polling data described above, Labor's 'no, but...' stance reflected public opinion more closely than the basic opposition in the streets.

2.3.5   Conclusion: explaining Australia's participation in the Iraq War

The government's decision to participate in the Iraq War of 2003 divided the Australian nation as only the Vietnam War had done before. This time, however, the nation was already divided before the ADF went into combat. But the differences between the two camps were narrower than it seems at first glance as both acted and argued on their respective understanding and interpretation of the concept of a middle power. For Howard, the most important aspect was to tighten the American–Australian alliance in troubled times as a 'middle power' relies on strong and powerful friends.

Despite the government's efforts to suggest that a formal decision to participate in war had only been reached on the very eve of war, most observers viewed this behaviour as masking the real decision-making process. Howard had, in fact, committed the ADF *informally* very early on in the process and pulling out would have caused great political damage in Washington – a risk the government was by no means willing

---

[62] Newspoll and *The Australian* survey, 'Thinking Now about Iraq and Australia's Involvement in Military Action against Iraq...', 4 March 2003. Online: www.newspoll.com.au/image_uploads/cgi-lib.15130.1.0301war.pdf.

[63] Kitney, Geoff 2003b. 'PM May Pay Price of His Convictions; Sydney on the March', *Sydney Morning Herald*, 17 February, p. 3.

to take. Furthermore, Howard's personal relation to President George W. Bush, and his aggressive rhetoric in the early phase of the stand-off locked Canberra onto a path of dependency from which it was practically impossible to break free. On the positive side, Howard's early indication of possible Australian participation in the 'coalition of the willing' maximised Australia's influence in the planning phase and gave Canberra much more influence than the sheer numbers of Australia's contribution suggested (Sheridan 2006), and Australia was an acknowledged ally in a league beyond its physical capabilities. Howard's early commitment enabled him to dictate his terms to Washington, effectively ruling out any long-term commitment in the occupation of Iraq. In retrospect, this policy paid off: without suffering any casualties in the Iraq campaign, the ADF returned home immediately after the cease-fire, as promised to the Australian people prior to the war.

Interestingly enough, however, neither Howard nor the Coalition MPs were stressing the alliance argument in public, at least not in proportion to its real relevance in the decision-making process. *The Australian*'s Paul Kelly commented on that contradiction after Howard made his case for war at the National Press Club on 14 March 2003. He argued: 'First, Australia is going to war because of the US alliance, not because Iraq represents a direct threat to this country', continuing:

Howard's speech said little about the alliance ... The alliance was 'a factor', yet it is far more. It is the main reason Australia will commit to war. Howard doesn't want to admit this because he fears it would be an electoral negative, yet he lacks the sense of domestic threat that Bush enjoys to mount a convincing threat-to-Australia case.[64]

The reason for this lay in the interpretation of 'middle power' by the majority of the public that stressed the aspect of legality and conformity with international law and UN procedures – the 'good international citizen' part of the middle power concept and Australia's self-image.

From this perspective, Labor's position of rejecting Australian participation in the war because of the lack of any clear UN mandate was swayed by public opinion. Fundamental pacifist reasons against the war were virtually absent in the Labor Party, arousing anger within the peace movement. However, the peace movement did not represent the majority opinion of the public since the majority of the Australian public would not shy away from military means – as long as they were employed within the UN framework. It is not too speculative to assume that a Labor PM would have sent the ADF to the Gulf as well, provided

[64] Kelly, Paul 2003. 'The Hapless Persuader', *The Australian*, 15 March, p. 30.

that there had been a second UN resolution. As the analysis of the parliamentary debates shows, the Coalition took great pains to give the
appearance of legality, as they were aware that they could not bypass
public sentiment on the issue. But, ultimately, faced with the choice
between alliance and legality, Howard chose the former.

3   Summary of results

Looking at all cases, Australia's behaviour is consistent with its self-
perception as a pragmatic *middle power* – trying to balance power politics with a normative orientation, leaning more to one side or the other
depending on the current government and not shying away from military means when the situation calls for strong resolve. Australia has
deeply internalised the idea of having only a limited leeway of independent action in the international realm and only a limited ability to
provide its safety unilaterally. To maximise both its safety and its freedom of manoeuvre, for example in disarmament policy, Australia is
willing to assist 'powerful friends' in cases where a small military contribution yields a high political profit. This allows Australia to 'punch
above [its] weight' (Thomson 2005) in international negotiations, and
the close proximity to the US guarantees Australia a more important
role in its region than its own military and economic capabilities alone
would allow. In addition, the strong US backing helps Australia to act
out the 'good international citizen' part of its self-image.

But, as all three cases have shown, this particular part of Australia's
self-image is not an independent element in itself but is instead subordinate to the more pragmatic – or realistic – element of the middle
power concept. Normative issues are taken into account but have to pass
rational scrutiny. Only a minority – which finds its political representation with the Democrats and the Greens – is willing to put its pacifist
beliefs before pragmatic considerations of national interest or the alliance at any cost. But the majority of Australians accepts war as a legitimate *means* of doing the normatively 'right thing'.

Consequently, a strong majority felt that in the case of the Gulf War
of 1991 there was a coming together of the normative and the pragmatic element, both leading to the same policy recommendation, giving
Labor its clear-cut support for the war. In 1999 the pragmatic side overruled the normative one when Australia decided not to participate in
the Kosovo War, despite there being a perceived humanitarian disaster.
Australia *could* have participated, as the regular, but rather lukewarm,
troop requests had shown, but decided not to because of the rather
small reward for a costly policy. Things might have been different,

however, if there had been a clear UN mandate or troop request. But given the situation as it was, the potential cost outweighed the benefits by far. In 2002/3, pragmatism once again overruled normative concerns, but this time the other way around. Australia participated in a very unpopular war because the Howard government reckoned that the rewards from America would outweigh international as well as national costs. Following a strategy with a very clear exit strategy and consequently minimal domestic risk, Howard knew he had reasonable chances of riding out the normative outcry to be anticipated when he ignored international law.

This element of pragmatism has its roots in Australia's perception of its strategic situation. Given Australia's limited resources, both major parties presume that at the end of the day Australia's safety rests on its close ties with mighty America. Participating in wars side by side with the US makes a virtue of necessity. Within this multifaceted concept of being a middle power, however, specific aspects are emphasised depending on whether Labor or the Liberals are in power. While Liberals accentuate the special relationship with the US and put normative issues second, Labor tries to balance material and normative elements – a view more consistent with Australia's public opinion. As the Australian public regards the use of military force as sometimes a necessary means to an end in international relations, as long as the cause appears to be a just one in moral and legal terms, public scrutiny permits the government a great deal of freedom – with the important caveat of low casualty rates among the ADF forces. Both the Hawke and the Howard governments used this freedom to their advantage.

The early decision granted the government a disproportional political leverage in comparison to the very limited number of forces deployed, and Hawke as well as Howard were able to dictate their terms of trade to their strong coalition partner in Washington. In 1990, the limitation on naval forces was the least dangerous option. In 2002/3, Howard got his way that the ADF would only contribute to the actual war fighting and not participate in the occupation of Iraq. With the prospect of having to fight mainly joint operations with technologically highly advanced US units, this was clearly the most promising way to keep Australian casualty rates low – a calculus most likely taken into consideration by both Hawke and Howard. From the US perspective, the Australian contribution was negligible in military terms but important as political support to generate the image of international approval. Canberra was aware of that and acted accordingly.

Given this strategy, any Australian government has a good chance of bypassing public scrutiny in the long run. If the engagement turns out to be bloodless, 'clean' and successful, the government might even get away with ignoring public opinion demanding a second UN resolution. Nonetheless, it is taking chances: the relevance assigned to formal legitimisation in terms of international law by both Hawke's Labor government and Howard's conservative Coalition is reflected in the newspaper commentaries as well as in public opinion. In 2003 in particular, the majority of commentators were sceptical – to say the least – over Bush's and Howard's interpretation of the UN resolutions and their disregard of the need for authorisation for war. Commentators as well as the Australian public were deeply uneasy about the prospect of being dragged into an illegal war, and only the final result of a seemingly flawless 'victory', an early Australian retreat and zero Australian casualties ensured Howard's political survival in the 2004 election. On the other hand, if there had been a second UN resolution, the case in Iraq would have been 'clear cut' once more and it would have been most difficult for any government not to participate.

REFERENCES

Abdiel, Douglas 2011. 'No News Is Good News: The Longevity of Australian Humanitarian Interventions', *Armed Forces and Society* 37 (4): 571–97

Altman, Dennis 2006. *51st State?* Carlton North: Scribe Short Books

Baldino, Daniel 2005. 'Australia and the World', in Chris Aulich and Roger Wettenhall (eds.), *Howard's Second and Third Governments: Australian Commonwealth Administration, 1998–2004.* Sydney: UNSW Press, pp. 189–207

Bellamy, Alex J. and Hanson, Marianne 2002. 'Justice Beyond Borders? Australia and the International Criminal Court', *Australian Journal of International Affairs* 56 (3): 417–33

Camilleri, Joseph A. 1991a. 'Problems in Australian Foreign Policy, July–December 1990', *Australian Journal of Politics & History* 37 (2): 183–99

1991b. 'Problems in Australian Foreign Policy, January–June 1991', *Australian Journal of Politics & History* 37 (3): 375–95

Department of Defence 2002. *The Australian Approach to Warfare.* Canberra: DoD, Public Affairs & Corporate Communications

DFAT (Department of Foreign Affairs and Trade) 1997. *In the National Interest: Australia's Foreign and Trade Policy. White Paper.* Canberra: Commonwealth of Australia

Dibb, Paul 2007. 'Australia – United States', in Brendan Taylor (ed.), *Australia as an Asia-Pacific Regional Power: Friendships in Flux?* London: Routledge, pp. 33–49

Evans, Gareth and Grant, Bruce 1991. *Australia's Foreign Relations: In the World of the 1990s.* Carlton: Melbourne University Press

Firth, Stewart 1992. 'The Peace Movement', in Murray Goot and Rodney Tiffen (eds.), *Australia's Gulf War.* Carlton: Melbourne University Press, pp. 97–113

2005. *Australia in International Politics: An Introduction to Australian Foreign Policy*. Crows Nest: Allen & Unwin

Garran, Robert 2004. *True Believer: John Howard, George Bush and the American Alliance*. Crows Nest: Allen & Unwin

Glanz, David 1991. 'Gulf War: Lessons of the Movement', *Socialist Review* 1991 (4): 126–51

Goot, Murray 1993. 'The Polls', in Murray Goot and Rodney Tiffen (eds.), *Australia's Gulf War*. Carlton: Melbourne University Press, pp. 140–79

Gurry, Meg 2003. 'Issues in Australian Foreign Policy, July to December 2002', *Australian Journal of Politics & History* 49 (2): 227–43

Gyngell, Allan and Wesley, Michael 2003. *Making Australian Foreign Policy*. Cambridge University Press

Hawke, Bob 1994. *The Hawke Memoirs*. Port Melbourne: Heinemann Australia

Hubbard, Christopher 2005. *Australian and US Military Cooperation: Fighting Common Enemies*. Aldershot: Ashgate

Huisken, Ron 2003. *The Road to War on Iraq*. Canberra: Australian National University

Kelly, Paul 2009. *The March of Patriots: The Struggle for Modern Australia*. Carlton: Melbourne University Press

Kelton, Maryanne 2008. *More Than an Ally? Contemporary Australia–US Relations*. Aldershot: Ashgate

Latham, Mark 2005. *The Latham Diaries*. Carlton: Melbourne University Press

Lindell, Geoffrey 2003. 'Authority for War', *About the House* 16 (May/June): 23–4, 36

McDonald, Matt 2010. '"Lest We Forget": The Politics of Memory and Australian Military Intervention', *International Political Sociology* 4 (3): 287–302

Malik, J. Mohan 1991. 'Australia, Asia and the Gulf', *Pacific Research* 4 (3): 29

Manne, Robert 1991. 'Can the Peace Movement Survive the Gulf?', *Quadrant* 35 (4): 2

Mason, Christine 2002. 'Issues in Australian Foreign Policy, January to June 2002', *Australian Journal of Politics & History* 48 (4): 528–38

O'Connor, Brendan and Vucetic, Srdjan 2010. 'Another Mars–Venus Divide? Why Australia Said "Yes" and Canada Said "Non" to Involvement in the 2003 Iraq War', *Australian Journal of International Affairs* 64 (5): 526–48

O'Neil, Andrew 2003. 'Issues in Australian Foreign Policy, January to June 2003', *Australian Journal of Politics & History* 49 (4): 540–57

Powell, Janet and Bolt, Richard 1992. 'The Case against Australian Participation', in Murray Goot and Rodney Tiffen (eds.), *Australia's Gulf War*. Carlton: Melbourne University Press, pp. 26–41

Schreer, Benjamin 2006. 'Australiens Sicherheits- und Verteidigungspolitik: Zwischen regionaler und globaler Sicherheit', *SWP-Studie* S 32, Berlin

2008. *The Howard Legacy: Australian Military Strategy, 1996–2007*. Frankfurt a.M.: Peter Lang

Scott, Shirley 1998a. 'Issues in Australian Foreign Policy, January to June 1998', *Australian Journal of Politics & History* 44 (4): 553–65

1998b. 'Issues in Australian Foreign Policy, July–December 1997', *Australian Journal of Politics & History* 44 (2): 225–32

Sheridan, Greg 2006. *The Partnership: The Inside Story of the US–Australian Alliance under Bush and Howard*. Sydney: University of New South Wales

Smith, Rodney 2001. *Australian Political Culture*. Frenchs Forest: Longman

Stephens, Alan 2007. 'The Defence of Australia and the Limits of Land Power', *Security Challenges* 3 (4): 29–44

Thomson, Mark 2005. 'Punching above Our Weight? Australia as a Middle Power', *Strategic Insights* 18, Barton: ASPI

Tiffen, Rodney 1992. 'News Coverage', in Murray Goot and Rodney Tiffen (eds.), *Australia's Gulf War*. Carlton: Melbourne University Press, pp. 114–39

Ungerer, Carl 2007. 'The "Middle Power" Concept in Australian Foreign Policy', *Australian Journal of Politics & History* 53 (4): 538–51

Walsh, Jim 1997. 'Surprise Down Under: The Secret History of Australia's Nuclear Ambitions', *The Nonproliferation Review* 5 (1): 1–20

6   Canada: standing on guard for international law and human security?

Una Becker-Jakob

Canada participated in the wars in the Gulf in 1990–1 and in Kosovo in 1998–9 but did not join the Iraq War in 2003. The Canadian democratic political culture and international role do not suggest participation in military action per se; instead, a perceived tradition of 'fighting for the good cause', which in the Canadian perspective includes the protection of international law, human rights and/or humanitarian values, represents an enabling condition for such action under certain circumstances. This chapter provides an analysis of the domestic context in which decision-making on war participation takes place in Canada, as well as an analysis of the actual decision-making processes, parliamentary debates, media reporting and public opinion prior to the three wars under scrutiny in the study.

1   Canada's foreign and security policy

1.1   Decision-making and political culture

Canada gained independence from the United Kingdom in 1931 but has remained a constitutional monarchy with the British sovereign as head of state. Its political system is modelled on the Westminster system, with strong elements of federalism and a multi-party system. The Liberal Party of Canada was for a long time the dominant party in Canadian politics. The conservative spectrum, with the Progressive Conservative Party (PC, Tories) as the major traditional party, was supplemented in 1987 by the more populist Reform Party that later became the Canadian Alliance in 2000. In 2003, it merged with the PC to form the Conservative Party of Canada. The third party represented in Parliament is the socialist–social democratic New Democratic Party (NDP). Finally, the separatist Bloc Québécois (BQ) has held seats in the House of Commons since its foundation in 1991. The BQ only runs for elections in the province of Quebec, and its main objective is Quebec's sovereignty.

Quebec represents one particularity in the Canadian polity: it is the only predominantly French-speaking province, accounting for about 25 per cent of the Canadian population, and separatist movements striving for independence have presented a latent and at times virulent challenge to the unity of the country. Public opinion in Quebec has traditionally and for historical reasons been more sceptical of military intervention than in the rest of Canada (Massie 2008: 24–7, 39). Given the particular nature of the Canadian political and electoral system, Quebec has frequently been attributed a 'special role' in Canadian politics, including in foreign and security policy (Boucher and Roussel 2008).

The Canadian legislative is formed by a bicameral parliament in which the House of Commons has far greater competencies than the Senate. General elections to the House are held through a majority vote. Coalition governments are virtually absent from Canadian political culture; if no party gains an absolute majority of seats, the strongest caucus usually forms a minority government that then has to depend on ad hoc support from other parties.

As in other Westminster systems, the Canadian foreign policy process is dominated by the executive and, in particular, the prime minister. The role of the House of Commons in foreign policy decision-making is marginal (Nossal 1997: 176–7, 185–9, 265–85); the Department of Foreign Affairs and International Trade (DFAIT) usually takes the lead – unless an issue is high on the prime minister's own agenda – and in security policy coordinates and consults with the Department of National Defence (DND) and other agencies as appropriate.

Decisions about troop deployment and war participation are the prerogative of the Crown and are exercised on its behalf by the cabinet and, ultimately, the prime minister. The House of Commons has no formal competencies in this decision-making process; the National Defence Act merely postulates that it be convened and notified when the army is put on 'active service', or at least within ten days after that (Dewing and McDonald 2006: 2). MPs can thus only impact upon decisions about war participation indirectly, through budgetary decisions or through votes of no confidence; but due to strict party and caucus discipline this is only relevant in minority government situations, if at all. Even if a government decides to hold a vote before deployment, the results may have political significance but are not binding. In practice,

[i]nvolvement of Parliament in this decision-making has ranged from no consultation at any time to a full debate and vote in the House before the making of a formal commitment. In many cases, however, debate came only after the government had made its decision, or so close to a deadline that it had little influence on the final decision. (Dewing and McDonald 2006: 3)

There is a tradition of public consultation and cooperation with civil society that also extends to foreign policy. It is mainly rooted in the Liberal Party and peaked under Foreign Minister Lloyd Axworthy in the mid-1990s, but has also been practised by Conservative governments (Tomlin *et al.* 2008: 208). Moreover, there is a tendency to anticipate, at least rhetorically, 'what Canadians expect', connected with a sense of accountability to the public. Hence, despite the centralisation of power in the executive, some elements of the Canadian political culture provide for a potential role for civil society and public opinion.

1.2   Foreign policy traditions and role conceptions

The two decades after the Second World War, often dubbed the 'golden age' of Canadian foreign policy, were the formative period of Canada's forcign policy tradition in which the crucial elements of its international role were constructed. Canada was an important player in the emerging international system and contributed substantially to the establishment of new institutions like the United Nations (UN), North Atlantic Treaty Organization (NATO) and the Bretton Woods system. This extensive influence was partly based on its disproportionately large contribution to the Second World War, which earned it a 'seat at the table', but also stemmed from a skilled and active policy and an idealist-pragmatic drive, in particular on the part of the Liberal prime ministers Louis St Laurent and Lester B. Pearson.

The 'liberal internationalism' as represented by St Laurent, Pearson and their staff has been the 'dominant idea' of Canadian foreign policy (Nossal 1997: 154–9) and one of the fundamentals of the country's identity (Munton and Keating 2001: 531), where it also served the function of distinguishing Canada visibly from the United States (US). While the concept of internationalism denotes a variety of elements in Canada, and while interpretations regarding its content vary, in a core definition it entails an 'active participation, multilateralism, commitment and pursuit of a common good' (Munton and Keating 2001: 531) in international affairs that translate into support of international institutions, law and regimes, human rights, peacekeeping, development aid and disarmament. It created an expectation that Canada should show leadership internationally and also entails pursuing an independent foreign policy as well as 'restraining the United States' unilateral tendencies' (Massie 2008: 23). At the same time, it commands respect for other cultures and identities. Such respect as well as the negotiation of compromises are part and parcel of the political culture of the Canadian multicultural and federalist polity and have fed into its internationalist role image (Dyck 2004: 217). This has precluded successive generations of policy-makers from developing and constructing strong enemy images and from defining international relations in Manichaean terms. While Canadian foreign policy lacks any militant missionary thrust, there does exist a preference for externalising Canadian domestic values such as democracy, tolerance, multiculturalism and the principles of 'peace, order and good government' (Dyck 2004: 214–15; Kirton 2007: 16).

This liberal-internationalist orientation and Pearson's practical implementation of it, for example in the form of UN peacekeeping, while resonating most strongly in the Liberal Party, have cast a 'long shadow' over Canadian foreign policy as a whole (Nossal 1997: 3).[1] In addition to an idealist perspective, it entails a more realist-informed foreign policy frame that also dates back to the Pearson years and in which it was argued that an internationalist foreign policy was in the Canadian national interest and the only viable strategy to ensure national security, maintain reliable international trade relations and balance the great powers, including the US. During the Cold War in particular, both frames converged in similar policy prescriptions, namely active support for and a contribution to international institutions. There was thus a broad consensus on an active multilateralism and internationalism as a guiding line, which was strongly supported by the Canadian public (Munton and Keating 2001). At times this was countered by the idea of continentalism, i.e. a preference for maintaining good relations with the US (Vucetic 2006: 142–3), whose influence on Canadian foreign policy is discernible, though not comparable to that of liberal internationalism.

Other elements of Canadian foreign and security policy include collective security, human security, the attitude towards war and peace, and the middle power concept. From his experiences in the League of Nations, Pearson concluded that a robust system of collective security was needed to ensure international security and stability. This idealist standpoint coalesced with the realist view that for a country like Canada with limited resources and capabilities, collective security and alliances were necessary to guarantee national security and prosperity in the long run (Gellman 1988/9). This created a commitment to and appreciation of institutions of collective security, in particular NATO

---

[1] UN peacekeeping, initiated by Pearson during the Suez crisis, subsequently even became one of the constituting elements of Canada's foreign policy identity and has remained so even though Canada's actual contributions to UN peacekeeping missions have declined significantly.

and NORAD (North American Aerospace Defense Command), which are also constitutive of Canadian foreign and security culture, and it adds the element of a 'good ally' to Canada's international role.

In the early 1990s, the concept of human security evolved with a strong resonance in Canada, in particular under Foreign Minister Axworthy, as a core element of Canadian foreign policy (McRae and Hubert 2001; Bosold and von Bredow 2006). The Canadian concept ultimately followed a narrower view on human security than, for instance, the 1994 UN Development Programme report (Paris 2001: 90). It focused mainly on the 'freedom from fear' aspect (MacFarlane and Foong Khong 2006: 226) or, in DFAIT's own language, on the 'freedom from pervasive threats to people's rights, safety or lives' (DFAIT website, quoted in Paris 2001: 90), and thus remained closer to traditional conceptions of security than other definitions.[2] Beginning with a shift in emphasis of Canadian foreign policy in the early 1990s, which prompted *inter alia* a transformed view on peacekeeping, state sovereignty and humanitarian intervention, human security became a guiding foreign policy principle, at least until 2000 when Lloyd Axworthy left office.[3] This had particular implications for the use of force: whereas Canada had for decades attached great importance to state sovereignty and had therefore been critical of humanitarian intervention, after 1990 the Conservative government under Prime Minister Brian Mulroney adopted a view that placed the protection of basic human rights (later to be expanded to human security) over such non-interventionism; this view was shared by the Liberals and NDP (Keating and Gammer 1993: 722–7). This trend continued and intensified under Liberal Foreign Minister Axworthy. The changed perspective also paved the way for the promotion of the 'responsibility to protect' (Tomlin *et al.* 2008: 202–61). While this added a different element to Canada's foreign and security policy culture, it did not represent a complete departure from liberal internationalism (see Roussel and Robichaud 2004: 152–3; see also Axworthy 1997: 185; Bosold and von Bredow 2006: 844).

Canada's foreign policy is guided by a primacy of peace, but it is not pacifist: Even before the 'human security turn' on humanitarian

---

[2] In the early days of his term, Axworthy seems to have followed a broader understanding of human security (Axworthy 1997: 184) but later discarded the developmental issues from the concept (Bosold and von Bredow 2006: 832–3).

[3] It is debated to what extent human security was part of the 'Axworthy agenda' or represented a continuous element in Canadian foreign policy also after 2000 (see, e.g., Bosold and von Bredow 2006; Furtado 2008). The Conservative government of Prime Minister Harper, who was first elected in 2006, abandoned the concept of human security in Canadian foreign policy (Cohen 2010: 4).

intervention, the experiences of the First World War, which has been framed as a defining moment for Canadian identity (see Massie and Roussel 2008: 73–4), of the Second World War, in which Canada (in a Pearsonian narrative) fought for humanity and democracy, and of the Korean War, which Pearson viewed as proof that the international system functioned (Gellman 1988/9: 86), had included 'fighting for a good cause' and 'standing up for one's values', with military means if necessary, as legitimate topoi in the Canadian foreign and security policy discourse.

Finally, the self-ascription of middle power status is an important element in Canada's foreign policy role connected with both the internationalist and the collective security frames. Even though Canada was in a position to strive for great power status after the Second World War, the middle power role was consciously constructed in a functionalist logic according to which there were countries that, while not being great powers, deserved a special place in the international hierarchy because of their larger contribution to international affairs (Chapnick 2000: 188–201). The concept was later enriched with a normative component: middle powers came to be those that filled a position between the great and small powers and could act as mediators, that pursued normative goals in addition to or instead of narrow national interests and that behaved like 'good international citizens' (Chapnick 2000: 193, 196). Since middle powers like Canada lack the resources and capabilities to guarantee their own security independently, they depend on alliances and international institutions. The self-image and perceived external expectations associated with being a middle power, with no colonial 'baggage' and with a certain status and influence in world politics, resulted in a strong feeling of responsibility to act as an 'honest broker' or 'helpful fixer' and to 'show leadership' internationally. The examples of Canada's policy towards the International Criminal Court (ICC), multilateral non-proliferation, arms control and disarmament and the UN, which are analysed below, serve to illustrate how these traditions and images translated into policy.

1.2.1   Canada and the International Criminal Court
Canada has traditionally attached great importance to international law and has long supported the establishment of a permanent international criminal court. In line with this, and as part of its human security agenda and 'good international citizenship', it was one of the earliest and most active proponents and key players in the international initiative that led to the creation of the ICC in 1998. In support of an effective court, Ottawa cooperated closely with civil society groups,

established and chaired the group of like-minded states, tried to secure US support for the court and played a pivotal role during the final round of negotiations in Rome in the summer of 1998. There, the head of the Canadian delegation, Philippe Kirsch, as chair of the Committee of the Whole, forged crucial compromises and was instrumental in producing the final draft statute of the new ICC (Axworthy 2003: 200–13). It is indicative of Canada's prominent role that Kirsch not only chaired the Preparatory Commission for the ICC between 1999 and 2002, but also became the court's first president in 2002.

1.2.2   *Canada and non-proliferation, arms control and disarmament (NACD)*

The traditional Canadian preference for multilateralism and a rules-based international order has also long found expression in its largely consistent and very active support for international non-proliferation, arms control and disarmament (NACD) that dates back to the 1950s and 1960s and continued well into the late 1990s. After 2001 and for some periods during the Cold War, the international context and/ or superpower policy limited the scope for activism for countries like Canada that in principle had not changed their positive attitude towards NACD.

Canada made crucial political and technical contributions to all NACD negotiations in the late 1980s and early 1990s (Fortmann *et al.* 2006: 238–52), including the 1990 Treaty on Conventional Forces in Europe, the 1992 Open Skies Treaty of which it is a depositary, the 1992 Chemical Weapons Convention, the 1996 Comprehensive Test Ban Treaty and the negotiating process of a compliance protocol to the 1972 Biological Weapons Convention, which was initiated in 1994 but failed in 2001. Canada also participated very actively and productively in all diplomatic conferences held in the existing international NACD regimes.

Canadian activism saw a shift in emphasis and reached a new peak in 1997, when Foreign Minister Axworthy partnered with the International Campaign to Ban Landmines and initiated the so-called Ottawa Process that led to the 'Ottawa Convention' banning anti-personnel mines (Tomlin 1998). With regard to nuclear disarmament, Canadian governments, though usually supportive of this goal, have with few exceptions not been as outspoken as on other issues. This is mainly due to Canada's membership of NATO, which maintains a nuclear posture, and its close relationship to the US, which is the world's largest nuclear power (Becker *et al.* 2008: 841, 849). These inconsistencies notwithstanding, Canadian policy has shown strong support for and proactivism in the international control and disarmament of weapons.

1.2.3   Canada and the United Nations

Active support for the UN and for its Charter has been considered of prime importance for normative as well as utilitarian reasons. Canada's foreign policy has been ascribed a 'preoccupation with international organization' that

> arguably exceeds anything observed in the foreign policies of other major industrialized democracies. Traditional prestige is not an adequate explanation. The United Nations has been not only an effective forum for advertising Canadian sovereignty (as was the League of Nations during the interwar period), but also the embodiment and source of principles which directed Canada's foreign policy after 1945. (Gellman 1988/9: 68–9)

Canada played a 'substantial and sometimes leading role' in the founding process of the UN in 1945 (Gordon and Wood 1992: 480; Keating 1993) and has made crucial contributions to the creation of core UN institutions such as the Charter of Human Rights or UN peacekeeping. This has enshrined a feeling of responsibility for and 'ownership' of the organisation in the Canadian self-image. Moreover, Canada has served six terms as a non-permanent member of the UN Security Council, more than any other Western UN member. All this has resulted in a very active participation in the various UN fora and in a foreign policy that generally supports a strong role for the organisation in international affairs.

1.2.4   Alliance, bilateral and regional relations

Canada and NATO: While the UN is perceived as the core of a stable and peaceful international system and a forum for mediation between different ideologies and political systems, NATO has been considered crucial for the maintenance of Canadian, but also Western, security and at the same time an extension of Canada's UN objectives. Canadian politicians together with the British promoted the idea of a Western collective defence organisation when it became clear in 1945 that the UN would not be equipped with an effective system of collective security. Canada initially proposed an alliance of all states 'willing to abide by its provisions' as long as they were democratic; and Article 2 of the North Atlantic Treaty (dubbed the 'Canadian article'), on the inclusion of which Canada conditioned its accession to NATO, reflects the fact that the Canadian negotiators wished to combine their internationalist orientation with their security concerns (Keating 1993: 76, 88–9). Moreover, NATO has also represented an important counterweight against US dominance and possible Canadian isolation in North American continental defence, and offers the possibility to maintain 'a seat at the table' in transatlantic security issues (Keating 1993: 78, 83–7, 95).

Canada's special bilateral and regional relations: The US is Canada's closest ally and most important point of reference, including in foreign and security policy-making. Apart from NATO, Canada's national defence rests largely on the integrated North American defence agreements, for example NORAD, first agreed in 1957 and last renewed in 2006. Roughly 80 per cent of Canadian exports go to the US, which highlights the importance of the southern neighbour as the biggest trading partner. This interdependence and the political, geographical, economic and cultural proximity notwithstanding, these relations contain an ambivalent component: while there is a strong desire in the Canadian political and public realm to 'be different', to be seen as being different and to exercise an independent foreign policy, there exists an equally strong desire in both realms not to alienate the closest friend and ally too much.

In addition to a regional focus on Europe that originated in Canada's historical ties to the UK and France, Canada maintains relatively close relations with various countries of the global South through its membership in the Commonwealth and *La Francophonie.* This has provided Canada with additional channels to promote some of its foreign policy objectives and with additional opportunities for mediation; it has also sensitised Canadian policy-makers to the concerns and problems of the 'Third World'.

1.3   Canada: the 'liberal internationalist' and 'close ally' and the use of force

Liberal internationalism has provided for a considerable consistency and continuity in Canadian foreign policy. The examples analysed above illustrate that this idea and the associated principles were also translated into policy between 1990 and 2003.[4] However, despite the broad consensus on the general thrust of Canadian foreign policy, several competing ideas, narratives and roles within the Canadian foreign policy tradition could have potential implications for Canada's participation in war. An active, UN-based internationalism could clash with the principle of collective security and the desire to maintain close

---

[4] However, Canada's material contributions to international affairs, for example, in peacekeeping or development aid and to NATO, formerly considered an integral part of Canada's internationalism, have decreased during this period.

relations with the US and NATO allies, if the preferences derived from the two related (and equally valid) concepts differ. Alliance relations in themselves could produce contingent outcomes given that demonstrating independence from the US *and* being a good ally are part of Canada's identity and foreign policy role. The focus on human security could represent a challenge in decisions on humanitarian intervention vis-à-vis the traditional emphasis on peacekeeping. This latter emphasis, a constitutive element of Canadian identity, stands in potential contrast to Canada's tradition of war-fighting. Canada's international role(s) hence provide for contingent outcomes with regard to the country's participation in wars between 1990 and 2003, as the following analyses will show.

2   Decision-making and public debates on the Gulf War, Kosovo War and Iraq War

2.1   *Canada and the war in the Persian Gulf 1990–1991*

2.1.1   *Domestic decision-making prior to the war*
Canada joined the multinational coalition that intended to force back Iraq and restore Kuwaiti independence at a very early stage; even though the Conservative government under Prime Minister Brian Mulroney hoped an offensive military confrontation could be avoided and made diplomatic efforts to that end, 'Ottawa had decided at an early stage in the crisis that if necessary, it would use force' (Kirton 1992: 382). It was of primary importance to the government that this crisis would be dealt with multilaterally and that the UN would play the central role (Rudner 1991: 268–70). As part of its diplomatic strategy and as a non-permanent member of the UN Security Council, Canada co-drafted and co-sponsored most and supported all of the resolutions pertaining to Iraq after 2 August 1990 (Cooper and Nossal 1997: 272). Canadian diplomats attached great importance to convincing the US and other allies to work through the UN, to refrain from unilateral action and to build and maintain a broad multinational coalition instead. The close personal relationship between Mulroney and US President Bush facilitated these efforts, but may also have rendered Mulroney reluctant to deviate too far from the US policy.

Constitutionally, the prime minister was in a strong decision-making position. Even though Secretary of State for External Affairs Joe Clark may initially have been less inclined to make a military contribution (Kirton 1992: 384), the decision to participate was largely consensual in government circles, and Mulroney was personally convinced of the eventual necessity of military action against Iraq. 'Parliament and the domestic body politic were given no role to play in the evolution of Canada's position' (Rudner 1991: 272). Politically, however, Mulroney was in a very weak position even though he held a majority in the House of Commons and elections were not scheduled for the next three years. He faced severe domestic problems, including uncertainty about the future unity of the country, and very low approval rates in opinion polls. Hence, he had to be receptive to the differing positions in the House of Commons, which was divided over the issue, and to public opinion, especially in Quebec.[5]

The domestic opposition to the war may have induced the government to put particular emphasis on diplomatic efforts. It may also have impacted upon the exact nature of Canada's contribution, most visibly in the decision to restrict the role of the Canadian forces to defensive tasks and to refrain from deploying ground troops (Cooper and Nossal 1997: 277; Kirton 1993: 427, 436). Ottawa had contemplated this latter option temporarily in November 1990, but the plans were abandoned for political reasons as well as due to structural operational problems and the reluctance of DND officials, who did not want to see Canada's peacekeeping tradition compromised (Maloney 2002: 8). The government's decision was also influenced by the belief that the Canadian public would be very sensitive to Canadian casualties (Kirton 1993: 436).

The decision-making process followed a pattern of balancing efforts to ensure a strong role for the UN, to meet allied preferences and to pay heed to the domestic political situation. First, the government announced its decision that Canada would contribute militarily to a sea blockade of Iraq following consultations with the allies; the fact that it had committed troops before the UN Security Council authorised the use of military means later elicited strong criticism from opposition MPs. However, at the UN Canada had apparently 'indicated that a new resolution authorising the use of force ... would be required before countries could legally use warships to enforce the sanctions',[6] thereby seeking at least *post facto* legitimisation through the UN.

---

[5] Mulroney faced criticism from Quebec MPs within his own caucus over his handling of the Meech Lake crisis that concerned the status of Quebec within the federation. To maintain his majority in Parliament, Mulroney had to pay special attention to the preferences of Conservative MPs from Quebec and to public opinion in this province. For the significance of the domestic situation for the Gulf War decisions, see Kirton (1993: 427–8).

[6] Lewis, Paul 1990. 'Confrontation in the Gulf: Order for Blockade Largely Isolates U.S. at Security Council', *New York Times*, 14 August, quoted by Minister of State Alan Redway in Commons Debates, Hansard, 27 September 1990, 13523.

Second, Mulroney delayed troop deployment and the definition of the despatched ships' and fighter jets' mission in order to avoid having to call the House of Commons from recess before it resumed its regular session in September. Hence, MPs did not become involved in the decision-making process until more than six weeks after the Iraqi invasion and after the government had decided to join the US-led coalition and engage militarily. This was another major point of criticism for the opposition, as was Clark's announcement in October 1990 that Canada might participate in a war against Iraq even without a UN mandate (Kirton 1992: 383). In early January 1991, the cabinet was apparently prepared to change the mandate of the troops to a more offensive role once the deadline set by UNSC Resolution 678 expired. The House, which was recalled from recess on 15 January for a debate that lasted several days, received the news of the allied attack on Iraq and Canada's participation in this attack in real time during sitting hours.

2.1.2   Parliamentary discourse[7]

Three debates, each initiated by a government motion, were held in the House of Commons. None of the motions mentioned the use of force by Canada; instead, they vaguely requested 'support for the UN'. This made outright rejection of the government's policy difficult for opponents of Canada's war participation, as apparently no one wanted to be seen as not supporting the UN, and it allowed those Conservative MPs who were reluctant to openly support a war to vote with their party. For this analysis, 49 speakers were coded; of those, 21 (Conservatives and one Liberal; see Table 6.1) supported Canada's involvement in war and 28 (all but one Liberal and members of the NDP; see Table 6.2) opposed it at the given points in time.

Hardly any speaker ruled out the option of war against Iraq; even the opposition accepted it as legitimate *ultima ratio* as long as all peaceful means had been exhausted, there was a UN mandate and command and Parliament was adequately involved in the decision-making.[8] No one questioned the fact that Canada would eventually 'take up its responsibility' and participate in a war should it also become justified and inevitable from the perspective of the Liberals and NDP. While the House was split regarding preferences for Canada's policy, the debate

---

[7] Only arguments used by at least 20 per cent of speakers are listed.
[8] Because of the general Canadian attitude to 'be counted' in such a case and in order not to distort the analysis, these speakers were coded as opponents provided they argued against participation under the given conditions.

Table 6.1 *Frequencies of arguments, Gulf War, Canada, supporters only (n = 21); extracts of results*[a]

Code	Argument	Number of speakers	Percentage of speakers
4101	Enforce international law/support UN	14	66.7
3101	Identity norms	14	66.7
1104	Show of force	11	52.4
5102	Threat to world order	11	52.4
4302	Peaceful means not exhausted	9	42.9
3201	Identity/role compatibility	8	38.1
4202	Peaceful means exhausted	7	33.3
1103	Regional stability	7	33.3
5201	Multilateral consensus pro	6	28.6
7101	Enemy image of adversary	6	28.6

[a] Full lists of results for this and all following tables are available from the author.

moved within a rather narrow framework, and war was neither rejected categorically nor supported enthusiastically.

As Table 6.1 reveals, most supporters of the war emphasised the need to enforce and reinforce international law and to support the UN. They saw it as Canada's responsibility to ensure that the UN can fulfil its role of providing collective security in an emerging new post-Cold War order, derived this from Canada's role in and contribution to the UN system and framed military action as necessary to protect world order. Historical analogies were frequently drawn from the failures of the League of Nations and from Canada's participation in the Second World War and the Korean War, fighting for 'the good cause'. The display of military force was seen as necessary to contain Saddam Hussein. A significant share of speakers conceded that peaceful means were yet to be exhausted. Coding of an enemy image was mostly triggered by a speaker's reference to Saddam Hussein's possession and use of weapons of mass destruction (WMD). National interests and security were cited as arguments only insofar as a stable and well-functioning international system of collective security was considered to be in Canada's interest and necessary to ensure national security. References to the allies, in particular the US, were conspicuously absent, while attention was drawn to the broad international consensus in support of the coalition's actions.

Opponents, depicted in Table 6.2, supported Canada's role in the military enforcement of the sanctions but complained that the government's policy merely followed US preferences, that Parliament and the public

Table 6.2 *Frequencies of arguments, Gulf War, Canada, opponents only (n = 28); extracts of results*

Code	Argument	Number of speakers	Percentage of speakers
4302	Peaceful means not exhausted	24	85.7
5303	Civilian casualties	15	53.6
5302	Pacifism/war damages global norms	12	42.9
6301	Democratic norms/procedures contra war	12	42.9
3301	Restraining identity/role norms	11	39.3
6302	Casualty aversion (own soldiers)	11	39.3
4301	No UN mandate/damage of UN	9	32.1
1303	Regional instability	6	21.4

were not adequately involved, that the government did not act with UN authorisation only and that there should be increased diplomatic efforts to prevent war. The argument used most frequently was that peaceful means were not yet exhausted and that sanctions would be effective if given more time. Many speakers anticipated and were not willing to accept high numbers of casualties (they usually expressed a universal reluctance to accept casualties, be it military or civilian, Canadian or other). A number of statements also referred to public opinion to support their anti-war stance. Damage was anticipated for world order, international law and the UN, and many speakers claimed that participation would not be compatible with Canada's identity, which required a stronger emphasis on diplomacy and a more neutral peacekeeping role. Some conceded that Saddam Hussein was indeed an enemy worth fighting and that the display of force might be necessary to contain him, but more speakers saw regional stability threatened by a war.

2.1.3 Newspaper discourse

The Canadian newspaper landscape is strongly regionalised; only two daily papers, the *National Post* and the *Globe and Mail*, have a country-wide distribution. Since the *Post* was founded only in 1998, it was not considered in this analysis. Instead, the *Toronto Star* was chosen in addition to the *Globe and Mail* because it has the highest circulation of all Canadian newspapers. Both papers can be located in the centre of the political spectrum, with the *Star* leaning more to the liberal-left than the *Globe*.

The editorials in the *Globe and Mail* accepted war as necessary and inevitable and framed it as a 'choice between victory for a dictator and victory for international law and security'.[9] While they acknowledged positively the government's efforts to find a peaceful solution, they later saw peaceful means exhausted and as a preferred but insufficient means of dealing with the crisis. In January 1991, they considered war to be the only way to liberate Kuwait and save the 'institutions of world order and peace'.[10] While the *Globe* editorials thus showed support for the government's policy, mirroring opposition arguments they also criticised its procedural approach, namely the inadequate involvement of Parliament, and through it of the Canadian public, in the decision-making process.[11]

In the *Toronto Star* editorials, there were no references to the need to uphold international law and to bolster collective security. Instead, it was emphasised that Mulroney should utilise his close relationship with US President Bush to convince him to work through the UN and refrain from unilateral action and a premature war. While the use of force was not rejected categorically and was explicitly endorsed to enforce the sanctions, the main argument, as among opposition MPs, was that peaceful means were not yet exhausted and that diplomacy and sanctions should be given more time.[12]

2.1.4   *Public opinion*

In correspondence with the stance of the parliamentary opposition, there was a marked difference in Canadians' support for involvement in the military enforcement of the sanctions and in a potential war.[13] The former enjoyed the support of around two-thirds of Canadians. Public opinion was initially also slightly in favour of Canadian participation in a war against Iraq, but later turned against it: in October 1990, a slim majority of 46 per cent agreed that 'if nothing else works, Canada

---

[9] Anonymous 1991. 'The Increasing Prospect of a War with Iraq', *Globe and Mail*, 10 January, p. A16.

[10] E.g. Anonymous 1991.'Sanctions Aren't Enough to Force Iraq to Leave Kuwait', *Globe and Mail*, 16 January, p. A14; Anonymous 1991. 'The World Unites against Saddam Hussein', *Globe and Mail*, 17 January, p. A16.

[11] E.g. Anonymous 1990. 'Flying Solo to the Gulf', *Globe and Mail*, 15 September, p. D6; Anonymous 1990. 'Preparing Canada for the Possibility of a Gulf War', *Globe and Mail*, 27 October, p. D6; Anonymous 1990. 'Time for Further Debate on the Gulf Crisis', *Globe and Mail*, 13 November, p. A16.

[12] Anonymous 1990. 'Caution in the Gulf', *Toronto Star*, 1 December, p. D2; see also, e.g., Anonymous 1990. 'Canada's Role in the Gulf', *Toronto Star*, 24 September, p. A16; Anonymous 1991. 'A Ray of Hope', *Toronto Star*, 5 January, p. D2; Anonymous 1991. 'The Case for War Is NOT Yet Made', *Toronto Star*, 12 January, p. D2; Anonymous 1991. 'War in the Gulf Not Inevitable', *Toronto Star*, 15 January, p. A20; Anonymous 1991. 'Limit Our Role in Gulf War', *Toronto Star*, 17 January, p. A24.

[13] For an overview of polling data, see Kirton (1993: 429).

[should] participate in a war to force Iraq out of Kuwait', while 44 per cent disagreed and 10 per cent were undecided. In Quebec, support stood at only 36 per cent, while 56 per cent opposed the proposition. In November 1990, support among Canadians for the use of force rose from 53 to 67 per cent if that force were backed by the UN.[14] A majority, albeit with a narrow margin, opposed the participation of Canadian forces in December 1990 (Martin and Fortmann 1995: 375–7); and in early January, a mere 37 per cent of Canadians country-wide favoured Canada going to war against Iraq, while 56 per cent (70 per cent in Quebec) opposed this.[15] Canadian public opinion thus apparently supported a tough stance towards Saddam Hussein, but was increasingly disinclined to support Canadian participation in a potential war, especially without a UN mandate.

2.1.5   *Conclusion: the Gulf War – fighting in support of international law and the UN*

For Ottawa, the Iraq crisis represented a test case for the UN system of collective security, to which Canadian foreign and security policy has traditionally attached great importance. It also presented an opportunity in the emerging post-Cold War world order to employ the UN Charter as it was originally intended, including the use of force under Chapter VII. Moreover, the war provided yet another opportunity for Prime Minister Mulroney to collaborate closely with the US. This setting resulted in a strategy that included the possibility of war from the beginning and simultaneously encompassed considerable efforts to enhance the role of the UN, even if that meant accepting an accelerated pace towards war.

The strong decision-making position of the prime minister was weakened by a serious domestic crisis that made Mulroney heed opposition and public preferences, especially in Quebec, and it probably also shaped the way the government presented its case publicly. The analysis yielded that elements of collective identity and foreign policy role, combined with some political-strategic considerations, played the most important role in shaping the Canadian policy: the strategic and

---

[14] For these figures, see Harper, Tim 1990. 'Canada Faces Lengthy Role in the Persian Gulf Analysts Predict', *Toronto Star*, 5 October, p. A3; Windsor, Hugh 1990. 'Battle of Sexes Extends to Views of War in Gulf', *Globe and Mail*, 30 October, pp. A1, A8; Stewart, Edison 1990. 'Vast Majority Absent as MPs Debate War', *Toronto Star*, 29 November, p. A2; Harper 1990. 'Give Iraq Sanctions Time to Work, 65% Say', *Toronto Star*, 28 November, p. A2; Delacourt, Susan 1991. 'MPs Struck Right Note, Pollsters Say', *Globe and Mail*, 17 January, p. A14.

[15] Oziewicz, Estanislao 1991. 'Bourassa Differs from Quebeckers on Gulf', *Globe and Mail*, 17 January, p. A14.

normative preferences for an effective system of collective defence and a solid role for the UN in international affairs as well as a strong belief in the legality and necessity of collective military action in this case appear as the major driving factors for the Mulroney government, supported by a desire to cooperate closely with the US.

The Canadian foreign policy tradition, which had included participation in wars in support of international law on previous occasions, allowed the government to frame this crisis in similar terms and to appeal to Canada's responsibility for the international system and the UN. Competing role elements of peacefulness, peacekeeping and mediation were invoked by opponents to the war in Parliament, the media and the public, but did not seem compelling enough to discredit the government's alternative narrative. The arguments most challenging for the government were those that claimed that peaceful means were not yet exhausted and that it was acting on command from the US and not independently. The latter argument points to another strong identity element, namely the US as principal 'Other', which influenced the government's decision-making and public justification. It is conspicuous that the government hardly ever cited Canadian interests, security or other, and never invoked the close alliance with the US or the UK to justify participation – even though this apparently played a role in its decision-making – but instead made great efforts to frame participation in terms of support for international law, appeals to humanitarian values and references to Canadian identity, which suggests that policymakers anticipated greater acceptance for these arguments than for any alliance or power-related ones.

2.2   Canada and the war in Kosovo 1998–1999

2.2.1   Domestic decision-making prior to the war

From the time when the Kosovo issue re-emerged on the international agenda in spring 1998, at the latest, Canada first accepted and then actively supported a robust military role for NATO even without a UN mandate (Dashwood 2000; Nossal and Roussel 2000). The Liberal Prime Minister Jean Chrétien was in a strong position given his majority in Parliament and a 'permissive domestic political environment' (Nossal and Roussel 2000: 190–1) in which there existed a broad consensus in Parliament as well as among the general public that the situation in Kosovo required a determined response (Roussel and Robichaud 2004: 155). While there are indications that Axworthy initially 'harboured reservations about unequivocally supporting NATO's actions in the Balkans' (Simpson 2000: 22), there was a broad consensus in the cabinet to support the NATO policy at all stages; the determination to act – by force if necessary – was never publicly called into question by any member of the executive. On the contrary, later on in the crisis Canada was one of the few NATO members that openly contemplated a ground offensive as a necessary supplement to the air strikes (Heinbecker and McRae 2001: 128, 130).

As during the Gulf crisis in 1990–1, Canada pursued a number of diplomatic initiatives in parallel to the military preparations (Axworthy 2003: 179). Ottawa also made considerable efforts – and emphasised this in the domestic discourse – to enhance the role of the UN, and from January 1999, in its capacity as non-permanent member, tried to design a meaningful role for the Security Council or at least have it endorse the NATO air strikes (Heinbecker 1999: 21). The government certainly would have preferred a UN mandate for any military action (Riekhoff 2002: 93), but, like the other NATO members, was willing to move ahead without it. Interestingly, given the traditional prominence of the UN in Canadian foreign policy, there was little opposition to this posture in the House of Commons and public opinion.

The dominant interpretation given was that in the present humanitarian crisis, international law combined with the existing UN resolutions provided sufficient justification for military action even without explicit UNSC endorsement (Heinbecker and McRae 2001: 123–4). Like many of its allies, Canada was concerned that it would be more damaging to the UN if NATO acted following a Russian veto than if the UNSC was circumvented altogether. Likewise, the idea of a 'Uniting for Peace' resolution in the UN General Assembly was considered in Ottawa but abandoned due to concerns that action could be delayed too long by a protracted negotiation process and that acting after a negative vote or with narrow majority support would cause more damage to the UN than acting outside the UN framework (Heinbecker 1999: 21; Riekhoff 2002: 92).

Given the severe humanitarian situation in Kosovo, the negative experiences with peacekeeping in the Balkans and the dominance of the human security paradigm in the Canadian foreign ministry at the time (Nossal and Roussel 2000: 192–4), there was a strong sense of the need to act, and to act militarily if necessary. Policy-makers justified the Canadian position as 'defence of universal principles of human rights and international humanitarian law' (Riekhoff 2002: 93) and with an emerging international norm of humanitarian intervention, and they considered 'yesterday's assumptions about sovereignty' to have been overtaken by 'today's imperative of human security' (Axworthy, quoted in Riekhoff 2002: 92). Canadian preferences and the NATO discourse converged, and the NATO actions (which Canada supported at all stages) continually narrowed the path towards military action for Ottawa, until air strikes came to be perceived as inevitable in March 1999.

2.2.2   Parliamentary discourse

In the period under consideration, only one debate in the House of Commons in October 1998 dealt with Canada's potential participation in a war against Serbia. Sixteen speakers were coded, all of whom supported the war and Canada's participation in it. The debate was conspicuously non-partisan and contained only sporadic and relatively mild criticism of the government's procedure and the lack of information provided to the Canadian public. While there was an all-party consensus to approve the motion of the Liberal government that formed the basis for the debate, apparently the Reform Party, the NDP and the Bloc Québécois would have supported even stronger wording calling explicitly for military action, which the Liberal motion did not do. No one opposed military action even without a UN mandate, and no one questioned the fact that Canada should participate in case NATO decided to authorise air strikes.

As Table 6.3 illustrates, by far the most speakers justified their position by referring to the humanitarian crisis and the inhumane actions of the Yugoslav forces. One of two speakers agreed that the time for military action had come since diplomatic efforts had failed and/or were unlikely to succeed in the future given Slobodan Milošević's known previous behaviour. Many MPs emphasised that military force would be necessary to stop Milošević and to bring him to the negotiating table, as such force was the only message he would understand. Reference was also made to Canada's identity and role, though this was less frequent and less explicit here than in the Gulf war debates. Also, Alliance solidarity and obligations were mentioned as reasons why Canada should participate in NATO air strikes.

Given the high prominence of support for the UN in the Gulf War debates, it is striking that relatively little room was accorded to debating the question of a UN mandate (or the lack thereof). Of the few speakers who mentioned this issue at all, several regretted that a UN mandate was unlikely to be obtained and conceded that air attacks might weaken the organisation, or could even be perceived as illegal under international law, but emphasised that they nevertheless supported military action. Others claimed that military action would be legitimate and covered by international law even without a UN mandate, since the Yugoslav actions represented crimes against humanity and since there was an emerging norm that entailed a responsibility to intervene

Table 6.3 *Frequencies of arguments, Kosovo War, Canada, all speakers (n = 16, all pro); extracts of results*

Code	Argument	Number of speakers	Percentage of speakers
5101	Humanitarian catastrophe	12	75
4202	Peaceful means exhausted	8	50
1104	Show of force	7	43.8
3101	Identity norms	7	43.8
2101	Alliance pro (internal aspects)	4	25
7101	Enemy image of adversary	4	25

in such situations. This shows that support for international law still figured as a subcutaneous factor in the debate, even though it was less prominent and, like the question of a UN mandate, was largely overlaid by the strong emphasis on humanitarian values.

2.2.3   Newspaper discourse

In the centre-left *Toronto Star*, two editorials dating from October 1998 supported military action against Milošević and Serbia in order to end the humanitarian catastrophe in Kosovo.[16] In this, they corresponded with the political discourse. In the more centrist *Globe and Mail*, most editorials remained vague in their attitude towards military action against Serbia. Before March 1999, they mainly discussed the dilemma in which Western states found themselves in trying to end the violence without supporting the Kosovo Albanians' claim to independence and in issuing threats that became less and less credible.[17] One of these editorials saw NATO 'troops on the ground' as the only possible solution, without, however, clarifying their exact role as combat or peacekeeping troops.[18] Another justified the air strikes and circumvention of the

---

[16] Anonymous 1998. 'Kosovo's Refugees Have Suffered Enough', *Toronto Star*, 1 October, p. A26; Anonymous 1998. 'Monitoring Kosovo', *Toronto Star*, 26 October, p. A20. For this analysis, an electronic search was carried out using the key words 'Kosovo', 'NATO', 'Canada' and 'war' in various combinations. Noticeably, a search that included 'war' as a keyword did not return any hits for the 2–3 weeks immediately preceding the NATO attacks.

[17] Anonymous 1998. 'Where to Go on Kosovo', *Globe and Mail*, 5 October, p. A16; Anonymous 1999. 'Crying Wolf in Kosovo', *Globe and Mail*, 1 February, p. A8; Anonymous 1999. 'The Limits of Power: Shoring up the Tentative Rambouillet Accords', *Globe and Mail*, 24 February, p. A14.

[18] Anonymous 1999. 'Balkan Sovereignty Association', *Globe and Mail*, 19 January, p. A18.

UNSC by claiming that a Russian veto could not have been tolerated in view of the nature of the crisis: 'In Kosovo, UN authorisation would have been better, but a Russian veto would have been worse. NATO was the appropriate answer.'[19]

2.2.4   Public opinion
There were no opinion polls or other primary sources available for this analysis covering the time before the NATO air campaign. Although, as Brawley and Martin state, 'there was even less willingness to accept casualties than in Britain' and '[t]he Canadian military was fairly secret-ive about its involvement in the early days, suggesting some fear that the Canadian public would not appreciate the job it was doing', the authors also claim that in Canada 'the public supported military operations fairly strongly' (Brawley and Martin 2000: 227; see also Nossal and Roussel 2000: 190–1). According to Simpson (2000: 22), there was a domestic public debate in Canada about the necessity and justifiability of NATO air strikes and a ground offensive, but unlike before the Gulf War in 1991, there does not seem to have been any strong, organised and outspoken opposition to the government's policy.

In several polls in early April 1999, i.e. after the war had begun, there was consistent majority support for NATO's actions in Yugoslavia (64–79 per cent) and for Canada's involvement (69 per cent). At least 'if this was the only way to stop the humanitarian crisis', Canadians even supported the deployment of NATO ground troops (59 per cent), including Canadian forces (61 per cent). Some 93 per cent supported the idea that Canada has a 'moral obligation in cases like Kosovo'.[20] Even in Quebec, public opinion did not differ from the rest of Canada (Nossal and Roussel 2000: 191). Heinbecker (1999: 25) attributes this strong public support to the fact that 'Canadians will support intervention, indeed will demand it, when they believe that the cause is just'.

2.2.5   Conclusion: the War in Kosovo – a 'just cause' for Canadians
The Canadian policy and decision-making processes during the Kosovo crisis cannot be viewed in isolation from the peacekeeping experiences in the Balkans in the early 1990s – or, for that matter, in Somalia and

---

[19] Anonymous 1999. 'Why the United Nations Was Ignored over Kosovo', *Globe and Mail*, 29 March, p. A12.

[20] IPSOS Reid poll, 8–10 April 1999, quoted in Everts, Philip (no date), 'The Kosovo Conflict in the Polls', data collection. Online: http://media.leidenuniv.nl/legacy/Poll%20Data%20Kosovo.pdf, p. 69; Nossal and Roussel (2000: 191); Brawley and Martin (2000: 232, fn. 2).

Rwanda.[21] These experiences fostered a changing perception of the possibilities and limits of traditional UN peacekeeping in post-Cold War conflicts and created a deep mistrust in Milošević's reliability as a negotiating partner. Canada's role image of peacekeeper had been challenged by these experiences and was subsequently transformed to include more robust actions. While peacekeeping thus changed, for Canada it remained within the same rationale of acting to enable and support peaceful settlements and hence could still be framed as compatible with traditional Canadian role elements.

To understand the Canadian policy, it is also essential to recognise the crucial role of the emerging concept of human security and how it dominated the discourse and shaped the policy within the foreign ministry, in particular (Nossal and Roussel 2000: 192–4; Nelles 2002). The Kosovo situation was being viewed almost exclusively in terms of humanitarian concerns (e.g. Axworthy 2003: 177–88), and this also led to the previously strong focus on the UN being overwritten by an even stronger belief in the necessity and legitimacy of, and indeed a responsibility for, humanitarian intervention.[22] International law thus remained an important factor in the Canadian decision-making process and public justification, but support was now based on a notion of changed and changing international law and norms after the Cold War. Moreover, the humanitarian focus resonated well in Canada where foreign policy in 1999 was still significantly influenced by the traditional Pearsonian idealism (Nossal and Roussel 2000: 192).

Even though NATO represented an, if not the most, important framework for decision-making, Alliance membership should be considered a sufficient rather than necessary condition. Even though NATO policy created a certain path dependency, Canada did not merely react to the preferences of NATO or some of the more powerful allies (see also Nossal and Roussel 2000: 189), but followed and helped shape the NATO course of action willingly and at times, for example regarding the question of ground troops, went further than most other members. Moreover, given the fact that Canadian politicians frequently referred to an obligation derived from Canada's being a founding member of NATO, it is difficult to differentiate clearly between a role- and an Alliance-based origin of this argumentation.

In sum, for Canada the Kosovo War was 'a war of values, not of interests' (Heinbecker 1999: 21; Axworthy 2003: 183) and an expression

---

[21] For a different view, see Nossal and Roussel (2000: 189–90).
[22] The Kosovo case was one catalyst for the development and promotion of the 'responsibility to protect' as a new international norm.

of the Canadian values of internationalism, democracy and the maintenance of international peace (Roussel and Robichaud 2004: 159). Hence, the most important factor in Canadian decision-making was a normative, humanitarian orientation reinforced by the dominance of the human security paradigm at the time. A diminished role of the UN was accepted for the sake of an emerging norm of humanitarian intervention in the post-Cold War world. This orientation was seen and portrayed as compatible with the Canadian self-image of peacekeeper and guardian of international law and humanitarian norms.

2.3   Canada and the war in Iraq 2003

2.3.1   Domestic decision-making prior to the war

On 17 March 2003, Liberal Prime Minister Jean Chrétien declared publicly that Canada would not participate in the war against Iraq.[23] The Canadian decision-making process in the Iraq case was longer and more convoluted compared to the wars in the Gulf in 1991 and in Kosovo. Prime Minister Chrétien was in a strong position, given his majority in Parliament and his personal style of governing. Many government members and officials, including Chrétien himself, had from the very beginning harboured reservations about a war of the kind the US was designing, in particular regarding the objective of regime change. This sceptical view was shared in the House of Commons by many Liberal MPs, the NDP and the Bloc Québécois.

At the same time, there were strong pressures from inside and outside the government to support the US as the closest ally and most important trading partner. Such pressures came from parts of the military, defence and trade establishments, the Canadian business community and, not least, from the US (see also Barry 2005: 224; Vucetic 2006: 143; Chrétien 2007: 310). In Parliament, only the (neo)conservative Canadian Alliance called for unequivocal support for the US policy. Public opinion was split over long periods of time and showed strong regional differences; yet the prime minister's eventual decision not to participate without a UN mandate met with approval from a large majority all over Canada. The different personal views, pressures from all sides and lack of an official government position until almost the last minute led to vague, at times contradictory and seemingly inconsistent presentations of government policy, which received much criticism

---

[23] Some observers claim that, the political 'no' notwithstanding, Canada still provided indirect support for the war through exchange officers and troops stationed in the region as part of the fight against international terrorism (e.g. Fawn 2006: 120).

from commentators, opposition parties and the media (Fawn 2006; Vucetic 2006: 143).

Several government officials and Chrétien himself had already indicated to the US in 2002 that Canada would require a UN mandate to participate in a war against Iraq (Barry 2005: 218). Yet, on several occasions mixed signals were sent to Washington, which gave rise to misperceptions and the expectation that Canada would support the US eventually. Canadian forces were even involved in the US's contingency planning and were caught by surprise by Chrétien's decision (Gross Stein and Lang 2007: 77).

Canadian policy-makers and diplomats had only limited chances in this case of inducing the US to remain within the UN framework through 'quiet diplomacy'. Ottawa supported Resolution 1441, which was drafted by the US and UK, in October 2002, arguably as an attempt to enhance the UN's role *and* to work with the US and UK. In keeping with Canada's previous policies, the Canadian ambassador to the UN, Paul Heinbecker, undertook a last-minute effort to reach a compromise in January/February 2003 (Gross Stein and Lang 2007: 74–5). He promoted a draft resolution that would have set deadlines for the inspections and requirements for Hussein's behaviour and would have included authorisation of military action in case these deadlines were not met. As in 1991, Canada apparently would have accepted the use of force (which it realised would ultimately be unavoidable), even though it might not have supported it wholeheartedly, in exchange for a process that followed international law and accorded the UN a central role.

Because the government hoped for a compromise and for a chance for the UN inspectors to conclude their mission, and because '[it] was attempting to strike a difficult balance between the views of the Canadian public and the needs of its most important ally' (Brunée and Di Giovanni 2005: 378), Chrétien avoided a final decision until the last minute. It seems highly probable, and Chrétien had already indicated this publicly in October 2002, that Canada would have participated in military action if there had been a UNSC decision or at least widespread support from its members for the use of force (Chrétien 2007: 308–9). In the given situation, however, when war was imminent (Barry 2005: 227) and in reaction to a UK enquiry whether Canada would join it (Gross Stein and Lang 2007: 75), Chrétien decided that Canada would not participate.

2.3.2   *Parliamentary debates*
The House of Commons held three debates on the issue of a war against Iraq between October 2002 and March 2003. Fifty speakers were coded,

14 of whom supported Canadian participation and 36 were against. All but one of the proponents were members of the Canadian Alliance. The NDP and the Bloc Québécois consistently opposed Canadian participation at least without a UN mandate, as did most Liberal MPs. It was conspicuous, however, that members of the (Liberal) executive hardly ever put forward a definitive position. Compared with the debates in the other two cases, the Iraq debates were much more polarised. Proponents and opponents of the war and of Canadian participation often departed from entirely different viewpoints: power-related arguments were now used by proponents of the war, while identity- and role-related arguments hardly appeared at all. As before, opposition parties criticised the government heavily for its inadequate involvement of Parliament.

As Table 6.4 shows, the majority of proponents of the war justified their position with the need to coerce Saddam Hussein into complying with his disarmament obligations, coupled with a strong enemy image in which they emphasised the cruel nature of his regime, his possession of WMD and his support for Al-Qaeda and international terrorism. In their support for war, the Canadian Alliance followed the neoconservative rhetoric of the Bush administration and introduced topoi hitherto alien to Canadian debates: the image of Saddam Hussein as evil dictator, the juxtaposition of democratic and non-democratic states, and the objective of regime change. Alliance speakers also emphasised the need to 'stand by Canada's allies' instead of alienating the US through an 'anti-Americanism' they claimed to detect in Liberal and other opposition statements. One-third of all speakers considered military action to be covered by existing UN resolutions, although some MPs conceded that a war might destabilise the region, that peaceful means had not yet been exhausted and that the Canadian military did not possess the necessary capabilities (the latter argument was usually used as criticism of the government's defence spending).

In opposing participation in a US-led war, the NDP, Bloc Québécois and most Liberals employed more of the traditional Canadian foreign policy rhetoric. Their statements contained a wide range of different arguments. As can be seen in Table 6.5, the argument used most frequently was that a war would cause intolerably high numbers of casualties and suffering among the Iraqi people. Many speakers also justified their position with references to public opinion in Canada and/or in their constituencies; and they considered a war without explicit UN endorsement (which many did not see in existing resolutions) illegal and potentially damaging to the UN and international law. They called for the continued employment of peaceful means, and while several conceded that Saddam Hussein was indeed a cruel dictator who might need to be

Table 6.4 *Frequencies of arguments, Iraq War, Canada, supporters only (n = 14); extracts of results*

Code	Argument	Number of speakers	Percentage of speakers
1104	Show of force	9	64.3
7101	Enemy image of adversary	9	64.3
1103	Regional stability	5	35.7
2101	Alliance pro (internal aspects)	5	35.7
4201	Covered by international law	5	35.7
1105	National security	3	21.4
6101	Regime change/democratisation	3	21.4
5201	Multilateral consensus pro	3	21.4
1303	Regional instability	3	21.4
1305	Lacking power capabilities	3	21.4
4302	Peaceful means not exhausted	3	21.4

Table 6.5 *Frequencies of arguments, Iraq War, Canada, opponents only (n = 36); extracts of results*

Code	Argument	Number of speakers	Percentage of speakers
5303	Civilian casualties	18	50
6301	Democratic norms/procedures contra war	17	47.2
4301	No UN mandate/damage of UN	15	41.7
4302	Peaceful means not exhausted	15	41.7
7301	Enemy image questioned	9	25
7101	Enemy image of adversary	9	25
1303	Regional instability	8	22.2
5302	Pacifism/war damages global norms	8	22.2

contained through a determined display of force, they did not consider his brute character a legitimate reason for war, and they did not appear convinced of his alleged possession of WMD. However, they, like the Progressive Conservatives, did not rule out the possibility of a war (and Canadian participation) should the evidence for an imminent threat become more convincing *and* should there be a UN mandate.

2.3.3 Newspaper discourse
The editorials in the *Toronto Star* were all critical of a war without a UN mandate and of US President Bush's doctrine of pre-emptive strikes,

and in this followed the line adopted by the government and most political parties. They argued that Canada should set a clear sign against such a policy but that participation might be acceptable (or unavoidable) if there was a UNSC mandate. Some agreed with the necessity of a tough stance against Iraq, though this was seen as the UNSC's purview. The editorials were not convinced that Iraq did indeed pose as big a threat as the US tried to convey nor that the US administration had sufficient evidence for the necessity of a war (which was accepted only in case a threat could be proven).[24]

In the *Globe and Mail*, the editorials did not assume a clear position on Canada's participation in an eventual war until after the government had decided against it in March 2003, when the *Globe* called Chrétien's decision 'the wrong choice'. Before that, the editorials criticised the government's ambiguous policy course and lack of a clear position, but mostly did not spell out a position of their own. Not unlike the majority in the polls and the *Star*, the *Globe* editorials supported a determined stance towards Saddam Hussein. While they sometimes questioned whether the evidence presented by the US was sufficient to justify war, in general the *Globe* seems to have been slightly more supportive of war than the *Toronto Star*.[25]

2.3.4 *Public opinion*

According to opinion polls conducted prior to the war, public preferences changed over time and displayed strong regional variances. Country-wide figures for autumn 2002 show a majority of Canadians (54–55 per cent) against war (e.g. Gross Stein and Lang 2007: 73). However, in winter 2002/3 public opinion was split: 41–43 per cent opposed a war and 40–44 per cent supported it; in several provinces in anglophone Canada, polls even yielded a majority support for war, while most Quebecers thought that Canada should stay out of it (e.g. Lachapelle 2003: 916–20; Haglund 2005: 194). Polls in January and

[24] E.g. Barthos, Gordon 2002. 'Stirring America's Coals of Rage', *Toronto Star*, 6 September, p. A24; Anonymous 2002. 'Bush Failed to Make Case for Starting Iraq War', *Toronto Star*, 13 September, p. A26; Anonymous 2003. 'War If Necessary, But Not Necessarily War', *Toronto Star*, 22 January, p. A22; Barthos 2003. 'Canada's Least Evil Iraq Option', *Toronto Star*, 30 January, p. A26; Anonymous 2003. 'Canada's Signal to Saddam', *Toronto Star*, 10 February, p. A22.

[25] E.g. Anonymous 2002. 'Questions for Bush, Questions for Chrétien', *Globe and Mail*, 9 September, p. A12; Anonymous 2002. 'Some Tough Talk, But After That?', *Globe and Mail*, 3 October, p. A20; Anonymous 2003. 'Canada Shows Up: What Kept It?', *Globe and Mail*, 11 January, p. A20; Anonymous 2003. 'Muddy, Aye Muddy', *Globe and Mail*, 16 January, p. A18; Anonymous 2003. 'Powell's Strong Case and the Coming Risk', *Globe and Mail*, 6 February, p. A16; Anonymous 2003. 'Canada's Iraq Policy: Inconsistency Ho!', *Globe and Mail*, 19 March, p. A22.

February 2003 showed that the conditions for a potential war were a crucial determinant for public opinion: when the question posited a UN mandate for military intervention, approval rates country-wide rose to 46 per cent in January (37 per cent in Quebec and 49 per cent in the rest of Canada; Jedwab 2003: 5; Lachapelle 2003: 917) and to 60–63 per cent in February (Barry 2005: 225; Vucetic 2006: 141), even in Quebec (Massie 2008: 38). *Without* UN authorisation, however, public opinion presented the inverse picture: only 25–26 per cent country-wide supported Canadian participation, while 60–67 per cent were against it (Barry 2005: 225; Vucetic 2006: 141). Support for intervention without UN backing averaged only 30 per cent (Massie 2008: 37) even in those provinces most prone to support Canadian participation, for example, Alberta.

2.3.5 Conclusion: the war in Iraq – an 'un-Canadian' war

Of the three cases under scrutiny in this study, the Iraq War proved the most difficult one for Canada. The government was caught between considerations of alliance solidarity and political and economic interests, on the one hand, and independence in foreign policy and traditional (Liberal) Canadian values and principles, on the other. Chrétien, his advisors and a number of government officials did not share the US perception of an immediate threat posed by Iraq and of its connections with international terrorism, or more generally the neoconservative worldview, and were not convinced of the intelligence evidence offered by the US and UK (to which they had access). They were unwilling to expand the 'war on terrorism' – to which they remained committed – to Iraq and/or to engage in a war without UN endorsement, did not approve of regime change as a justification for war and warned against a 'clash of civilisations' if the US went ahead with its plans. Moreover, they were concerned about the circumvention of the UN, the legality of a pre-emptive war without UN authorisation and the repercussions for international law. In short, from Chrétien's personal perspective and from how he and his officials perceived Canada's liberal-internationalist foreign policy tradition, participation in a war under the given circumstances was just 'not the right thing to do'.

For the Canadian Alliance, which did not follow the liberal-internationalist logic but displayed a strong continentalist orientation, these arguments were overwritten by the primacy of alliance solidarity and national interests and security, as well as by a very different threat perception. The resonance that the two former arguments in particular found among the general public in some provinces and even within some government quarters can probably account for the government's vague and at times evasive presentation of its (non-)position. However, it was not strong enough to overrule the view that prevailed in the government, especially in the Prime Minister's Office and Department of Foreign Affairs, in the House of Commons and in the public, in particular in Quebec. Continentalism is also reflected in the fact that the government (unlike several MPs) refrained from criticising the US openly or publicly declaring the war illegal and that it took a legalistic viewpoint to justify its position instead. While such legalism may at first glance seem surprising given the Canadian willingness to fight in Kosovo without UNSC authorisation, it nevertheless follows a certain pattern: unlike in the Kosovo case, Ottawa did not see a humanitarian catastrophe that could (or had to) be prevented or ended by military action. There was no international norm available to replace the UN Charter as a legitimate source for legalising a war, and there was no broad Western/NATO, let alone international, consensus that could make up for single dissenting positions on the UNSC. At the same time, concern for civilian casualties and damage to international law were counter-indicative of a war and Canadian participation in it. Neither humanitarian concerns nor the protection of international law could hence be called upon to justify the country's participation.

3   Conclusion: Canada's participation in wars 1990–2003

According to democratic peace (DP) theory, democracies would be expected to avoid war due, *inter alia*, to their citizens' normative and utilitarian considerations that translate into policy through the democratic processes and institutions. Contrary to these prima facie expectations, Canada participated in two of the three wars under scrutiny, namely in the Gulf in 1991 and in Kosovo in 1999, but stayed out of the war against Iraq in 2003.

In all three cases, international law and, in particular in the latter two, humanitarian concerns played a prominent role in the public justification of the decisions and were frequently connected with various elements of Canada's foreign policy traditions. The Gulf War was perceived as a model case of collective security in which the aggression of one UN member against another member had to be ended through a collective military effort sanctioned by the UNSC. Protection of the international system of collective security, which Canada had helped to create after the Second World War, and of international law were among the crucial motives of the Conservative government at the time for participating in the war even against an initial majority opposition in the Canadian public. In the Kosovo case, international law again played a role, albeit in a different perspective: whereas in the former case the UN was the central point of reference, it was all but marginalised in the 1999 debates. Here, emerging norms of international law – humanitarian intervention, human security and a responsibility to protect – were at the centre, and humanitarian concerns trumped the previously essential condition of a UN mandate. The UN was restored to its central role in the official justification for Canada's non-participation in the Iraq War in 2003, when the government officially took a legalistic viewpoint and argued that, for Canada, participation was not legitimate without a UNSC mandate.

The political system of Canada with its strong centralisation of decision-making power in the executive and the Prime Minister's Office makes it difficult to argue for a special effect of democracy in these decisions. Parliament has virtually no constitutional role in decisions on troop deployments overseas and on Canada's participation in wars. This seems to limit the potential impact of the citizens' preferences on political decisions as postulated by DP theory. However, while the prerogative of the executive is mostly accepted in principle even by Members of Parliament, there exists a strong expectation in the political culture that Parliament, and through it the Canadian public, is to be involved in decision-making about troop deployment at least through debates and the possibility for MPs to express their views and those of their constituents. Adequate involvement of parliament was frequently considered a precondition for the legitimacy of Canada's war participation by all political parties, and discussions about procedural questions and the (in)adequate actual involvement of Parliament took up much time in the parliamentary debates on all three events.

Nor is there a formalised role for public influence or for the direct impact of citizens. Yet, the Canadian political culture allows for an impact of public opinion (as measured by opinion polls or as anticipated by politicians). It comprises a strong element of 'accountable government' and, depending on the disposition of the government and the prime minister, this allows for a considerable, though not imperative, impact of public opinion (which can show significant regional differences). In the Gulf War, the conviction of the government that it was doing the right thing in support of the international system and in accordance with Canada's foreign policy tradition overruled the initial (narrow) public majority opposition to the war and Canada's participation. In the Kosovo case, the public supported the government's course. In 2003, public opinion was split over long periods of time but eventually turned against the war in the way it was initiated and justified by the US. While the (indirect) influence of democratic processes and culture should hence not be completely neglected, it is not sufficient to explain the Canadian behaviour in the three cases; first, because there is no institutionalised role for Parliament and/or citizens' involvement and hence room for contingency; and second, because, with the exception of the Kosovo case, political, public and published opinions are not sufficiently congruent to explain the respective decisions.

Of the other potential explanatory factors taken into account in this study, power, national security and national interests did not figure prominently in the justifications of the respective government or opposition positions, with the sole exception of the neoconservative Alliance Party during the Iraq crisis; apparently these arguments are not expected to help garner broad support in the Canadian public for a chosen policy course. The analysis of the decision-making processes beyond the public presentation, as far as they could be traced, did not yield any hints, either, that these factors played more than a minor, modifying role, if at all. Only if one takes into account the Canadian view that the country's national security can only be guaranteed through a stable and secure international system with a strong rule of (international) law might the policy in some cases be construed as an expression of national interests and national security; nevertheless, other factors have to be considered in order to fully grasp the respective positions.

References to alliance obligations are conspicuously absent in most statements, in particular in statements by members of the executive, regardless of whether a Liberal or Progressive Conservative government was in power. On the contrary, speakers often went to great lengths to stress the independence of Canada's positions.[26] While alliance considerations obviously did play a role in the internal decision-making processes in all three cases, speakers apparently did not expect to win support for their positions by emphasising alliance obligations publicly – unless they were connected with Canada's role and tradition in founding and supporting alliances, in particular NATO. The alliance aspect can thus not be viewed in isolation from Canada's self-image, foreign policy tradition and perceived international roles; it works through a corresponding logic of appropriateness, and its effects are contingent.

For the purposes of this study, the impact of the foreign policy role conception needs to be viewed in terms of the relationship with the US as well as Canada's foreign policy traditions and self-constructed international roles. Concerning the US, regardless of their personal preferences, policy-makers were careful to appear to act independently

---

[26] This is even true for the Canadian Alliance that in 2002/3 otherwise built its position on the need to support Canada's closest ally 'no matter what'.

of US pressures. This is most probably due to the identity-based wish to differentiate and delimit Canada from the US and to emphasise Canada's independence from the US, which at times clashed with the role- and interest-based perspective of appropriate behaviour as close friend, trading partner and ally that also impacted on the decision-making processes in our cases. In instances where US policies requiring a Canadian positioning did not correspond to Canada's perceived foreign policy tradition, as was the case in nuances during the Gulf crisis and fundamentally in the Iraq case, Canadian policy-makers tried to balance expectations arising from Canada's role as a good ally against the country's own traditions. The search for compromises, for example in the form of compromise UN resolutions or through quiet diplomacy with the US, was one typical strategy in these cases.

Foreign policy traditions are another vital element to consider. The principles of peacekeeping, collective security and defence of international law and human rights, all strongly connected with Lester B. Pearson and the 'golden age' of Canadian foreign policy (and as such part of the myths and definitions of Canadian-ness), have created path dependencies, yet with potentially conflicting outcomes. In the Gulf crisis, the government and proponents of war mainly justified participation in the military build-up and in the war with references to Canada's military history in support of international law and the UN, while opponents tried to discredit the government's approach through references to Canada's peacekeeping (as opposed to war-fighting) tradition. In Kosovo, the 'robust' peacebuilding as pursued by NATO was portrayed as a logical extension of this peacekeeping tradition under new international circumstances. Again, international law and Canada's responsibility to guard and promote it, as derived from its policy tradition, played a central role in the justifications, as did the new elements of human security and humanitarian intervention. Policy-makers emphasised the compatibility even of these relatively recent principles with traditional Canadian approaches to foreign policy. In the Iraq case, the liberal-internationalist attitude eventually prevailed over alliance concerns, and the decision not to participate without a UN mandate was justified by portraying such participation as 'un-Canadian', meaning incompatible with the country's foreign policy traditions and principles.

In all three cases under scrutiny here, political and public support for Canada's stance on participation in war between 1990 and 2003 rested on an expectation of Canada's commitment to international law, to a rules-based international system with strong multilateral institutions and to humanitarianism. This commitment developed at a time that was crucial for the construction of a Canadian role as an independent, active and influential international actor; despite some modifications, in the period under scrutiny it remained in essence constitutive of Canada as a 'good international citizen' and 'benign middle power'. Similarly, the conditions that appear vital to justify Canadian participation in wars domestically are mostly rooted in Canada's roles and self-image rather than in rationalist, utilitarian considerations: there has to be a collective effort with an objective beyond immediate and material self-interest; it must be construed as being in accordance with international law as derived from the UN Charter or other sources; there has to be a broad international consensus; and there needs to be a plausible moral/humanitarian justification. A central role for the UN is important; however, the Kosovo case showed that it is no *conditio sine qua non* as long as there are other compelling legal and/or humanitarian arguments available. The definition of an enemy has to be credible on the basis of international law and humanitarian concerns and is much less likely to succeed if framed in culturalistic terms.

Provided that these conditions are met, war participation may be considered legitimate or even imperative by Canadians. Consequently, while Canadians consider their country a 'peaceable country' with a clear preference for multilateralism, international law and diplomacy and with an international role of liberal-internationalist, honest broker and benign middle power, and expect international leadership as part of this role, the Canadian foreign and security culture is not pacifist, but entails a commitment to military means for providing security and a willingness to fight, as a last resort, in support of the international institutions that Canada helped to found and maintain.

REFERENCES

Axworthy, Lloyd 1997. 'Canada and Human Security: The Need for Leadership', *International Journal* 52 (2): 183–96
     2003. *Navigating a New World: Canada's Global Future*. Toronto: Vintage Canada
Barry, Donald 2005. 'Chrétien, Bush, and the War in Iraq', *American Review of Canadian Studies* 35 (2): 215–45
Becker, Una, Müller, Harald and Wisotzki, Simone 2008. 'Democracy and Nuclear Arms Control: Destiny or Ambiguity?', *Security Studies* 17 (4): 810–54
Bosold, David and von Bredow, Wilfried 2006. 'Human Security: A Radical or Rhetorical Shift in Canada's Foreign Policy?', *International Journal* 61 (4): 829–44
Boucher, Jean-Christophe and Roussel, Stéphane 2008. 'From Afghanistan to "Quebecistan": Quebec as the Pharmakon of Canadian Foreign and

Defence Policy', in Jean Daudelin and Daniel Schwanen (eds.), *What Room for Manoeuvre? Canada among Nations 2007*. Montreal: McGill-Queen's University Press, pp. 128–56

Brawley, Mark R. and Martin, Pierre 2000. 'Balancing Acts: NATO's Unity and the Lessons to Learn', in Pierre Martin and Mark R. Brawley (eds.), *Alliance Politics, Kosovo, and NATO's War: Allied Force or Forced Allies?* Basingstoke: Palgrave, pp. 221–33

Brunée, Jutta and Di Giovanni, Adrian 2005. 'Iraq: A Fork in the Road for a Special Relationship?', *International Journal* 60 (2): 375–84

Chapnick, Adam 2000. 'The Canadian Middle Power Myth', *International Journal* 55 (2): 188–206

Chrétien, Jean 2007. *My Years as Prime Minister*. Toronto: A. A. Knopf Canada

Cohen, Andrew 2010. 'A Conservative Revolution? The State of Canadian Politics in 2010', *FES Perspective Canada* No. 01/2010, Washington/Berlin

Cooper, Andrew F. and Nossal, Kim Richard 1997. 'The Middle Powers in the Gulf Coalition: Australia, Canada, and the Nordics Compared', in Andrew Bennett, Joseph Lepgold and Danny Unger (eds.), *Friends in Need: Burden Sharing in the Persian Gulf War*. Basingstoke: Macmillan, pp. 269–89

Dashwood, Hevina S. 2000. 'Canada's Participation in the NATO-Led Intervention in Kosovo', in Maureen Appel Molot and Fen Osler Hampson (eds.), *Vanishing Borders: Canada among Nations 2000*. Don Mills: Oxford University Press, pp. 275–302

Dewing, Michael and McDonald, Corinne 2006. 'International Deployment of Canadian Forces: Parliament's Role', Parliamentary Information and Research Service PRB 00–06E, Ottawa

Dyck, Rand 2004. *Canadian Politics: Critical Approaches*. Scarborough: Nelson

Fawn, Rick 2006. 'Canada: Outside the Anglo-American Fold', in Rick Fawn and Raymond Hinnebusch (eds.), *The Iraq War: Causes and Consequences*. London: Lynne Rienner, pp. 115–25

Fortmann, Michel, Hogg, William and Jobin, Catherine 2006. 'Le Canada et le contrôle des armaments durant les annéed 1990', in Serge Jaumain and Éric Remacle (eds.), *Mémoire de guerre et construction de la paix: Mentalités et choix politiques*. Brussels: Peter Lang, pp. 235–54

Furtado, Francis J. 2008. 'Human Security: Did It Live? Has It Died? Does It Matter?', *International Journal* 63 (2): 405–21

Gellman, Peter 1988/9. 'Lester B. Pearson, Collective Security, and the World Order Tradition of Canadian Foreign Policy', *International Journal* 44 (1): 68–101

Gordon, Nancy and Wood, Bernard 1992. 'Canada and the Reshaping of the United Nations', *International Journal* 47 (3): 479–503

Gross Stein, Janice and Lang, Eugene 2007. *The Unexpected War: Canada in Kandahar*. Toronto: Viking Canada

Haglund, David G. 2005. 'Relating to the Anglosphere: Canada, "Culture", and the Question of Military Intervention', *Journal of Transatlantic Studies* 3 (2): 179–98

Heinbecker, Paul 1999. 'Human Security', *Canadian Foreign Policy* 7 (1): 19–25

Heinbecker, Paul and McRae, Rob 2001. 'Case Study: The Kosovo Air Campaign', in Rob McRae and Don Hubert (eds.), *Human Security and the New Diplomacy: Protecting People, Promoting Peace*. Montreal: McGill-Queen's University Press, pp. 122–33

Jedwab, Jack 2003. 'Canadian Opinion on the Possible Invasion of Iraq: Between Old and New Europe', Association for Canadian Studies. Online: www.acs-aec.ca/oldsite/Polls/Poll16.pdf

Keating, Tom 1993. *Canada and World Order: The Multilateralist Tradition in Canadian Foreign Policy*. Toronto: McClelland & Stewart

Keating, Tom and Gammer, Nicholas 1993. 'The "New Look" in Canada's Foreign Policy', *International Journal* 48 (4): 720–48

Kirton, John 1992. 'Liberating Kuwait: Canada and the Persian Gulf War, 1990–91', in Don Munton and John Kirton (eds.), *Canadian Foreign Policy: Selected Cases*. Scarborough: Prentice-Hall, pp. 382–93

1993. 'National Mythology and Media Coverage: Mobilizing Consent for Canada's War in the Gulf', *Political Communication* 10 (4): 425–41

2007. *Canadian Foreign Policy in a Changing World*. Toronto: Nelson

Lachapelle, Guy 2003. 'Pourquoi le gouvernement canadien a-t-il refusé de participer à la guerre en Irak?', *Revue Française de Science Politique* 53 (6): 911–27

MacFarlane, S. Neil and Foong Khong, Yuen 2006. *Human Security and the UN: A Critical History*. Bloomington, IN: Indiana University Press

McRae, Rob and Hubert, Don (eds.) 2001. *Human Security and the New Diplomacy: Protecting People, Promoting Peace*. Montreal: McGill-Queen's University Press

Maloney, Sean M. 2002. 'War with Iraq: Canada's Strategy in the Persian Gulf, 1990–2002', *Martello Papers* No. 24, Kingston

Martin, Pierre and Fortmann, Michel 1995. 'Canadian Public Opinion and Peacekeeping in a Turbulent World', *International Journal* 50 (2): 370–400

Massie, Justin 2008. 'Regional Strategic Subcultures: Canadians and the Use of Force in Afghanistan and Iraq', *Canadian Foreign Policy Journal* 14 (2): 19–48

Massie, Justin and Roussel, Stéphane 2008. 'Au service de l'unité: Le rôle des mythes en politique étrangère canadienne', *Canadian Foreign Policy Journal* 14 (2): 67–93

Munton, Don and Keating, Tom 2001. 'Internationalism and the Canadian Public', *Canadian Journal of Political Science* 34 (3): 517–49

Nelles, Wayne 2002. 'Canada's Human Security Agenda in Kosovo and Beyond: Military Intervention versus Conflict Prevention', *International Journal* 57 (3): 459–79

Nossal, Kim Richard 1997. *The Politics of Canadian Foreign Policy*. Scarborough: Prentice-Hall

Nossal, Kim Richard and Roussel, Stéphane 2000. 'Canada and the Kosovo War: The Happy Follower', in Pierre Martin and Mark R. Brawley (eds.),

Alliance Politics, Kosovo, and NATO's War: Allied Force or Forced Allies?
Basingstoke: Palgrave, pp. 181–99

Paris, Roland 2001. 'Human Security: Paradigm Shift or Hot Air?' *International
Security* 26 (2): 87–102

Riekhoff, Harald von 2002. 'Canada and the United Nations Security
Council, 1999–2000: A Reassessment', *Canadian Foreign Policy Journal*
10 (1): 71–106

Roussel, Stéphane and Robichaud, Chantal 2004. 'L'État postmoderne par
excellence? Internationalisme et promotion de l'identité internationale du
Canada', *Revue Études internationales* 35 (1): 149–70

Rudner, Martin 1991. 'Canada, the Gulf Crisis and Collective Security',
in Fen Osler Hampson and Christopher J. Maule (eds.), *After the Cold
War: Canada among Nations 1990–91*. Ottawa: Carleton University Press,
pp. 241–80

Simpson, Erika 2000. 'Canada's NATO Commitment: Current Controversies,
Past Debates, and Future Issues', *Behind the Headlines* 57 (2–3): 20–7

Tomlin, Brian W. 1998. 'On a Fast Track to a Ban: The Canadian Policy
Process', in Maxwell A. Cameron, Robert J. Lawson and Brian W. Tomlin
(eds.), *To Walk without Fear: The Global Movement to Ban Landmines*.
Toronto: Oxford University Press, pp. 185–211

Tomlin, Brian W., Hillmer, Norman and Hampson, Fen Osler 2008.
Canada's International Policies: Agendas, Alternatives and Politics. Oxford
University Press

Vucetic, Srdjan 2006. 'Why Did Canada Sit out of the Iraq War? One
Constructivist Analysis', *Canadian Foreign Policy Journal* 13 (1): 133–53

7 French ambiguities: of civilising, diplomatic and military missions

Johanna Eckert

French foreign policy since the end of the Cold War has revealed ambiguities and dilemmas. France's claim to remaining an independent great power that acts autonomously and keeps its distance from the United States is at odds with the country's resources and with the international political constellation after 1990. This chapter shows that French reasons for going to war and for rejecting war are often linked to international law and to an 'exceptional' self-conception of protecting universal values. Power considerations are far from absent from the French discourse, but they often appear in synthesis with a normative posture.

1   Institutional and ideational determinants of France's foreign and security policy

1.1   Regime-type features and decision-making

In 1958, the constitution of the Fifth French Republic established a political system with a dual-headed executive consisting of the president, who is directly elected by the people, and the prime minister, who emerges from separate parliamentary elections and is responsible to parliament. In order to avoid the political instability of the Fourth Republic, this political system limited the powers of parliament while strengthening executive powers. 'Rationalized parliamentarism' gave rise to a constitutional practice of a dominant presidential executive, rendering France a semi-presidential democracy (Kimmel 2005: 248–56). The president appoints the prime minister and is entitled to initiate referendums and to dissolve the first chamber of parliament (*Assemblée Nationale*).

According to the constitution, the president is the guarantor of national independence and territorial integrity and commander-in-chief of the armed forces. He decides on the use of nuclear weapons and presides over the higher national defence councils and committees.

The government also has substantial, but only vaguely couched, powers in foreign and security policy: the prime minister is 'responsible for national defence', and the government, which is to determine and conduct national policies, 'shall have at its disposal the civil service and the armed forces' (Articles 20 and 21 of the constitution).

The contrast between the letter of the constitution and political practice is remarkable: although the constitution divides powers in the realm of foreign and security policies between the president and the government, the president (due to Charles de Gaulle's imprint) has acquired a prerogative in this domain (*domaine réservé*; Tümmers 2006). However, when the president and the parliamentary majority (the prime minister) do not belong to the same political camp, conflicts within the dual-headed executive arise and the prime minister usually manages to some extent to redress the asymmetrical power relationship between the heads of the executive (Kimmel 2005: 259–62).[1]

Parliamentary oversight of military deployments is limited, although the constitution does stipulate in Article 35 that a 'declaration of war' shall be authorised by parliament (Treacher 2003: 19). Since military actions short of war are not explicitly mentioned, French governments are at liberty to decide whether authorisation is required. For example, while President Mitterrand asked for a (symbolic) vote at the beginning of the Gulf War in 1991, Prime Minister Jospin refused a vote in the Kosovo crisis (Rozenberg 2003: 126). Article 35 has in reality lost its meaning as none of the French military engagements since the 1950s has been based on the declaration of a 'war'. Parliament can only influence foreign policy by way of budget decisions or through the ratification of international treaties. Since the president is not responsible to parliament, he retains great discretionary powers; the role of parliament is weak and debates on security policy rare (Stahl 2006: 109).

The influence of the political parties on French foreign and security politics is also limited, as is their degree of organisation. There have been numerous splits and regroupings of political parties in the Fifth Republic (Schild 2005). The party system was fragmented during the 1990s: with a strong leftist camp, formed by the *Parti Socialiste* (PS) and the *Parti Communiste Français* (PCF); a strong centre-right camp, formed by several Gaullist and centre-right parties such as the *Rassemblement pour la République* (RPR) and the *Union pour la Démocratie Française* (UDF); and with the establishment of the Green Party (*Les Verts*) and

---

[1] The Fifth French Republic has seen *cohabitations* in 1986–8 (President Mitterrand/Prime Minister Chirac), 1993–5 (President Mitterrand/Prime Minister Balladur) and 1997–2002 (President Chirac/Prime Minister Jospin).

the far-right *Front National* (FN). The elections in 2002 led to a higher concentration of the party system as the centre-right camp reorganised itself under the umbrella of the newly founded Gaullist *Union pour un mouvement populaire* (UMP).

French politics are shaped by an administrative-political elite educated in exclusive *grandes écoles*. This elite is socialised into a shared political consensus that is still modelled on de Gaulle's 'certain idea of France' (see below), but this also leads the public to perceive it as a detached political class. French foreign policy is conducted by an executive network dominated by a powerful president, is implemented by an administrative elite and is rather secluded from parliamentary influence or the impact of public opinion and NGOs (Treacher 2003: 20; Morisse-Schilbach 2006: 66–72).

1.2   Role conception and role profile in foreign and security policy

1.2.1   Foreign policy traditions, guidelines and role conception[2]

France emerged from the Second World War as one of the victorious powers, but the traumatic experience of occupation by Nazi Germany left a deep imprint on the collective identity and led General de Gaulle to define supreme goals of French foreign policy that are still valid today: the invulnerability of the nation, the promotion of national glory and the pursuit of a global status (*rang*) and greatness (*grandeur*) (Roche 2000: 394–7). 'La France parce qu'elle le peut, parce que tout l'y invite, parce qu'elle est la France, doit mener au milieu du monde une politique qui soit mondiale.'[3] National and international interests are merged into one. 'Its self-interest and universal mission were one. Assisting France's quest for *grandeur* was in the interest of other states too' (Hoffmann 1974: 46). De Gaulle declared that France's 'greatness is the condition sine qua non of world peace' (cited in Rathbun 2004: 125).

De Gaulle also drew from Republican traditions that stress that France is the cradle of modern democratic values and has a special mission to promote the values of the French revolution abroad. France regards itself as a unique nation and a cultural 'exception', as the guardian of democracy, human rights, the rule of law and republicanism. Such values are considered as being at the same time special (to France) and universal (for all) (e.g. Jospin 1999: 7–8). This self-image is similar to that enshrined in missionary conceptions of US foreign

---

[2] A useful contemporary introduction by a former official is de Villepin (2003b).

[3] De Gaulle in a New Year's Address on 31 December 1963, cited in Grosser (1989: 319).

policy,[4] placing the two countries in an ambivalent relationship, ranging from a mild rivalry to anti-Americanism (Kolboom and Stark 2005: 380–1). This rivalry is expressed in the global politics of culture that France pursues in its former colonies and that pits a francophone against an anglophone world.

For decades after the Second World War, French foreign policy pursued three aims: containing Soviet as well as US influence in Europe, integrating West Germany into transatlantic – increasingly European – structures and asserting French independence and sovereignty (Meimeth 1997). France's national independence was founded on its permanent seat in the UN Security Council, its nuclear deterrent and its leadership in the global francophone network. Its retreat from NATO's military structures in 1966 and its special relations with its former colonies and overseas territories underlined France's ambition to position itself between the two superpowers, the US and the USSR, as an independent power with a global outreach (Kolboom and Stark 2005: 365–7). It still seeks to prevent the rise of a single hegemon and envisions a multipolar world order, in which France retains a high rank, and strengthens the UN as a central multilateral arena. Not even France's humiliation in the wars in Indochina (1954), Suez (1956) and Algeria (1962) was able to impair the country's pursuit of global '*grandeur*' (Heuser 1998).

The Gaullist legacy also influenced parties of the moderate left: central foreign policy tenets remained valid during the socialist presidency of François Mitterrand (1981–95). However, the end of the Cold War and globalisation changed international power constellations to the disadvantage of France. Initially, German reunification and Germany's push for EU Eastern enlargement aroused French suspicion. The insight that France was a great power in decline slowly gained ground during the 1990s. The *cohabitation* government under President Mitterrand and Prime Minister Balladur started a gradual rapprochement with NATO; and since Neo-Gaullist President Chirac assumed office in 1995 (until 2007), France has increasingly relied on multilateralism, primarily enacted within the EU and the UN. This multilateralism is intended to compensate for France's loss of international influence and now extends to its development policies towards its former African colonies (Schmidt 2000: 246–50). Chirac put emphasis on North–South *problématiques* and a reform of France's African policies, which had long been shaped by clientelism and collusion with autocrats. The notorious economic–political networks with elites in the former colonies had

---

[4] See the chapter on the United States in this book.

personalised France's developmental policies in francophone Africa and were often accused of sleaze (Brüne and Mehler 1998).

Following the sobering experience of European powerlessness in the Balkan wars, Chirac encouraged the development of a *European Security and Defence Policy* at the end of the 1990s. The promotion of a muscular *l'Europe puissance* mirrors the traditional French policy vision of a multipolar world that requires strengthening Europe as a counterpart to the US. At the same time, Chirac pursued further ties with NATO. France has been a large contributor of troops to NATO's missions since the 1990s. This accelerated France's efforts to restructure its military for a broader mission spectrum. The 1994 White Book on national defence and security policy described new threats since the end of the Cold War and announced a reappraisal of France's force structure. In 1996, Chirac declared that the French military would be profoundly reformed and turned into a professional army. This marked a break with the myth of general conscription as a Republican 'school' and a service to the nation. However, the population did not protest against the professionalisation of the armed forces; military deployments are an accepted, traditional element of pursuing French national interests (Gauzy-Krieger and Meyer 2003: 5, 24).

Intermediate agencies such as parties, trade unions or civil associations only play a moderate role in French politics. The Gaullist emphasis on the unity of the nation, the public will and the global status of the country all imply a strong state and discourage the evolution of a sectional, intermediate tier of politics. Citizens are used to articulating their protests on the street (Mény 2005: 286–301). However, there is a fundamental consensus on foreign and security policy. Opinion polls usually measure high consent rates on the president's foreign policies. The population at large shares the elite's identity conception of France as guardian and defender of universal values. The catchwords of the French revolution in 1789, '*liberté, égalité, fraternité*', still encapsulate the core beliefs anchored within the country's cultural identity (Treacher 2003: 9–22).

1.2.2   *France's approach to international law: the example of the International Criminal Court*

Given France's traditional emphasis on its national sovereignty and independence, it might hardly be surprising that France was sceptical towards the creation of a strong, independent International Criminal Court (ICC). During the negotiations on the Rome Statute, it belonged to the small camp of 'sovereignist' states concerned about losing sovereign rights to the new court and facing new restrictions regarding military activities. After the new Labour government changed the UK's position in 1997, the French remained exceptional among the European states in their enduring opposition to central 'progressive' proposals of the 'like-minded' group of states (Deitelhoff and Burkard 2005: 21). The French delegation sought several opt-out clauses, favoured a 'state consent regime' for each trial, which would have rendered the court a mere paper tiger, and opposed the right of the ICC prosecutor to initiate an investigation (Weschler 2000: 102–3).

In a last-minute about-turn during the Rome conference, France finally supported the more progressive concept for the court after it managed to introduce a significant transitional provision in Article 124 of the Rome Statute: a signatory state may declare that, for a period of seven years after the statute has entered into force for the state concerned, it does not accept the court's jurisdiction with respect to war crimes when a crime is alleged to have been committed by its nationals or on its territory. France signed the Rome Statute in July 1998 and ratified it in June 2000.

1.2.3 *France's approach to international regimes: arms control and disarmament*

The so-called *force de frappe* generated a national myth, inspired by de Gaulle: the possession of nuclear weapons is closely related to the French identity and symbolises France's independence, international rank and invulnerability (Wisotzki 2002: 274–7). Following the end of the Cold War, French nuclear policy has highlighted the tensions between the doctrine of a strictly defensive nuclear deterrent and multilateral obligations resulting from the country's late accession (in 1992) to the Nuclear Non-proliferation Treaty (Wisotzki 2004: 9–12). President Mitterrand initiated several important unilateral disarmament measures such as the reduction of France's nuclear arsenal, the moratorium on testing and the halt on production of fissile material for military purposes. President Chirac continued this policy to some extent, but caused an international outcry when he ordered new nuclear weapons tests in the South Pacific. In 1998, France together with the UK ratified the nuclear test ban. The French leadership claims that it has to retain a 'minimal deterrence' to secure French independence and security as well as international peace and stability (Wisotzki 2004: 13–23). After the terrorist attacks of 11 September 2001, the French government re-emphasised the importance of nuclear weapons and tacitly welcomed the opposition of the Bush administration to further initiatives for disarmament and arms control.

In contrast, France actively supported the Biological Weapons Convention (BWC). Its late accession in 1984 was primarily due to the

BWC's lack of verification measures rather than to any French opposition to the prohibition of biological weapons (Hunger 2005: 15). After all, France was among the first states to prohibit these weapons by law (Littlewood 2005: 16). France was crucially involved in establishing an investigation mechanism of the UN Secretary-General in cases of the alleged use of biological and/or chemical weapons in 1982, and in initiating, and participating actively in, the negotiations on a verification protocol to the BWC in 1991 (Hunger 2005: 221–2; Littlewood 2005: 48, 101, 109).

France was an early advocate of dealing with the global landmine issue; one of the first measures taken by France in 1993 was President Mitterrand's announcement of a moratorium on the export of anti-personnel (AP) landmines and an official request to stage a review conference. During the 1995 conference, the French government announced that it would ban the production and trade of AP mines but not their use. However, it gradually changed its position between 1995 and 1997, partly due to public pressure from the French NGO campaign, and partly as a result of a political persuasion process within the government (Renoldner 2007: 116–31). France's late 'turn' towards the Ottawa Process in June 1997 was facilitated by the change of government following the 1997 parliamentary elections: the *cohabitation* executive of President Chirac with the socialist Jospin government defied opposition from the French military. Once on board, France 'became a strong advocate of the [Ottawa] Process and a member of the expanded core group'.[5]

1.2.4   France's approach to the UN

As one of the five permanent members of the Security Council ('P5'), France bears a strong responsibility for the UN. The permanent seat along with its status as a nuclear weapon state is crucial for France's claim to be a major power (Tardy 2002: 932–5). The relationship between the UN and France was not always tension-free: on the one hand, the UN embodies the universal values that are inscribed in French national identity and that France claims to defend in the international realm; on the other hand, there were a number of conflicts in the era of decolonisation. From the 1960s onwards, however, the relationship improved. The UN has provided a forum for France to express its '*vocation mondiale*' – and at times also to present itself as

---

[5] 'Landmine Monitor, France Mine Ban Policy, 1999'. Online: www.the-monitor.org/index.php/publications/display?act=submit&pqs_year=1999&pqs_type=lm&pqs_report=france&pqs_section=%23Heading10062#Heading10062.

a political alternative to the US. The UN is highly appreciated as it constitutes a multiplier for France's international power (Tardy 2002: 939). The end of the Cold War did not reduce this important role of the UN; on the contrary, France became one of the most active members of the UN, including its offer in 1991 to provide a quick reaction force of 1,000 soldiers on a standby basis (Pitette 1990: 74). The intention was to strengthen the UN as the central actor in international crisis management since France regards the Security Council as conducive to pursuing French foreign policy interests (Tardy 2002: 936–40).

1.2.5 Alliance, bilateral and regional relations

The United States and NATO: Unlike Britain and Germany, the French political elite after 1945 felt a permanent need to pursue and assert French autonomy and keep some distance vis-à-vis the US. Consequently, France's attitude towards NATO has been ambivalent: De Gaulle saw NATO as an instrument of the US to exert its hegemony within Europe, but he also recognised it as a useful military alliance. France aimed at establishing a European security arrangement under French leadership so as to limit US influence in Europe, but failed in these attempts. France left the military structures of NATO in 1966 but remained in NATO's political structures. After the end of the Cold War, President Mitterrand continued to be critical towards NATO as he considered that the Alliance had lost its purpose (Schmidt 2000: 244–6). France initially also opposed the enlargement of NATO's missions and membership (Woyke 2000: 132–43). However, a gradual rapprochement with NATO began during the *cohabitation* government of Mitterrand and Prime Minister Balladur, which was pursued further by the subsequent Chirac presidency. France participated in NATO's missions in the Balkans in the early 1990s. In 1995, it took up its seat on the military committee and took full part in meetings of defence ministers, finally rejoining NATO's integrated military structure in 2009.[6] These concessions resulted from France's interest in not becoming marginalised in the Alliance when NATO played a crucial role in international security affairs. Nevertheless, the strengthening of a European pillar of defence remained central to France and shaped its policy towards the EU (Wisotzki 2002: 384–6).

---

[6] This rapprochement culminated in President Sarkozy's announcement in March 2009 that France would rejoin NATO as a full member. Sarkozy argued that France would be better off having a say in NATO's actions rather than committing resources without any influence; 'Sarkozy: France Will Return to NATO', 11 March 2009. Online: www.cnn.com/2009/WORLD/europe/03/11/france.sarkozy.nato/index.html.

EU and Franco-German relations: Ambivalence is also a characteristic of France's policy towards the EU: on the one hand, France advocates a strong, autonomous Europe; on the other hand, France is reluctant to give up sovereignty and prefers intergovernmental forms of cooperation (Boniface 1998: 81–4). French politicians played a crucial role in establishing the European Communities in the 1950s, which were designed to integrate and control West Germany. Under de Gaulle, French policy towards Europe became more instrumental; the vision of an intergovernmentally coordinated 'Europe of Nations' under the leadership of France was to provide a counterweight to the two superpowers, the US and the USSR. De Gaulle clung to a 'sovereignist' notion of Europe and rejected supranational elements. Presidents Giscard d'Estaing and Mitterrand accepted the need for further steps towards integration and close cooperation with integration-friendly Germany (Müller-Brandeck-Bocquet 2005: 385–9).

Following the end of the Cold War and German unification, which initially caused concern in France, France sought to contain united Germany within a political union and an economic and monetary union, despite the fact that this would also imply a loss of its own sovereignty. Under the presidencies of Mitterrand and Chirac, France accepted the enhanced status of the European Parliament and the extension of majority decisions in the Council. In the light of the failure of the Europeans in the Kosovo crisis, Chirac, together with his British partners, pushed for a European Security and Defence Policy (ESDP). The older French concept of an independent, powerful '*Europe puissance*' as a counterweight to the US re-emerged in this initiative for a common military force, but again highlighted the dilemma that France remains averse to giving up its sovereignty – and that its preferences often differ from those of its closest partner, Germany (Müller-Brandeck-Bocquet 2008).

Franco-German relations proved to be the driving force of European integration for decades. The former 'hereditary enemies' established numerous bilateral institutional links and staged their reconciliation after the Second World War as a steadfast friendship that would endure all setbacks and crises that tried it time and again (Buffet and Heuser 1998). Since Germany and France had many opposing interests, their informal coordination was most crucial for achieving compromises at the highest European level (Müller-Brandeck-Bocquet 2008). Despite Germany's larger population and stronger economy, France is able to demonstrate a degree of superiority in the military sector (in addition to its P5 status), and through its significant participation in multilateral military operations and unilateral deployments in its African zone of influence.

Close relations with Arab countries: In contrast to other European countries in our sample, France has long-standing privileged relations with many Arab countries (Meyrede 1999; Styan 2006). This is an important aspect in understanding its position towards the two wars against Iraq (Bonnefous 1998: 60–2; Styan 2006: 174–82). The French *politique arabe* encompasses the Maghreb, the Middle East and the Gulf region, where France pursues different interests. Due to its colonial history, France entertains the closest relations with the Maghreb states, which remained an important zone of influence after decolonisation. As far as the Middle East is concerned, French diplomacy is quite active in the Palestinian–Israeli conflict.

1.3   Conclusion: France's foreign policy role profile

French foreign policy has for decades been marked by ambiguities. Gaullist ideas about France's exceptional status in world politics still prevail in French national identity, although the status of the country has been perceived as declining since the end of the bipolar world order. France regards itself as a cultural exception, distinguished by its leadership of the francophone world. The notion that France, as the cradle and guardian of human rights, liberty and democracy, has a global *mission civilisatrice* still exists (Roche 2000: 394–7), but has not prevented French elites from collaborating with dictators. As a former colonial power with a large zone of influence in francophone Africa and Asia and as one of the P5 in the UN Security Council, France pursues an active diplomacy in many conflicts in the world. In particular, it has sought to conduct an independent pro-Arab policy that demonstrates its claim to remaining a great power in Africa and the Middle East (Styan 2006).

Following the end of the Cold War and under the increasing pressure of globalisation, France has been searching for a new role in the world, without renouncing the Gaullist idea of *grandeur*, of France as a 'special nation' and a great power (Kessler and Charillon 2002: 104). France has increasingly been making use of the EU to compensate for its own loss of national power, building '*l'Europe puissance*' as an independent counterpart to the US '*hyperpuissance*'. French foreign policy today is more committed to multilateralism, and the concept of French exceptionalism is complemented by a European exceptionalism (Treacher 2003: 2–5; Morisse-Schilbach 2006: 77).

2   Decision-making and public debates on the Gulf War, Kosovo War and Iraq War

2.1   *France and the Gulf War 1990–1991*

2.1.1   *The road to war*

From the 1970s onwards, France had built up amiable political and profitable economic relations with Iraq. French oil companies had invested hugely: France was Iraq's third-largest trading partner, supplied the Tammuz nuclear research centre (which provided the basis for teaching Iraqi experts skills that could be used in the country's nuclear weapons programme) and emerged as a significant arms supplier, notably during the Iraqi war against Iran. French–Iraqi relations thrived not least because the French government observed a strict policy of non-interference, keeping silent on the violent suppression of the Kurdish minority and the extensive human rights violations under Saddam Hussein (Morizet 1990). There were concerns that a war would weaken France's competitive position in the Gulf region in favour of their Anglo-Saxon 'rivals' (Bonnefous 1990: 39). Thus, France sought to mediate a peaceful settlement to the Gulf crisis until the very end; after these efforts failed, it participated in the war with substantial forces.

Following Iraq's invasion of Kuwait in August 1990, Mitterrand supported UN sanctions against Iraq and dispatched the aircraft carrier *Clemenceau* to the Gulf. While French frigates helped enforce the naval blockade, French diplomats initially pursued a mediating strategy that built upon France's traditionally close relations with the Arab countries and a well-functioning, informal information network within the region. France attempted to prevent an escalation and an expansion of the Gulf conflict, not least because many people of Arab origin live in France. Yet, Mitterrand and Prime Minister Rocard made clear from an early stage that Iraq's blatant breach of international law had precipitated the world into a 'logic of war' (Gresh and Vidal 1991: 270–2). French policies were shaped by cooperation with the Western allies, the embargo, military support for states on the Arab peninsula and negotiations for a peaceful settlement to the conflict (Hadas-Lebel 1991: 16–20; Portelli 1991: 28; Frémeaux 1995: 120–2). The French executive was convinced that the invasion of Kuwait must not be tolerated, but also concerned that France's friendly relations with Iraq and other Arab countries were at stake; this excluded an overly offensive strategy (Styan 2006: 176–9).

France began to play a more active role during the September meeting of the countries that had agreed to participate in *Operation Desert*

Shield. It gave up its defensive posture after the Iraqi assault on the French embassy in Kuwait on 14 September forced Mitterrand to demonstrate that France would not accept such aggression (Gresh and Vidal 1991: 278; Frémeaux 1995: 121–5). He significantly raised the number of ground troops, tanks and aircraft in the Gulf, starting the military build-up that would later became *Opération Daguet,* which included the dispatch of the Sixth Light Armoured Division and Foreign Legion troops. Parallel to this military build-up, France utilised its multiple informal negotiating channels with Arab leaders to launch several peace initiatives.

Mitterrand irritated the US by cautiously linking a negotiated withdrawal by Iraq with the Palestinian issue and suggesting an international conference on several conflicts in the Middle East. In a speech to the UN on 24 September, he indicated that a broader Middle East settlement was desirable (Wood 1993: 34–5). France insisted on Iraq releasing all Western hostages before further negotiations would be possible. French envoys used their relations with Palestinian leader Yasser Arafat to obtain this release, but this initially only involved the freedom of 330 French hostages, at the end of October. This was heavily criticised by the US (Gresh and Vidal 1991: 281–3).

Over a period of months, France continued its diplomatic activities for a peaceful settlement, but as a permanent member of the UN Security Council it also supported the ultimatum for an Iraqi withdrawal in UN Resolution 678. Shortly before this ultimatum expired on 15 January 1991, France used several channels to avoid war at the last minute (Styan 2006: 177–8). Mitterrand sent another envoy to Baghdad to meet with Saddam Hussein on 5 January, but without results. In parallel, French Foreign Minister Dumas conveyed a formal peace proposal to the Iraqi ambassador in Paris on 10 January. In a futile last-ditch attempt on 14 January, Mitterrand proposed a UN draft resolution, still seeking a peaceful solution through an international conference. After all French initiatives had failed, Mitterrand accepted war as inevitable (Frémeaux 1995: 123–5).

France's ambivalent policy was also a result of domestic concerns: participation in a war against Iraq was controversial because it could jeopardise the country's traditionally close relations with the Arab world and because France seemed to be subordinating itself to the US. A prospective war aroused strong protests in France; the largest anti-war demonstration on 12 January 1991 mobilised 100,000 people in Paris. The political executive was divided. Mitterrand's Defence Minister Chevènement criticised the president's policy and resigned after the war had started. He refused to accept the change in French strategy from defensive to offensive during the crisis and was particularly concerned that France would surrender its independent strategy and military command to the US (Frémeaux 1995: 185–8; Styan 2006: 179). President Mitterrand dominated the domestic decision-making process; his strategy was broadly in line with Gaullist traditions (Hadas-Lebel 1991: 17–19). During the crisis, Mitterrand prepared the French for a potential war in addresses to the people; after all negotiations had failed, a majority supported the president's decision to participate in the war (Frémeaux 1995: 155). A majority of parliamentarians also supported the president's policy, with the exception of the MPs of the Parti Communiste and the Front National. Parliament was called to a (purely symbolic) vote on French participation in the war on 16 January, only hours before fighting began. Out of 568 MPs, 523 voted for and 43 against participation, with two abstentions.

2.1.2   Content analysis of parliamentary debates

The Assemblée Nationale held two major debates on the Gulf crisis, on 27 August 1990 and on 16 January 1991. Out of the 22 coded speeches, 16 speakers supported French participation in a military action (Table 7.1) and 6 speakers rejected it (Table 7.2).

As Table 7.1 reveals, three of the four most frequent arguments used by supporters of military action belong to the field of international law. Many supporters declared that France must enforce international law and strengthen the role of the UN in this precarious transitional period following the end of the Cold War (93.8 per cent). The breach of international law by Iraq was unacceptable and war inevitable after peaceful means had been exhausted (56.3 per cent). Nearly two-thirds of the supporters also argued that French attempts to settle the conflict needed to be backed by a military show of force in the Gulf region. Half of the supporters recognised a threat to world order emerging from Iraqi aggression. Closely connected were references to France's identity as guardian of universal values and as a country with a special international *rang*: France as one of the P5 should bolster the UN and assume responsibility for protecting world order. One-third of supporters also expressed concern for regional stability in the Gulf region. In sum, French advocates of the war relied heavily on 'order'-related arguments.

The six speakers who rejected French participation in the war (depicted in Table 7.2) most frequently appealed to universal or democratic values. Opponents feared that a war would claim many casualties among French soldiers (all speakers) and among Iraqi civilians (two-thirds of the speakers). They doubted that peaceful means had

Table 7.1 *Frequencies of arguments, Gulf War, France, supporters only (n = 16); extracts of results*[a]

Code	Argument	Number of speakers	Percentage of speakers
4101	Enforce international law/support UN	15	93.8
1104	Show of force	10	62.5
4201	Covered by international law	9	56.3
4202	Peaceful means exhausted	9	56.3
5102	Threat to world order	8	50
3101	Identity norms	6	37.5
1103	Regional stability	6	37.5
2201	Alliance consensus	6	37.5

[a] Full lists of results for this and all following tables are available from the author.

Table 7.2 *Frequencies of arguments, Gulf War, France, opponents only (n = 6); extracts of results*

Code	Argument	Number of speakers	Percentage of speakers
6302	Casualty aversion (own soldiers)	6	100
5303	Civilian casualties	4	66.7
4302	Peaceful means not exhausted	4	66.7
6301	Democratic norms/procedures contra war	4	66.7
1303	Regional instability	3	50

really been exhausted. Two-thirds of the speakers criticised the fact that the French executive had marginalised parliamentary powers in the crisis; in particular they objected that the parliamentary vote had been scheduled so late in the process and had only symbolic meaning. Half of the opponents foresaw regional instability caused by a war in the Gulf.

2.1.3   Newspaper debates

The commentaries in both the liberal *Le Monde* and the conservative *Le Figaro* condemned the Iraqi invasion of Kuwait. *Le Figaro* anticipated the necessity of a war more clearly, while *Le Monde* also published more critical positions. Both newspapers left no doubt that Saddam Hussein was a brutal aggressor. Commentaries in *Le Monde* held military force as necessary to back up economic sanctions;[7] but the newspaper also made the Arab side heard, which was critical of a total condemnation of Iraq and pointed to the roots of the conflict in Western imperialism. It was feared that the Gulf crisis would expand into a large military conflict involving the entire Middle East. Commentaries saw an increasing probability of French participation in the war following the Iraqi assault on the French embassy in Kuwait. In January 1991, more commentaries argued against a war, stating that one had to deal with the roots of the regional conflicts. Advocates of a war argued that France carried a responsibility for international order; they pointed to the brutal aggression of Saddam Hussein's regime and to the military superiority of the Western allies.[8]

Commentaries in *Le Figaro* initially dealt with the challenges posed by a new world order, which might imperil France's standing in the world.[9] France should thus strengthen the UN and international law and respond unambiguously to Iraq's breach of international law. From October onwards, positions advocating war became more frequent:[10] international law had to be enforced, democratic values should be promoted in the Gulf region and diplomatic efforts had to be backed by credible signals of military resolve. But in a similar way to the president's policy, the newspaper expected viable chances for a peaceful solution if Saddam were to back down.

2.1.4   Public opinion polls

There were numerous public opinion polls on the attitudes of the French towards participation in a war in the Gulf region. French public opinion was rather volatile during the crisis.[11]

---

[7] E.g. Alain Frachon 1990. 'Jérusalem: le prochain objectif de M. Saddam Hussein est la Jordanie', *Le Monde*, 6 August; Theo Klein 1990. 'Amis arabes, choisissez', *Le Monde*, 22 August; Rafic Boustani and Philippe Fargues 1990. 'Proche Orient entre golfe et méditerranée', *Le Monde*, 13 October.

[8] E.g. Jean Louis Dufour 1991. 'Golfe: La guerre sera courte', *Le Monde*, 8 January; Jean Pierre Langellier 1991. 'La double exigence de M. Mitterrand', *Le Monde*, 11 January; Bernard Kouchner 1991. 'Démocraties L'après-guerre a commencée', *Le Monde*, 16 January.

[9] E.g. Jacques Jacquet-Francillon 1990. 'Gendarmes du monde?', *Le Figaro*, 4 August; François Hauter 1990. 'George Bush: porté par histoire, c'est maintenant son heure de vérité', *Le Figaro*, 10 August; Marcel Merle 1990. 'L'Irak et le droit international', *Le Figaro*, 26 August; Jacques Jacquet-Francillon 1990. 'Guerre ou paix?', *Le Figaro*, 9 September.

[10] E.g. Thierry de Montbrial 1990. 'Nous ne sommes pas à Munich', *Le Figaro*, 5 October; Jacques Jacquet-Francillon 1990. 'Ne pas céder', *Le Figaro*, 24 October; Michel Massenet 1990. 'Golfe: le parti de la guerre', *Le Figaro*, 5 November.

[11] For all following data, see: *IPSOS/Le Point*: 'Les français et la crise du Golfe Persique', 8, 9 August 1990; *IFOP/Le Figaro*: 'Les français et la crise du Golfe Persique', 14, 16

The Iraqi attack on the French embassy in Kuwait in mid-September caused an outcry in France and prompted a majority of the respondents (59 per cent) to favour French military action in the following weeks. After the Iraqi regime apologised and released the French hostages, a majority of respondents once again opted against military action, leading to a drop in military support to 36 per cent in November. In the first weeks of January, a majority of 57 per cent still rejected participation in a war and hoped for a last-minute peaceful solution. This attitude changed, however, with the expiry of the UN ultimatum of 15 January and the beginning of the war one day later. Some 65 per cent of the respondents now backed Mitterrand's decision to take part in the war. This change in public attitude reflected the numerous attempts by the French government to negotiate a peaceful settlement until the very end. Once this had failed, the public accepted the military enforcement of international law as inevitable.

2.1.5   Conclusion: explaining France's participation in the Gulf War

France's participation in the Gulf War was controversial; critics feared that France would endanger its long-standing relations with Arab countries and would surrender too much autonomy to the US. Consequently, the French security elite lamented the US 'power monopoly' once the war was over (e.g. de la Gorce 1991). President Mitterrand, who dominated the decision-making process, sought to mediate a peaceful solution to the crisis until the last minute, but after having failed, he supported the war with significant military forces. Mitterrand's policies signalled ambivalent messages to his Western allies (Styan 2006: 176), but he acted in accordance with majority public opinion and parliament. Although the newspapers published a number of critical voices, by and large they supported the president's policy.

Most crucial for France's participation in the Gulf War was Iraq's blatant breach of international law, which required a firm response. Iraq's

---

August 1990; *IFOP/Profession Politique*: 'La crise dans le golfe persique et la position des hommes politiques français', 13–14 September 1990; *SOFRES/Le Figaro*: 'Les français et la crise du Golfe Persique', 22–23, 28 August, 22–26 September 1990; 'La crise dans le Golfe', 7, 8 November 1990; 'La crise du Golfe Persique', 20–22 November 1990, 7–9 January 1991, 'La guerre du Golfe Persique', 17 January 1991; *CSA*: 'La crise dans le golfe persique', 27, 29 August, 10, 11, 25, 26 September, 29, 30 October 1990; 'La guerre du Golfe Persique', 18 January 1991; *HARRIS/Le Nouvel Observateur*: 'La crise dans le golfe persique', 28, 29 September 1990; *BVA/Paris-Match*: 'La crise du golfe persique', 1–4, 15–19 October 1990; 'Baromètre: Coté du Président, du 1e ministre, Action gouvernementale et confiance', 23–25 October 1990; *BVA*: 'La crise du golfe persique', 4–5, 12, 13 January 1991; *BVA/Libération*: 'La guerre du Golfe Persique', 18 January 1991.

aggression should not be allowed to set a precedent in international politics following the end of the Cold War. France sought to strengthen the UN, which it regarded as a decisive player in the new world order and an arena for its own global leadership ambitions (Bonnefous 1991: 62). Mitterrand saw the risk that France might be isolated among the Western allies and might lose its international *rang* if it abstained from the war. Nevertheless, the French executive demonstrated French autonomy by launching numerous negotiations in the Arab world in order to avert a war and by proposing an international conference until the very end, to the dismay of the US.

2.2   France and the Kosovo War 1998–1999

2.2.1   The road to war

France played an active role throughout the Kosovo crisis, using bilateral initiatives with Germany and the UK or multilateral fora such as the Balkan Contact Group and the UN Security Council. Against the historical background of close relations with Serbia, the French *cohabitation* government under neo-Gaullist President Chirac and socialist Prime Minister Jospin sought a neutral mediator role during most of the run-up to the war and tried to keep Russia on board; nevertheless, it proved a reliable ally to the US once bombing had started.

When the Kosovo crisis intensified with the massacres in Dreniça in February/March 1998, the Balkan Contact Group condemned the Serbian actions and worked on drafts for a political solution and sanctions. Against the background of its close relations with Serbia, France tried to prevent a harsh policy line against Slobodan Milošević and wanted to accord Serbia more time to comply with the demands of the Contact Group. While the EU decreed sanctions, France departed from cooperative actions against Milošević's regime and then increasingly bypassed the EU by pursuing a national negotiating line (Tardy 2000: 5; Maull and Stahl 2002: 96–8; Stahl 2006: 191–3). As a permanent member of the UN Security Council, France supported the arms embargo against Yugoslavia in Resolution 1160 at the end of March 1998. One month later, President Chirac addressed Milošević directly in a personal letter, making clear how serious the situation was. Whereas NATO developed an increasingly high profile in the crisis, the French government continued to play an active mediator role, seeking diplomatic solutions and refraining from military threats (Roux 1999; Maull and Stahl 2002: 96).

France strongly criticised NATO's decision to prepare for military action despite the fact that UN Resolution 1199 of 23 September 1998 contained no clear mandate for the use of force. The French insisted on authorisation by the UNSC and demanded the involvement of Russia in case of an intervention (Tardy 2000: 7–8; Maull and Stahl 2002: 98). France actively supported the Holbrooke–Milošević agreement of October 1998 and contributed half of the troops for the subsequent observer mission. While this agreement contained the conflict for a short while, fighting intensified again during December and January. The turning point was the so-called 'massacre of Račak' on 15 January 1999, which was attributed to the Serbs and caused an international outcry. From then on, the hitherto hesitant France, like all Western allies, pursued a harsher course. During a visit to London, President Chirac and British Prime Minister Blair stated that military intervention might be necessary. The French government was now prepared to accept a limitation of Serbian sovereignty in Kosovo, but deemed a revision of borders and a regime change in Serbia unacceptable (Maull and Stahl 2002: 95).

The Contact Group summoned the conflict parties to negotiate with each other to avert a military intervention. The US, UK and France, though disagreeing on several crucial issues, exerted pressure on the conflict parties to push through an agreement, the conditions of which the Serbs found unacceptable. The fact that the negotiations took place in Rambouillet and later in Paris underlined the major role that France sought to play in mediating a peaceful settlement (Tardy 2000: 4, 9). The French and British foreign ministers, Védrine and Cook, chaired the negotiations, but they disagreed on several matters. In contrast to the UK, France did not consider a mediator from the EU desirable. The French also strongly criticised the massive American interference in the negotiations. France rejected US demands for a firm stance and military threats against Milošević. French ministers stressed at the outset of the conference that France saw no automatic triggering of air strikes if the negotiations failed. Only after the ultimate breakdown of the talks did Chirac blame this outcome on the Serbian side (Stahl 2006: 200, 214). When war started, France once again proved a reliable ally, and accounted for about 10 per cent of NATO's forces (Rynning 2000: 64; Lukic 2003: 353–4).

The Kosovo crisis posed a domestic challenge for President Chirac. The traditionally strong presidential position was weakened by a *cohabitation* government. Chirac had to govern with a 'pluralist left', composed of the socialists, Greens, radicals, communists and a new party founded by the former socialist Chevènement. While many left-wing parliamentarians justified the war, the communists demanded an end to the air strikes and the resumption of negotiations just a few days after the beginning of air operations (Rathbun 2004: 146–51). The neo-Gaullist Chirac had disagreements with his socialist prime minister, but Jospin's foreign political role remained limited (Rynning 2000: 62–70). Chirac used the Kosovo crisis to demonstrate his dominance of the French executive; he shaped the decision-making process together with a close circle of associates (Rouleau 1999: 7). Remarkably, there was no substantial parliamentary debate in the run-up to the war. Since the NATO intervention was not formally declared a 'war', the Assemblée Nationale had no formal decision-making powers (Tardy 2000: 10–12).

2.2.2   Content analysis of parliamentary debates

As the French parliament had conducted no substantial debate prior to the war, there were only few speeches eligible for content analysis. It was only *after* the war had begun that a controversial debate took place (Stahl 2006: 206–8, 219). We thus had to include speeches beyond our actual period of investigation.[12] Although many speakers acknowledged that a humanitarian disaster had to be prevented, conservative and Liberal Party members feared France's loss of independence in a NATO-led military campaign, while some MPs of the ruling left-wing parties rejected the war, blaming it on the US and complaining about the damage done to the UN by NATO's act of self-empowerment. This created a difficult situation for the *cohabitation* and in particular for Prime Minister Jospin, who had justified the air strikes as an exceptional humanitarian emergency (Kempin 2008: 65–76). Critics on the left and right demanded a quick initiative to achieve a non-violent solution and limit the growing US influence in Europe. Such arguments were often connected with demands for strengthening an independent European power that could pacify the continent on its own.

Out of the 26 speeches coded, 20 were in favour of (Table 7.3) and 6 (from the left wing) against an intervention in Kosovo (Table 7.4).

As Table 7.3 shows, most war supporters argued that peaceful means had been exhausted (no surprise, as most speeches were made after the war had started) and that a humanitarian catastrophe had to be prevented. Nearly a third of the supporters depicted Milošević as a dangerous enemy and two-thirds of the speakers deemed a military threat necessary to compel him to give in. A third of the supporters also referred to France's international rank and responsibility to play a leadership role in ending the conflict. Although there was no UN

---

[12] Additional speeches by President Chirac were also included since the French president does not speak to parliament.

Table 7.3 *Frequencies of arguments, Kosovo War, France, supporters only*
(n = 20); extracts of results

Code	Argument	Number of speakers	Percentage of speakers
4202	Peaceful means exhausted	14	70
5101	Humanitarian catastrophe	14	70
1104	Show of force	13	65
3101	Identity norms	7	35
4201	Covered by international law	7	35
2201	Alliance consensus	6	30
7101	Enemy image of adversary	6	30

Table 7.4 *Frequencies of arguments, Kosovo War, France, opponents only*
(n = 6); extracts of results

Code	Argument	Number of speakers	Percentage of speakers
4302	Peaceful means not exhausted	5	83.3
4301	No UN mandate/damage to UN	4	66.7
1303	Regional instability	3	50
5303	Civilian casualties	3	50
6301	Democratic norms/procedures contra war	3	50

authorisation for using force, a third still argued that military action was covered by international law and that there was an alliance consensus to take a firm stance towards Serbia.

The opponents, depicted in Table 7.4, most frequently referred to international law and universal and democratic values to justify their rejection of the war: five out of six opponents considered peaceful means not yet exhausted, and four out of six pointed to the lack of a mandate from the UN. Half of the opponents feared that the intervention would cause many civilian casualties and a further destabilisation of the Balkan region. In addition, they criticised the fact that the executive had prevented parliament from exerting its democratic powers in the process.

2.2.3   Newspaper debates

The commentaries in the liberal newspaper *Le Monde* and the conservative *Le Figaro* were sometimes not clear about support for or rejection of a war, but often discussed the broader setting such as its legality, the future of NATO, a new concept for the EU or the implications for transatlantic relations. *Le Monde* initially addressed problems of an intervention without UN authorisation, an expansion of NATO missions and the weakness of the EU during the crisis. While it was hoped that the Holbrooke–Milošević agreement would avert war, a credible military threat was deemed necessary to enforce compliance. Following the 'massacre of Račak', more commentaries advocated military intervention to stop Milošević.[13] Preventing a humanitarian disaster was cited as the lesson learnt from the Bosnian war. *Le Monde* also emphasised the importance of collective European action and France's leadership role in dealing with this humanitarian crisis. The lines of argumentation in *Le Figaro* were similar;[14] the particular focus was on Europe as a political actor. The commentaries demanded an independent, powerful Europe, where France would have a leading position and where the US would lose its influence. Commentaries debated the dilemma that the intervention was not mandated by the UN, but that non-intervention would damage NATO's credibility. While advocates pointed to the catastrophic humanitarian situation in Kosovo, some accepted the overall goals of an intervention as laudable, but still criticised the use of force.

2.2.4   Public opinion polls

The Kosovo conflict aroused moderate public attention during 1998; only Foreign Minister Védrine accentuated the role of France as a major power, important mediator and counterweight to the US in public. Jospin and Chirac only turned their attention to the French public from February 1999 onwards (Stahl 2006: 209, 233). Reflecting the lack of parliamentary debate prior to the war, there were no opinion polls available for this period, only polls conducted after the start of the war; for this reason we had to deviate from our rule only to look at pre-war polls. This might inflate approval rates by a temporary 'rally around the flag' effect. Although some intellectuals and politicians heavily criticised the war, polls indicated that a majority of the population supported it. At the end of March 1999, 57 per cent of the respondents endorsed the air strikes, mainly because they deemed them necessary to end the

---

[13] E.g. Martin Plichta 1999. 'Seul un déploiement de forces militaires peut changer la situation', *Le Monde*, 20 January; Emmanuel Wallon 1999. 'Kosovo: guérir du syndrome de répétition', *Le Monde*, 27 February; Jean-Christophe Rufin 1999. 'L'OTAN, les humanitaires et la mort', *Le Monde*, 20 March.

[14] E.g. Michel Barnier 1998. 'La leçon de Sarajevo', *Le Figaro*, 21 September; Thierry de Montbrial 1998. 'Kosovo: les puissances paralysées', *Le Figaro*, 8 October; Arnaud de la Grange 1999. 'Conflits; La déraison des armes', *Le Figaro*, 25 February.

humanitarian disaster. A majority also approved French participation in NATO's intervention.[15] Other polls showed that 60 per cent would have even supported the deployment of ground troops if the bombing had not had the desired effect (Stahl 2006: 239).

2.2.5   Conclusion: explaining France's participation in the Kosovo War

Generally considered to be pro-Serbian, France pursued an active diplomacy in several multilateral and bilateral settings and, similarly to the situation in the Gulf conflict, the French president hoped to avert war until the end. As a lesson learnt from the Bosnian War, the prevention of a humanitarian disaster was the supreme justification for French participation in the military intervention. The French government attempted to strengthen France's leadership position in Europe, but it failed to keep the US out of this violent crisis on Western Europe's doorstep. Due to its traditionally reserved attitude towards NATO, France initially also sought to limit NATO's role and to strengthen the UN. The lack of an explicit UN mandate for NATO's intervention was quite controversial in France, which had hoped to keep Russia involved in a consensual solution to the Kosovo conflict. Finally, the French had to resign themselves to the insight that Europe was still too weak as a collective political actor to handle the crisis on its own and that the humanitarian catastrophe called for firm action; thus, the country joined the Western allies in bombing the Federal Republic of Yugoslavia. As with participation in the Gulf War, the French leadership wanted to prevent France from becoming isolated from its Western allies, but to still demonstrate the country's independence and international standing.

The Kosovo crisis touched on core values encapsulated in France's collective identity: its proclaimed *mission civilisatrice*, the ambition to be a major power and thus to have a special responsibility, as well as its geopolitically inspired image of Europe as a counterweight to the US (Maull and Stahl 2002: 105). In justifying military intervention, French speakers usually linked the promotion of French interests with the promotion of universal objectives. The humanitarian crisis overshadowed even France's defence of the prerogatives of the UN Security Council (Jospin 1999: 12). President Chirac could count on a large national consensus that France had a particular responsibility as a European great power to stop a humanitarian catastrophe. His policy was supported

[15] *IPSOS/JDD*, 'L'opinion Français à l'égard de la situation en Yougoslavie', 26–27 March 1999; *CSA/Le Parisien*, 'Kosovo: Les bombardements inquiètent les Français', 26–27 March 1999; *IFOP/L'Express*, 'Oui à une intervention terrestre au Kosovo', 29 March 1999.

by a majority in parliament and the public. It must be noted, however, that it was due to the precarious arrangement of a right-wing/pluralist left-wing *cohabitation* government that there was little resonance to the Kosovo crisis in parliament and among the population prior to the war. The public debate only intensified after the war had started and showed that the national consensus on the use of force was rather fragile. Once more, a stronger Europe was seen as the political requirement emerging from the war (Gnesotto 1999).

2.3   France and the Iraq War 2003

2.3.1   Domestic decision-making process

During the Iraq crisis of 2002/3, the French neo-Gaullist government under the leadership of re-elected President Chirac and Prime Minister Raffarin acted as a powerful counterweight to the US–British allies who were pressing for military action against Saddam Hussein from summer 2002 onwards. France recognised that Iraq might pose a threat *if* the regime was *proved* to have weapons of mass destruction (WMD) or to be active in related weapon programmes – and the French government suspected that this was the case just as much as anybody else (Raffarin 2002: 7–8). Nevertheless, Iraq was to be given due time to cooperate with the UN weapons inspectors again and to be disarmed peacefully. Chirac sought to prevent a hasty decision to use force and rejected a forcible regime change that was not mandated by UN resolutions (Kempin 2008: 171).

French diplomats, who once again made use of their close relations with the Arab world, again actively sought to mediate a peaceful solution and to place the UN in the driving seat. France as a P5 member was crucial in submitting UNSC Resolution 1441 of 8 November 2002, which demanded the immediate and complete disarmament of Iraq and the declaration of all its WMD to the Security Council. The resolution was passed unanimously as a 'final warning'. While US President Bush considered that this resolution mandated military action in case of non-compliance, France refused 'automaticity', demanded more time for the UN weapons inspectors and insisted upon a second resolution as necessary authorisation of the use of force (Colard 2004: 213–15; Cogan 2005: 235–7). France kept open the possibility of military action until the beginning of 2003 if Iraq were not to comply. But from January 2003 onwards the French defied the 'pre-emptive' US strategy and positioned themselves as leader of the 'coalition of the unwilling' (Styan 2006: 188–9). Although Chirac saw no 'logic of war' resulting from Resolution 1441, he assured the US and UK of French support in case of an attack involving Iraqi chemical or biological weapons and granted flyover rights.

When the US and UK governments intensified their plans for military action at the end of 2002 on the grounds of alleged Iraqi non-compliance, France together with Russia and Germany developed several initiatives in the UNSC to halt this escalation and allow time for more intensive inspections. However, France indicated that it would support a second resolution authorising military action if Iraq did not fully cooperate and peaceful disarmament proved impossible (Styan 2006: 189). Strengthening the UN was a supreme French goal. From January to March 2003, France played a key role as veto power in the UNSC.

French Foreign Minister de Villepin levelled heavy criticism at the US in several speeches to the UNSC. On 20 January 2003, he declared that military action was absolutely not justified at that time and that France would consider using its veto (Cogan 2005: 239–41). Chirac hoped that the US and UK would depart from their plans if it was clear that they would not get a majority in the Security Council. Responding to US Secretary of State Colin Powell's controversial presentation of 'evidence' for Iraq's putative WMD programmes to the Security Council on 5 February, de Villepin suggested an intensification of inspections and a peaceful solution to the conflict. He resolutely refuted the alleged tie between Iraq and Al-Qaeda (de Villepin 2003a: 10). As the US and UK failed to present evidence of Iraq's WMD, France developed practical proposals to continue the inspections (de Villepin 2003a: 8) while explicitly threatening to use its veto against a resolution authorising the use of force – a position shared by China and Russia. After UNMOVIC chairman Hans Blix reported progress in cooperation with Iraq on 7 March 2003, Chirac told the French people in a televised address on 10 March that the French government would reject a war if there was no evidence for the possession of WMD (Styan 2004: 382; Cogan 2005: 238): 'Ma position c'est que quelles que soient les circonstances, la France votera "non" parce qu'elle considère ce soir qu'il n'y a pas lieu de faire une guerre pour atteindre l'objectif que nous avons fixé, c'est-à-dire le désarmement de l'Irak.'[16]

Chirac acted in accordance with the opinions of the majority of the French public and politicians. A war against Iraq without a UN mandate was very unpopular. However, there was relief that France actually did not have to use the veto, as the supporters of military action

---

[16] President Chirac on TF1 and France 2, cited in 'Quelles que soient les circonstances, la France votera non', *Le Monde*, 11 March 2003.

withdrew the draft resolution when it became clear that there was no majority in favour. The French used the Franco-African summit in February in Paris as well as de Villepin's trips to the capitals of all three African members of the UNSC on 10 March to secure their votes (Styan 2006: 191). The run-up to, and the aftermath of, the war indicated the degree of alienation from the US. There was the perception that the Bush administration wished to humiliate France, an attack on French identity that one would only expect from an enemy (Chaigneau 2004).

2.3.2   Content analysis of parliamentary debates

Twenty-nine speeches were identified as eligible for the content analysis. Out of these, only two supported credible threats or eventually the use of force (Table 7.5) while 27 argued against French participation in a war (Table 7.6). While the left-wing parties opposed war, some members of the ruling neo-Gaullist UMP – including Prime Minister Raffarin and Foreign Minister de Villepin – remained more ambivalent (Styan 2006: 189; Kempin 2008: 171, 174–5). They deemed it necessary to signal credible threats of force towards Iraq, but refused hasty military action.

Given only two speeches advocating participation, the results shown in Table 7.5 are hardly telling. Remarkably, even the few supporters put forward many counter-arguments. However, they viewed Saddam Hussein as a highly dangerous enemy acquiring WMD and believed that he would only comply following a credible threat of force. They viewed this aspect as more important than the lack of a UN mandate or the non-exhaustion of peaceful means.

As Table 7.6 reveals, the opponents of a war most frequently referred to arguments connected with international law and universal norms. Most speakers argued that peaceful means had not yet been exhausted and that there was no UN mandate for using force. About half of the speakers recalled that, like the French people, many other countries rejected the use of force. They also feared that a war that lacked UN authorisation would damage global norms and cause regional instability in the Middle East. The opponents doubted that Saddam Hussein was really acquiring WMD; hence they questioned his status as a dangerous enemy.

The French parliamentary debate invoked aspects not covered by our category scheme. Many speakers dealt critically with the 'pushy' behaviour of the US, with the weakness of Europe and with the future of the international community in the light of a fatal US unilateralism. The US was accused of desiring this war for geopolitical and economic reasons. The disunity of Europe was another grievance; speakers demanded

Table 7.5 *Frequencies of arguments, Iraq War, France, supporters only*
(n = 2); extracts of results

Code	Argument	Number of speakers	Percentage of speakers
1104	Show of force	2	100
1303	Regional instability	2	100
4301	No UN mandate/damage to UN	2	100
4302	Peaceful means not exhausted	2	100
7101	Enemy image of adversary	2	100

Table 7.6 *Frequencies of arguments, Iraq War, France, opponents only*
(n = 27); extracts of results

Code	Argument	Number of speakers	Percentage of speakers
4302	Peaceful means not exhausted	23	85.2
4301	No UN mandate/damage to UN	16	59.3
5304	Multilateral war rejection	14	51.9
5302	Pacifism/war damages global norms	13	48.1
6301	Democratic norms/procedures contra war	13	48.1
7301	Enemy image questioned	13	48.1
1303	Regional instability	11	40.7

(like in the Kosovo case) a strengthening of Europe as a counterweight to US hegemony. They once again underlined that they considered it France's historical mission to play a leadership role in Europe, to bolster the UN and to defend universal values in the world.

2.3.3 Newspaper debates

Most commentaries in *Le Monde* and *Le Figaro* positioned themselves against a war in Iraq. From August to December 2002, the focus was on the costs and benefits of a preventive war and on the roles of the US, Europe and France. Commentaries in *Le Monde* acknowledged that Saddam Hussein's regime was unsavoury, but warned that a war would damage the 'moral' and political world order.[17] Commentaries

---

[17] E.g. Cormac Murphy-O'Connor 2002. 'Irak: au risque d'un combat douteux', *Le Monde*, 7 September; Moncef Kdhir 2002. 'Vers la fin du droit international?', *Le Monde*, 12 September; Amir Jahanchahi 2002. 'Il n'y a pas que l'Irak', *Le Monde*, 25 September; Ran Halevi 2002. 'L'unité dans la confusion', *Le Monde*, 10 December.

in *Le Figaro* presented similar lines of argumentation: a war would cause regional instability.[18] US unilateralism was condemned, the 'true' motives were believed to be US greed for oil and global hegemony; in contrast, France's role as a counterweight in the UN was praised, but the French should be careful not to become isolated internationally. France and the Europeans should strive to bring the US back to multilateralism.

As the controversies between the US and France intensified in February and March 2003, the newspapers focused even more on US–French/European relations. *Le Monde* commended France's role as leader of the peace-prone countries and saw US–French relations as being in their biggest crisis since the end of the Cold War. Commentaries in *Le Figaro* discussed the questionable (geopolitical, self-centred) motives of the US for pushing for this war.[19] The French government's rejection of the war was encouraged; France would only strengthen its international reputation by pronounced opposition to an unlawful war. France and Europe should not act as US vassals.

2.3.4   Public opinion polls

Opinion polls on the Iraq War showed that the French population was very critical towards a war from August 2002 onwards.[20] Whereas initially more than 70 per cent rejected a war, well over 80 per cent of respondents did so in the first month of 2003. When asked about French participation in a potential war, majorities of 65–75 per cent said 'no'. As the debate on a potential second, authorising UN resolution and a

---

[18] E.g. Renaud Girard 2002. 'Irak: pas maintenant, pas comme ça', *Le Figaro*, 27 August; François Géré 2002. 'Bush, Saddam Hussein et l'Orient compliqué', *Le Figaro*, 3 September; Yves Thréard 2002. 'La raison américaine', *Le Figaro*, 9 November.

[19] E.g. Alain Minc 2003. 'Irak: un désastre atlantique?', *Le Figaro*, 6 February; Jean de Belot 2003. 'Irak: la ligne de Paris', *Le Figaro*, 10 Februrary; Guillaume Bigot 2003. 'La France qui dit non', *Le Figaro*, 15 March.

[20] Analysed were polls conducted by *IFOP/Le Journal du Dimanche*: 'Les Français et l'éventualité d'une intervention américaine en Irak', 8–9 August 2002; 'Les Français et la guerre contre le terrorisme', 12–13 September 2002; 'Les indices de popularité', 10–18 October 2002; 'Les indices popularité', 6–14 February 2003; 'Jugement sur le droit de veto de la France', 13–14 February 2003; 'L'état d'esprit des Français à l'égard des Américains et de la guerre en Irak', 20–21 February 2003; 'Les objectifs de guerre en Irak', 21–22 March 2003; by *IFOP/Le Figaro*: 'Le jugement des Français sur l'intervention américaine en Irak', 20 March 2003; by *IPSOS/France 2*: 'La perception par les Français de la crise irakienne', 15 February 2003; 'Le gouvernement Raffarin: Première Impression', 20–21 September 2002; 'Que pensent les Français des Etats-Unis et de la crise irakienne?', 7–8 March 2003; by *GALLUP International*: 'L'opinion publique face à la perspective d'une intervention en Irak', 15–16 January 2003 and by *SOFRES/Le Pèlerin Magazine*: 'Les Français et le conflit irakien', 13–15 March 2003. However, no questions related to the Iraq War or French participation were asked in these polls between October and December 2002.

French veto intensified in February/March 2003, questions and answers grew more differentiated, but also more contradictory: while an over-whelming majority rejected a war as such (as stated above), about 60 per cent were against French participation *without* a UN mandate. However, 44 per cent of respondents were willing to support French participation if such a mandate were available, while 42 per cent still refused. Yet, more than 80 per cent still supported France's opposition to the highly unpopular US government and approved of President Chirac's threat to veto a second resolution. As these figures indicate, the war (as well as the US president) aroused very negative opinions.

2.3.5   Conclusion: why France abstained

The French policy in the 2002/3 Iraq crisis was to a large extent shaped by the French perception of a dangerous US unilateralism and concern about a world order shaped by the unfettered hegemony of the US. As in the Gulf in 1991 and in Kosovo in 1999, France sought to mediate by peaceful means until the very end – but in contrast to the two other crises, this time the French perceived no blatant breach of international law or a humanitarian catastrophe. Consequently, they saw no mandate emerging from international law to fight such a 'pre-emptive' (in fact, preventive) war. As a permanent member of the UNSC, France played a key role in the conflict; conversely, the UN was the key stage for French international influence. Gaullists as well as Leftists celebrated France's insistence upon a UN prerogative and the 'showdown' with the US as an indicator of the country's regained independence and global stand-ing. 'Dans leur très large majorité, les Français ont été fiers d'entendre à nouveau la voix de la France, absente il est vrai depuis longtemps des grandes affaires du monde' (Lellouche 2003: 21).

There was a large domestic consensus on President Chirac's 'no' pos-ition, visible in parliament, newspaper commentaries and opinion polls. As one civil society leader remarked: 'Il est remarquable de constater combien le refus de l'intervention militaire en Irak a traversé les familles politiques, associatives et syndicales au point de provoquer une sorte d' "unité nationale" derrière le président de la République' (Tubiana 2004: 79). It is difficult to fathom to what degree domestic consider-ations influenced the government's position, but its position certainly was highly popular among the Arab immigrants (Ghaleb 2004).

Arguments against the war referred primarily to international law and universal values. In addition, the relations between France and the US and between Europe and the US were a constant theme. In a traditional Gaullist vein, differences between the US and Europe were highlighted and demands for an independent, militarily strong Europe under the leadership of France were again put forward (Colard 2004: 216–18; Cogan 2005: 246–8). Indeed, when political leaders of the opposition criticised the president's policy in the aftermath, this referred to the perceived mistake of pursuing a national policy rather than taking the lead in Europe (Fabius 2004; Rocard 2004). As in the previous wars, there was an almost unanimous conclusion: Europe must grow stronger in military and political terms. The French perceived this war as aggression aimed at regime change, which was incompatible with international law and would have dangerous consequences for regional and international security. The French goal was not to topple Saddam Hussein's regime but only to disarm him – if possible by peaceful means (Styan 2006: 188).

3   Conclusion: ambiguities of a global mission

France participated in two of the three wars analysed in this book, and abstained in one case. The justificatory frames for all three decisions were similar: references to international law, to universal values and to the French self-perception of being an exceptional major power with a global responsibility were used to legitimise both participation and non-participation. In all three conflicts, there was at the point of decision a '*union sacrée*', a large national consensus on the policy pursued by the president. The democratic checks and balances assumed by democratic peace theory are rather weak in France: the president dominates the decision-making process in foreign and security policy. Chirac also demonstrated the overwhelming power of the president in the *cohabitation* government that ruled during the Kosovo crisis. Compared to other democracies analysed in this book, there was little debate in parliament or in public prior to the wars (more after the wars had started). A small circle of the political elite with similar views on France's role in international politics managed to shape decisions; public opinion was often presented with *faits accomplis* (Sur 2000: 279–80; Stahl 2006: 111).

France's foreign and security policies appear primarily oriented towards elements of its collective identity (Stahl 2006: 112). Crucial determinants for the decisions in our three cases were France's concern about its global standing after the end of the Cold War, the fear of being marginalised and that of being subordinated to the US. Following in the footsteps of Charles de Gaulle, both the socialist and the neo-Gaullist presidents Mitterrand and Chirac merged normative arguments with national interest motives. Promoting France's status is always portrayed as conducive to promoting universal goals and values such as the strengthening of the UN, the enforcement of international law, the protection of human rights or the creation of a multipolar world order. Hence one does not usually find 'naked' power motives in the justification of French military actions; instead these are integrated in normative semantics: 'Notre pays ... met son statut de puissance au service de la prospérité et de la sécurité du monde' (Jospin 1999: 6; Roche 2000: 392; Treacher 2003: 11–12).

It is striking that there are only a few public references to external expectations in the French discourses on the wars. This underlines the nation's self-perception as an independent major power. Allies play a moderate role (Stahl 2006: 112). This is probably due to France's ambivalent relationship to NATO, which has only gradually improved since Chirac's presidency. If partners are mentioned, they are usually located within the European framework. The insight that Europe as a collective actor is too weak to handle international crises motivated Chirac to promote (together with the UK and later Germany) the project of a common European Security and Defence Policy.

French foreign policy is marked by various ambiguities. Many stem from the discrepancy between France's claim to remain a major power after the end of the Cold War and its limited capabilities (Roche 2000: 399–402; Gournay 2002). Today, the attempt to develop a counterweight to the liberal hegemon (the US) can only be pursued within a European framework. Following the failure of the Europeans in the Balkan wars of the 1990s, French leaders have re-accentuated an older Gaullist idea: the need to create a unified, independent European military force to contain US influence in the world. As France had to recognise after 1990 that it was a great power in decline, a 'Europe' in which France was to play a leadership role became the new point of reference for regaining lost influence (Boniface 1998: 91; Sur 2000: 284–5). 'L'Europe est pour la France – bien plus que toute autre instance multilatérale – un surgénérateur de puissance' (Boniface 1998: 101). Consequently, each of the wars was followed by complaints about US superiority and European impotence, an emphasis that is found in no other European discourse (e.g. de la Gorce 1991; Touchard 2003: 85).

French attempts to limit US hegemony not only motivate the country's support for a stronger unified European force, but also lead to a remarkable commitment to the UN. The UN offers a multilateral framework in which France can demonstrate its global standing as a permanent member of the UNSC. In all three conflicts, France sought to contain US or NATO (in Kosovo) dominance by insisting on the UN prerogative; this stance is also related to France's emphasis on international law (Raffarin 2002: 11). In the Kosovo case, France did finally participate in a war without a UN mandate; the humanitarian disaster was perceived as overriding. For a country that regards itself as the cradle and defender of human rights, the Kosovo case in the neighbouring region appealed to core values of French identity – aggravated by the experience of France's own failure in the preceding Bosnian war. Lessons learnt from Bosnia were cited to justify the military intervention in Kosovo (Rathbun 2004: 129–52). In contrast, the 2003 Iraq War was unacceptable for France, as it was perceived to be a war for regime change and for US geopolitical interests, not for disarming Iraq in accordance with prior UN resolutions – a goal that France shared unequivocally.

A commonality in all three cases is the very active French diplomacy and the search for a non-violent solution. France used a multiplicity of formal and informal negotiation channels in order to avert war until the very last minute, in strong contrast to the 'Anglo-Saxons'. Nonetheless it also proved a reliable military ally to the US/NATO in the Gulf War and the Kosovo War once war had started, and not only with token contributions, but with significant forces. This might seem contradictory, but as Chirac emphasised in the 2003 Iraq crisis, where France was stylised as the 'pacifist' leader of the 'coalition of the unwilling' together with Russia and Germany, France is neither pacifist nor anti-American (Styan 2006: 191).

Given the fact that France belongs to the group of liberal democracies that are frequently involved in military actions, it can definitely not be called pacifist: 'France's willingness to intervene militarily is still shaped by its tradition as a former colonial power which emphasises its national independence and global outreach, and which regards military means as a legitimate element of foreign policy' (Gauzy-Krieger and Meyer 2003: 38–9). At the same time, French actors often highlight the differences between France and the 'imperialistic' US, contrasting alleged French affinities to multilateralism, cooperation, diplomacy and peaceful means of conflict resolution with alleged affinities of the US to unilateralism, imperialism and the latent arrogance of a '*hyperpuissance*', as Foreign Minister Védrine once called the US (Boniface 1998: 60; Sur 2000: 283–4).

Although the French attempted in all three cases to mediate peaceful solutions, military options do not contravene the norms of domestic political culture; they are acceptable under certain circumstances, preferably when they are mandated by the UN. French foreign policies combine diplomatic, military and 'civilising' missions, resulting in a number of ambivalences. As Adrian Treacher succinctly summarises this 'missionary' trait of French political culture: it contains a 'strong motivation to pass on its special message to the rest of the world, and a belief in the prerogative of the French nation to speak on behalf of humanity' (Treacher 2003: 13).

REFERENCES

Boniface, Pascal 1998. *La France est-elle encore une grande puissance?* Paris: Presses de Sciences Po

Bonnefous, Marc 1990. 'Actions, déclarations et contradictions devant la crise du Golfe', *Défense nationale* 46 (12): 23–42

1991. 'Golfe 1991', *Défense nationale* 47 (5): 59–66

1998. 'Réflexions sur une politique arabe', *Défense nationale* 54 (8): 44–67

Brüne, Stefan and Mehler, Andreas 1998. 'Die neue französische Afrikapolitik: Face-lifting oder außenpolitische Wende?', in Institut für Afrika-Kunde and Rolf Hofmeier (eds.), *Afrika-Jahrbuch 1997*. Opladen: Leske + Budrich, pp. 46–58

Buffet, Cyril and Heuser, Beatrice 1998. 'Marianne and Michel: The Franco-German Couple', in Cyril Buffet and Beatrice Heuser (eds.), *Haunted by History: Myths in International Relations*. Oxford: Berghahn, pp. 175–205

Chaigneau, Pascal 2004. 'L'Irak après la seconde chute de Saddam', *Défense nationale* 60 (2): 93–9

Cogan, Charles G. 2005. *Diplomatie à la française*. Paris: Jacob-Duvernet

Colard, Daniel 2004. 'L'axe Paris-Berlin-Moscou: Le "camp du refus" dans la crise iraquienne (2002–2003)', in *Annuaire Français de Relations Internationales*, vol. v. Brussels: Bruylant, pp. 212–22

Deitelhoff, Nicole and Burkard, Eva 2005. 'Europa vor Gericht: Die EU-Außenpolitik und der Internationale Strafgerichtshof', *HSFK-Report* No. 13/2005, Frankfurt a.M.

de la Gorce, Paul-Marie 1991. 'Présentation', *Défense nationale* 47 (6): 23–30

de Villepin, Dominique 2003a. 'Intervention au Conseil de la Sécurité', *Défense nationale* 59 (3): 5–11

2003b. *Un autre monde*. Paris: L'Herne

Fabius, Laurent 2004. 'Diplomatie Française: Passer de la posture à la stratégie', *Revue internationale et stratégique* 53 (1): 53–6

Frémeaux, Jacques 1995. *Le monde arabe et la sécurité de la France depuis 1958*. Paris: Presses Universitaires de France

Gauzy-Krieger, Florence and Meyer, Berthold 2003. 'Wege und Umwege zur Professionalisierung: Ein Vergleich der Militärreformen in Frankreich und Deutschland', *HSFK-Report* No. 16/2003, Frankfurt a.M.

Ghaleb, Bencheikh 2004. 'Une position française imperturbable et courageuse', *Revue internationale et stratégique* 53 (1): 35–8

Gnesotto, Nicole 1999. 'Introduction: l'OTAN et l'Europe à la lumière du Kosovo', *Politique étrangère* 64 (2): 207–18

Gournay, Pierre 2002. *Exception culturelle et mondialisation*. Paris: Presses de Sciences Po

Gresh, Alain and Vidal, Dominique 1991. *Golfe: Clefs pour une guerre annoncée*. Paris: Le Monde

Grosser, Alfred 1989. *Affaires extérieures: La politique de la France 1944–1989*. Paris: Flammarion

Hadas-Lebel, Raphaël 1991. 'La Ve République et la guerre', *Pouvoirs* 58: 5–24

Heuser, Beatrice 1998. 'Dunkirk, Diên Biên Phu, Suez or Why France Does Not Trust Allies and Has Learnt to Love the Bomb', in Cyril Buffet and Beatrice Heuser (eds.), *Haunted by History: Myths in International Relations*. Oxford: Berghahn, pp. 157–74

Hoffmann, Stanley 1974. *Decline or Renewal? France since the 1930s*. New York, NY: Viking Press

Hunger, Iris 2005. *Biowaffenkontrolle in einer multipolaren Welt: Zur Funktion von Vertrauen in internationalen Beziehungen*. Frankfurt a.M.: Campus

Jospin, Lionel 1999. 'La politique de défense de la France', *Défense nationale* 55 (12): 5–17

Kempin, Ronja 2008. *Frankreichs neue Sicherheitspolitik*. Baden-Baden: Nomos

Kessler, Marie-Christine and Charillon, Frédéric 2002. 'France: un "rang" à réinventer', in Frédéric Charillon (ed.), *Les politiques étrangères: Ruptures et continuités*. Paris: Documentation Française, pp. 101–32

Kimmel, Adolf 2005. 'Der Verfassungstext und die lebenden Verfassungen', in Adolf Kimmel and Henrik Uterwedde (eds.), *Länderbericht Frankreich*. Bonn: BpB, pp. 247–67

Kolboom, Ingo and Stark, Hans 2005. 'Frankreich in der Welt: Weltpolitik zwischen Anspruch und Wirklichkeit', in Adolf Kimmel and Henrik Uterwedde (eds.), *Länderbericht Frankreich*. Bonn: BpB, pp. 365–83

Lellouche, Pierre 2003. 'La France et l'après-Saddam', *Revue des deux mondes* 6: 9–28

Littlewood, Jez 2005. *The Biological Weapons Convention: A Failed Revolution*. Aldershot: Ashgate

Lukic, Renéo 2003. *L'Agonie Yougoslave (1986–2003): Les États-Unis et l'Europe face aux guerres balkaniques*. Québec: Presses de l'université de Laval

Maull, Hanns W. and Stahl, Bernhard 2002. 'Durch den Balkan nach Europa? Deutschland und Frankreich in den Jugoslawienkriegen', *Politische Vierteljahresschrift* 43 (1): 82–111

Meimeth, Michael 1997. 'Frankreichs Sicherheitspolitik unter den Bedingungen des Ost-West-Konflikts', in Hanns W. Maull, Michael Meimeth and Christoph Neßhöver (eds.), *Die verhinderte Großmacht: Frankreichs Sicherheitspolitik nach dem Ende des Ost-West-Konflikts*. Opladen: Leske + Budrich, pp. 37–52

Mény, Yves 2005. 'Interessengruppen in Frankreich: Von Pluralismus keine Spur', in Adolf Kimmel and Henrik Uterwedde (eds.), *Länderbericht Frankreich*. Bonn: BpB, pp. 286–301

Meyrede, Laurent 1999. 'France's Foreign Policy in the Mediterranean', in Stelios Stavridis, Theodore Couloumbis, Thanos Veremis and Neville Waites (eds.), *The Foreign Policies of the European Union's Mediterranean States and Applicant Countries in the 1990s*. Basingstoke: Macmillan, pp. 40–72

Morisse-Schilbach, Melanie 2006. *Diplomatie und europäische Außenpolitik: Europäisierungseffekte im Kontext von Intergouvernementalismus am Beispiel von Frankreich und Großbritannien*. Baden-Baden: Nomos

Morizet, Jacques 1990. 'Vingt ans de relations franco-irakiennes', *Défense nationale* 46 (12): 53–63

Müller-Brandeck-Bocquet, Gisela 2005. 'Frankreich in der Europäischen Union', in Adolf Kimmel and Henrik Uterwedde (eds.), *Länderbericht Frankreich*. Bonn: BpB, pp. 384–401

2008. 'Deutsch-französische Beziehungen und das Projekt "Friedensmacht Europa"', in Peter Schlotter, Wilhelm Nolte and Renate Grasse (eds.), *Berliner Friedenspolitik? Militärische Transformation – zivile Impulse – europäische Einbindung*. Baden-Baden: Nomos, pp. 233–60

Pitette, Yves 1990. 'Les interventions extérieures', *Arès* 13 (5): 73–8

Portelli, Hugues 1991. 'Union sacrée?', *Pouvoirs* 58: 25–32

Raffarin, Jean-Pierre 2002. 'La politique de défense de la France', *Défense nationale* 58 (11): 5–22

Rathbun, Brian C. 2004. *Partisan Interventions: European Party Politics and Peace Enforcement in the Balkans*. Ithaca, NY: Cornell University Press

Renoldner, Simeón 2007. *Regimebildung in der Landminenfrage und der Einfluß von Nichtregierungsorganisationen: eine Untersuchung des Ottawa-Prozesses unter besonderer Berücksichtigung der Rolle Österreichs und Frankreichs*. Frankfurt a.M.: Lang

Rocard, Michel 2004. 'La France dans la crise Irakienne: de l'apprentissage de la mesure', *Revue internationale et stratégique* 53 (1): 73–8

Roche, Jean-Jacques 2000. 'La France et l'universel', in *Annuaire Français de Relations Internationales*, vol. I. Brussels: Bruylant, pp. 390–406

Rouleau, Eric 1999. 'Errements de la diplomatie française au Kosovo', *Le Monde diplomatique*, 12 December, pp. 6–7

Roux, Michel 1999. *La guerre du Kosovo: Dix clés pour comprendre*. Paris: La Découverte

Rozenberg, Olivier 2003. 'French Parliamentary Participation in Foreign, Security and Defense Policy: Anemic National Performance and European Potential', in Jürgen Mittag (ed.), *The Parliamentary Dimension of CFSP/ ESDP: Options for the European Convention*. Brussels, pp. 125–36

Rynning, Sten 2000. 'French Defence Reforms after Kosovo: On Track or Derailed?', *European Security* 9 (2): 61–80

Schild, Joachim 2005. 'Politische Parteien und Parteiensystem im Wandel', in Adolf Kimmel and Henrik Uterwedde (eds.), *Länderbericht Frankreich*. Bonn: BpB, pp. 268–85

Schmidt, Peter 2000. 'Frankreichs Schwierigkeiten mit den Vereinigten Staaten und der NATO: Entwicklungstrends einer mühsamen Partnerschaft', in Jens van Scherpenberg and Peter Schmidt (eds.), *Stabilität und Kooperation: Aufgaben internationaler Ordnungspolitik*. Baden-Baden: Nomos, pp. 234–55

Stahl, Bernhard 2006. *Frankreichs Identität und außenpolitische Krisen*. Verhalten und Diskurse im Kosovo-Krieg und der Uruguay-Runde des GATT. Baden-Baden: Nomos

Styan, David 2004. 'Jacques Chirac's "Non": France, Iraq and the United Nations, 1991–2003', *Modern & Contemporary France* 12 (3): 371–85

2006. *France and Iraq: Oil, Arms and French Policy Making in the Middle East*. London: Tauris

Sur, Serge 2000. 'La puissance et le rang revisités', in *Annuaire Français de Relations Internationales*, vol. I. Brussels: Bruylant, pp. 269–90

230   *Johanna Eckert*

Tardy, Thierry 2000. 'La France, l'Europe et la guerre du Kosovo', *Regards sur l'actualité* 257 (1): 3–18

2002. 'La France et l'ONU, entre singularité et ambivalence', *Politique Étrangère* 67 (4): 931–47

Touchard, Georges-Eric 2003. 'L'intervention en Irak: Un faux débat pour de vraies questions?', *Défense nationale* 59 (4): 71–88

Treacher, Adrian 2003. *French Interventionism: Europe's Last Global Player?* Aldershot: Ashgate

Tubiana, Michel 2004. 'La société civile face à la définition d'un nouvel ordre mondial', *Revue internationale et stratégique* 53 (1): 79–81

Tümmers, Hans J. 2006. *Das politische System Frankreichs.* Munich: Beck

Weschler, Lawrence 2000. 'Exceptional Cases in Rome: The United States and the Struggle for an ICC', in Sarah B. Sewall and Carl Kaysen (eds.), *The United States and the International Criminal Court: National Security and International Law.* Lanham, MD: Rowman & Littlefield, pp. 85–111

Wisotzki, Simone 2002. *Die Nuklearwaffenpolitik Großbritanniens und Frankreichs: Eine konstruktivistische Analyse.* Frankfurt a.M.: Campus

2004. 'Abschreckung ohne Ende? Die ambivalente Nuklearwaffenpolitik Großbritanniens und Frankreichs', *HSFK-Report* No. 11/2004, Frankfurt a.M.

Wood, Pia Christina 1993. 'France and the Israeli–Palestinian Conflict: The Mitterrand Policies, 1981–1992', *Middle East Journal* 47 (1): 21–40

Woyke, Wichard 2000. *Deutsch-französische Beziehungen seit der Wiedervereinigung: Das Tandem faßt wieder Tritt.* Opladen: Leske + Budrich

8 Burdens of the past, shadows of the future: the use of military force as a challenge for the German 'civilian power'

Anna Geis

From a democratic peace perspective, post-Second World War Germany seems prima facie like a model case for democratic peace: the (West) German parliamentary democracy has institutionalised numerous legal constraints on the use of military force; norms of peaceful conflict resolution are deeply entrenched in the polity and the population is noted for its anti-militarist attitude. The country is one of the wealthiest in the world and firmly embedded in a multitude of international organisations. However, since unification in 1990 and following its abstention from the Gulf War, Germany has gradually been expanding its engagement in military missions, culminating in its participation in the Kosovo War. On the other hand, Germany's staunch opposition to the Iraq War in 2003 puzzled many observers.

1 Institutional and ideational determinants of Germany's foreign and security policy

1.1 Regime-type features and decision-making in Germany's security policy

Following Germany's total defeat in the Second World War, the occupational forces aimed at redesigning West Germany's political institutions in a way that reflected 'lessons learnt'. In 1949, the Basic Law (*Grundgesetz*) of the Federal Republic of Germany (FRG) founded a federal type of regime that combines a parliamentary democracy with an institutionally strong chancellor and a weak president. The Basic Law explicitly encourages the integration of Germany in international and supranational organisations. Germany's polity is characterised by a high degree of vertical and horizontal power fragmentation. During the period of our investigation (1990–2003), Germany had a moderately polarised multi-party system, with five parties elected to the federal parliament (*Bundestag*): two large 'people's parties' (*Volksparteien*) at the centre, the moderately left Social Democratic Party (*SPD*) and the conservative parliamentary group consisting of the Christian Democratic Union/Christian Social Union (*CDU/CSU*); a smaller liberal party (*FDP*) and two small left-wing parties, the Green Party (*Bündnis 90/Die Grünen*) and, following German unification, the Socialist Party (*PDS*).

As in other countries, German foreign and security policies are substantially shaped by the federal executive. While the federal president formally represents the Federal Republic of Germany in terms of international law, the chancellor has the formal powers to set the guidelines for all domestic and foreign policies and he/she is the commander-in-chief of the armed forces in the event of a so-called case of defence. The minister of defence is the commander-in-chief in peacetime and is responsible for defence policy guidelines.[1] The German parliament possesses important budget, participation and oversight powers that exceed those of a number of Western parliaments (Wagner 2006). All cabinet proposals to deploy armed forces on missions abroad for other than purely humanitarian aid purposes require the prior approval of a simple majority in the Bundestag. Parliament approves or rejects a mission's mandate and general operational issues: it has the right to visit troops abroad and to decide on the duration of the mission.

This 'parliamentarisation' of security policy was established in a seminal judgement by Germany's highest court in 1994. Until unification, the dominant political interpretation of the Basic Law held that the constitution precluded 'out-of-area' deployments (i.e. outside NATO territories) of armed troops of the Bundeswehr. Changes in the expectations of Germany's allies served to intensify the debate on Bundeswehr deployments of the future. While some political parties sought a clarification by the judiciary or an amendment to the constitution, the Kohl government started by deploying troops with UN authorisation at a low level of intensity in Cambodia, Somalia and, more controversially, in Bosnia (Baumann and Hellmann 2001). In its ruling, the Federal Constitutional Court in July 1994 declared all these missions to be constitutional to the extent that they were carried out within the framework of collective security systems.

---

[1] These were officially documented in the period 1990–2003 in a White Book on Germany's Security Policy (1994) and two Defence Policy Guidelines (1992, 2003).

*1.2   Germany's role conception and role profile in foreign and
          security policy*

1.2.1   Foreign policy traditions, guidelines and role conception

Following the end of the Second World War, (West) Germany's foreign policy was strongly influenced by the burdens of its Nazi past and
by being the (divided) front-line state in the Cold War. German leaders had to learn how to strike a balance between very heterogeneous
interests in the West and the East and to avoid any political move that
might be interpreted as the resurgence of a new, inappropriate power
politics. Germany's location in the centre of Europe and its division
during the Cold War made the German leadership a quasi-natural
bridge-builder between West and East Europe. The intensification of
relations with the Russians following the end of the Cold War causes
occasional irritations with some Western partners, but also with the
new Eastern members of the European Union (EU). While post-Cold
War relations between Germany and Russia have tended to be rather
friendly, the Soviet Union and communism posed a powerful 'enemy'
for West Germany during the Cold War when the country felt directly
threatened by the communist menace. Following the collapse of the
Soviet Union, German political discourses have not featured a com-
parably strong enemy image: it is rather Germany's own Nazi past that
serves as the ultimate 'other' of the unified, 'civilian' Germany.

In the precarious constellation of the Cold War, a defeated, occupied
and outlawed West Germany gradually developed a distinctive form of
exercising 'soft' power that enabled its rehabilitation and integration
into the Western community. For decades, West Germany, which had
developed into one of the richest states in the world, was considered an
economic giant but a political dwarf. The reliance on soft power and
a highly internationalised state identity has characterised Germany's
foreign policy profile ever since (Katzenstein 1997: 19–29). Whereas
unified Germany is regarded by other European states as a major
power in Europe, its own elites usually describe it as a middle power
(*Mittelmacht*).[2] Strikingly, the German elite often tries to avoid explicit 'realist' language: 'The Germans have eliminated the concept of
"power" from their political vocabulary. They speak the language of
"political responsibility" instead' (Katzenstein 1997: 2).

---

[2] It should, however, be noted that the German term '*Mittelmacht*' is not equivalent to
the distinctive foreign policy role conception of 'middle powers' such as Canada and
Australia. See the case studies on Canada and Australia for further explanations of the
'middle power' concept.

These traits of German foreign policy have led some scholars to call Germany a 'civilian power'. This foreign policy role conception is based on the assumption that international relations changed fundamentally with the end of the Cold War. Problems in international politics were now considered to arise predominantly in economic, social and cultural spheres. Such problems could best be tackled by the establishment of multilateral, participatory arrangements, the strengthening of the UN system, the juridification of international relations and the promotion of democracy, human rights and sustainable development. Civilian powers pursue a value-oriented foreign policy in terms of goals, means and policy style. They are prepared to give up sovereignty and to subordinate their short-term, narrow self-interests to the achievement of collective goods. Although civilian powers have strong reservations about the use of force, they are not *pacifist* powers. Since they are actors who are willing and able to actively shape international relations, they might also use force, if need be, to implement their principles on the basis of collective decision-making (Maull 2000: 69, 75).

The role ideal type 'civilian power' is used to highlight characteristics of (West) German foreign policy since 1949: West Germany had completely renounced all the negative traits of its past policy and culture. It acted multilaterally, it abandoned sovereignty, it featured a 'culture of restraint' and its population had 'anti-militarist' attitudes (Baumann and Hellmann 2001). This concept is also used to assess continuity and change within German foreign policy after unification. Many students of German foreign policy argue that there is a relative high level of continuity in most fields of foreign policy (e.g. Rittberger 2001). Drawing on constructivist theoretical approaches, they usually locate reasons for this in 'soft' factors such as identity, norms, role conceptions, worldviews and learning processes (Duffield 1999).

The self-conception of German foreign policy can be summarised by the two phrases 'never again war' and 'never alone' (Maull 2004: 19–20). The former refers to the break with the past, i.e. gives highest priority to the maintenance and promotion of peace; the latter refers to Germany's integration into the Western multilateral frameworks of NATO and EC/EU. It was in West Germany's interest to become integrated in international institutions and organisations since this self-commitment alleviated the fears of its neighbours and facilitated confidence-building (Haftendorn 2001). Over time, West Germany's predominantly instrumental multilateralism acquired increasingly normative traits, rendering its commitment to international institutions, in particular the EC, an element of its state identity and *raison d'état*.

1.2.2   Germany's approach to international law: the example of the International Criminal Court

It is characteristic of a 'civilian power' that it sets out to advance the juridification of international relations. In this vein, the German government strongly advocated the establishment of the International Criminal Court (ICC). Germany was one of the initiating actors in the international negotiations on the establishment of the ICC from 1992 onwards. The German diplomat Hans-Peter Kaul led the German negotiations for six years and has been described as 'one of the most passionate proponents of a strong court' (Weschler 2000: 104–5). Germany was co-founder of the coalition of like-minded states, a group that opted for a strong, independent court and asserted this position against powerful opposing states such as the US (Deitelhoff and Burkard 2005: 10–13, 20).

The German delegation received much acclaim for their proactive, constructive activities during the negotiations; their close cooperation with non-governmental organisations (NGOs) and like-minded state delegations was widely acknowledged. German delegates submitted very progressive proposals for the draft of the statute, for example with regard to the crime of aggression or universal jurisdiction and the competencies of the chief prosecutor. The German delegation also succeeded in obtaining acceptance for a detailed record of war crimes (Kaul 1998: 126–7). Germany signed the Rome Statute on 10 December 1998 and ratified it on 11 December 2000 without major public debate. In sum, Germany is one of the most pronounced supporters of the ICC and has significantly contributed to its establishment and financing. In this context, official rhetoric and the actual behaviour of a German 'civilian power' corresponded very closely.

1.2.3   Germany's approach to international regimes: arms control and disarmament

Although (West) Germany had officially renounced the production and possession of nuclear weapons, its leadership was not 'anti-nuclear' but believed in the importance of nuclear deterrence. During the 1970s and 1980s when the FRG developed into a prospering trading state, Germany behaved according to the letter of the Non-Proliferation Treaty but kept its domestic export control system 'in a very permissive state' (Müller 2003: 4). In the early 1990s, however, the German government radically altered its export control policies. The strengthening of multilateral regimes was the clear priority of German non-proliferation policy in the 1990s. Germany engaged proactively in the fields of nuclear arms control and disarmament, which increased tensions with its nuclear allies.

However, a number of progressive initiatives were quickly stymied by the nuclear powers, notably the US (Müller 2006).

Germany played a leading role in the negotiations of the Conference on Disarmament resulting in the Chemical Weapons Convention (CWC), and was also instrumental in establishing the CWC verification system. Following this first very active phase between 1990 and 1994, Germany became significantly less active and restricted itself mainly to supporting the process.[3] In the field of biological weapons, Germany has shown consistent and active support for the Biological Weapons Convention (BWC) and for the various efforts to strengthen its regime, for example through the Confidence-Building Measures or through a legally binding compliance protocol (Littlewood 2005: 14, 48, 53, 100–2). Germany is among the most active states in the BWC regime in terms of participation and number of papers submitted. It often assumes the role of a mediator in differing multilateral settings.

As regards Germany's attitude towards the ban on anti-personnel (AP) landmines, Germany was the first major power in Europe to very actively support the ban from 1994 onwards. It was a member of the proactive core group. The German NGO Medico was co-founder of the international NGO campaign and managed to put the government under heavy public pressure to support a ban. On 22 April 1996, Germany renounced the use and production of AP mines and the last German AP mine stockpiles were destroyed in December 1997. However, the government came under heavy criticism from the national campaign since it focused on AP mines only and sought to complement the fast-track approach of the Ottawa Process with other traditional arms control fora favoured by the US (Long and Hindle 1998: 254–5, 264). Germany pursued the inclusion of strong verification mechanisms in ban negotiations and ratified the Mine Ban Treaty (MBT) on 23 July 1998.[4]

In sum, Germany's non-proliferation and arms control policies since 1990 have been largely high profile, proactive and in accordance with the criteria of a 'civilian power'. Its goal is to strengthen multilateral regimes. However, in the nuclear field the 'civilian power' has difficulty reconciling its allegiance to the allies, its adherence to NATO's nuclear sharing arrangements and its normative preference for nuclear disarmament.

---

[3] Lohrberg, Malte, 'Fallstudie Deutschland: Chemische Waffen', unpublished manuscript 2007, PRIF, Frankfurt.

[4] 'Landmine Monitor, Germany Mine Ban Policy, 1999'. Online: www.the-monitor. org/index.php/publications/display?url=lm/1999/germany.html.

1.2.4   Germany's approach to the United Nations

The United Nations, along with NATO and the EU, provides one of the three crucial multilateral frameworks for German foreign policy. It took rather a long time before Germany (that is to say, the two Germanys) was granted membership of the UN in 1973. As one of the 'enemy states' mentioned in the UN Charter, post-war Germany had first of all to earn international trust. In particular, the existence of two Germanys complicated matters considerably (Knapp 2007: 730–1). During the Cold War, West Germany contributed significantly to the advancement of development and human rights policies, but its UN engagement also remained shaped by the bloc confrontation.

After 1990, all leaders of a unified Germany have pledged their strong commitment to the UN, pointing out Germany's expanding multiple activities in many policy fields. With reference to these political activities and Germany's financial significance as contributor of the third-largest subscription to the UN budget (nearly 9 per cent), consecutive German governments started to bid for a permanent seat on the Security Council. Germany was elected to the Security Council in 1995/6 and 2003/4 and used the second tenure in particular (in the midst of the crisis over the Iraq War) to demonstrate its ability to assume a leadership role in the UN.

Hence, although Germany's proactive policies to strengthen the UN have been acknowledged for their own virtue (e.g. with regard to human rights, environmental protection, development policies, arms control/disarmament), unified Germany's approach to the UN is also to be considered in instrumental terms of gaining more influence internationally. In addition, Germany's actual commitment lags behind the high-profile rhetoric in some respects, so Germany's material contribution to UN-led peace missions, to development assistance or to crisis prevention measures is comparatively modest.

1.2.5   Alliance, bilateral and regional relations

Germany has established two special relationships that reflect the burdens of its past: its 'friendship' with its former 'arch enemy' France and its historic responsibility for the existence of Israel, which is regarded as part of Germany's *raison d'état*. Very close relations to the US as West Germany's supreme 'guarantor state' against the communist threat have constituted a third cornerstone of special bilateral relations, outlasting the end of the Cold War and indicating unified Germany's firm integration in the West. In addition to such bilateral relations, (West) Germany has developed a very strong affiliation to NATO and the EU.

NATO: The highly controversial rearmament of West Germany and its accession to the Western European Union (WEU) and NATO in 1955 were seen as necessary for the containment of Soviet expansionism. NATO provided West Germany with security and at the same time provided other countries with a safeguard against Germany. The German military was then not regarded as an instrument of a 'normal', sovereign state, but has since been firmly integrated into NATO command structures like no other national force. Germany geared its national security strategies to NATO's strategies during the Cold War, but tensions between the allies arose time and again, for example over nuclear armament or rapprochement with the Soviet Union. Since France had resigned from NATO's military integration in 1966, Germany faced the structural dilemma of having to mediate between Atlanticists and Gaullists within both Europe and its own ranks.

The end of the Cold War changed the situation completely for NATO as well as for Germany; unified Germany met with rising expectations regarding its military contribution to the 'new NATO'. However, since the constitutional stipulations for such an engagement had not yet been clarified, the Kohl government primarily played a decisive, proactive role in the 'politicisation' of NATO as guarantor of European democracy, peace and stability during the 1990s (Tewes 2002). The government considered the integration of the new East European democracies into NATO as crucial for the stabilisation of its regional neighbourhood. Germany contributed significantly to the 'partnership for peace' programme and helped to integrate Russia into the process and later on to establish the NATO–Russia Council.

The successive SPD–Green government engaged in ever more military missions, but it seemed to be mainly reactive and lagged behind with the transformation of its armed forces. The new Defence Policy Guidelines of May 2003 only codified what had been developing over a number of years. Although the transformation of the Bundeswehr strengthened the latter's integration in NATO, the Schröder government eventually sought to demonstrate greater political independence from the transatlantic community by strengthening the European pillar of military integration (Overhaus 2006).

European Union: West Germany was one of the six founding members of the European Communities in the 1950s. All German governments since Konrad Adenauer have conducted Europe-friendly policies and advocated further integration. European policy has become the *raison d'état* across all of Germany's political parties. Germany was (together with France) a crucial force in transforming the predominantly economic EC into a political community (Woyke 2000). Although Germany had always aimed to deepen integration, it also proactively propelled the first wave of Eastern enlargement, which promised more economic benefits than political costs.

The recent intensification of the European Security and Defence Policy (ESDP) project was successfully put on the agenda by France and the UK in 1998 following the sobering experience of European weakness in the Kosovo crisis, but Germany quickly joined this initiative. It helped to set up the Helsinki Headline goal of 1999 under which the EU committed itself to providing military forces, but a future 'militarisation' of Europe was not in line with Germany's and the EU's self-image of a 'civilian power'. Germany hence also advocated a civilian pillar of the ESDP, but in these activities it lagged behind smaller states such as Finland and Sweden. France's more muscular concept of a *'Europe puissance'* should be merged with a German preference for a 'European power for peace' (*Friedensmacht*) (Müller-Brandeck-Bocquet 2008).

The 'German–French friendship' was the nucleus and subsequently the driving force of European integration for decades and was sealed by the Elysée Treaty in 1963. Despite the great political and symbolic enactments of this friendship, the relationship has been marked by 'ups and downs' (Woyke 2000). Since Germany and France had opposing interests in many respects, their prior coordination served as an important 'clearing station' for compromises to be negotiated later at the highest European level. Although the celebrated 'engine of integration' has lost much of its power and clearing functions since the realisation of monetary union and Eastern enlargement, this special relationship remains crucial for Europe.[5]

1.3   Conclusion: Germany's foreign policy role profile

As the brief review of several fields of foreign policy has shown, Germany's foreign policy between 1990 and 2003 resembles the ideal type of a 'civilian power'. It showed a high profile in all central international organisations and engaged proactively in non-proliferation, the ban on landmines and the establishment of the ICC. It actively promoted the integration and enlargement of the EU and NATO. As to policy style, it preferred to exercise 'soft power' and for the most part renounced unilateral actions. The dominant worldview of its political elites tended to be pluralistic and cooperative. This is not to say

---

[5] As is currently demonstrated in the eurozone debt crisis, which is labelled as the worst crisis integrated Europe has ever seen.

that German foreign policy was 'flawless': although high aspirations were declared in a number of fields, only relatively low resources were assigned, such as in the commitment to foreign aid, crisis prevention or the restructuring of the armed forces. In addition, in contrast to the rhetorically often exaggerated normative basis of German self-commitment strategies, Germany's 'model' multilateralism has always also had instrumental underpinnings.

2   Decision-making and public debates on the Gulf War, Kosovo War and Iraq War

2.1   *Germany and the Gulf War 1990–1991*

2.1.1   *Domestic political situation and decision-making process*
The 1990–1 Gulf crisis coincided with a unique historical situation for the Germans. When Iraq invaded Kuwait in August 1990, German diplomats were preoccupied with the negotiations on the 'Two-plus-Four' Treaty. Rapid unification and the bestowal of full sovereignty were to take place on 3 October 1990. The elections to the first all-German parliament were held on 2 December 1990 and the sensitive constitutional question of the participation of German troops in out-of-area operations was postponed.

The German government had to balance a number of contradictory expectations and positions that resulted in a rhetoric and a behaviour that many observers perceived as 'shirking its responsibilities': many Germans were largely averse to the use of military force in general, but the Western allies, in particular the US, expected the Germans to contribute actively to solving the crisis. The Soviets represented an especially sensitive partner since various treaties had not yet been ratified and large numbers of Soviet troops were still stationed on German territory. The German government did not want to send out any signal that might encourage the hardliner opposition in Moscow (Kaiser and Becher 1992: 39, 44–5).

Shortly after Iraq's invasion of Kuwait, the US started a military build-up in the Gulf. The German government strongly supported and assisted the use of US bases on its territory but was much more hesitant when asked to contribute troops. A possible German contribution to a joint naval task force was deliberated in the run-up to a WEU meeting on 21 August 1990. On 16 August, a German minesweeping detachment was sent to the Mediterranean in order to replace US forces that had left for the Persian Gulf. Speculations about whether the German ships might eventually be deployed in the Gulf came to a halt on 20

August when the government announced that the constitution precluded sending German troops to the Gulf. This decision was taken to protect the government coalition of the CDU/CSU and the FDP from severe conflict and to adjourn this difficult issue until after the first all-German elections. Chancellor Kohl (CDU) was the dominant figure in these decisions. He marginalised Defence Minister Stoltenberg (CDU), who deemed participation in the Gulf constitutional (Oldhaver 2000: 240–2). Foreign Minister Genscher and many of his FDP colleagues considered such a deployment unconstitutional. On 20 August, the governing coalition informally agreed to address the issue again in the new electoral term and to seek a constitutional clarification by way of an amendment.

On 30 August, the US government asked other countries to at least share the financial burden of the crisis measures. The German response irritated the allies since it remained unclear for more than two weeks until US Secretary of State James Baker visited Germany on 15 September. When Baker announced at the North Atlantic Council meeting on 10 September that the US would also appreciate its European allies deploying ground troops to Saudi Arabia, Germany announced that it would contribute some *Fox NBC* reconnaissance vehicles (without troops) and airlift and sealift capacities and participate in the economic aid programme that the EC had agreed to provide. The government offered 3.3 billion Deutsche marks to help the US military effort and aid countries affected by the embargo in the Middle East. German military aid included the delivery of 60 *Fox* vehicles to the US forces and further transport and engineering equipment.

The contribution issues were made worse for the German government when, on 20 December 1990, Turkey requested that NATO deploy the Allied Command Europe Mobile Force's Air component (AMF-A) to south-eastern Turkey. NATO approved this request on 2 January 1991. The AMF-A included 18 German *Alphajets* and 200 soldiers. The reluctant German government at first hesitated to make this contribution lest the Soviets could possibly misinterpret this German engagement within NATO, but eventually justified it as a sign of solidarity with the allies. The opposition rejected this deployment as a dangerous move, arguing that Germany might be drawn into a future war. Germany also participated with ships in the mine countermeasure forces of NATO's Standing Naval Force Channel dispatched to the Mediterranean.

From August 1990 to January 1991, German politicians conveyed a rather confusing picture to their observers and, at times, their own public (Oldhaver 2000: 136–8). Many allies missed signs and acts of 'real' and unequivocal solidarity since they considered the aims of the war to also be in the German interest. On the other hand, Germany *did* make a considerable contribution to the Gulf crisis and war effort but concealed the full extent of this from the public at the time (Inacker 1991). German military, economic and financial contributions to the Gulf War and related crisis measures amounted to the remarkable sum of more than 17 billion Deutsche marks, i.e. Germany paid 12.2 per cent of the overall costs.

Apart from these contributions, Germany also clearly backed the resolutions issued by the UN politically, and actively cooperated within the EC, WEU and NATO. It made another important indirect contribution to the success of the war coalition by cooperating very closely with the Soviets, by paying large sums for the Soviet withdrawal from Central Europe and for the stabilisation of Eastern Europe. This enabled the transfer of a major part of the allied troops to the Gulf. Germany's function as the major deployment base for many of the allied troops and the considerable logistical assistance provided by the Germans meant that, from the perspective of international law, Germany 'was far more directly involved in the Gulf war ... than admitted by the German government' (Kaiser and Becher 1992: 54).

In mid-January 1991, large sections of the German public and leadership were still hoping for a peaceful solution to the conflict. Chancellor Kohl and Foreign Minister Genscher emphatically backed the attempt at mediation by French President Mitterrand. Although the US had already taken the decision to fight the war, Kohl applauded these last-minute, 'passionate efforts' to hopefully prevent military action. The strong German peace movement of the early 1980s was 're-awakened' by the Gulf crisis and voiced quite audibly, though rather briefly, the much-cited 'anti-militarist consensus' of the German public.

2.1.2   Content analysis of parliamentary debates

In the German debate on the Gulf War we could detect only 26 speeches that qualified for coding; 9 speeches supportive of a German military contribution *of some kind* (depicted in Table 8.1) and 17 speeches opposing this (shown in Table 8.2). But even the nine supportive speeches remained strikingly vague about the exact nature of this contribution.

The most frequent argument mentioned in the *whole* debate was that peaceful means had not been exhausted.[6] This was used by both supporters (55.6 per cent) and opponents (82.4 per cent). It is remarkable

---

[6] For reasons of space the overall frequencies are not reproduced here but can be deduced from the individual tables.

Table 8.1 *Frequencies of arguments, Gulf War, Germany, supporters only (n = 9); extracts of results*[a]

Code	Argument	Number of speakers	Percentage of speakers
4101	Enforce international law/support UN	8	88.9
3101	Identity norms	7	77.8
4202	Peaceful means exhausted	5	55.6
4302	Peaceful means not exhausted	5	55.6
2101	Alliance pro (internal aspects)	4	44.4
1104	Show of force	4	44.4
5102	Threat to world order	4	44.4
1101	National interest	3	33.3
1103	Regional stability	3	33.3

[a] Full lists of results for this and all following tables are available from the author.

Table 8.2 *Frequencies of arguments, Gulf War, Germany, opponents only (n = 17); extracts of results*

Code	Argument	Number of speakers	Percentage of speakers
4302	Peaceful means not exhausted	14	82.4
3301	Restraining identity/role norms	12	70.6
5302	Pacifism/war damages global norms	9	52.9
4101	Enforce international law/support UN	6	35.3
5303	Civilian casualties	7	41.2
1303	Regional instability	5	29.4

how emphatically even supporters of the war stressed that absolutely every chance for a peaceful solution must be taken. At that time, shortly after the Cold War, there was widespread unease about waging wars again. The second most frequent argument, the enforcement of international law, is also prominently used by both groups (88.9 vs 35.3 per cent): more than one in three opponents accepted the general idea that international law must be enforced in the crisis. Every opponent of the war clearly condemned Iraq's annexation of Kuwait as a criminal act of aggression, but a number of opponents from the left-wing parties also expressed a fundamental aversion to war.

Supporters as well as opponents referred frequently to their understanding of the German identity/role (77.8 vs 70.6 per cent), drawing support for two fundamentally antagonistic positions. While those in favour of war stressed the historical German guilt of utmost aggression and the failure of appeasement, those against war emphasised the norm of self-restraint embedded in the German constitution. However, some of those speakers proclaimed a willingness to amend the constitution in the future so that Germany might participate in UN missions.

As was to be expected from the foreign policy role profile, 'classic' power arguments such as national interests, national security or the balance of power were far less used. The 'securing of the oil supply' as a motive for the war was essentially played down in the official parliamentary discourse. References to an enemy image were also comparatively few in the Bundestag (though they figured more prominently in the media debate).

2.1.3   Newspaper debates

The main lines of arguments in the left-liberal *Süddeutsche Zeitung* (SZ) and conservative *Frankfurter Allgemeine Zeitung* (FAZ) newspaper commentaries and editorials were as follows.

Saddam Hussein figured in many newspaper accounts as an evil and extremely dangerous enemy, sometimes explicitly likened to Hitler. The recourse to German history, the Second World War and analogies to the current crisis represented an important stream of moralising arguments. Opponents of the war referred to only one lesson from German history: 'Never again war!' Advocates of the war invoked the Saddam–Hitler analogy to legitimise a potential war against Iraq since the Germans should know best that dictators of that kind can only be stopped by force. Historical lessons and German guilt were then intensified as topics in the debate on the threat to Israel from German-aided weaponry (Schallenberger 1999: 115–22, 132–56).

A second line of arguments voiced concern about what the 'others' think of 'us'. In particular the FAZ, but partly also the SZ, criticised the non-participation of Germany, stressing the notion of the German 'shirkers', 'cowards' and 'cheque-book diplomats' who damaged the country's reputation with the allies. The argument of 'alliance solidarity' and enhanced responsibility for a unified Germany figured prominently in the liberal and conservative newspaper editorials. A third line in the public discourse was pacifism and the expression of 'fear' (*angst*). The fundamental opponents of the war envisioned apocalyptic consequences for themselves, the environment and the world at large. The slogan of the peace movement, 'No blood for oil', was brusquely rebutted by those advocating a war (though not advocating German participation in it!). The counter-argument was that aggression must be confronted unequivocally and that this war was being fought in order to enforce international law and to advance a new world order.

2.1.4   Public opinion polls

Although the Germans had at the time been labelled a largely 'pacifist' people, *at the beginning of the war*, polls showed that the Germans supported the war to a similarly high extent as citizens in other countries. The visible protest against the anti-Iraq coalition thus spoke for a minority. Depending on the individual poll, majorities of 57 per cent (Emnid), 64 per cent (with 75 per cent of West Germans) (ZDF-Politbarometer) and even 80 per cent (Wickert-Institut) were identified in January and February 1991 (see Oldhaver 2000: 203–4). Such high rates of consent were not scored in earlier phases of the crisis; on the contrary, in October 1990, only 35 per cent of West Germans agreed to the use of military means, and only 32 per cent in January 1991. On the other hand, 44 per cent in October 1990 and 50 per cent in January 1991 said that war should be avoided under all circumstances; 21 per cent in October 1990 and 18 per cent in January 1991 were undecided (Noelle-Neumann and Köcher 1993: 1086). A Gallup poll at the end of December identified 63 per cent of Germans as being against a war.[7] What remained comparatively constant from August 1990 to January 1991 was a high majority rejecting the *participation of German troops* in the Gulf (Kaiser and Becher 1992: 48). The differentiation between support for the war in principle and German participation in it was crucial in all the polls during the crisis.[8]

2.1.5   Conclusion: explaining Germany's non-participation in the Gulf War

It was completely unclear in 1990–1 what international role unified Germany should and would adopt and how much continuity or how much change to its multilateralist policy traits and 'culture of restraint' were 'appropriate'. Polls showed that *public* opinion during the Gulf crisis was polarised between more pacifist and more 'we need to take on more responsibility' attitudes, but that a large majority was against the participation of German troops in the Gulf. While the coalition government was 'hiding' behind a complicated legal debate, the *published* opinion did not hesitate to construct clear-cut images of friend and foe

---

[7] Cited in Kleine-Brockhoff, Thomas, Kostede, Norbert and Schwarz, Birgit 1991. 'Die Kinder des Friedens', *Die Zeit*, 25 January. Online: www.zeit.de/1991/05/die-kinder-des-friedens.

[8] A summary of public opinion polls concerning the Gulf War is presented in Oldhaver (2000: 203–15).

and to put the government under pressure with putative expectations on the part of Germany's 'friends and allies'.

Hence, the main reasons for non-participation lay in identity/role conceptions and in a special situational reason: politicians argued about the interpretation of Article 87a of the Basic Law that stated that the armed forces were bound to purposes of self-defence. Article 87a was commonly related to Article 24 [2] of the Basic Law that permitted the German federation to enter a system of mutual collective security in order to maintain peace. The dispute here was whether this implied the allowance for participation in UN missions, and if so, in which. This legal ground for restraint was sometimes bolstered by the normative belief that the 'culture of restraint' would also suit unified Germany very well as the ultimate lesson from the Nazi past. Such speakers saw themselves in line with a majority of German citizens who were believed to be deeply averse to war. In a time of electoral campaigning and restructuring of the German polity, it would have been risky for the government to have acted against the will of the majority.

The special situational reason in the transition phase from divided Germany to unification lay in the political challenge not to estrange the Soviets by making any false move in the crisis. This balancing of the needs and expectations of Western and Eastern allies and counterparts proved awkward. Although many German officials kept on stressing that Germany would have to accept more responsibilities and burdens, the political elite did not yet know how to meet these new tasks appropriately.

2.2   Germany and the Kosovo War, 1998–1999

2.2.1   The road to war

The participation of German ECR-Tornados in NATO's bombing of the Federal Republic of Yugoslavia from 24 March 1999 to 10 June 1999 has been considered a landmark in German foreign policy. For the first time since 1945, German military forces took part in an offensive combat mission and did so without a clear UN mandate. Remarkably, it was a coalition government of Social Democrats and Greens with strong traditions of a pacifist culture in their parties, just elected into office after 16 years of Chancellor Kohl's conservative incumbency, who were leading their country into its first war – against a state that had been attacked by Nazi Germany in the Second World War.

Germany's membership in the Balkan Contact Group secured the country central opportunities to shape the crisis within a multilateral framework in 1998–9. Germany kept trying to mediate between the

Western powers and Russia in the Contact Group. 'To keep Russia on board' was proclaimed an important German goal (Joetze 2001: 69–70). As the number of refugees rose further, Germany's Foreign Minister Kinkel (FDP), during an EU meeting in Palermo on 4 June 1998, called upon NATO to decide quickly on military action in Kosovo. In addition to this, he demanded safeguards to keep the refugees in the region since Germany had already received 140,000 Kosovar Albanians and would not provide further capacities.

On 11 June 1998, NATO's defence ministers decided to mandate their military agencies to work out concrete military options for the region and announced aircraft manoeuvres over Albania and Macedonia. Some accounts underline that NATO's eventual concrete military actions can be attributed to German initiatives (Loquai 2003: 44–5). German politicians, who were in the midst of the election campaign for the federal election on 27 September 1998, heavily debated during the summer the necessity of a UN mandate. While Kinkel initially insisted on a mandate, Defence Minister Rühe (CDU) declared repeatedly that NATO might have to act without a mandate. Rühe accused Kinkel of weakening the credibility of deterrence by insisting on a mandate. On 24 August, the government finally agreed on the line that participation in a military action in Kosovo without a mandate could become necessary in the event of a further escalation.

After NATO had issued an 'activation warning' to signal its resolve, the Kohl government decided on 30 September 1998 to participate with Tornados. As the election had yielded a majority for a coalition government of SPD and Greens, this decision was taken in coordination with the presumptive next chancellor, Gerhard Schröder (SPD), and next foreign minister, Joseph Fischer (Green Party) (Friedrich 2005: 50, 57). Crucial steps towards Germany's participation in the war were taken now and in the next weeks in an interregnum since neither the newly elected Bundestag nor the new government had yet been constituted. The Western allies observed Germany's transitory phase from the Kohl to the Schröder government with concern since Richard Holbrooke had been quoted during his negotiations in Belgrade as saying that Slobodan Milošević placed his hopes on a hesitant Germany.

On 9 October 1998, a delegation from the designated new government, which included Schröder and Fischer, was invited to the White House. Fischer later claimed that because of the precarious situation for the coalition negotiations and the pressure from his party, the Greens, he had hoped for a chance to somehow circumvent the NATO decision on an 'activation order' or to at least avoid military involvement. Fischer also reports that US President Clinton indicated to Schröder in a private conservation that he would understand if the Germans were not able to decide immediately because of the constitutional 'void' (Fischer 2007: 103–4). Schröder himself, however, claims in his memoirs to have assured Clinton that the new German government would adopt the Kohl government's position of 'a limited participation in a military intervention' (Schröder 2006: 110). The exact content of this one-to-one talk has been delivered in different, contradictory versions (Friedrich 2005: 53).

On 12 October 1998, Schröder and Fischer were, according to the Foreign Office's account, taken aback by a 'sudden' change of mind in the White House. Holbrooke would need NATO's complete unity behind him to put Milošević under credible pressure. Kohl thus summoned Fischer and the SPD leaders Schröder, Lafontaine and Verheugen to the Chancellery to coordinate the decision with Rühe, Kinkel and the parliamentary leaders of the CDU/CSU and FDP. The representatives of the new government gave their consent, but this decision to take part in potential air strikes required the approval of the Bundestag, which had not yet been constituted in its new composition. In a legally controversial move, the 'old' Bundestag assembled on 16 October for this special vote; an overwhelming majority of 500 MPs voted in favour of participation.

Following the Holbrooke–Milošević agreement there were efforts to build up the OSCE mission and to ensure that the 'extraction force' could be deployed to Macedonia. Germany agreed to participate in the extraction force, providing 200 soldiers and 200 OSCE observers. The violence intensified again in December and January, although NATO's activation order was still in force. The 'turning point', as it was labelled in the German media and by leaders such as Fischer, came with the 'massacre of Račak' on 15 January 1999. NATO accelerated its preparations for an intervention in order to increase the pressure on Milošević. The escalation of the conflict was to be prevented by one last opportunity for negotiations, which were prepared in the Contact Group but basically led by the US, French and British. Although the Germans felt marginalised during the negotiations in Rambouillet and Paris, they claimed to have provided the biggest impulses for staging this kind of 'Dayton II' negotiations (Fischer 2007: 123, 128–31).[9]

2.2.2   Content analysis of parliamentary debates

In the German parliamentary debates on the Kosovo crisis we identified 45 speeches qualifying for coding; 30 speeches advocating the

---

[9] Hofmann, Gunther 1999. 'Wie Deutschland in den Krieg geriet', *Die Zeit*, 12 May, pp. 17–21.

participation of the Bundeswehr in several proposed deployment missions (Table 8.3) and 15 rejecting this (Table 8.4). The central debate took place on 16 October 1998 in the 'constitutional void' and yielded a large majority of 500 MPs approving participation while 62 rejected it and 18 abstained. The 62 no-votes included the complete PDS group (29), 21 SPD MPs, 9 Green MPs and one each from the FDP and CDU/CSU and one non-affiliated MP.

The most frequent argument mentioned overall was that the humanitarian catastrophe had to be stopped (68.9 per cent), which was used by supporters (80 per cent) and also by a considerable number of opponents (46.7 per cent). While this was the argument most frequently used by supporters, many opponents conceded that a humanitarian disaster was impending but feared that the lack of a UN mandate would cause irreparable damage to international law and the world order. Lack of UN backing was the second most prominent argument (55.6 per cent) in the *whole* debate. For the opponents, it was their absolute central counter-argument (93.3 per cent), while only 36.7 per cent of advocates referred to this argument. Opponents were concerned that NATO's act of self-mandating and self-empowerment would constitute a negative precedent for the future. Many advocates emphasised that an intervention would be an exceptional act of emergency help. The third most used argument was that a credible show of force was needed (44.4 per cent of all speakers). This was predominantly put forward by supporters (63.3 per cent). They referred to negative experiences with Milošević in the past and claimed that he would give in only to credible military threats. Two-thirds of the opponents, however, claimed that peaceful means had not been exhausted.

The arguments of alliance solidarity and a special German obligation to take part in the military action were used quite frequently: 50 per cent of the advocates maintained that Germany must not 'stand aside' in NATO if the Alliance decided to strike; 43.3 per cent of the supporters referred to German lessons from the past dictatorship and the failure in Bosnia. Some opponents from the PDS and the Green Party argued the other way around: that NATO would damage its credibility by intervening since it had no legal mandate and since the selectivity of Western 'humanitarian interventions' was so blatant (26.7 per cent). As regards identity arguments, a number of opponents instead highlighted the prohibition of the preparation and conduct of wars of aggression in the German constitution (33.3 per cent).

Again, 'classic' power arguments were hardly used. The prevention of a large influx of refugees from the Balkans was an important motive of German policy but mentioned rather *in passing* in the parliamentary

Table 8.3 *Frequencies of arguments, Kosovo War, Germany, supporters only (n = 30); extracts of results*

Code	Argument	Number of speakers	Percentage of speakers
5101	Humanitarian catastrophe	24	80
1104	Show of force	19	63.3
2101	Alliance pro (internal aspects)	15	50
3101	Identity norms	13	43.3
4301	No UN mandate/damage to UN	11	36.7
6302	Casualty aversion (own soldiers)	8	26.7

Table 8.4 *Frequencies of arguments, Kosovo War, Germany, opponents only (n = 15); extracts of results*

Code	Argument	Number of speakers	Percentage of speakers
4301	No UN mandate/damage to UN	14	93.3
4302	Peaceful means not exhausted	10	66.7
5101	Humanitarian catastrophe	7	46.7
3301	Restraining identity/role norms	5	33.3
1303	Regional instability	4	26.7
2302	Alliance contra (external aspects)	4	26.7
5302	Pacifism/war damages global norms	4	26.7
6301	Democratic norms/procedures contra war	4	26.7

debate. In addition, casualty aversion arguments were used rather seldom (26.7 per cent) and notably only by supporters of the war. This might be due to the fact that most advocates reckoned with limited air strikes, and Germany's participation with Tornados was a comparatively small contribution to NATO's military forces. Still, it seems remarkable that the opponents did not capitalise on this issue but focused rather on international legal questions.

Arguments referring to enemy image were not significant in the selected parliamentary speeches (only 6.7 per cent mentioned it). This is surprising since the clear-cut enemy image of Milošević was widespread in the German media. This difference might be due to the fact that the German parliamentary debates were held at times when it was still hoped that Milošević would give in. Before and after the beginning of the air strikes, however, leading German politicians used an unequivocal language that likened the Serbian military operations in Kosovo to genocide and Auschwitz (e.g. Schröder 2006: 110–11; Fischer 2007: 184–5).

2.2.3   Newspaper debates

The editorials of the conservative FAZ from July 1998 to March 1999 articulated from an early stage clear demands *for* a military intervention in Kosovo. Milošević had no credit left whatsoever with the commentators following the catastrophe of the Bosnia war.[10] There was no doubt that a humanitarian disaster on an incredible scale was occurring in Kosovo. The FAZ positions went much further than most NATO politicians, not only with regard to this explicit and straightforward pro-war approach but also with regard to the future of Kosovo. Some commentators advocated a protectorate for Kosovo at a very early stage, or even independence.[11] Milošević and his Serbian troops presented a constant enemy image for the FAZ; he was represented as a brutal dictator with whom one could not negotiate.

The editorials of the left-liberal SZ pursued a slightly more reserved line towards a military intervention but also clearly saw the necessity to draw the lessons from the Bosnia War that such violence can only be stopped by force and that a humanitarian disaster must be averted.[12] The editorials also complained about the indecisive behaviour of NATO and criticised the fact that Milošević was fooling about with 'the West'. While the SZ also described the crimes by the Serbian military and police forces in strong language, the tenor was sometimes less moralistic than in the FAZ and the commentators also pointed to the share of guilt that the Kosovar KLA bore in the escalation of violence.[13]

2.2.4   Opinion polls

In contrast to the Gulf War, there were no large demonstrations in the German public against the Kosovo War. The public believed in the news and pictures of the humanitarian disaster in Kosovo. Germans felt a special obligation to protect human rights, especially since this was being done in agreement with their allies (Maull 2001). Another reason why there was relative quiescence can be traced to the fact that it was an SPD–Green government that was fiercely advocating the war.

---

[10] E.g. Author Nm 1998. 'Das Dilemma der NATO', FAZ, 25 September.
[11] E.g. Author Rm 1998. 'Entwaffnen', FAZ, 19 December. Author W. A. 1999. 'Bittsteller', FAZ, 21 January; Author Rm 1999. 'Nichts anderes hilft', FAZ, 28 January.
[12] Münch, Peter 1998. 'Moral und Militärintervention', SZ, 8 October.
[13] E.g. Münch, Peter 1999. 'NATO in Fesseln', SZ, 19 January.

Left-wing opponents within the peace movement had thus lost their former allies in the Bundestag.

In contrast to the Gulf War, there are hardly any polls available before the Kosovo intervention; for this reason, a poll taken after fighting started is considered here. An early Dimap poll of July 1998 produced the result that 48 per cent of Germans were against the participation of the Bundeswehr in a NATO intervention and 48 per cent supported it.[14] But after the beginning of the air strikes, opinion polls measured public approval of about 60 per cent for the intervention as well as for Germany's participation. However, the observation that a large majority of Germans had at least acquiesced to the war requires some differentiation. Many supporters of the Greens did not support the war, and the opposing PDS could count on a large rejection of the war in East Germany. Attitudes between East and West Germans differed considerably towards NATO and the Kosovo War.[15] While in April 1999 66 per cent of West Germans found that the German government 'behaved rightly' in the Kosovo crisis, only 27 per cent of East Germans shared this view (Noelle-Neumann and Köcher 2002: 988).

2.2.5   *Conclusion: explaining Germany's participation in the Kosovo War*
In summary, there were four sets of reasons why the German government decided to take part in the Kosovo War. Domestically, the most important decisions were taken within the transitional phase from the Kohl government to the new 'inexperienced' left-wing government. The Kosovo crisis put the new government to a severe test of its ability to govern. Though one can sometimes read that the road to war had largely been prepared by the former government, leading SPD–Green politicians such as Schröder, Scharping and Fischer declared that they advocated the war out of the conviction that there was no alternative and that it was in line with Germany's values and obligations.[16] As has been shown above, the government could draw upon the support of a majority of citizens when deciding in favour of an intervention.

News and pictures of atrocities in Kosovo generated a strong sense of moral and political responsibility towards the human suffering in Kosovo. It was felt that one could not just stand by and watch such crimes happen in the middle of 'civilised' Europe, in particular because

---

[14] Quoted in Associated Press Worldstream (German), 'Kinkel befuerchtet Fluechtlingsstrom wegen Kosovo-Krise', 31 July 1998.

[15] Köcher, Renate 1999. 'Der Kosovo spaltet Ost und West', FAZ, 16 June.

[16] E.g. see Hogrefe, Jürgen, Leinemann, Jürgen, Lersch, Paul, Pörtner, Rainer and Szandar, Alexander 1999. 'Aus freier Überzeugung', *Der Spiegel*, 19 April, pp. 22–29.

memories of the failure of the West in Bosnia were still too vivid. The parallels drawn between the worst Nazi crimes and the situation in Kosovo once again encouraged, as a follow-up to the Bosnia debate, a reflexive and moralistic German discourse about the lessons to be drawn from the Nazi past. The German 'civilian power' was hence confronted with central dilemmas between its normative core beliefs of 'Never again war' and 'Never again Auschwitz' (Maull 2001: 118): which one was to be given priority in case they should clash?

While the humanitarian motive was usually ranked highest by German advocates of the war, the argument 'alliance allegiance' (*Bündnistreue*) was the second salient public justification for a German participation. While members of the Kohl government even appeared among the most proactive NATO members with regard to military action in Kosovo in spring and summer 1998, the SPD–Green government did not leave the slightest doubt that they would also be a reliable NATO member. The SPD–Green government professed to continue Kohl's recognised foreign policy of strong multilateral bonds and thus underlined that being a good multilateralist had become part of Germany's identity and role conception (Maull 2001: 117).

Germany's participation in the intervention was also motivated by regional stabilisation interests. Another large-scale civil war in Yugoslavia with uncontrollable consequences for Albania and Macedonia was seen as too big a threat for the rest of Europe. Connected to this was the less openly discussed concern in Germany that a new wave of refugees would head for Germany (Hyde-Price 2001: 22). This was a sensitive topic since it was perceived that Germany had been receiving the bulk of refugees from the Balkans during the 1990s. An intervention in Kosovo therefore implied a clear self-interested motive for Germany: tackling the problem where it was located before it 'migrated' to one's own country.

2.3   Germany and the Iraq War 2003

2.3.1   Domestic decision-making process

The behaviour of the SPD–Green government during the Iraq crisis 2002/3 cannot be understood without considering the wider context of other military engagements. The left-wing government, in office from 1998 to 2005, had continued Chancellor Kohl's strategy of slowly expanding the quality and scope of Bundeswehr missions. One of the Bundeswehr's most extensive missions is its Afghanistan engagement following the terror attacks of 11 September 2001, which had prompted Chancellor Schröder to pledge US President Bush Germany's 'unrestricted solidarity'. Schröder's radical policy shift in the Iraq crisis of August 2002 onwards seemed puzzling, but the chancellor had already declared on 19 September 2001 that Germany would not take part in 'adventures'.

Schröder stated during a meeting with President Bush in the White House on 31 January 2002 that Germany would back US military action against Iraq in case of clear evidence that the Iraqi regime supported the Al-Qaeda terror network.[17] Bush later claimed in his memoirs (Bush 2010) that he took Schröder's statement as one of support and expressed his disappointment at Schröder's 'different take' when the German elections arrived later that year. When he told the chancellor that he would use military force should the need arise, Schröder replied, according to Bush, 'What is true of Afghanistan is true of Iraq. Nations that sponsor terror must face consequences. If you make it fast and make it decisive, I will be with you.' Schröder responded to this passage in Bush's memoirs by stating that Bush 'is not telling the truth' and added: 'Just as I did during my subsequent meetings with the American president, I made it clear that, should Iraq ... prove to have provided protection and hospitality to al-Qaida fighters, Germany would reliably stand beside the US. This connection, however, as it became clear during 2002, was false and constructed.'[18]

While the US administration was trying to put a war on Iraq on the political agenda by linking it to the terror attacks from 2001 and incorporating it into an 'axis of evil', Schröder declared in March 2002 that he would not support a unilateral military action by the US and that any German commitment to such an action had to be based upon a UN mandate. At the same time, he conceded that German *Fox NBC* reconnaissance vehicles in Kuwait would provide aid in case of a war. In the following months, the Iraq issue largely vanished from the official governmental agenda in Germany until the chancellor addressed it again during the federal election campaign in August 2002. Polls indicated that the SPD was facing the loss of its majority in the election on 22 September 2002. Schröder capitalised on the widespread attitude of citizens against an Iraq war and positioned himself on 5 August for a long time to come as he stated that Germany would not participate in a war against Iraq, even if this was mandated by the UN. He repeated

---

[17] Westdeutscher Rundfunk 2011. 'Broadcast "Fischer, Schily: Mein 11. September. Als der Anschlag die deutsche Regierung traf"', ARD, 5 September, transcript p. 10, quotations Karsten-Uwe Heye and Wolfgang Ischinger.

[18] All quotations taken from Hawley, Charles 2010. 'The Legacy Battle: Bush–Schröder Enmity Continues in Memoirs', *SPIEGEL online*, 10 November. Online: www.spiegel. de/international/world/0,1518,728336,00.html.

that under his leadership Germany would not take part in 'adventures'. The Green Foreign Minister Fischer stated that Iraq was the false priority. The CDU foreign policy expert Schäuble did not preclude German participation, but only on the basis of a UN mandate. Schröder's challenger Stoiber (CSU) initially wavered on the Iraq issue, then tried to catch up with Schröder's position but claimed that German soldiers had not been requested at all in Iraq. The FDP insisted that the Iraq crisis had to be addressed within the UN context.

The federal election eventually yielded a very slim majority for the SPD–Green government. Analysts of the election agreed that the handling of the Iraq War issue, together with that of the flood disaster in some parts of Germany, had finally turned the vote in favour of the incumbents.[19] Schröder and his Green Foreign Minister Fischer differed on noticeable aspects during the election campaign and during the whole Iraq crisis. While Fischer largely avoided acid rhetoric and kept his position towards an Iraq War more flexible over time, Schröder (and parts of the SPD) used a rhetoric that was widely accused of anti-Americanism, latent unilateralism and an irritating self-assertiveness.

When the German government was formally requested by the US in November 2002 to support a potential military action, it still refused an active participation but promised to provide assistance such as granting the allies overflight rights, usage rights for the allied military bases and the protection of allied barracks in Germany. Later on, the government also agreed to keep German personnel aboard NATO's AWACS aircraft over Turkey and to leave the NBC reconnaissance vehicles in Kuwait. All these forms of indirect and direct German assistance to a potential war effort once again – as was the case with the first Gulf War – triggered a political debate about several legal aspects of such support. The German government had obviously manoeuvred itself into a politico-legal dilemma. While it officially stuck to its rejection of the war under all circumstances, it equally referred to certain alliance obligations that Germany would also have to meet on the basis of international agreements.[20]

---

[19] Dettmer, Markus, Hammerstein, Konstantin von, Hornig, Frank, Leinemann, Jürgen, Neubacher, Alexander, Palmer, Hartmut, Reiermann, Christian, Sauga, Michael, Schäfer, Ulrich, Schult, Christoph and Steingart, Gabor 2002. 'Mehrheit ist Mehrheit', *Der SPIEGEL*, 24 September, pp. 10–12.

[20] At the end of 2005, it became public that two agents of the German intelligence service, Bundesnachrichtendienst (BND), had been in Baghdad from February to April 2003 and supplied reconnaissance information to the US military. The Bundestag then set up a committee of inquiry to investigate the former SPD–Green government's activities in the US 'war on terror' and in the Iraq War. While the SPD still denies any participation whatsoever in the Iraq War, it remains controversial as to

Importantly, in January 2003, Germany assumed its two-year seat as a non-permanent member of the UN Security Council, which it would chair in February 2003, hence putting Germany into a central UN position for a limited but decisive period. This responsibility at first seemed to soften up Germany's strict anti-war attitude. At the end of the year, Fischer and German UN diplomats indicated that under 'unforeseen circumstances' a German approval of an Iraq War in the UN Security Council 'could not be precluded'.[21] During January, however, Fischer and Schröder reaffirmed their position of rejection and agreed with France that the weapons inspections needed more time.

From January 2003, Germany and France commenced close cooperation to avoid a war, thus alleviating Germany's international isolation. As a temporary member of the Security Council, Germany launched several counter-initiatives in the UN in association with France and Russia. A common European perspective on the Iraq issue was lacking (Harnisch 2004: 188–9). Initial signals that the German government might change its attitude were finally disclaimed when Schröder once again used an election campaign rally in Goslar to establish his position. On 21 January, he declared that he had told Germany's allies that Germany would not approve a resolution that legitimated a war. The sudden launching of a putative plan by France and Germany for an alternative, robust weapons inspections concept aggravated tensions with the US, leading to an outright controversy at the Munich Conference on Security Policy (7–9 February). While US Secretary of Defense Donald Rumsfeld declared that diplomacy had been exhausted, Fischer argued to the contrary. The opposition CDU leader Angela Merkel, however, stated at the Munich Conference that she would advocate military action and German participation if all peaceful means were exhausted.

2.3.2   Content analysis of parliamentary debates

The debates in the Bundestag on the Iraq crisis were rather difficult to code since it was often difficult to pin-point the positions of the CDU/CSU and FDP opposition speakers. We selected 47 speeches from the parliamentary debates qualifying for coding. A large majority of 76.6 per cent (36 speeches) were against a war and Bundeswehr participation in

what extent the information provided by the German agents was 'relevant' for the US war effort. The evidence collected in the committee of inquiry suggests an 'indirect' war participation. See Blechschmidt, Peter 2009. 'Indirekt am Krieg beteiligt', SZ, 27 May, p. 5.

[21] Cited in 'Welt von Freunden', FAZ, 30 December 2002, p. 12.

Table 8.5 *Frequencies of arguments, Iraq War, Germany, opponents only (n = 36); extracts of results*

Code	Argument	Number of speakers	Percentage of speakers
4302	Peaceful means not exhausted	23	63.9
4301	No UN mandate/damage to UN	14	38.9
6301	Democratic norms/procedures contra war	13	36.1
5302	Pacifism/war damages global norms	11	30.6
5303	Civilian casualties	8	22.2
5304	Multilateral war rejection	8	22.2

Table 8.6 *Frequencies of arguments, Iraq War, Germany, supporters only (n = 11); extracts of results*

Code	Argument	Number of speakers	Percentage of speakers
4101	Enforce international law/support UN	8	72.7
1104	Show of force	7	63.6
3101	Identity norms	4	36.4
1105	National security	4	36.4
4202	Peaceful means exhausted	4	36.4
7101	Enemy image of adversary	4	36.4

it (Table 8.5), while only 23.4 per cent (11 speeches) declared that they would advocate a credible threat of force and, later in the process but becoming more vague, eventually a war as the last resort (Table 8.6).

As Table 8.5 indicates, the opponents most frequently argued that peaceful means had not been exhausted (63.9 per cent). Following this argument was the reference to the lack of UN authorisation to use force (38.9 per cent) and the reference to the German public's rejection of the war (36.1 per cent). The supporters (depicted in Table 8.6) most frequently argued that someone had to enforce compliance with UN resolutions, by force if need be, and that the use of force against Iraq posed such an instance following many years of the dictator's defiance. Related to this is the second most used argument by supporters: that such a dictator can only be made responsive by credible threats of force or eventually the use of force.

Which arguments were less used? The debate overall was dominated by references to 'international law', 'universal values' (here, world order) and 'democracy'. Once again, classic power arguments appeared relatively rarely. Interesting to note is that, in contrast to Anglo-Saxon advocates of the war, the arguments of 'regime change' or 'humanitarian disaster' were not used at all by German supporters of the war. Equally interesting is the relative insignificance of the usually prominent alliance arguments. Such arguments tended to be concealed as 'identity obligation' arguments, which were less prominent in this debate than in former debates.

The sharply edged controversy between the left-wing government and the FDP and CDU/CSU opposition revolved around the following lines of arguments: the government rejected the US allegation that Iraq was cooperating with terrorists and claimed instead that effective inspections and an effective international disarmament regime would contain the Iraqi threat. An important issue for the government was the damage to the world order and international security that would be caused by a war. They referred to a dangerous slippery slope as a result of war: this would destabilise the region, harm the anti-terror coalition with Muslim states and fuel terrorism all around the world.

The CDU/CSU and FDP opposition focused less on US policy than on the 'failure' of the German government in the Iraq crisis: they deemed it a big mistake that the government had precluded German participation in military actions under any circumstances, even if a second resolution were to be obtained. This would damage the UN and international law since law always required someone to enforce it, if necessary by means of force. Whereas the FDP demanded a clear UN mandate for any military action, the Conservatives remained quite vague or contradictory over this issue.

2.3.3 Newspaper debates

The FAZ editorials rejected the US concept of a war for regime change. They pointed to the high risks of such a war without precedence and to the unconvincing reasons put forward by the US. In contrast to the 1990–1 Gulf crisis, the FAZ did not convey striking enemy images of the regime any more. While Saddam Hussein was regarded as a threat, it was equally conceded that (for the time being) there was insufficient evidence of the scale of this threat and that a 'war on suspicion' was inadmissible. At the same time, both FAZ and SZ editorials advocated a robust and credible threat of force since Saddam Hussein would otherwise never comply with all the UN resolutions. Both newspapers strictly separated the enforcement of UN disarmament resolutions (acceptable) and a violent regime change (unacceptable). The SZ rejected the 'regime change war' as a 'war of aggression' and a breach of international law.[22]

Many FAZ editorials dealt with Schröder's early positioning of 'total denial',[23] assessing this stance as imprudent and unnecessary, reducing Germany's international influence to nil, splitting the Western community and in the end only benefiting the Iraqi dictator. The German government should keep its policies more flexible since evidence of Iraq's WMD programme might emerge in the coming months. The SZ criticised the SPD–Green government in a less scathing tone than the FAZ and, in principle, did not find fault with the greater emancipation of Germany from the US. But the left-liberal newspaper was also worried about Germany's isolation. Although the SZ showed some sympathy for the government's line of 'no participation in adventures', their editorials were often critical of the misplaced rhetoric as well as the inconsistencies and dilemmas resulting from its policies.

2.3.4   Opinion polls

Rejection of the Iraq War by the German population was tremendous. No other military action since 1990 has been as unpopular as this war. Demonstrations against the Iraq War were well attended. The biggest demonstration assembled 500,000 people in Berlin on 15 February 2003. Many polls published from late August 2002 onwards show relatively stable high rejection rates, with 70–75 per cent of Germans against a war – or of even more than 84 per cent in the first months of 2003[24] – and, if asked, a majority against a German participation. In East Germany, the rates of disapproval were, as with former military actions, even higher than in West Germany. An Emnid poll in January 2003 showed 73.4 per cent of West Germans but 89.2 per cent of East Germans stating that Germany should not participate in any form if the US were to attack Iraq.[25] A Gallup poll in January 2003 found that 89 per cent of Germans dismissed the idea of German participation in a US-led war without a UN mandate, and a small majority of 52 per cent regarded participation as unjustified (45 per cent deemed it justified) even in the event of a UN mandate.[26] In a Politbarometer poll in

---

[22] E.g. Ulrich, Stefan 2003. 'Im Club der Unbeugsamen', SZ, 17 March, p. 4; Cornelius, Stefan 2003. 'Kreislauf des Zorns', SZ, 21 March, p. 4; Prantl, Heribert 2003. 'Recht bleibt Recht, aber nur solange es passt', SZ, 22 March, p. 4.
[23] Author Bko 2002. 'In der Sackgasse', FAZ, 8 November, p. 1.
[24] E.g. Infratest dimap 2003. 'DeutschlandTREND März 2003'.
[25] Emnid poll, presented in Wittich (2003: 3).
[26] EOS Gallup Europe 2003. 'International Crisis Survey Report', 21–27 January. Online: http://paks.uni-duesseldorf.de/Dokumente/International-Crisis-Survey_ Rapport-Final.pdf.

February 2003, respondents were asked about their attitudes towards a UN-mandated war and here 50 per cent of Germans disapproved of German participation *of any kind*, while 33 per cent advocated financial and material aid and 14 per cent participation involving soldiers.[27]

2.3.5 Conclusion: why Germany abstained

The German government's 'surprising' behaviour during the Iraq crisis in 2002/3 entailed much debate on the foreign policy ambitions and style of the left-wing government as well as the future of the transatlantic and European community. The following factors contributed – to differing extents and at differing points in time – to Germany's abstention.

Most observers agree that the SPD instrumentalised the Iraq issue for election campaigning purposes in summer 2002. This is not to say that the government did not present substantial reasons for rejecting the war. But the SPD was aware of the immense public unpopularity of such a war and capitalised on the issue to avert its anticipated loss of power. The reiteration of this strong position led to a rhetorical self-entrapment that finally committed German diplomacy to this line, otherwise Germany might have faced a loss of credibility. The war was not only unpopular with the public, participation in it would probably also not have won the approval of the coalition MPs in parliament. Earlier than during the Iraq crisis, elements of the SPD–Green security policy at large had generated discontent with MPs of both parties. The government's difficulties in procuring its own Bundestag majority for the Bundeswehr deployment to Macedonia and Afghanistan indicated how much more difficult it would have been to convince the MPs of the necessity of an Iraq war (Harnisch 2004: 174, 192).

Many analyses claim that German citizens today still have strong anti-militarist and anti-war sentiments that characterise the 'culture of restraint' (e.g. Harnisch 2004; Forsberg 2005), and that the German political elite largely retains rather 'amicable' worldviews that render them distinct from their closest allies in France, the UK and the US (Malici 2006). US foreign policy following the terror attacks of 11 September 2001 had shaped world policy in a way that did not fit in with the dominant German foreign policy culture. The militarisation of international politics by the US 'war on terror', growing unilateralism, the pre-emptive use of force and violent regime change stand in

---

[27] Cited in Anonymous 2003. 'Front der Kriegsgegner wird immer breiter', *SPIEGEL online*, 21 February.

sharp contrast to the entrenched norms and values of German foreign policy (Risse 2004: 30).

In contrast to this explanation, some scholars have interpreted Chancellor Schröder's attitude in the Iraq crisis as an articulation of a self-assertive policy style indicating a transformation of the culture of reticence into a more 'nationalist' political culture (e.g. Buras and Longhurst 2004; Hellmann 2004). They argue that, in 1998, the left-wing government brought a new generation into power, who facilitated a gradual dissociation from the burdens of Germany's past. In foreign policy, this transformation of political culture implies an 'emancipation' from the West German protective power, the US (Forsberg 2005). Although Schröder indeed emphasised the new self-confidence of a 'grown-up' 'great power' in an unprecedented way, with the benefit of hindsight it is questionable to interpret this much criticised personal style of the chancellor as evidence of a transformed political culture: the successive grand coalition government of the CDU/CSU and SPD with Chancellor Merkel (CDU) and Foreign Minister Steinmeier (SPD) has displayed a different (moderate and cooperative) foreign policy style, although members of the same younger (SPD) generation have retained power positions.

3   Summary of results

In the German case, *each* of the three decisions by the government was in accordance with the majority will of the people, i.e. peaceful *and* coercive policies were supported by the majority. Reviewing the reasons for Germany's (non-)participation, one finds special situational factors, but also some commonalities in each of the cases. With regard to military actions, unified Germany remains a precarious power (Hellmann 2001), which leads to numerous controversies about issues of appropriateness: to what extent is a 'culture of restraint' still appropriate for Germany? What do legal norms suggest as appropriate? What does the country owe to its allies and partners?

3.1   *Domestic accountability: the government and the will of the people*

Citizens/public opinion: in each of the three cases the decision of the German government was supported by a majority of citizens. The public was not constantly averse to war during our period of investigation, as classic democratic peace theory would assume. Also the proponents of a 'culture of restraint' or even the claim that the Germans were (still) 'pacifist' run into difficulties in explaining the Kosovo case: why was there so little public protest against a war without a UN mandate? It seems more plausible to assume that a majority of Germans are not simply 'pacifist' but that their consent can be won if the justification for a military action presents reasons that they consider legitimate. A 'democratic war' justified by the prevention of gross violations of human rights (likened by some even to the prevention of a 'new Auschwitz' in Kosovo) could be accepted, but not a war justified by regime change.

Parliamentary arena: in none of the cases did the government face serious criticism from within their own parliamentary parties; its position enjoyed the support of the MPs. In some cases, the government was even backed by the opposition: in 1990/1, the CDU/CSU–FDP government did not face a war-mongering opposition; on the contrary, the leftist opposition was still quite pacifist at that time. The SPD–Green government in 1998/9 could draw upon a broad consensus with the CDU/CSU and FDP, making the radical left PDS the only real 'opposition' in this case. The constellation in 2002/3 was more intricate: while the SPD–Green government consistently pursued a policy that was averse to war, only surpassed by the PDS, who did not accept any indirect war participation whatsoever, the positions of the CDU/CSU and FDP remained diffuse over long periods of time. They tended partly in the direction of the US but tried to evade the issue of the UN mandate.

Newspaper commentaries: the relationship of the government to published opinion (the press) was differentiated in each of the three cases. In 1990/1, left-liberal as well as conservative commentaries were dissatisfied with the behaviour of the German government towards their allies and partners. They accused the Kohl government of hesitancy, of shirking and of damaging Germany's reputation, but it remained partly unclear what exactly they expected their government to contribute to the war effort. In 1998/9, the FAZ pronouncedly advocated an (early) intervention; the SZ was somewhat more cautious but also in favour of an intervention. Both newspapers criticised NATO's hesitancy to act, the German government included. Through their coverage of the atrocities in Kosovo, both newspapers contributed actively to the legitimation of Germany's participation in the war. In 2002/3, the SZ clearly rejected the war, as did the general tendency of the FAZ, at least in the absence of a UN mandate. Both newspapers, the FAZ far more than the SZ, however, criticised the 'bad policy style' of Chancellor Schröder and complained about the dangerous isolation of the Germans and the damage to German–US relations.

3.2   The substantial reasons for (non-)participation

3.2.1   Gulf War 1990–1991

Germany was preoccupied with its unification process when the military build-up in the Persian Gulf started. Many constitutional issues
such as the out-of-area deployment of the German armed forces had
not yet been clarified. The dominant political interpretation at the
time denied that such a deployment was constitutional. The German
government justified its position with reference to this interpretation.
The public debate on a (non-)participation in the Gulf War was largely
shaped by legal and pacifist arguments, pointing to the necessity of a
self-reflexive debate on the future role of unified Germany in international politics. Hence, Germany's non-participation in 1990–1 can
be explained as follows: first, reasons that resulted from the specific
situation of 'rapid unification'; second, reasons that refer to the identity
and role conception of a 'civilian power', whose fragility in the light of
new political challenges came to the fore for the first time. Germany's
power position was relevant for the decision in a rather negative sense.
A 'power' that was just in the process of developing from two extremely
different German polities, and that was partly observed with distrust
due to its Nazi past, could only become aware of itself at that time as
an insecure power.

3.2.2   Kosovo War 1998–1999

The decision to participate in the Kosovo War can partly also be traced
back to a special domestic situation. The decision was taken at a time
of a power transition from the liberal-conservative Kohl government
to the left-wing SPD–Green government. The newly elected parliament had not yet been constituted. The war decision was regarded
at home and abroad as the first critical test of the new government.
The German Kosovo debate was dominated by the assumption that
there was a humanitarian disaster taking place in Kosovo that had
to be stopped and by the weighing up of international legal issues of
legality and legitimacy. Speakers often referred to lessons learnt from
Western failure in the Bosnia War. The German debate featured ever
more moralistic traits; the atrocities in Kosovo were compared to the
war crimes of the Germans in the Second World War. That a majority of Germans advocated the war can be attributed to the persuasive
power of humanitarian arguments. News and pictures from Kosovo
gave credibility to NATO's claims that it was fighting this war for
humanitarian reasons. The new left-wing government emphasised the

continuation of Kohl's foreign policy and reassured the allies that they would not have to fear the Germans taking 'separate paths'. Quite 'typical' for the German Kosovo debate (as for the two others as well) is the fact that motives of 'national interests' were hardly mentioned in the official political debate. As a main receiving country for refugees, Germany had a massive self-interest in keeping refugees from the Balkans in their own region, i.e. preventing a further destabilisation of the Balkans in any event.

3.2.3   *Iraq War 2002–2003*

In 2002 it was again a federal election that played a significant role in the decision-making process. The SPD–Green government utilised the issue of German (non-)participation for electoral reasons. The war was immensely unpopular with the public, and the government would probably also not have won the support of their own members of parliament for the war. The fact that the re-elected government managed to stick to its distinctive 'no' position until the very end even in the case of a UN mandate was partly due to the dominant leadership of Chancellor Schröder. He had often marginalised the more 'moderate' Green Foreign Minister Fischer.

This time the German debate was less marked by explicit lessons from the German past or by explicit references to alliance solidarity and more by arguments concerning the 'poisoning' of transatlantic relations as well as the splitting of the EU. Germany's much appreciated 'soft power' seemed to have vanished from the scene. The actual content of this debate revolved around the issue of what a world order should look like in times of a US 'war on terror'. The non-participation of the Kohl government in 1990–1 and that of the Schröder government were thus worlds apart: the former compensated for its 'shirking' with extensive financial and material aid and altogether kept a controversial low political profile in the Gulf crisis; the latter sought head-on confrontation with its most powerful ally, forged its own counter-coalition and refused to make direct contributions to the war (Dalgaard-Nielsen 2005: 351).

3.3   *Commonalities across the three cases: the search for 'appropriateness'*

There are two constant themes in all three cases. One concerns legal issues. The German decision-making process is characterised by numerous domestic constitutional law and international law controversies. Since unified Germany has no long-standing practice of out-of-area missions, since the German parliament enjoys considerable oversight powers and since the Federal Supreme Court plays a significant role in German politics, issues of constitutionality, legality and legitimacy usually figure prominently in the German debates on military deployment (Liste 2012). Constitutional law and political practice had for decades stabilised the (West) German 'culture of restraint'. Against the background of the Nazi past, the controversies about the lawfulness of unified Germany's military missions indicate that the elite still has a particular confidence in the law as providing guidance on what is 'appropriate' in this precarious field.

The other constant theme refers to another issue of appropriateness: Germany's relationships with its allies and partners. The self-styled 'model multilateralist' Germany acts within a dense web of relations with significant other states, which means balancing highly complex expectations and reconciling these with its own interests. Remarkably, such German self-interests are usually played down in the public debate. In the debate on the Iraq War, the concern about Germany's isolation could only resonate so prominently because Germany is characterised by a highly internationalised state identity (Katzenstein 1997: 19–29).

In all three cases, the German government faced role conflicts due to completely new contexts of action: in the Gulf War, the 'culture of restraint', which is rooted within the German legal constitution, became problematic for solidarity with the Western allies, who expected a more pronounced burden sharing. In the Kosovo War – the ground having already been prepared by the preceding debate on the Bosnia War – the principle of 'never again war' was at odds with the self-conception of Germany as an international guardian of human rights. In addition, the principle of alliance allegiance implied a violation of international law in this case. In the Iraq War, the world order notions that are typical for a 'civilian power' came into conflict with solidarity with Germany's most powerful ally, the US.

Such role conflicts are by no means unusual since a foreign policy role is a bundling of different role segments that can produce tensions between each other. The political elite then has to solve these tensions through decisions that in turn and in the case of 'formative events' might trigger a long-term change within the role conception (Tewes 2002: 8). Like any other role concept, the 'civilian power' contains the possibility of numerous norm collisions, as the empirical analysis of war/peace decisions has just shown and as the 'creators' of the German civilian power concept have themselves pointed out (Harnisch and Maull 2001).

REFERENCES

Baumann, Rainer and Hellmann, Gunther 2001. 'Germany and the Use of Military Force: "Total War", the "Culture of Restraint" and the Quest for Normality', in Douglas Webber (ed.), *New Europe, New Germany, Old Foreign Policy? German Foreign Policy since Unification*. London: Cass, pp. 61–82

Buras, Piotr and Longhurst, Kerry 2004. 'The Berlin Republic, Iraq, and the Use of Force', *European Security* 13 (3): 215–45

Bush, George W. 2010. *Decision Points*. New York, NY: Crown

Dalgaard-Nielsen, Anja 2005. 'The Test of Strategic Culture: Germany, Pacifism and Pre-Emptive Strikes', *Security Dialogue* 36 (3): 339–59

Deitelhoff, Nicole and Burkard, Eva 2005. 'Europa vor Gericht: Die EU-Außenpolitik und der Internationale Strafgerichtshof', *HSFK-Report* No. 13/2005, Frankfurt a.M.

Duffield, John S. 1999. 'Political Culture and State Behavior: Why Germany Confounds Neorealism', *International Organization* 53 (4): 765–803

Fischer, Joschka 2007. *Die rot-grünen Jahre: Deutsche Außenpolitik – vom Kosovo bis zum 11. September*. Cologne: KiWi

Forsberg, Tuomas 2005. 'German Foreign Policy and the War on Iraq: Anti-Americanism, Pacifism or Emancipation?', *Security Dialogue* 36 (2): 213–31

Friedrich, Roland 2005. *Die deutsche Außenpolitik im Kosovo-Konflikt*. Wiesbaden: VS-Verlag für Sozialwissenschaften

Haftendorn, Helga 2001. *Deutsche Außenpolitik zwischen Selbstbeschränkung und Selbstbehauptung: 1945–2000*. Stuttgart: DVA

Harnisch, Sebastian 2004. 'Deutsche Sicherheitspolitik auf dem Prüfstand: Die Nonproliferationspolitik gegenüber dem Irak', in Sebastian Harnisch, Christos Katsioulis and Marco Overhaus (eds.), *Deutsche Sicherheitspolitik: Eine Bilanz der Regierung Schröder*. Baden-Baden: Nomos, pp. 173–200

Harnisch, Sebastian and Maull, Hanns W. 2001. 'Conclusion: "Learned Its Lesson Well?" Germany as a Civilian Power Ten Years after Unification', in Sebastian Harnisch and Hanns W. Maull (eds.), *Germany as a Civilian Power? The Foreign Policy of the Berlin Republic*. Manchester University Press, pp. 128–56

Hellmann, Gunther 2001. 'Precarious Power: Germany at the Dawn of the Twenty-First Century', in Wolf-Dieter Eberwein and Karl Kaiser (eds.), *Germany's New Foreign Policy: Decision-Making in an Interdependent World*. Basingstoke: Palgrave, pp. 293–311

2004. 'Von Gipfelstürmern und Gratwanderern: "Deutsche Wege" in der Außenpolitik', *Aus Politik und Zeitgeschichte* B 11/2004: 32–9

Hyde-Price, Adrian 2001. 'Germany and the Kosovo War: Still a Civilian Power?', in Douglas Webber (ed.), *New Europe, New Germany, Old Foreign Policy? German Foreign Policy since Unification*. London: Cass, pp. 19–34

Inacker, Michael J. 1991. *Unter Ausschluß der Öffentlichkeit? Die Deutschen in der Golfallianz*. Bonn: Bouvier

Joetze, Günter 2001. *Der letzte Krieg in Europa? Das Kosovo und die deutsche Politik*. Stuttgart: DVA

Kaiser, Karl and Becher, Klaus 1992. 'Germany and the Iraq Conflict', in Nicole Gnesotto and John Roper (eds.), *Western Europe and the Gulf: A Study of Western European Reactions to the Gulf War.* Paris: Institute for Security Studies of WEU, pp. 39–69

Katzenstein, Peter J. 1997. 'United Germany in an Integrating Europe', in Peter J. Katzenstein (ed.), *Tamed Power: Germany in Europe.* Ithaca, NY: Cornell University Press, pp. 1–48

Kaul, Hans-Peter 1998. 'Durchbruch in Rom: Der Vertrag über den Internationalen Strafgerichtshof', *Vereinte Nationen* 4/1998: 125–30

Knapp, Manfred 2007. 'Vereinte Nationen', in Siegmar Schmidt, Gunther Hellmann and Reinhard Wolf (eds.), *Handbuch zur deutschen Außenpolitik.* Wiesbaden: VS, pp. 727–45

Liste, Philip 2012. *Völkerrecht-Sprechen: Die Konstruktion demokratischer Völkerrechtspolitik in den USA und der Bundesrepublik Deutschland.* Baden-Baden: Nomos

Littlewood, Jez 2005. *The Biological Weapons Convention: A Failed Revolution.* Aldershot: Ashgate

Long, David and Hindle, Laird 1998. 'Europe and the Ottawa Process', in Maxwell A. Cameron, Robert J. Lawson and Brian W. Tomlin (eds.), *To Walk without Fear: The Global Movement to Ban Landmines.* Toronto: Oxford University Press, pp. 248–68

Loquai, Heinz 2003. *Weichenstellungen für einen Krieg: Internationales Krisenmanagement und die OSZE im Kosovo-Konflikt.* Baden-Baden: Nomos

Malici, Akan 2006. 'Germans as Venutians: The Culture of German Foreign Policy Behavior', *Foreign Policy Analysis* 2 (1): 37–62

Maull, Hanns W. 2000. 'Zivilmacht Deutschland: Vierzehn Thesen für eine neue deutsche Außenpolitik', in Dieter Senghaas (ed.), *Frieden machen.* Frankfurt a.M.: Suhrkamp, pp. 63–76

  2001. 'Germany's Foreign Policy, Post-Kosovo: Still a "Civilian Power"?', in Sebastian Harnisch and Hanns W. Maull (eds.), *Germany as a Civilian Power? The Foreign Policy of the Berlin Republic.* Manchester University Press, pp. 106–27

  2004. '"Normalisierung" oder Auszehrung? Deutsche Außenpolitik im Wandel', *Aus Politik und Zeitgeschichte* B 11/2004: 17–23

Müller, Harald 2003. 'Germany and WMD Proliferation', *The Nonproliferation Review* 10 (2): 1–20

  2006. 'Germany and the Proliferation of Weapons of Mass Destruction', in Hanns W. Maull (ed.), *Germany's Uncertain Power: Foreign Policy of the Berlin Republic.* Basingstoke: Palgrave MacMillan, pp. 49–65

Müller-Brandeck-Bocquet, Gisela 2008. 'Deutsch-französische Beziehungen und das Projekt "Friedensmacht Europa"', in Peter Schlotter, Wilhelm Nolte and Renate Grasse (eds.), *Berliner Friedenspolitik? Militärische Transformation – zivile Impulse – europäische Einbindung.* Baden-Baden: Nomos, pp. 233–60

Noelle-Neumann, Elisabeth and Köcher, Renate (eds.) 1993. *Allensbacher Jahrbuch der Demoskopie, 1984–1992.* Munich: Saur (eds.) 2002. *Allensbacher Jahrbuch der Demoskopie, 1998–2002.* Munich: Saur

Oldhaver, Mathias 2000. *Öffentliche Meinung in der Sicherheitspolitik: Untersuchung am Beispiel der Debatte über einen Einsatz der Bundeswehr im Golfkrieg.* Baden-Baden: Nomos

Overhaus, Marco 2006. 'Civilian Power under Stress: Germany, NATO, and the European Security and Defense Policy', in Hanns W. Maull (eds.), *Germany's Uncertain Power: Foreign Policy of the Berlin Republic.* Basingstoke: Palgrave MacMillan, pp. 66–78

Risse, Thomas 2004. 'Kontinuität durch Wandel: Eine "neue" deutsche Außenpolitik?', *Aus Politik und Zeitgeschichte* B 11/2004: 24–31

Rittberger, Volker (ed.) 2001. *German Foreign Policy since Unification: Theories and Case Studies.* Manchester University Press

Schallenberger, Stefan 1999. *Moralisierung im Kriegsdiskurs: eine Analyse von Printmedienbeiträgen zum Vietnamkrieg und zum Golfkrieg.* Frankfurt a.M.: Peter Lang

Schröder, Gerhard 2006. *Entscheidungen: Mein Leben in der Politik.* Hamburg: Hoffmann & Campe

Tewes, Henning 2002. *Germany, Civilian Power and the New Europe: Enlarging NATO and the European Union.* Basingstoke: Palgrave

Wagner, Wolfgang 2006. 'Parliamentary Control of Military Missions: Accounting for Pluralism', *DCAF Occasional Paper* No. 12, Geneva

Weschler, Lawrence 2000. 'Exceptional Cases in Rome: The United States and the Struggle for an ICC', in Sarah B. Sewall and Carl Kaysen (eds.), *The United States and the International Criminal Court: National Security and International Law.* Lanham, MD: Rowman & Littlefield, pp. 85–111

Wittich, Dietmar 2003. 'Angst und Skepsis: Öffentliche Meinung in Deutschland vor einem neuen Irak-Krieg', *rls Standpunkte* No. 1/2003, Berlin

Woyke, Wichard 2000. *Deutsch-französische Beziehungen seit der Wiedervereinigung: Das Tandem fasst wieder Tritt.* Opladen: Leske + Budrich

9   Moving beyond neutrality: Sweden's changing attitude towards the military use of force

Carmen Wunderlich

In accordance with the policy of neutrality traditionally pursued by the country, Sweden was not involved in any of the three wars examined. However, the country's concept of foreign policy and its self-image both contain contradictory elements. While humanitarian intervention such as that in the 1999 Kosovo conflict does fit in with Sweden's perceived role as the 'world's moral conscience', an increased trend to military intervention is, however, at odds with the pacifism deeply anchored in the country's self-image and with its legalistic UN policy.

1   Institutional and ideational determinants of Sweden's foreign and security policy

1.1   Decision-making competencies in foreign and security policy

Sweden is a constitutional monarchy with a parliamentary governmental system. Since the constitutional reform in 1975, the king as head of state has a merely representative function. The power to make political decisions lies with the parliament (*Riksdag*), which consists of one chamber with 349 seats that is re-elected every four years according to a system of proportional representation with a 4 per cent exclusion clause. One feature of the Swedish party system is the formation of factions on the basis of a left-wing/right-wing spectrum. Traditionally, a distinction is made between the non-socialist bloc, consisting of the Moderate Party (*Moderata samlingspartiet*), the Liberal Party (*Folkpartiet liberalerna*), the Centre Party (*Centerpartiet*) and the Christian Democrats (*Kristdemokraterna*) and the socialist bloc, made up of the Social Democratic Party (*Socialdemokraterna*) and the Left Party (*Vänsterpartiet*). In 1988, the entry into the Riksdag of the Green Party (*Miljöpartiet de Gröna*), a party located in the centre of the spectrum, undermined what had, until then, been a stable political landscape.

In Sweden, the Riksdag is in a strong position vis-à-vis the executive, reinforced by the fact that, unlike in most other European countries, minority governments are the rule. Thus, in voting situations the government is dependent upon the support of one or several other parties, which gives the opposition a large influence on the country's policies and generates a consensual and corporative style of politics (Jahn 2003: 99).

The Riksdag's work is largely determined by its committees. All parliamentary affairs need initially to pass through one of the committees before being put to the vote and it is here that the political debates actually take place. Particularly when there are minority governments, compromises and agreements are reached in the committees. The strong position of the Riksdag is also visible from the distribution of competencies between government and parliament in questions of foreign policy. Accordingly, although negotiating international agreements is primarily the responsibility of the executive, it does require the approval of the Riksdag if any agreements reached fall into the latter's sphere of competence (legislation and state budget) or are 'of particular significance' to the country.

With regard to the right to deploy troops, the situation in Sweden is somewhat ambivalent. Admittedly the constitution does involve a parliamentary proviso that means that before deploying troops abroad the executive is obliged to seek the Riksdag's approval. However, there are two special regulations in force – apart from cases of self-defence – that allow the executive to act without this authorisation. The first concerns putting troops on standby on the basis of an international agreement approved by the Riksdag: for example, the deployment of troops on the basis of Article 43 of the UN Charter (provision of standby forces and support of the Security Council). The Law on Armed Force for Service Abroad also allows the government to put up to 3,000 soldiers on standby for peace*keeping* operations decided on within the framework of the UN or the OSCE without prior parliamentary approval.[1] By contrast, peace-*enforcing* measures, such as Sweden's participation in UNPROFOR, IFOR or ISAF, do require the authorisation of the Riksdag (Wagner 2006: 53).

---

[1] 'Lag (1992:1153) om väpnad styrka för tjänstgöring utomlands'. Before 1992, Swedish military staff members were only allowed to take part in peacekeeping operations under UN command in accordance with Chapter VI of the Charter; moreover, nobody could be ordered to take part in military operations abroad; see Jakobsen (2006: 183). Revisions to the law in 2003 and 2010 concerned organisational issues within the army.

Even in cases that do not require parliamentary approval, in the run-up to any decisions to deploy troops, as a rule, appropriate consultations take place in the *Committee on Foreign Affairs* in order to guarantee the greatest possible degree of political support. Since the government is obliged to seek the authorisation of the Riksdag to finance these missions abroad the latter does have an indirect say in these matters and performs a control function. This is complemented by the strong role of the *Council for Foreign Affairs* whose primary function is to advise the government on matters of foreign affairs (Siedschlag 2001: 8).

Since the end of the Cold War Sweden's foreign and security policy has been largely based on a political consensus that transcends the affiliations of party blocs. Although public interest in questions of foreign and security policy has declined in recent years, the Swedish public is described as relatively 'attentive' (Anthonsen 2003: 187).

1.2 *Traditions, role conception and national identity in Swedish foreign policy*

1.2.1 *Traditions and guiding lines*

Sweden's identity with regard to foreign policy has been shaped by its traditionally pursued policy of neutrality and by the associated peacefulness of its relationships with other countries – since the end of the Napoleonic Wars in 1814, Sweden has not been involved in any violent conflict. At least between 1949 and 1992, the security policy doctrine summarised in the formulation 'non-participation in military alliances in peacetime aiming at neutrality in the event of war' was designed to preserve the country's independence and increase the chances of non-involvement in a war. Moreover, neutrality was considered to have the effect of promoting stability in Europe. Since the neutrality was not anchored in international law Sweden was obliged to provide it with credibility by means of a universal foreign policy orientation and to demonstrate political, economic and military independence (Schüngel 2005: 6–7).The country's neutral status simultaneously allowed it to act as a mediator between the antagonistic superpowers and, through its active foreign policy as 'conscience of the world' (Bjereld *et al.* 2008; translation by the author), to garner international reputation and trust. The country's policy of neutrality has thus increasingly been of identity-shaping significance as a 'super-ideology' (Agius 2006: ch. 4); the combination of a security policy oriented towards neutrality and a progressive, internationalist foreign policy has become the determining factor in post-war Swedish policy.

The basic features of this policy of 'active internationalism' are rooted in the socio-political concept formed during the Second World War, at the core of which is the idea of the people's home (*folkhemmet*), namely 'the vision of a government as a home that protects the nation's people as much as a family's home protects each of its members' (Åsard and Bennett 1997: 86). The result of this was a particular understanding of democracy, characterised especially by consensus politics and mechanisms for solving conflicts peacefully, plus a firm belief in core values such as solidarity and equality. The 'Swedish model' was profoundly influenced by the Social Democratic Party, which was in government almost without interruption for a period of four decades and, through this continuity, anchored Social Democratic standards deep in society (Agius 2006: 100). In parallel to the country's active foreign policy, as part of which Sweden stood up for democracy, international conflict prevention, disarmament and mediation work in conflict situations, what soon came to light was a characteristic typical of Scandinavian countries: a preference for multilateral, value-driven solutions rather than a need to satisfy purely material, national interests (see Agius 2006: 70). A recurring motif of Swedish activism is the export of national values and standards 'to change the world to fit Swedish ideals' (Sundelius 1990: 117). In Sweden, solidarity with the underprivileged is seen as a moral duty. Sweden's Lutheran/Protestant roots favour this attitude, and consequently a pursuit of social justice and solidarity was anchored in society even before the establishment of the welfare state. Among other things, Sweden's role as 'the advocate of the weak' has been expressed in the country's development aid, which has always been exemplary and, in view of the country's size, exceedingly generous (Eliæson 2002: 9; translation by the author).

After the end of the Cold War and the changes in Europe as a consequence of the collapse of the Soviet Union, Sweden adapted its foreign and security policy to the changed circumstances. At the beginning of the 1990s, the national security doctrine was reformulated with a view to watering down the classic neutrality policy and challenging classic Social Democrat standards and institutions while simultaneously reinforcing efforts to create a 'European identity' (Agius 2006: 143). The security policy formula was officially replaced by 'non-participation in military alliances aiming at making it possible to remain neutral in the event of war in our vicinity', thus liberating itself from ideological undertones. Neutrality in the event of war was declared *one* possibility among several and restricted to wars in the immediate vicinity – predictable politics were replaced by the freedom for Sweden to act as it sees fit (Bjereld *et al.* 2008: 323).

In the wake of continued European integration, neutrality became less and less justifiable, was perceived as an anomaly and interpreted by the political elite as a hindrance. Accordingly, in 2001 there was another revision of the concept behind the security policy with the intention of 'harmonising the security policy guidelines with the actual circumstances by stretching the neutrality concept to a great extent and assuring the Europeans of Sweden's loyalty and reliability' (Schüngel 2005: 12; translation by the author). Although nonalignment is still an objective, a willingness to participate in military operations within the framework of the European Union (EU) can now be discerned. The fact that the country still clings to nonalignment is interpreted by many as a difficult undertaking. Whereas politically speaking joining NATO remains a taboo subject and extensive collaboration within the framework of the Partnership for Peace Agreement and the Euro-Atlantic Partnership Council is considered enough by Swedish politicians, the obligations undertaken by Sweden within the framework of European security and defence policy render the military nonalignment meaningless. Sweden's foreign policy has undergone a transformation in accordance with changed outside conditions – the country is increasingly prepared to move away from traditional attitudes to further world peace and international security (Hallenberg 2000: 26–7). However, despite changed determinants of foreign policy, the fundamental principles of Swedish politics based on norms and values have not changed; and thus, for example, the UN remains the cornerstone of foreign policy and the guarantor of international security.

1.2.2 Sweden's attitude to international law: the case of the International Criminal Court

The United Nations and international law are among the cornerstones of Swedish foreign policy. For a small country such as Sweden, adherence to international standards is the equivalent of protection from exploitation and is thus in the national interest of the country (Ahlin 1993: 351–2). Sweden's attitude to international law can be illustrated on the basis of the nation's position on the International Criminal Court (ICC), whose establishment it supported from the outset. Together with other middle powers Sweden became an active voice in the 'like-minded group', which demanded an independent and strong ICC (Deitelhoff and Burkard 2005) and succeeded, together with an active non-governmental coalition (Coalition for the International Criminal Court, CICC), in considerably advancing the negotiation process between 1995 and 1998. Sweden held the view that initially the ICC should be responsible for 'core crimes', suggesting that other crimes could later be included in the ICC's jurisdiction as part of a review process. Moreover, it was argued that the court should receive an independent prosecutor and should complement the national legal system. Sweden signed the Statute of Rome, which served as the basis for the set-up of the ICC, on 7 October 1998; ratification took place on 28 June 2001.

1.2.3   Sweden's attitude towards international regimes: the case of arms control and disarmament

For over 30 years now, Sweden has continually been speaking out in favour of a policy of nuclear disarmament and non-proliferation. The significance that Sweden attaches to the non-proliferation regime is visible from the country's above-average commitment displayed at review conferences, in disarmament committees and at other relevant fora (Prawitz 2000). Sweden regularly speaks out in favour of the objective of complete nuclear disarmament in the framework of the New Agenda Coalition (NAC), an Irish–Swedish initiative established in 1998. After the Non-Proliferation Treaty was prolonged indefinitely in 1995 the NAC succeeded at the 2000 review conference in forcing the nuclear states to agree to an action plan for gradual nuclear disarmament. Sweden has also been actively supporting a Comprehensive Test Ban Treaty (CTBT) since the 1960s, presenting various draft texts on the subject at the Conference on Disarmament (CD). Importantly, the Swedish government established the Weapons of Mass Destruction Commission in 2003, chaired by Hans Blix, with the aim of providing new impetus for attempts at global disarmament and non-proliferation. Further examples are the EU WMD Strategy, initiated in 2003 by Foreign Minister Lindh, and repeated demands for the EU to play a proactive role in the field of nuclear disarmament and non-proliferation.

Sweden is also very active in the field of chemical weapons control and disarmament policy. Within the UN Sweden pleaded for banning chemical weapons as far as possible, played an active role in treaty negotiations because of its national technical expertise and thus made a fundamental contribution to the successful conclusion of negotiations (Salander 1992: 35). From the outset, Sweden advocated a comprehensive ban on biological weapons but criticised the unsatisfactory verification arrangements in the established treaty text as weak and, for this reason, delayed signing the Biological Weapons Convention itself (Roffey 2002). Since Sweden signed the treaty after some delay in February 1975, the country has been lobbying for the establishment of an effective verification system. With regard to banning landmines, Sweden is also active at a high level. Sweden was one of the first nations (1994) and one of the few countries to demand a global ban on mines at an early stage. After various civil society groups had demanded a ban on landmines, in June 1994 the Riksdag commissioned the government to lobby for a ban on anti-personnel mines within the framework of the Convention on Certain Conventional Weapons (CCW). In 1993, together with France and the Netherlands, Sweden called upon the UN General Assembly to initiate a review of the CCW and its protocol on mines. Sweden was the first country to present a draft text for a complete ban on anti-personnel mines at the CCW's review conference in August 1994, but the document was rejected in October 1995. The Swedish government finally decided to implement a unilateral ban and completed the destruction of national stockpiles in 2002. Nonetheless, Sweden was only moderately involved in the Ottawa Process and was not part of the core group of like-minded states that initiated treaty negotiations in 1997 (ICBL 1999: 655–7). Sweden signed the Ottawa Convention on 4 December 1997; ratification followed on 30 November 1998.

Sweden's proactive commitment to the field of arms control and disarmament shows how very important multilateral collaboration in international regimes is considered there.

1.2.4   Attitude towards the United Nations

Ever since the accession in 1946, the United Nations forms the framework of Sweden's foreign and security policy, since the UN is considered a suitable forum for 'active neutrality' (Bring and Mahmoudi 2001). Not only was Sweden's concept of security policy regarded as compatible with membership in a collective security system, it soon came to be perceived as an advantage as regards international mediating efforts. 'Neutrality gives Sweden the unmatched opportunity to enter arenas and areas normally reserved for other actors under the cover of the international mediator, negotiator, moralist, and pacifist' (Nilsson 1988: 30). UN membership made it possible for Sweden to externalise solidarity and to practise internationalism, which was achieved most successfully in the domains of peacekeeping and conflict prevention (see Björkdahl 2007). Accordingly, Sweden provided active support both financially and personally to the UN in the course of its history and has long since counted among its most generous contributors.

Considerable significance is attached by Sweden particularly to mediating efforts between conflicting parties; ever since UN peacekeeping operations began, Swedish involvement in peacekeeping operations has indeed been disproportionate – 12 per cent of the 530,000 soldiers who participated in UN operations before 1991 were Swedish (Lindström 1997: 6). Until 2004, a total of 80,000 Swedes participated

in UN missions (Jakobsen 2006: 189, 248–50). After initial controversies, the move away from traditional peacekeeping to more peace-
enforcing measures witnessed during the mid 1990s also met with
Swedish consent, albeit under the official guise of a continued traditional security policy.

1.2.5   Sweden's relations with alliances

NATO: Sweden's official collaboration with NATO began after the
end of the Cold War when, in 1994, the country joined the Partnership
for Peace programme (PfP; Dahl 2002a: 144). Since 1997, Sweden has
participated regularly in consultations on security policy issues in the
Euro-Atlantic Partnership Council and in what is referred to as the
'enhanced PfP'. Despite the fact that full membership with NATO is
excluded on the basis of Sweden's continued nonalignment policy, special significance is attached nonetheless to close cooperation and long-
term integration in the structures of NATO as regards building a stable
European security architecture.

Even though Sweden meets all the relevant criteria for joining
NATO and several members of the Alliance have repeatedly advocated
Swedish NATO membership in the past, accession is not expected to
occur in the near future. Full membership would contradict the norm
of neutrality deeply rooted within the country's political self-image.
However, declining membership is not to be equated with rejecting
the Alliance per se. Since joining PfP, all governments – regardless of
party affiliation – have been emphasising NATO's significance in providing European security. To date, Swedish soldiers have performed
several peacekeeping missions under NATO command, while closer
cooperation beyond the PfP programme is envisaged. Even though
the Swedish government seeks to circumvent practical difficulties by
excluding any military exercises conducted on the basis of the mutual
assistance clause pursuant to Article 5 (Dahl 2002b: 230–1), Sweden's
adherence to a policy of nonalignment is increasingly coming into conflict with a strong overall wish to enhance cooperation. In doing so,
the Swedish government is putting at stake its credibility as a reliable
European and transatlantic partner.

European Union: Whereas in the time of the Cold War, Sweden's accession to the European Community was perceived to be irreconcilable
with its claim to neutrality, a change in its stance came about when the
confrontation between the Eastern and Western Blocs ended. Sweden
joined the EU on 1 January 1995, a step considered necessary mainly
in order to master economic difficulties; moreover, Sweden also wished

to partake in establishing a new security architecture in Europe. EU membership turned out to be ambivalent for Sweden. While, on the one hand, previously unexpected opportunities of action and influence were opening up, the tensions arising from the clash between the country's continued nonalignment and a common European security policy simultaneously presented a challenge since Sweden was expected to give up its sovereignty (Schüngel 2005: 14–15; Folz 2011). Accordingly, the executive attempted to mitigate the future Common Foreign and Security Policy, particularly as regards a common security and defence policy, aiming for a stronger emphasis on (civil) crisis management instead (Björkdahl 2007). Difficulties may nonetheless arise from the 'Solidarity Clause' established in the course of European integration, which obliges EU member states to show mutual solidarity. Even though solidarity was interpreted by the Swedish government in a purely political sense, it is equally affirmed that, in the event of an EU member being attacked, Sweden's role would not be that of neutrality (see Rieker 2002: 32).

1.3   Conclusion: Sweden's self-perception as 'conscience of the world'

Ever since the 1970s and 1980s, when Olof Palme coined the phrase 'force for good in the world' to illustrate Sweden's global reputation (Dahl 2002a: 140), the country's self-image and perception by others have portrayed Sweden's foreign policy tradition as highly value-oriented. Within the framework of 'active internationalism', Sweden pursues a value-based foreign policy that is characterised by a preference for achieving multilateral, cooperative solutions, a commitment to the juridification and regulation of international relations, international solidarity, protection and promotion of international law and, finally, *good international citizenship*. Sweden's foreign policy culture always has been and indeed still is substantially influenced by its policy of neutrality, a tradition essential in shaping the country's identity and thus widely endorsed. That this policy of neutrality must in no case be equated with neutrality of opinion is illustrated by Sweden's diplomats who, on the international stage, have been very persistent in advocating a just world order. Sweden's role as a (self-appointed) 'moral superpower' (Nilsson 1991; translation by the author) or 'conscience of the world' (Bjereld *et al.* 2008: 21; translation by the author) is also expressed in the fields of international law and international regimes examined in this chapter, where Sweden has shown above-average commitment. Interesting in this regard is that Sweden lacks a pronounced enemy image – despite still-lingering effects of latent reservations about

Russia, Sweden's attitude towards non-democratic governments is, in general, not founded upon strong concepts of an enemy.

2   Analysis of decision-making processes and public debates in the run-up to the three wars

2.1   Sweden and the Gulf War 1990–1991

2.1.1   Domestic decision-making process

Sweden participated indirectly in *Operation Desert Storm* by deploying a field hospital; a decision that, according to Niklas Ekdal and Jonas Ekströmer, went down in Swedish history as the country's first participation in a conflict since 1814, namely 'in a war sanctioned by the UN to protect the rights of small nations' (Ekdal and Ekströmer 1991: 7; translation by the author). However, the government did not classify Sweden's contribution as participating in acts of war, but as a humanitarian commitment.[2]

From the outset, Sweden strongly condemned the invasion of Kuwait, calling instead for a peaceful resolution of the conflict within the UN framework until the very end. However, national sanctions against Iraq were not applied until the day after Security Council Resolution 661 was passed – the fact that the Social Democratic government led by Ingvar Carlsson had thus held off until the Security Council's decision was strongly criticised, even though the tactic itself was anchored deeply within the country's traditions (Ahlin 1993: 194). Predominantly, Sweden set the focus on making full use of peaceful means within the UN's framework – above all economic sanctions – and on providing humanitarian aid for the suffering population in Iraq. Resolution 665, which, all else failing, sanctioned the use of violence to enforce the UN embargo, albeit without explicitly drawing on Article 42 of the UN Charter,[3] was adopted on 25 August 1990 and put Sweden's commitment to the UN to the test. Per T. Ohlsson (1991: 9; translation by the author) spoke in this

---

[2] It is therefore a matter of controversy to what extent Sweden's participation can in fact be regarded as participation in *war*. While several authors – the majority of them Swedish (see Ekdal and Ekströmer 1991: 7) – and a number of scientists/politicians interviewed as part of this project do endorse this view, the deployment of the field hospital is not, in the operationalisation of 'war participation', considered participation for the purposes of our research project (for further information, see Chapter 2).

[3] Pursuant to Article 42 of the UN Charter the Security Council has the right, after all peaceful means in accordance with Article 41 of the UN Charter have been fully exhausted, to resort to military measures to maintain or restore world peace and international security and to call upon all member states to deploy armed forces to this end. In contrast, in Resolution 665, all member states are authorised by the Council to act on its behalf.

context of the 'most heated – and possibly the most important – debate on foreign policy held in Sweden since the Vietnam War'.

Since there was no mandatory request for military assistance by the Security Council pursuant to Article 42, the Swedish government did not see the need to offer military support and conducted a legalistic interpretation of the Charter instead (Ahlin 1993: 199). However, in the absence of legal obstacles to rule out military participation, the opportunity could have been seized regardless. Swedish government representatives repeatedly called for a peaceful resolution of the conflict, demanding that all avenues be explored in doing so. At the same time they declared, however, that, in the event of a failure of these efforts, Sweden would be prepared to participate with peacekeeping troops in a military operation, should the Security Council call upon its member states to do so.

Resolution 678 was interpreted in accordance with Resolution 665 to the effect that, since no reference was made to Article 42 of the UN Charter, the Council's request for participation was not deemed binding, and authorisation to use violence was given merely to a US-led coalition of the member states. Accordingly, the executive decided, in addition to providing financial support for refugee assistance, to contribute to the effort by setting up and running a field hospital,[4] which was made available before the date due upon British request (Ekdal and Ekströmer 1991: 8). The government strongly emphasised that Sweden's commitment should be regarded as humanitarian and that Sweden could not be considered as being at war. Sweden's decision to deploy hospital staff, albeit armed for reasons of self-defence, was in fact interpreted as a peacekeeping measure (Engdahl and Lind 2005), and thus did not require approval by the Riksdag; moreover, it was based on overarching political consent.[5]

That Sweden abstained from active participation in the military operation by not deploying its own armed forces was met with heavy criticism, particularly in the United States (US) – conversely, some time later the Swedish government was able to argue that Sweden had not participated in the war when seeking the release of Swedish hostages in Iraq.

---

[4] Field hospitals had already been supplied as means of humanitarian aid in conflicts in Korea (1951–3), in the Lebanon (1980–92) and in Somalia (1993).

[5] In the Riksdag, only the Greens and the Left Party raised objections against such a commitment. While the Greens held the view that the mission should be carried out not by the Swedish defence forces but by the Red Cross, the Lefts claimed that it represented an act of war rather than humanitarian aid.

The confusion of the Swedish debate is reflected particularly in the different positions assumed by Minister for Foreign Affairs Sten Andersson and Prime Minister Ingvar Carlsson after the bombing began. Whereas Andersson expressed his regret at the intervention, while at the same time defending its legitimacy on the basis that the Iraq invasion was a breach of international law and that the UN had a mandate, Carlsson was sorry that a peaceful solution had not been reached, and he seemed worried about the potential repercussions of such a war. Accordingly, for the entire duration of the war he never once expressed his consent for the allied operations. Instead, a number of the executive's spokesmen repeatedly pointed out that Sweden would have preferred more scope for economic sanctions to take effect (Ohlsson 1991: 64). Perceived as hesitant by both the public and the non-socialist political opposition, the Swedish government's attitude was met with harsh criticism.

2.1.2   Content analysis of the parliamentary debates

Only 17 speeches were eligible for coding. Within this spread, a majority of 13 members of the Riksdag argued against a Swedish participation or military intervention (Table 9.1).

The parliamentary group of the Social Democrats, the Greens and the Left (depicted in Table 9.1) spoke out against the possibility of intervention to free Kuwait, primarily highlighting the fact that peaceful means of conflict resolution had not yet been fully exhausted (69.2 per cent). Moreover, they pointed to the danger of spillover effects feared to take hold in the region (61.5 per cent) and the possibility of civilian casualties (23.1 per cent), thus advancing a fundamental opposition to the war (38.5 per cent). Rather than supporting military intervention, Sweden was to fulfil its traditional role as a neutral mediator and the expectations arising therefrom (23.1 per cent), and engage in seeking a peaceful conflict resolution. Particularly the Lefts accused the executive of avoiding serious debate so as to dodge disputes with the Liberals and Moderates. The Greens and the Lefts insisted repeatedly that Swedish participation in the operation by way of deploying troops was inconceivable, even if such were authorised by the Security Council.

Whereas before it commenced, the war was endorsed by only the Liberal Party and the Moderate Party, a favourable (albeit legalistic) stance was assumed also by the executive after the legitimised UN intervention began. Although the two non-socialist parties highlighted the importance of maintaining sanctions and thus exhausting peaceful means, they considered a credible threat of force necessary for Saddam Hussein to give in (see Table 9.2). If he would not retreat, the parties

Table 9.1 *Frequencies of arguments, Gulf War, Sweden, opponents only (n = 13); extracts of results*[a]

Code	Argument	Number of speakers	Percentage of speakers
4302	Peaceful means not exhausted	9	69.2
1303	Regional instability	8	61.5
5302	Pacifism/war damages global norms	5	38.5
3301	Restraining identity/role norms	3	23.1
5303	Civilian casualties	3	23.1
4301	No UN mandate/damage to UN	2	15.4
6301	Democratic norms/procedures contra war	2	15.4

[a] Full lists of results for this and all following tables are available from the author.

Table 9.2 *Frequencies of arguments, Gulf War, Sweden, supporters only (n = 4); extracts of results*

Code	Argument	Number of speakers	Percentage of speakers
1104	Show of force	3	75
4302	Peaceful means not exhausted	3	75
4101	Enforce international law/support UN	2	50
4201	Covered by international law	2	50
3303	Restraining expectations by others	1	25
4202	Peaceful means exhausted	1	25
5101	Humanitarian catastrophe	1	25

endorsed the international community's intervention under UN mandate. The position taken by the Social Democratic executive, however, remained ambivalent. Before the outbreak of the war, government representatives – backed by the Centre Party – were strictly opposed to intervention, arguing that spillover effects may occur and emphasising the necessity to make full use of peaceful strategies. When the war had commenced, Minister for Foreign Affairs Andersson, as a representative of the executive, took a clear stance in justifying it, saying that it was incumbent upon Sweden as a loyal member of the UN to endorse the intervention on the basis of Resolution 678 so as to prevent the only recently revived association of member states from weakening.[6]

[6] Notwithstanding, it was not implied that Swedish forces would be deployed.

The reasons previously raised against the war were now considered less important vis-à-vis the need to preserve the UN's authority.

2.1.3   Newspaper debates

Beyond the scope of the two newspapers analysed in this chapter (i.e. the left-inclined *Aftonbladet* and the conservative *Svenska Dagbladet*) the public debate on the Gulf crisis was driven by two opposing camps in Sweden. On the one hand, military intervention was justified as the only possibility to defeat the 'reckless despot' that was Saddam Hussein and, consequently, to free Kuwait.[7] On the other hand, the main point of criticism presented was that the economic sanctions had not been given sufficient time to take effect, that a peace organisation like the UN should never be allowed to sanction war and that the military intervention was based on issues very different from the concern about maintaining international law.

The majority of commentaries from the *Aftonbladet* take a clearly negative stance towards war; only a few commentaries were sufficiently backed by factual arguments. Many commentators took a personalised approach to describing the conflict. Saddam Hussein was unanimously depicted as a threat to world peace and international security; ultimately, however, this negative characterisation may not be regarded as synonymous with approving war. Saddam Hussein was referred to as 'the Baghdad butcher', 'the ruthless despot of Iraq' and a 'bloody murderer' whose invasion of Kuwait showed gross disrespect for the international rule of law,[8] yet the right to use military force inherent in this reasoning was immediately counteracted by other arguments. One line of argumentation pointed to the double standards or 'moral hypocrisy' of the US and its allies, submitting this as a reason against military intervention.[9]

Moreover, the right to use military force that had come to be legitimised vis-à-vis the despotic personality of the enemy was null and void in light of the fear of spillover effects or conflict escalation and the hope of avoiding unnecessary suffering among civilians. The only article to endorse military intervention criticised the Swedish government mainly for asserting that Resolution 678 in fact did not entail an obligation to deploy troops (pursuant to Article 42). Hence the article concluded

---

[7] See, for example, Fredriksson, Gunnar 1990. 'Varför tar vi så lätt på krigshotet?', *Aftonbladet*, 16 November, p. 18; translation by the author.

[8] Fredriksson, Gunnar 1990. 'Våld löner sig: ibland' *Aftonbladet*, 17 August, p. 14; translation by the author.

[9] *Ibid.*

that the 'refusal' to join the international forces was synonymous with 'hypocrisy at the highest possible level'.[10]

Contrary to the *Aftonbladet*'s position, the *Svenska Dagbladet* seemed inclined to support the war throughout the entire period of investigation; however, the paper's line of reasoning is almost exclusively tied to the existence of a UN mandate. As already observed in the *Aftonbladet*, the despotic personality of Saddam Hussein, paired with his striving to possess weapons of mass destruction (WMD), was considered such a severe threat to global security that it justified the use of military force. In light of the possibilities that arose from the end of the bloc confrontation, some commentators saw the opportunity to set a precedent on the basis of taking legitimised UN military action against Saddam Hussein. However, it was absolutely crucial to this end that peaceful means were fully exhausted first.[11]

2.1.4   Public opinion polls

The refusal to engage in military intervention as proclaimed particularly in the social-democratic press culminated in a call for a 'new' peace movement similar to that witnessed during the Vietnam War. However, there was no public support; on the contrary, opinion polls revealed that after the beginning of the war a narrow majority of Swedes not only stood behind the course of action taken by the UN, but also backed the US and their allies (Ohlsson 1991: 65), and were hence more inclined than the Swedish executive to take steps against Iraq.[12] In the period from January to March 1991, opinion polls recorded a constant rise in support from the Swedish public for the actions taken by the UN and the US and their allies.[13] Investigations carried out in early March showed that the foreign policy tack taken by the Social Democrats was no longer being approved by the Swedish people – a development attrib-

---

[10] Wolkoff, Robert L. 1991. 'Freden har alltid ett pris', *Aftonbladet*, 17 January, p. 3; translation by the author.

[11] E.g. Huldt, Bo 1991. 'Kuwaitkrisen hotar regionala balansen', *Svenska Dagbladet*, 11 January; Bring, Ove and Melander, Göran. 1990. 'FN hanterar krisen väl', *Svenska Dagbladet*, 26 August.

[12] One should note that the opinion polls did *not* broach the issue of potential Swedish participation.

[13] An opinion poll conducted at the beginning of February 1991 showed that a 64 per cent majority of the population fully or largely endorsed the action taken by the US, and 69 per cent that by the UN. An opinion poll conducted at the beginning of March 1991 even recorded a rise in support during the hostilities. Only in January 1991, a mere 41 per cent (February: 51 per cent) had fully backed UN action, and 36 per cent (February: 50 per cent) US action (Ohlsson 1991: 65).

uted also to the manner in which the Kuwait crisis was handled by the Social Democratic government (Ohlsson 1991: 65).[14]

2.1.5   *Conclusion: explaining Sweden's policy towards the Gulf War*

Even though the intervention in the Gulf region was mandated by the UN, Sweden was faced with a problem scenario. It is true that the political support for the use of violence – as long as it was authorised by the Security Council in accordance with Chapter VII of the UN Charter – did not contradict the traditionally pursued policy of neutrality. Regarding the intervention, however, the – at times rather convoluted – Swedish debate illustrated that the country found itself in a quite difficult situation. As a result of the bipolar world order opening up, the role inhabited by Sweden was undergoing a process of redefinition. While, by vehemently endorsing a peaceful solution to the conflict within a UN framework, the political establishment was trying to hold on to the old political structures, there was nevertheless a strong sense of awareness of the potential obligation inherent in a UN mandate. These conflicting roles are likewise reflected in the content analysis of the parliamentary debates: those opposing war, in addition to naming regional instability and their preference for a peaceful solution to the conflict, presented Sweden's role as a neutral mediator as their main argument and even partly advanced a fundamental opposition. The reasons given by those advocating war, however, also comprised elements of Sweden's role, namely that a humanitarian catastrophe was at hand and that all attempts of settling the conflict peacefully had been fruitless. Interestingly, differing positions prevailed within the executive – at least after the bombing had started. Whereas Foreign Minister Andersson, in agreement with the people of Sweden, justified the intervention as the only possible option to free Kuwait, Prime Minister Carlsson refrained from showing official support for the hostilities by the allies. Instead, he highlighted the potential risks presented by military action and expressed his regret that peaceful means had not been used to their full potential.

Even though the majority of the Riksdag rejected the US-led intervention, the government did find a way of participating in accordance with Swedish tradition, namely by deploying a field hospital. Not only did this solution conform to humanitarian tradition, it also afforded an opportunity to demonstrate loyalty vis-à-vis the UN without

---

[14] In fact, on 15 September 1991, the Social Democratic government was replaced in early elections by a new government under Carl Bildt; however, foreign policy matters account for only one of several reasons.

compromising the country's self-image as an essentially neutral state in foreign politics. Therefore, from the perspective of international law, Sweden was not considered a nation at war. It was a compromise made by the government to catch up with the people of Sweden, who had been quick in signalling their support for intervention.

2.2 Sweden and the 1999 Kosovo War

2.2.1 Domestic decision-making process

Concerns over European stability meant that Sweden also had a national interest in keeping a close eye on the conflicts in the Balkans; in 1995, the government even went so far as to deploy troops to Bosnia under NATO command (and with UN mandate; SFOR). In the conflicts that were to follow in the territory of former Yugoslavia, Sweden took on a special role by accepting a large number of political refugees into the country; however, as there was no UN mandate, the country did not partake in any military operations.

During its two-year membership in the Security Council, Sweden demanded as early as March 1998 that the situation in Kosovo be treated by the council as a threat to peace and international security. To this end, Sweden worked closely with the extended Balkan Contact Group by presenting its own suggestions in addition to using its good relations with Russia to achieve unity among all permanent council members (Utrikesdepartementet 1999a: 14; 112–13). It was under Swedish council presidency that, in September 1998, UN Resolution 1199 was adopted.

In October 1998, the Social Democratic government led by Prime Minister Göran Persson announced that Sweden would essentially be willing to send troops for the OSCE Verification Mission in the Kosovo – provided that a mandate be issued by the Security Council or that a peace agreement be reached between the two conflicting parties (Granholm 1999).[15] In December 1998, Minister for Foreign Affairs Anna Lindh said that a NATO-led intervention would be a necessary reaction to a 'situation of extreme emergency', arguing that the prerogative to use violence issued by the Security Council would be overridden not only in cases of self-defence but also in other exceptional situations.[16] Prime Minister Persson emphasised that, in situations of extreme emergency, the community of states could not remain passive

---

[15] 'Pressmeddelande 1998–10–22. 80 svenskar till OSSE-missionen i Kosovo', 1998, Stockholm, reprinted in Utrikesdepartementet (1999b), 133–4.

[16] Lindh, Anna. 'Sweden in Europe'. Address at the Swedish Institute of International Affairs, 16 December 1998, Stockholm. Online: www.regeringen.se/sb/d/4042.

even if the Security Council were blocked. The fact that reference was made to 'situations of extreme emergency' to justify an intervention, even in the absence of a mandate from the Security Council, meant that Sweden was departing from its traditional legalistic line of adhering to the UN – a change that was met with public criticism (Norlin 1999).

At the NATO conference held for the troop-deploying countries in late February 1999, Sweden not only declared its willingness to contribute to the international peace troops for Kosovo (KFOR) together with SWERAP (Swedish Rapid Reaction Force), provided that such participation were authorised by UN mandate or that a relevant peace agreement had been issued, but also offered to temporarily receive up to 5,000 refugees. Particular significance was attached to the participation of neutral states in the NATO-led peace troops. Sweden consequently advocated a political solution to the conflict, backing the corresponding demands made by the Balkan Contact Group. As late as two days before the outbreak of the war, Lindh made it very clear that the sole responsibility lay with the Serbian military forces and the police and that the Rambouillet Agreement represented the best possible option (Møller 1999). When, on 24 March 1999, the NATO-led intervention finally went ahead without a UN mandate, the executive officially endorsed the action on the grounds that all peaceful means had been exhausted, arguing that, ultimately, the sole responsibility lay with the regime in Serbia. Persson 'expressed his regret' that the negative attitude stated by China and Russia left the Security Council unable to agree on a mandate.[17]

In the Riksdag, the Left Party was not the only one to strongly reject the planned offensive – the Moderates equally expressed a critical view of the bombardment strategy. After the war had started, the government initially held back with criticism of the attacks launched by NATO, which can be read as a sign of consideration for the EU member states, the majority of which were involved in the NATO action (Hallenberg 2000: 26). In agreement with the Independent International Commission on Kosovo initiated by the Swedish government some time later, the Swedish government regarded the intervention as *legitimate*, albeit *illegal*. Notwithstanding, the baseline of Swedish foreign policy continued to be postulated, following which military intervention could only be justified as a last resort – namely, when all means for a peaceful settlement of the conflict had been exhausted and a mandate had been issued by the Security Council. Accordingly, the government conceded

---

[17] Persson, Göran, 'Pressmeddelande den 24 mars: Statsminister Göran Persson om Kosovo', 1999, Stockholm, reprinted in Utrikesdepartementet (2000), 92–3.

that the NATO intervention had been contrary to international law; however, it also explained that, in the face of mass murder and ethnic cleansing, the international community did have the responsibility to act. The government was confronted with a dilemma: on the one hand, in the face of what was perceived as genocide, moral concerns rendered the option of non-action unthinkable, while the Swedish foreign policy tradition simultaneously required that international law and the UN Charter be observed. The problem was solved only imperfectly, namely by declaring the NATO intervention as a special situation and by vehemently denying that this situation may potentially constitute a precedent.[18] Insistently treating the intervention as a special situation, the government shirked its duty of providing a deeper analysis for this problem scenario, pointing out that, should any such situations arise in the future, they were to be evaluated on a case-by-case basis.

2.2.2 Content analysis of parliamentary debates

With so little debate in the Riksdag on the matter of the Kosovo conflict, only eight speeches were eligible for coding. Of these, four speakers voted against military intervention (Table 9.3) while another four expressed their agreement with military intervention (Table 9.4). Due to the small number of pertinent speeches, the following percentages are of only limited value.

At the end of January 1999, Foreign Minister Lindh did not yet regard the military intervention as a matter of urgency and referred to efforts embracing a long-term political solution as part of an EU strategy aiming to achieve a negotiation-based conflict settlement. Nonetheless, the possibility of military intervention – provided it was under UN or OSCE mandate – could not be ruled out, she further explained. Whereas the government was essentially pro-war, the only party to take a rigorous stance against military action (without a UN mandate) was the Left Party – albeit only after the intervention had begun. Moreover, the Left pointed out that bombardments would result in unnecessary civilian casualties, only contributing to a worsening of the humanitarian catastrophe, if anything.

The main argument used by those endorsing intervention was, as Table 9.4 shows, the existence of a humanitarian catastrophe (75 per cent) that called upon the international community to put an end to the suffering of the Kosovo Albanians.

---

[18] Lindh, Anna, 'Speech by Foreign Minister Anna Lindh in the Parliamentary Security Policy Debate 26 May 1999'. Online: www.sweden.gov.se/sb/d/4045/a/25899.

Table 9.3 *Frequencies of arguments, Kosovo War, Sweden, opponents only (n = 4); extracts of results*

Code	Argument	Number of speakers	Percentage of speakers
4301	No UN mandate/damage to UN	2	50
4302	Peaceful means not exhausted	2	50
1306	Lacking military strategy	1	25
5201	Multilateral consensus pro	1	25
5303	Civilian casualties	1	25

Table 9.4 *Frequencies of arguments, Kosovo War, Sweden, supporters only (n = 4); extracts of results*

Code	Argument	Number of speakers	Percentage of speakers
5101	Humanitarian catastrophe	3	75
4202	Peaceful means exhausted	2	50
1104	Show of force	1	25
4101	Enforce international law/support UN	1	25
4302	Peaceful means not exhausted	1	25
6101	Regime change/democratisation	1	25

The government, together with the Liberal Party and Centre Party, argued that, should a UN mandate be issued, Sweden had to be ready and willing to become involved in military action. The Centre Party was rather cautious in stating that, even though it welcomed the negotiations held in Rambouillet, the party did not insist upon making full and unconditional use of peaceful means, given the situation of humanitarian emergency at hand. In contrast, the Liberal Party regarded the same as having already been fully exhausted (50 per cent), hence demanding that military action be taken against Slobodan Milošević (specifically emphasising the necessity of democratisation to drive ahead the peace process in the Balkans) in order to prevent 'a second Bosnia' from happening. The party argued that, even in the absence of a UN mandate, Sweden had no right to thwart intervention but rather was obliged to express its willingness to deploy military resources. After NATO had started the intervention, cabinet member Pierre Schori justified the action taken on the basis of the humanitarian catastrophe and the exhaustion of peaceful means.

2.2.3   Newspaper debates

The commentaries published in the liberal daily newspaper *Dagens Nyheter* – used here to supplement the relatively poor Swedish newspaper commentaries records – and in the *Svenska Dagbladet* tended to support a peaceful settlement of the Kosovo conflict. Despite the fact that both papers discussed and even compared and contrasted the pros and cons of intervention, it is difficult to identify a clear position. The same must be said, albeit to a lesser extent, for the *Aftonbladet* – a paper more definitely opposed to war.

For the full period of investigation, the distinction was made in the *Dagens Nyheter* and in the *Svenska Dagbladet* between a long-term conflict solution derived on the basis of negotiation and a short-term perspective considering the use of military force. In the latter case, the aforementioned basic 'opposition to war' was superseded mostly by the following two arguments: first, the prevention of a humanitarian catastrophe was called for – a task that required special responsibility from the international community.[19] Moreover, given that all diplomatic means had been exhausted to no avail, military intervention was often seen as the last resort;[20] although the mere threat of force was favoured in order to obtain compliance by the conflicting parties. The worst possible scenario imaginable was not the possibility of war, but the passivity displayed vis-à-vis civilian suffering.[21]

Milošević was given the sole responsibility for the – potentially violent – development of the conflict. The possibility that he, 'the notorious liar'[22] and 'psychopath',[23] may himself initiate a peaceful resolution to the conflict was ruled out. Bo Hugemark even went so far as to draw parallels between Milošević and Hitler.[24] Although we

[19] E.g. Anonymous 1998. 'Tiden börjar rinna ut i Kosovo: Hot om militära insatser har bara effekt om de någon gång kan realiseras', *Dagens Nyheter*, 3 October, p. 2.; Anonymous 1998. 'Sverige kräver snabba insatser av säkerhetsrådet', *Aftonbladet*, 2 October; Oseku, Shqiptar 1998. 'Kosovokonflikten: Sverige bör ge sitt stöd för en väpnad Natoinsats i Kosovo', *Svenska Dagbladet*, 6 October.

[20] E.g. Anonymous 1999. 'Ingen ideal lösning i Kosovo: Det sämsta alternativet är att statssamfundet passivt åser övergrepp mot civila', *Dagens Nyheter*, 19 January, p. 2.

[21] E.g. articles published in *Dagens-Nyheter*: Anonymous 1999. 'Ingen ideal lösning i Kosovo: Det sämsta alternativet är att statssamfundet passivt åser övergrepp mot civila', 19 January, p. 2; Anonymous 1999. 'Tiden åter ute i Kosovo: För NATO kan det vara farligare att förhålla sig passiv än att sätta bombhoten i verket', 20 March, p. 2.

[22] Cervin, Ann-Marie 1998. 'Milosevic notorisk lögnare', *Svenska Dagbladet*, 22 October; translation by the author.

[23] Ahlin, Per 1999. 'Katastrofen i Kosovo är Europas skam', *Dagens Nyheter*, 24 January; translation by the author.

[24] Hugemark, Bo 1999. 'De tanklösa och hjärtlösa', *Svenska Dagbladet*, 31 January, p. 2.

can easily elicit the image of 'good against evil' from the commentaries, the enemy image was never the crucial factor in deciding in favour of military intervention. Even though the commentaries published in the *Aftonbladet* painted a predominantly negative image of Milošević, this did not result in endorsing military action. Quite the contrary, the paper expressed the view that taking military action would be synonymous with punishing the civilian population for crimes committed by Milošević. While the use of military force through NATO was endorsed mainly as leverage, there was a consensus among the commentators of the *Dagens Nyheter* and the *Svenska Dagbladet* that the use of ground forces was the preferred strategy over the launching of air raids. On the other hand, the *Aftonbladet* commentators condemned any military operation on the grounds of potential civilian casualties and the fear of spillover effects.

2.2.4   Public opinion polls

There are no opinion polls available for the period preceding the war. The ambivalent attitude expressed by Sweden's political elite is equally reflected by the people (Jakobsen 2006: 184). Following opinion polls conducted after the onset of war in March 1999, NATO's military intervention was rejected by a narrow relative majority of 41 per cent, with 33 per cent of the population being in favour of the bombardments.[25] When the air raids began, 52 per cent strongly opposed Sweden's involvement in military action.[26] The fear of negative spillover effects (60 per cent) and the fact that it was not anchored in international law (Fischer 2003: 21) constituted the main reasons for rejecting the intervention. Furthermore, in March, 48 per cent of the population backed the use of ground forces if the war were to be continued (27 per cent were against this). Emphasising the humanitarian tradition of their country, 65 per cent of Swedes also welcomed the limited reception of Kosovo Albanian refugees.

2.2.5   Conclusion: explaining Sweden's policy towards the Kosovo War

During the Kosovo conflict, Sweden again found itself torn between the different conceptual elements underpinning its foreign policy role conception – a situation not unlike that in 1991. The divide in public opinion and the ambivalence of the newspaper commentaries account

---

[25] SIFO Research International (Svenska Institutet för Opinionsundersökningar), 'Kriget i Jugoslavien', 31 March 1999.

[26] Wendel, Per 1999. 'Svenskar ska inte vara med i bombanfallen', *Expressen*, 25 March, p. 12.

for this fact, which is furthermore borne out when analysing the contents of the parliamentary debates. Justified by humanitarian reasons, an intervention appealed to Sweden's moral conscience on the one hand, even more so as peaceful solution-based negotiations seemed out of reach. On the other hand, however, the blocking of the Security Council, and hence the lack of UN legitimisation for military action, put Sweden severely under pressure: in line with the legalistic foreign policy traditionally pursued in the country, a mandate issued by the Security Council was the mandatory condition for endorsing military action. Doubts as to whether this was firmly rooted in international law rendered the (albeit anticipated) participation of Swedish troops in the intervention unthinkable – the domestic political price to pay for such a participation would have been too high.

The fact that, faced by this dilemma, no individual strategy was devised by the government on the Kosovo issue has been termed 'timid indecisiveness' (Bjereld 2002: 277; translation by the author) – government statements expressing regret about the lack of a UN mandate contrasted with those that deemed intervention absolutely necessary and inevitable (Jakobsen 2006: 184). Nonetheless, the absence of a UN mandate meant that the government could rule out Swedish participation from the outset. The government's political support for the NATO-led intervention – which was declared an exceptional case on the grounds of the humanitarian emergency suffered by the people in the Kosovo – meant departing from prior positions and hence encountered sharp criticism (Møller 1999).

2.3   Sweden and the Iraq War, 2003

2.3.1   Domestic decision-making process
During the Iraq conflict, Sweden relied for its strategy mostly on the United Nations Monitoring, Verification and Inspection Commission (UNMOVIC) under the leadership of the Swede Hans Blix. The commission was to investigate whether Iraq had in fact complied with the 1991 obligations to destroy its arsenal of WMD. In accordance with its foreign policy tradition, from the outset Sweden was fundamentally opposed to taking action without a UN mandate. Consequently, the government under the leadership of Social Democratic Prime Minister Göran Persson lobbied for the continuation of weapons inspections and for treating the problem under a UN framework (Granholm 2003: 55). If there were no compliance, the Security Council as the sole legitimate authority to permit the use of force would have to face up to its responsibilities – after all, the credibility of the UN depended on the success

of disarmament efforts in Iraq.[27] Accordingly, Minister for Foreign Affairs Anna Lindh welcomed the acceptance of Resolution 1441 in November 2002.

At the same time, Persson declared with reference to Saddam Hussein and the latter's repeated human rights violations that, even though Sweden would as a last resort endorse the Security Council's potential decision to use military force, a troop request by the UN was not expected.[28] In late November, Persson even ensured the deployment of a field hospital if the situation demanded it – what he did not consider, however, was that these capacities were exhausted already in 1999. Even though at the time this position presumably served to postpone a decision, it is remarkable that for the entire duration of the crisis the Swedish military remained on standby (Granholm 2003: 55–6). In December 2002, the prime minister attracted renewed criticism when he commented in a radio interview that, although military action was deeply regrettable, a short war may indeed have a positive effect on the international world order and the economy.[29]

At the international level, Sweden was still fully committed to seeking a solution under a UN framework. Repeatedly, attention was drawn to the danger that the world organisation's authority could be undermined by a unilateral approach adopted by the US and the UK. First and foremost, Sweden emphasised the need to afford more time to the weapons inspectors and called upon Saddam Hussein to grant them free access. Only after the inspectors had come to a conclusion would the Security Council be obliged to consider 'serious consequences'. The high turnout among Swedish people in the demonstrations on 15 February 2003 was accordingly welcomed by the government.

In line with Sweden's traditionally legalistic attitude towards the UN, Lindh explained in the days running up to the war that, should a new draft resolution by the US and the UK be accepted, Sweden would not approve of military action but support the decision made by the UN nonetheless.[30] When talks in the Security Council collapsed in early

---

[27] See Lindh, Anna 2002. 'Speech by Foreign Minister Anna Lindh at the Fifty-Seventh Session of the UN General Assembly', 19 September. Online: www.sweden.gov.se/sb/d/1111/a/4146.

[28] Persson, Göran, 'North Europe: A Blueprint for Peace and Security', lecture given by Prime Minister Göran Persson at Jyväskylä University, 8 November 2002, Finland. Online: www.regeringen.se/persson.

[29] Åström, Sverker 2003. 'Göran Persson mumlar om kriget', *Svenska Dagbladet*, 9 January, p. 5.

[30] See Lindh 2002. 'Speech by Foreign Minister Anna Lindh at the Fifty-Seventh Session of the UN General Assembly'; Lindh, Anna 2003. 'Än kan ett krig mot Irak undvikas', *Aftonbladet*, 14 February.

March, Persson was asked in an interview the hypothetical question of where Sweden would position itself were it a council member with veto power. He responded by saying that a resolution mandating the use of force had of course been vetoed (Granholm 2003: 55). With the outbreak of war looming, the government assumed a position of growing scepticism on legalistic grounds, and Persson adopted a harsher stance towards the US due to President Bush's implicit threat to ignore the UN should the Security Council not follow the line of policy pursued by the US and the UK. The way in which the US repeatedly cast doubts on the reports issued by the International Atomic Energy Agency and, most of all, Blix himself, served to fuel at least latent anti-American sentiments.

When the war finally started, Persson condemned the approach taken by the US as constituting a clear violation of international law. He also called for the Iraq issue to be placed in the hands of the UN as soon as possible, emphasising that Sweden would be willing to provide support in rebuilding the country. Hence, Foreign Minister Lindh emphasised that participating in a war of the '*coalition of the willing*' was not 'currently on the agenda' for Sweden.[31] Sweden criticised the US for making a solo effort that failed to receive unanimous backing even from the Western states.

Meanwhile, the intervention was not condemned as an act against international law by all parties; Carl Bildt, for example, chairman of the Moderates, called for a parliamentary debate in order to reconsider the matter, thus even countermanding UN Secretary-General Kofi Annan's position (who himself regarded the intervention as contrary to international law). He also accused the government of condemning the attack without having consulted with the Committee on Foreign Affairs beforehand, which constituted a breach of Swedish Constitutional Law.

2.3.2   Content analysis of parliamentary debates

Relative to the little attention the 1991 Gulf War and the 1999 Kosovo conflict received in the Riksdag, the Iraq conflict sparked a lively debate indeed. A total of 48 speeches could be coded overall. The majority of members of the Riksdag opposed the option of war (37 speeches, or 77 per cent), whereas 11 speakers (22.9 per cent) endorsed military intervention.

---

[31] Ministry for Foreign Affairs 2003. 'The Swedish Government's View on the Iraq issue', 20 March. Online: www.ud.se/inenglish/frontpage/Governments_view_on_Iraq.htm.

Table 9.5 *Frequencies of arguments, Iraq War, Sweden, supporters only (n = 11); extracts of results*

Code	Argument	Number of speakers	Percentage of speakers
1104	Show of force	6	54.5
7101	Enemy image of adversary	6	54.5
5102	Threat to world order	5	45.5
5101	Humanitarian catastrophe	4	36.4
1103	Regional stability	3	27.3
4101	Enforce international law/support UN	3	27.3
4302	Peaceful means not exhausted	3	27.3

Moderates and Christian Democrats spoke out in favour of military intervention as early as autumn 2002 (see Table 9.5), giving as their main argument the need to show military force, a strategy that was hoped to force Saddam Hussein to fulfil his obligations (54.5 per cent). More than half of those backing the military option justified this on the grounds of Saddam Hussein being a brutal and dangerous enemy (54.5 per cent); while, in relation to this and Iraq's WMD programme, 45.5 per cent gave the threat to world peace and international security as a reason. Furthermore, 36.4 per cent named the calamitous situation for the people in Iraq and 27.3 per cent the danger for regional stability emanating from Saddam Hussein's regime and the need to enforce UN resolutions.

While the Left was the only party to fundamentally demonstrate its opposition to war, radically rejecting any kind of military intervention (even under a UN mandate), the Social Democratic parliamentary party, the Greens and – to a markedly lesser extent – the Liberal Party and the government ruled out war in the present situation but did not exclude military action at a later stage. Table 9.6 gives an overview of the arguments used.

Almost 65 per cent pointed out that peaceful means had not yet been fully exhausted, thus they demanded that more time be given to the weapons inspectors. Even though as many as 40.5 per cent of those opposed to war expressed their full support for a credible threat of force and accepted the use of military means as a last resort, they justified their negative stance on the basis that, at the time, military action did not present a feasible option due to the absence of a UN mandate (43.2 per cent). Opposing arguments basically included collateral damage incurred mostly by the Iraqi civilian population (21.6 per cent), specific

Table 9.6 *Frequencies of arguments, Iraq War, Sweden, opponents only (n = 37); extracts of results*

Code	Argument	Number of speakers	Percentage of speakers
4302	Peaceful means not exhausted	24	64.9
4301	No UN mandate/damage to UN	16	43.2
1104	Show of force	15	40.5
5303	Civilian casualties	8	21.6
3301	Restraining identity/role norms	7	18.9
6301	Democratic norms/procedures contra war	7	18.9
5304	Multilateral war rejection	6	16.2
5302	Pacifism/war damages global norms	5	13.5
7101	Enemy image of adversary	5	13.5
7301	Enemy image questioned	5	13.5

elements of identity (18.9 per cent) – namely, Sweden's nonalignment policy and active foreign policy traditionally based on peaceful conflict resolutions – and, finally, the violation of democratic principles as war would contravene the beliefs held by a majority of the people (18.9 per cent). Some 13.5 per cent of those opposed to war conceded that Saddam Hussein was a dangerous enemy but they gave anti-war arguments more weight.

2.3.3 Newspaper debates

A considerable majority of commentaries in both papers took a clear stance against military action, however, with only a minority of articles being fundamentally anti-war and relatively few anti-war arguments being presented – both papers concentrated mainly on weakening the pro-war arguments made by the US (Nohrstedt 2004). Predominantly, it was pointed out that Saddam Hussein's threat potential was deliberately exaggerated so as to convince the international community of the necessity of war, and that, as yet, there was no sufficient evidence to suggest that Iraq was in fact in possession of WMD.[32]

What is equally striking is that in both papers, even though Saddam Hussein's dangerous character and crimes are essentially recognised as pro-war arguments, a variety of counter-arguments are simultaneously presented to render them obsolete. For the commentators, the

---

[32] E.g. Hansson, Wolfgang 2002. 'Men svenska experter tror inte Iraq kan skada världen', *Aftonbladet*, 20 September, p. 13; Berntsson, Lennart 2002. '11 september motiv för anfall mot Iraq', *Svenska Dagbladet*, 4 November, p. 56.

fact that the US-led unilateral approach was in breach of international law seemed to carry more weight than the deposition of the Iraqi dictator – which could have been a desirable alternative. Similarly, the fear of imminent civilian casualties and potential refugees as well as instabilities in the region caused by military action, the strengthening of terrorism and the radicalisation of the Muslim community were considered more important than the deep disdain for Saddam Hussein.[33] Even though the *Aftonbladet* took a clear stance against military action (with only a single commentary in favour of intervention),[34] only a minority of commentators was fundamentally anti-war, whereas the majority of commentators did not rule out a UN-mandated military action as a last resort per se, but criticised the attitude of the US and the disrespect shown for the UN.

The majority of commentaries in the *Svenska Dagbladet* also argued against attacking Iraq. In contrast to the *Aftonbladet*, however, some commentators tied their anti-war attitude to Sweden's identity; in doing so, not only the tradition of nonalignment, but also pacifism as something rooted deeply within the country's political culture and the preference for peaceful conflict resolutions were mentioned.[35] Pro-war commentators mostly referred to Saddam Hussein's character, his striving for and possession of WMD and his previous crimes.

While the *Aftonbladet* adopted a pro-government perspective by insinuating – far more than the *Svenska Dagbladet* – that the executive took a strong anti-war stance, several commentators in the latter paper were very critical of Sweden's official position. Both papers directed criticism at the legalistic approach adopted by the executive to endorse the final decision of the Security Council – regardless of its contents – while avoiding an in-depth debate as to whether military action was basically justified.

2.3.4   Public opinion polls

The Swedish people took a clear stance against the war in Iraq from very early on. In an opinion poll conducted in September 2002, 62 per cent declared that Sweden must refrain from supporting the US war against terrorism, should the next step involve violent action against Iraq; while

---

[33] E.g. Svenning, Olle 2002. 'Han vill krig', *Aftonbladet*, 12 October, p. 2; Kohnstamm, Max 2003. 'Bush utlöser religionskrig', *Svenska Dagbladet*, 1 January, p. 5.

[34] Wiesel, Ellie 2003. 'Vi är skyldiga att ingripa mot ondskan Irakkriget', 20 March, p. 32.

[35] See Gröning-Degerlund, Lotta 2002. 'Sverige ska inte delta i något krig mot Iraq', 23 November, p. 5; Dahlberg, Anna and Kleine, Helle 2003. 'Moodysson har fel. Säg nej till kriget!', 6 February, p. 5.

only 24 per cent approved of such action.[36] In January 2003, the issue as to whether contemplating military action without a Security Council mandate was right or wrong was decided in favour by a mere 5 per cent of the population, while 37 per cent agreed to military action with a UN mandate.[37] Half of those polled spoke out against taking military action per se.[38] Asked what kind of strategy should be pursued by the Swedish government as regards the conflict in Iraq, in February 2003, 40 per cent of Swedes requested more time for the weapons inspections, and 39 per cent wished for a peaceful resolution of the conflict. By contrast, only 14 per cent of those asked said that Sweden had to remain neutral, while 4 per cent preferred military intervention. Accordingly, in an opinion poll carried out in mid-February, 38 per cent of those asked said that they were satisfied with the diplomatic or political action taken by the government; however, as the war unfolded, an increasing number of people considered the government's political approach 'insecure, vague, hesitant and without a clear focus'. [39]

Opinion polls suggest a slight swing in public opinion since the beginning of the war. Whereas on 20 March, as many as 68 per cent of the people were against US military action (with 14 per cent in favour), only one week into the war the number had declined to 62 per cent (with 20 per cent in favour).[40]

2.3.5 Conclusion: explaining Sweden's policy towards the war in Iraq

In contrast to the other two wars analysed, the war in Iraq did not confront Sweden with a dilemma situation. As early as in autumn 2002, the government declared that, being a loyal UN member, Sweden was going to follow the world organisation's decisions – thus not per se ruling out the option of taking military action against Iraq. According to the legalistic UN policy traditionally pursued in such situations, the condition of rendering such action legitimate was a mandate from the Security Council. The large proportion of members of the Riksdag who

[36] SIFO Research International, '11 September', 2–5 September 2002.
[37] An investigation performed by the Swedish Gallup Institute in February 2003 indicated that 64 per cent were against a war under a UN mandate, while only 24 per cent were in favour of such; see Stridsman, Sofia 2003. '64 procent av svenskarna: Vi vill ha fred', 15 February. Online: www.expressen.se/nyheter/64-procent-av-svenskarna-vi-vill-ha-fred.
[38] SIFO Research International 2003. 'NATO/Rätt att USA angriper Irak?/Kärnkraft', 13–16 January.
[39] Styrelesen för psykologiskt försvar 2003. 'SPFs kommentarer till studie nr. 2 avseende befolkningens inställning till och syn på konflikten med och stridigheterna i Iraq', 2 April 2003; translation by the author.
[40] SIFO Research International, 'Kriget i Irak', 20 March 2003, and 'Kriget i Irak', 27 March 2003.

did not per se rule out military action can be seen as supportive of the executive's position. It is striking nonetheless that, with the outbreak of war looming, the position assumed by the government – expressed mainly through statements issued by Prime Minister Persson – was that of increasing scepticism, which ultimately culminated in the official condemnation of the unilateral intervention strategy pursued by the US and its allies as breaching international law. The mission was therefore condemned by the Swedish government as both illegal and illegitimate (as motives were unclear).

The analysis of the public opinion polls showed nonetheless that the official position of the government did not reflect that of the wider population. From very early on, the majority of Swedes had spoken out against any form of military intervention – with or without a UN mandate. This stance was furthermore supported in the press: commentaries focused mainly on criticising the pro-intervention arguments presented by the US. Most likely, there is a connection between this unanimous criticism and the repeated repudiation of Hans Blix. Moreover, in contrast to the official government position, the newspaper commentaries hardly made the claim that the power of decision-taking on any future action should lie solely with the UN.

3   Summary of the results

As illustrated above, Sweden adopted in the international arena the role of an active 'civilian power', preferring political over military solutions and, in matters regarding foreign and security policy, following the UN as a superordinate authority over war and peace. The analysis of decision-making processes and public debates in the run-up to the three wars investigated here equally points to patterns of behaviour and justifications corresponding to those of an active 'civilian power'. Accordingly, in the run-up to all interventions, the Swedish executive typically insisted on achieving a peaceful conflict resolution under a UN framework and the need for a mandate from the Security Council. Sweden's foreign policy is shaped predominantly by the country's self-perception as a 'moral superpower' (Nilsson 1991; translation by the author) and, consequently, the corresponding elements of identity – there were hardly any arguments put forward in public that were linked to the power position of the country or to external alliance relations. Even though the EU has been assuming an increasingly dominant role in Swedish (foreign and security) policy and the European Security and Defence Policy may indeed present possible 'predicaments' for a continued Swedish nonalignment policy, it is true that in the two conflicts investigated since Sweden's EU accession in 1995, the EU as a united collective actor has not figured prominently yet.

Ultimately, the foreign policy role conception of the active 'civilian power' is crucial also with regard to the position assumed by the country in the conflicts at hand. During the 1990s, due to the altered security constellation following the end of the Cold War, Sweden's role conception was becoming increasingly contradictory. On the one hand, humanitarian-based interventions constituted an appeal to Sweden's moral conscience; on the other hand, the peaceful attitude deeply anchored within the Swedish conception of neutrality as well as a legalistic UN policy prevented Sweden from becoming more inclined towards intervention. This divide created situations of political dilemma in recent international conflicts.

Within the context of the 1991 Gulf War, the Swedish government succeeded in overcoming the dilemma by way of compromise: according to Swedish legal opinion, the allied forces' military intervention was not based on Article 42 of the UN Charter; hence it was possible for Sweden to fulfil the UN Charter's general obligation of providing assistance and the demands voiced by the public by deploying a field hospital – in other words, of providing humanitarian aid. Nevertheless, the Swedish population did not call for military participation; an option that, given the lack of resources at the time, would not have been feasible in the first place.

The Kosovo conflict also confronted the Swedish government with a difficult situation. Even though the NATO-led intervention, due to the blockade of the Security Council, was not explicitly legitimised by international law, it was nevertheless regarded as a 'moral responsibility' for the international community to stop a humanitarian catastrophe, a perception that many Swedes also agreed with. The difficult position into which Sweden had been thrust by these dilemmas is reflected both by the ambivalent positions held by the Members of the Riksdag and by the divide in public and published opinion. That NATO acted without a mandate from the Security Council was what ultimately helped to solve the dilemma, weaving together the different strands of discourse – and simply ruled out Swedish participation. The Swedish government, in declaring the intervention a 'situation of extreme emergency' and an exceptional case on the basis of the humanitarian crisis suffered by the people in Kosovo, indeed supported the action at least in a political sense; something which, in view of the absence of a UN mandate, marked a change from previous positions.

Finally, the 2003 Iraq War turned out to be relatively unproblematic from a Swedish point of view: not only was it illegal (due to the absence of a UN mandate), but it was also illegitimate (as motives were unclear). That Sweden was this time not faced with a dilemma situation was, moreover, due to the fact that the intervention was not motivated by humanitarian concerns and thus appealing to moral conscience – the intervention was rejected purely on the grounds of being in breach of international law.

The actions taken by the Swedish executive in the Iraq conflict illustrate that Sweden's support for the UN can at times be characterised as 'opportunistic'. Even though a number of high-ranking politicians repeatedly pointed out that a peaceful resolution would indeed be preferable over military action and sought to employ the pertinent diplomatic means, Minister for Foreign Affairs Lindh declared as early as in autumn 2002 that Sweden would endorse any decision made by the UN, irrespective of the outcome. In line with the traditional legalistic UN policy, Sweden was thus awaiting a decision from the Security Council, a position that was repeatedly criticised as lacking a firm personal stance on the Iraq issue. Exaggerated as this criticism may seem, for a country that traditionally pursues an independent, active foreign policy, these manoeuvring tactics seem slightly disconcerting indeed.

In conclusion, of the three wars investigated in this chapter, the Kosovo conflict, which led to the dissolution of the traditional primacy of the principle of sovereignty, can be regarded as moving the goalposts for any future shaping of Swedish foreign policy. In its wake, several Swedish politicians repeatedly urged that, in the face of severe human rights violations, the international community could not be allowed to take a passive stance. Notwithstanding the problem of the somewhat sparse data obtained from the analysed primary sources, it has been demonstrated that in the Swedish discourse arguments in favour of participating in wars legitimised by international law are becoming increasingly more relevant.

This is not intended to conceal the fact that Sweden still continues to adhere to its principle of UN policy – namely that, for Sweden, any such participation in war shall be considered a possible and conceivable option under UN mandate only. However, there is an increasing willingness to deviate from this position in the case of humanitarian crisis situations, in which intervention is considered legitimate even in the absence of a UN mandate. This means that Sweden's UN policy – legalistic in principle – can be overruled by moral concerns in exceptional situations of humanitarian emergency.[41] It remains to be seen

---

[41] Personal interview with a Social Democratic member of the Riksdag: 'We are legalistic, but not idiotic legalistic, naïve', December 2006, Stockholm.

how such emergencies will impact decisions on Swedish involvement in interventions that have no UN mandate but have been initiated by NATO or the EU. Particularly in light of Sweden's participation in and leadership of the EU Nordic Battle Group within the European Rapid Reaction Concept, there is a possibility that, should a 'second Kosovo' occur, Sweden's legalistic policy of adhering to the UN will also be undermined in practice.

REFERENCES

Agius, Christine 2006. *The Social Construction of Swedish Neutrality: Challenges to Swedish Identity and Sovereignty*. Manchester University Press
Ahlin, Per 1993. *Folkrätten i svensk säkerhetspolitik*. Stockholm: Juristförlaget
Anthonsen, Mette 2003. *Decisions on Participation in UN Operations: Do Media Matter? Danish and Swedish Response to Intra State Conflicts in the 1990s.* Gothenburg: Göteborgs Universitet
Åsard, Erik and Bennett, Lance W. 1997. *Democracy and the Marketplace of Ideas: Communication and Government in Sweden and the United States.* Cambridge University Press
Bjereld, Ulf 2002. 'Mellan folkrätt och moral? Kosovokriget och nordisk säkerhetspolitik', in Sven Eliæson and Hans Lödén (eds.), *Nordisk säkerhetspolitik: inför nya utmaningar*. Stockholm: Carlsson, pp. 273–8
Bjereld, Ulf, Johansson, Alf W. and Molin, Karl 2008. *Sveriges säkerhet och världens fred: Svensk utrikespolitik under kalla kriget*. Stockholm: Santérus
Björkdahl, Annika 2007. 'Constructing a Swedish Conflict Prevention Policy Based on a Powerful Idea and Successful Practice', *Cooperation and Conflict* 42 (2): 169–85
Bring, Ove and Mahmoudi, Said 2001. *Sverige och folkrätten*. Stockholm: Norstedts Juridik
Dahl, Ann-Sofie 2002a. 'Activist Sweden: The Last Defender of Non-Alignment', in Ann-Sofie Dahl and Norman Hillmer (eds.), *Activism and (Non)Alignment: The Relationship Between Foreign Policy and Security Doctrine.* Stockholm: Utrikespolitiska Institutet, pp. 139–50
2002b. 'Det kontroversiella NATO: varför och för vem?', in Sven Eliæson and Hans Lödén (eds.), *Nordisk säkerhetspolitik: inför nya utmaningar*. Stockholm: Carlsson, pp. 229–50
Deitelhoff, Nicole and Burkard, Eva 2005. 'Europa vor Gericht. Die EU-Außenpolitik und der Internationale Strafgerichtshof', *HSFK-Report* No. 13/2005, Frankfurt a.M.
Ekdal, Niklas and Ekströmer, Jonas 1991. *Desert Blues: Boken om det svenska Fältsjukhuset i Saudiarabien 1991.* Karlskrona: Fredsbasker
Eliæson, Sven 2002. 'Inledning', in Sven Eliæson and Hans Lödén (eds.), *Nordisk säkerhetspolitik: inför nya utmaningar*. Stockholm: Carlsson, pp. 7–49
Engdahl, Ola and Lind, Gustaf 2005. *Regeringens befogenheter att sända väpnad styrka till andra länder*. Stockholm: Totalförsvarets forskningsinstitut
Fischer, Maria 2003. *Schweden und die NATO*. Berlin: Institut für Internationale Politik und Regionalstudien

Folz, Rachel 2011. 'Does Membership Matter? Convergence of Sweden's and Norway's Role Conceptions by Interaction with the European Union', in Sebastian Harnisch, Cornelia Frank and Hanns W. Maull (eds.), *Role Theory in International Relations: Approaches and Analyses*. London: Routledge, pp. 147–64

Granholm, Niklas 1999. 'Det politiska priset kan bli högt för att vi kom så sent till Kosovo', *FOA-tidningen (Framsyn)* No. 5/1999, Stockholm

2003. 'Sverige och Irakkrisen: Ett svenskt dilemma?', in Bo Ljung (ed.), *Irakkriget 2003: en preliminär analys*. Stockholm: Totalförsvarets Forskningsinstitut, pp. 52–8

Hallenberg, Jan 2000. 'Swedish Foreign and Security Policy', in Lee Miles (ed.), *Sweden and the European Union Evaluated*. London: Continuum, pp. 19–32

ICBL (International Campaign to Ban Landmines) 1999. *Landmine Monitor Report: Toward a Mine-Free World*. New York: Human Rights Watch

Jahn, Detlef 2003. 'Das politische System Schwedens', in Wolfgang Ismayr (ed.), *Die politischen Systeme Westeuropas*. Opladen: Leske + Budrich, pp. 93–130

Jakobsen, Peter Viggo 2006. *Nordic Approaches to Peace Operations: A New Model in the Making?* London: Routledge

Lindström, Gustav 1997. 'Sweden's Security Policy: Engagement – the Middle Way', *Institute for Security Studies WEU Occasional Papers* 2, Paris

Møller, Bjørn 1999. 'The Kosovo Crisis and the Northern Tier: Denmark, Norway, Iceland, Sweden and Finland', *COPRI Working Papers* 24/1999, Copenhagen

Nilsson, Ann-Sofie 1988. 'Swedish Foreign Policy in the Post-Palme Era', *World Affairs* 151 (1): 25–33

1991. *Den moraliska stormakten: En studie av socialdemokratins internationella aktivism*. Stockholm: Timbro

Nohrstedt, Stig A. 2004. 'Media Reflexivity in the War on Terror: Three Swedish Dailies and the Iraq War', in Stig A. Nohrstedt and Rune Ottosen (eds.), *Global War–Local Views: Media Images of the Iraq War*. Gothenburg: Nordicom, pp. 223–44

Norlin, Margareta 1999. 'Svenska fredstraditioner', in Örjan Appelqvist (ed.), *Fredsbomber över Balkan: Konflikten om Kosovo, historia, analys, debatt*. Stockholm: Manifest, pp. 159–63

Ohlsson, Per T. 1991. *Landet utanför: Saddam och ståndpunkterna*. Stockholm: Timbro

Prawitz, Jan 2000. 'Svensk kärnvapenpolitik under 50 år', Stockholm: Olof Palme International Center

Rieker, Pernille 2002. 'From Territorial Defence to Comprehensive Security? European Integration and the Changing Norwegian and Swedish Security Identities', *NUPI Paper* No. 626, Oslo

Roffey, Roger 2002. 'Threats from Chemical and Biological Weapons a Swedish View', Swedish Defence Research Agency

Salander, Henrik 1992. *Nedrustningspolitik och rustningskontroll i en ny tid*. Stockholm: Utrikesdepartementet

Schüngel, Daniela 2005. 'Schwedens Sicherheitspolitik im Wandel: Zwischen militärischer Allianzfreiheit, NATO und ESVP', *HSFK-Report* No. 14/2005, Frankfurt a.M.

Siedschlag, Alexander 2001. 'Innenpolitische Entscheidungsprozesse bei Streitkräfteeinsätzen im Rahmen der Petersberg-Aufgaben der Europäischen Union: Deutschland, Frankreich, Großbritannien, Italien, Schweden', Berlin: SWP

Sundelius, Bengt 1990. 'Sweden: Secure Neutrality', *Annals of the American Academy of Political and Social Science* 512: 116–24

Utrikesdepartementet 1999a. 'Sverige i Förenta Nationernas säkerhetsråd 1997–1998: Aktstycke utgivna av Utrikesdepartementet', Ny serie II: 54, Stockholm

Utrikesdepartementet 1999b. 'Utrikesfrågor: Offentliga dokument m.m. rörande viktigare svenska utrikesfrågor 1998', Ny serie I:C 48, Stockholm: Norstedts Tryckeri AB

Utrikesdepartementet 2000. 'Utrikesfrågor: Offentliga dokument m.m. rörande viktigare svenska utrikesfrågor 1999', Ny serie I:C 49, Stockholm: Norstedts Tryckeri AB

Wagner, Wolfgang 2006. 'Parliamentary Control of Military Missions: Accounting for Pluralism', *DCAF Occasional Paper* No. 12, Geneva

Part III

Conclusion

10 Liberal democracies as militant 'forces for good': a comparative perspective

Anna Geis, Harald Müller and Niklas Schörnig

This chapter outlines the reasons for participation and non-participation in the three wars in a comparative perspective and discusses the implications of these findings for democratic peace (DP) research. Further original data are presented in order to assess similarities and differences between the national public discourses: the results from a correlations analysis depicting 'similarity' in the use of the arguments in the respective parliaments as well as seven national 'argumentative maps' that depict the relative importance of the arguments most frequently used. The analysis of these justificatory discourses contributes to identifying and differentiating the norms that are prevalent in the political culture and institutions of a given democratic polity. This procedure allows deeper insights into the variation among democracies.

The chapter proceeds as follows. It briefly recalls the theoretical assumptions that were set out in the introductory chapter (Section 1). The next section outlines the reasons that have led the democratic governments to participate in, or to abstain from, the wars. In particular, it discusses in more detail the respective institutions that provide for accountability in the warring democracies, questioning some rationalist-institutional approaches to democratic peace (Section 2). A separate comparison of the dominant arguments shaping the national parliamentary discourses on war (no war) elucidates which domestic justifications have been submitted for (non-)participation in the three wars (Section 3). The section also discusses the implications of some striking findings of the aggregate data on DP research and the key similarities/differences between the democracies. The concluding section summarises the implications of our findings for both rationalist and normative assumptions of DP research (Section 4).

1 A shift of perspective: from democratic peace to democratic war

As outlined in the Introduction, we adopt a dyadic democratic peace perspective, assuming that monadic features of a democratic polity – utilitarian preferences, institutional constraints, inhibiting norms – play out differently in different interaction constellations: whereas democracies are peaceful with one another, they wage wars against non-democracies, but *some* democracies fight (much) more frequently than other democracies and they are not bellicose towards *all* non-democracies but only towards *some* of them. How is this variation to be explained?

We infer from domestic analogies on the use of force within democratic polities that it is essential for DP research to investigate the procedural and substantial 'legitimising requirements' that also structure the external use of force by democracies (Müller and Wolff 2006: 61; see also Brock *et al.* 2006: 197–204): the use of force is not prohibited per se within democracies, but its legality and legitimacy are made contingent upon the respective legal order and politico-cultural norms of the polity. In analogy, we expect that decisions on war participation must, first, be in accordance with procedural requirements, i.e. meet procedural standards of domestic lawful decision-making and of international law, and, second, must be justified publicly with 'good reasons' that are accepted as legitimate by the majority of the respective democratic public.

Normative-cultural explanations of democratic *peace* assume that democratic actors externalise the domestic norms of peaceful conflict resolution, tolerance and fairness in international interactions (Russett 1993: 31–3; Friedman 2008). In differentiation of this normative-cultural explanation, we focus on democratic *war* instead and consider liberal-democratic norms to be inherently ambivalent, i.e. depending on the interacting regime, and legitimating peaceful policy options as well as militancy beyond self-defence (Müller and Wolff 2006).

According to traditional *normative-cultural explanations* of DP research, democratic actors take recourse to force primarily in reaction to the offensive behaviour of non-democracies that do not play by the same rules as democracies. A democracy that is facing a conflict with a non-democracy may 'feel obliged to adapt to the harsher norms of international conduct of the latter, lest it be exploited or eliminated by the nondemocratic state that takes advantage of the inherent moderation of democracies' (Russett 1993: 33; see Rummel 1979: 292). In contrast, we have analysed escalations of conflicts into war under the less benign perspective that democracies might also contribute their share to such escalations. As will be discussed below (Section 3.1.1), our data show that 'coercive diplomacy' and the description of the adversary regime in pejorative language, denoting its 'enemy character' in 'unjust enemy' terms, figure prominently among the reasons leading democratic actors onto the road to war.

The second strand of 'classic' DP explanations, *rationalist-institutionalist approaches*, argues that democratic citizens as well as their leadership are rational actors who are averse to costs and risks (Bueno de Mesquita *et al.* 1999; Rousseau 2005: 20–7). While citizens eschew the material and human costs of a war (beyond self-defence), governments are primarily interested in securing their power, so that war-prone democratic executives will feel restrained by various checks and balances and constitutional safeguards that feed back the peaceful preferences of citizens into the executive decision-making process. Empirical studies, however, provide no support for the thesis that wars prove *ex post* inefficient for leaders (Chiozza and Goemans 2004: 605). What is more relevant for the wars analysed in this book – which are not regarded as 'lost' wars by the democratic belligerents – is that parliaments, public opinion or the media do not invariably function as constraining factors for war-prone governments since deputies, people and journalists can and do support decisions to use force under certain circumstances (see Section 2.2). It would be wrong to assume prior and unchangeable peaceful preferences in democratic publics as conventional DP research has often done. Depending on the type of military action at issue, democratic publics have displayed a variety of attitudes towards the use of force (Rosato 2003: 594–5).

2   Liberal militancy and liberal restraint: roads to participation and non-participation in war

2.1   *Reasons to fight or to abstain in a comparative perspective*

2.1.1   *The Gulf War: a liberal ca(u)se for world order*
The participation rate in the 1991 Gulf War was high among the seven democracies. The United States, the United Kingdom and France, all of whom bore responsibility for the UN Security Council (UNSC) mandate to use force, sent considerable contingents into battle. Australia and Canada also participated. Only Germany and Sweden abstained, though Sweden opted for 'semi-participation' by sending a field hospital, but no combat units, thereby simultaneously participating and not participating. Germany supported the war indirectly by providing financial assistance and by replacing US troops in some missions such as the presence in the Mediterranean. But no German soldier went to the Persian Gulf. One can thus state the 'participation rate' as '5.5' out of 7.

Looking at the paths to participation and non-participation, it is clear that the main drivers for punishing the Iraqi aggression by force, the US and the UK (each at that time governed by a conservative executive), both had a strong interest in restoring order, but also combined this (universalist) interest in a very specific way with their national interests. The negotiations at the UN on the US side were tactical-opportunistic – to facilitate broader participation and reduce opposition at home and abroad through the legitimacy provided by the UN – and reluctant on the British side, at least as regards Prime Minister Thatcher. For France, Canada and Australia, UN consent was probably a necessary condition for participation, even though the Canadian and Australian leaders had decided to send troops long before the UN authorised the use of force and even before the US requested their participation. For these two nations, the 'good cause' coincided with their national interest in closing ranks with their most important ally. For the governments of Germany and Sweden, UN authorisation meant that the case was worthy of support, but both limited their assistance to financial and logistical aid (Germany) and a token, non-combat contribution (Sweden) due to domestic legal constraints and residual pacifism as strong ingredients of their national cultures.

Military action against Saddam Hussein was supported by clear majorities in public opinion polls in the US, the UK and Australia. In Canada and France, the majorities were less clear-cut and at some points in the run-up to the war, there were small majorities against. While in France a majority backed their troops once the war began, the Canadian case is of particular interest since the Canadian public, and notably the citizens of the province of Quebec, supported a tough stance towards Saddam Hussein but were increasingly disinclined towards their own country's participation in a war. Prime Minister Mulroney decided to participate in the war against an initial domestic majority and despite the difficult domestic situation that he was facing in the province of Quebec. The fact that the mission of the Canadian troops was projected as being of a more defensive nature and that the deployment of ground troops was eventually ruled out was a concession to a reluctant public. In Germany, only a minority advocated a potential war, but a clear majority approved of the allied effort once the fighting began. Nevertheless, there were always clear majorities against German participation in the war. In Sweden, public opinion supported the US approach and showed a relative majority in favour of military operations after the war had started. One could speculate that public opinion might have even supported Swedish participation.

Conservative newspapers in the participating democracies were largely supportive of their governments, while the newspapers of the centre-left camp tended to be more critical of their governments and often argued that peaceful means had not yet been exhausted. Left-leaning papers in Australia and Canada tended to back the overall policy line of their governments but criticised what they regarded as an overly indulgent attitude on the part of their governments towards the wishes of their US ally. The only clear, consistent anti-war position was presented by the leftist *Guardian* in the UK (where public opinion was most 'hawkish'). Even in the non-participating states of Germany and Sweden, newspaper editorials often leaned towards endorsing the use of force, with the exception of the Swedish *Aftonbladet*. In Germany, the abstention of the Kohl government was repeatedly criticised as 'shirking'. This variation of attitudes among the newspapers on the centre-right and centre-left quite accurately mirrors the variation in political positions adopted by the respective political parties of the seven countries.

Government policies and public opinion were largely in line. While support for war was not overwhelming everywhere in the warring countries, (narrow) majorities did exist, at the latest when the fighting started – with Canada remaining a remarkable exception. But although public opinion did back the government policy line in most cases, governments decided on war largely independently of the formation of public opinion; a fact that was quite notable in the early determination of the US, the UK, Canada and Australia to confront Saddam Hussein. Apart from the case of Canada, the only instance of a possible disconnection between the government and the public, surprisingly, was Sweden, where public opinion was more 'militant' than the government anticipated. However, the fact that the government acted in the tradition of time-honoured Swedish policy prevented any major rift, and under these circumstances its half-hearted semi-participation was enough to satisfy the Swedes.

All in all, the balance shows that 'order wars' in favour of a regional or world order in reaction to an undisputed, grave breach of international law and sanctioned by the UN are within the realm of appropriate behaviour as seen by liberal-democratic citizens and elites. Apart from the high visibility of several large demonstrations in Germany, France and the US, opposition to the war did not dominate overwhelmingly either public opinion or the selected newspaper editorials in the non-participating countries. The factors that impeded both (full) German and Swedish participation in combat were idiosyncratic norms of national identity, the constitution enshrining military restraint in the German case – a position that would be reconsidered during the later 1990s – and neutrality in the Swedish case.

This 'order war' was also fought by some non-democracies, indicating that the liberal preference for a law-based order might be shared with those non-democracies that also perceive themselves as having a stake in orderly relations based on international law. This also applies to economic interests: when it comes to the Persian Gulf, oil is always relevant, though not in the form of the primitive popular conspiracy thesis that always suspects US military action of serving the profit interests of the big US companies. Quite the reverse: US policies, at least since the rise of OPEC in the late 1960s, have focused persistently on the strategic interest of keeping access to reasonably priced crude oil open for the world economy and preventing the resources of the Gulf from falling under a politically motivated monopoly. In a broader sense, this is also an order consideration; this time not one of restoring international law, but of preserving the prerequisite of a liberal world market economy – an interest that is shared not only by democratic states.

2.1.2   *The Kosovo War: a liberal ca(u)se for human rights*

The participation rate in the Kosovo War in 1999 was again fairly high: five out of seven countries deployed air forces over Serbia. The two democracies that abstained, Sweden and Australia, nevertheless supported NATO's actions politically without feeling compelled to take an active part in the operations. This political unity among the democracies is all the more remarkable as the mission lacked an explicit mandate from the UNSC and the lawfulness of the war was thus very much in doubt.

All the participating countries were NATO members. The decision was prepared within the Alliance – very much in the sense of entering a slippery slope (see below, Section 3.1.1). This chain of collective decision-making, together with the necessity to demonstrate NATO's credible *unified* resolve to the Serbian leader Slobodan Milošević, left hardly any real chance of evading participation, even if member countries might have preferred to stay out. The deliberations by the governments involved, however, pointed to a strong conviction that helping the Kosovar population was genuinely believed to be 'the right thing'. There were also other interests involved such as asserting the importance of NATO in post-Cold War European security and stemming the flow of refugees. But evidence suggests that the humanitarian motive was strong within the executives, and it dominated the public discourse.

The crucial difference in this case was the participation of Germany, one of the two countries most reluctant to go to war in our sample. The new German left-wing government had political reasons for and against participation. It was running a considerable domestic risk in terms of intra-party opposition and domestic aversion to involvement in war. Its decision to participate can to a considerable extent be explained by the particular need of a leftist executive to prove their capacity to behave as a reliable ally. After the so-called 'massacre of Račak' on 15 January 1999, government rhetoric increasingly compared the 'genocide' in Kosovo to Auschwitz, rendering German participation in the war quasi the equivalent of fighting the country's dark past.

Canadian participation, in contrast, rested on no such ambiguities: supported by a broad consensus in public and Parliament, the Canadian government pursued a new philosophy of limited sovereignty and the 'responsibility to protect' in the interest of a humanitarian cause.[1] This cause reigned so supreme that the absence of UNSC authorisation was overruled, despite regrets that a mandate was not available. Canadian legalism required the reasoning that the recent evolution of humanitarian law in fact made the one-sided intervention a legal undertaking.

The British government, which together with US Secretary of State Madeleine Albright was the driving force for the war, was willing to add ground troops to the air campaign (as initially were the Canadians), and was critical of the US refusal to do so. It expanded the legal argument: the use of force to remedy the humanitarian crisis would be justified once the UNSC had determined the situation in Kosovo as a threat to peace and security. If the Security Council then proved unable to follow the logic of its own decisions, individual states were legally authorised to help. As in Canada, there was broad support within the public and political arena.

France was in a special situation as the country had traditionally good relations with Serbia and was very concerned about the circumvention of the UNSC. As a consequence, France tried longer than the rest to find a diplomatic solution. However, the humanitarian cause – which France traditionally claims as its national mission and which enjoyed broad political support – together with the fear of being isolated in the Western alliance induced President Chirac to lead France into this war and provide a significant contribution. Members of the socialist-led cabinet within the executive under the left-wing/right-wing *cohabitation* did not like following US leadership, but could not prevail.

US President Clinton was facing a difficult domestic situation and allegations that he was intending a 'diversionary war'. The militant faction in the executive, led by Secretary of State Albright and Ambassador Holbrooke, pushed for a humanitarian-driven confrontation. Alliance cohesion and the need to preserve US leadership in the face of British activism were important aspects. The scepticism among the public and

---

[1] Following the Kosovo War, this 'responsibility to protect' (R2P) has been actively advanced by a larger number of actors (see ICISS 2001), with Canada in a proactive and leading position, and has made a remarkable career as a new emergent norm in the international normative structure (Bellamy 2008). The 'R2P' was endorsed by the UN General Assembly at the World Summit in 2005.

Congress led Clinton to emphasise casualty aversion, which explains the categorical exclusion of ground operations.

To summarise, the humanitarian aspect was the strongest force in the mix of political reasons and a helpful legal reference in the public justifications of all governments, with the 'Račak massacre' driving decisions in Germany, France and the US. Alliance considerations of various forms played an important role in Germany, France and the US, proving helpful for all three to substitute Western multilateralism for UN legalism.

What about the abstentions? Given Australia's 'war record', one could have expected participation were it not for the weight of national interest aspects in the Australian political calculus: the cause was morally right and worth supporting, but there was no urgent pressure from the important ally, and the site of the conflict was well beyond the orbit where Australia locates its vital interests. Thus, Australians wished the allies well, but did not consider participation as useful. Sweden, in contrast, faced another dilemma: the cause was good, no doubt, and corresponded to the highest values enshrined in Swedish culture. On the other hand, the lack of a UN mandate prohibited consideration of any form of Swedish participation, and Alliance membership was not available as a substitute for this neutral country. Sweden thus endorsed legal and moral justifications as put forward by Britain or Canada, but still insisted on abstention (which helped fend off a major domestic controversy that would otherwise have been likely).

Public opinion in Canada, the UK and France strongly endorsed military intervention to help the Kosovars. It was divided in the US and Germany, but once the war started, the 'rally around the flag' effect turned public opinion in favour of the operation with (slim) majorities. There was medium to strong support from the newspapers in Germany, Canada, the UK, France and the US. In the US newspapers, there was a switch in the roles between liberal and conservative media: while the liberal *New York Times* tended to advocate war, a majority of articles in the conservative *Washington Times* expressed support, although a significant number expressed dissent; this clearly reflected the domestic climate. The Australian public and press were indifferent, mirroring the government's view of the national interest, while in Sweden, public opinion was slightly disposed against the war and strongly objected to any Swedish participation. The Swedish press wavered between support and criticism, echoing the basic dilemma that the Swedes faced in a conflict where two cherished values confronted one another: providing humanitarian relief while lacking an explicit UN mandate.

Humanitarian intervention appears to strike a uniform chord in Western democracies: it is a powerful motivator for military action, evoking moral obligations emerging from one's own collective identity as a liberal democracy. Even in Canada, the doubtful legality of this operation did not give rise to a single dissenting voice among the coded statements in Parliament, although Canada has been a country that faithfully abides by international law. The fact that opposition in even the more militarily restrained nations gave way to (moderate) majority support in the late phase of the preparations for the war is a further indication of the power of the humanitarian motive. Yet, the need for multilateralism appears strong even under these circumstances. The reference to NATO, which was made by war proponents in all participating countries, is evidence of this. Significantly, only two non-members of the Alliance, Australia and Sweden, did not participate. Equally, the need for legal justification is uniform, and where this is not available via the letter of international law, actors refer to legitimacy derived from the 'spirit' of international law. The Kosovo War is a strong hint of just how powerful the potential for governments is to frame the image of a war as a legitimate action: this was demonstrated in their public presentation of the (still ambiguous) 'Račak massacre', which played a key role in reducing opposition and gaining majority public support for the use of force.

2.1.3   The Iraq War: a liberal ca(u)se for regime change

The Iraq War in 2003 had the lowest participation rate (three out of seven) and was the only case of open and effective opposition from all absentees; it is singular in both aspects. It is also noteworthy that two out of three participants took part in defiance of majority public opinion, and that all opponents rejected participation in agreement with the overwhelming majority of the public.

In the run-up to the war, five out of the seven democracies were poised to engage in Iraq through a proper UN procedure; only the US would have been prepared to circumvent the Security Council altogether and acquiesced to seeking a UN mandate only at the intense request of the British and, to a lesser extent, the Australian governments. The split became ever more visible at the end of 2002 and the beginning of 2003: led by the primary objective of removing Saddam Hussein from power, the three war parties tried to utilise the UN procedure in order to build a strong legal case for their intention to topple the Iraqi regime. While the Australian government differed from the British government in being slightly less committed to the UN route, it differed from both Britain and the US in refusing any role in post-war Iraq. The fear of having to justify casualties to a divided country is likely to have been the primary reason for this stance.

War opponents tried hard to use the interplay between the inspections and pressure from the Security Council to complete the disarmament of Iraq. The German government alone refused any participation in a military operation even if Iraqi behaviour and an ensuing UNSC resolution were to make military enforcement inevitable. This attracted considerable domestic and international criticism, but also demonstrated the persistence of the German 'culture of restraint'. Disarming Iraq was the only appropriate objective that the four dissenting governments accepted. Regime change was not a legitimate goal in their eyes.

Public opinion was opposed to this war, in most cases very strongly so. The US was the only country where majorities supported the use of force throughout the run-up to the war. The growing commitment of countries to the 'coalition of the willing' and US President Bush's increasing propaganda activities in 2003 to frame the Iraq case as a 'pre-emptive' war of 'self-defence' helped to dispel scepticism among the population. According to most polls conducted weeks before the war started, majorities finally even supported a war without a UN mandate; however, there was never any general public pressure on the government to invade Iraq. In other democracies, there was considerable opposition to the war as such, but this opposition rose to very high levels (two-thirds plus) when participation in a war without a UN mandate was at stake. In Germany, France and Sweden, participation even with a UN mandate shifted only the relative strengths of those for or against, but did not lead to majorities in favour of either a military operation or national participation. In Britain, Australia and Canada, a mandate would apparently have led to majority support, while its absence sealed strong majority opposition.

Newspapers' reactions were divided along partisan lines in states participating in the war. Left-of-centre newspapers promoted strict opposition to the war. In the US, some of the *New York Times* articles opposed Bush's policy and some were supportive, while the conservative *Washington Times* demonstrated stronger support; arguments of national interest and national security dominated the debate. In Australia, the conservative *Australian* shifted its position, vague at first, to a clear 'yes' only in parallel with the executive's policy becoming clear.[2] In the UK, the conservative *Times* advocated a war, even against considerable opposition in the population and Parliament, while *The Guardian* rejected the war. The issue of legality and the inappropriateness of regime change as a war objective dominated counter-arguments within the newspapers; regional stability issues and concern about civilian casualties came

---

[2] A similar move occurred in anti-war Canada where the centrist *Globe and Mail* only adopted an attitude supportive of war once the government's opposition to military operations became unambiguous (it is noteworthy that the newspaper argued that way in line with a parliamentary opposition that had recently turned neoconservative).

second. Swedish and French newspapers emphasised arguments related to national identity and foreign policy role conceptions such as neutrality and military restraint (Sweden) and independence and responsibility for the UN (France). In Germany, not only were right- and left-of-centre newspapers largely united in their scepticism towards US war aims, but also in their criticism of Chancellor Schröder's unconditional 'no' without regard for the situation on the ground and the stance of the UN. Concern about alliance relations mitigated the conservative FAZ's opposition to the war. By and large, there was a high level of correspondence between German public opinion, published opinion and government policy, at least as far as participation in the war was concerned.

As this record of the Iraq War demonstrates, 'regime change' wars are bound to split democracies. While this is the most genuine '*democratic*' motivation to take up arms – probably no autocracy would feel compelled to democratise an adversary by force – it is also the most contested objective in terms of its legitimacy (MacMillan 2005). Significantly, the ubiquitous argument put forward by war critics that 'peaceful means are not exhausted' referred to a different objective, namely to that of disarming Saddam Hussein and thereby implementing the related resolutions of the UNSC. This is an 'order' concern, an indication that regime change was not accepted at all as the goal of pre-war diplomacy by people opposed to war, that is, by majorities in the bulk of the countries. In addition, legal procedures erect a strong barrier to participation for many democracies: the problem of legality will remain a barrier for participation since a UNSC mandate for this purpose is fairly unlikely – after all, why should a non-democracy like China or a semi-democracy like Russia condone the use of force for an objective that could be used against it?[3] Political leaders, the press and public opinion were remarkably united in these concerns.

Pro-war governments, in contrast, not only embraced regime change, but pushed aside legal concerns as being virtually irrelevant (in the US) or sought self-empowerment as the supreme interpreters of substantive international law, which implied standing above international procedural law. Self-empowerment extended to the domestic debate where the executives disregarded majority opinion or set out to 'frame' or even to manipulate it: if necessary, using distorted facts, half-truths or outrightly false allegations.[4]

---

[3] In the 2011 Libya case, Russia and China condoned by abstention a mandate to protect civilians by force, but were strongly critical when NATO turned the aims of the war into overthrowing Colonel Gaddafi's regime.

[4] In a BBC interview of December 2009, the former British Prime Minister Blair, facing the Chilcot Inquiry in 2010, declared that he would have invaded Iraq even without

2.2   *Qualifying some assumptions of democratic peace: democratic accountability mechanisms*

As outlined in the introduction to this chapter, rationalist-institutionalist variants of DP theory assume that democratic leaders as well as their constituencies are actors who are averse to costs and risks. In this model of the democratic process, the preference of the leadership to be re-elected and the preferences of the citizens to avoid costs are tied to each other by institutional accountability mechanisms such as elections, parliamentary oversight powers, public opinion polls and control via the media (Auerswald 2000; Elman 2000). Such models are often linked to a prior definition of citizens' preferences as being peaceful (Czempiel 1996: 90): governments that are interested in re-election will pay regard to such preferences and refrain from war. It has become obvious in our empirical analysis that such assumptions require qualification in various respects (Müller and Wolff 2006).

When the democracies analysed went to war, it was not because there was a strong popular demand for this course of action (Hils 2008: 258–61). In all cases of war participation, the executive was in the lead; the 'CNN effect' was not at work. This does not prove that this effect is irrelevant, but it does not appear to be the rule. There was one single case where the people appeared to be more ready to support war than the government, Sweden in 1991, and this resulted in a convenient compromise solution. In all other cases, governments made their case for war, with the effect of rallying majority public opinion around their position, sometimes late, as in the US and Germany in 1999. The doubtful validity of government allegations (e.g. the 'Račak massacre' in 1999 and Saddam Hussein's non-existent weapons of mass destruction (WMD) in 2003) did not inhibit their mobilising impact.

Can a critical press constrain governments pursuing military missions? The country chapters show that at least one of, if not even both, the leading newspapers usually supported the government's policy. This is not to say that published opinion was uniform or uncritical; critical editorials were found in most newspapers. In our cases, the press often reflected the spectrum of arguments for and against war that were also presented in the national parliaments (see below, Section 3.2). However, in contrast to most politicians, many editorials did not contain clear-cut positions

---

evidence of WMD and would have found a way to justify the war to Parliament and the public, emphasising: 'I would still have thought it right to remove him [Saddam Hussein].' See 'Tony Blair Admits: I Would Have Invaded Iraq Anyway', *The Guardian*, 12 December 2009.

but engaged in deliberating possibilities, assessing the policies of other states or backing/criticising the national government in broader terms.

The attitudes of political elites and citizens towards the use of force appear to be changing *gradually* (Finnemore 2003: ch. 5). Liberal-democratic elites put forward a whole range of legitimising reasons for military actions; and, according to opinion polls, 10 out of the 13 cases of military participations were supported by the majority of the citizens, although none of the wars presented clear cases of self-defence. Hence, it would be a mistake to assume *prior* peaceful preferences of a liberal-democratic public.

Remarkably, the three governments that participated in wars without popular support (Canada in 1991, the UK and Australia in 2003) paid no political price related to that decision: Blair and Howard were even re-elected with solid majorities; this is at odds with the key argument of institutionalist DP theory. Canadian Prime Minister Mulroney resigned from office in 1993, but for domestic reasons: he stepped aside as party leader, facing a general election that his party would probably have lost under his unpopular leadership. Mulroney's low approval rates at that time resulted from his economic and constitutional policies during his second term, not from his stance on the Gulf War.

As regards parliamentary oversight powers, it should be emphasised that these exist to very varying degrees in our sample of democracies (Born and Urscheler 2004; Houben 2005; Peters and Wagner 2011): the 'Westminster' models in the UK, Canada and Australia and the constitutional practice of the semi-presidential system in France render the deployment of troops the prerogative of the executive (partly leaving it to the goodwill of the head of government whether he or she would like to involve parliament through debates or symbolic votes). The presidential political system of the US, in contrast, grants considerable competencies to Congress by way of the 'War Powers Resolution' of 1973, but these powers remain legally controversial between parliament and the presidents (Grimmett 2009: 14–17). The presidents, as commanders-in-chief, have often exercised their supreme authority and consulted with Congress inconsistently or ignored the provisions of the War Powers Resolution, while the courts are reluctant to address this issue. Given that US presidents have not been obliged to ask for prior parliamentary authorisation for military action, the parliamentary control of the use of force in the US is in practice comparatively weak (Born and Urscheler 2004: 63; Fisher 2004).

In our sample, the parliamentary democracies Sweden and Germany possess the relatively strongest *formal* parliamentary oversight powers in deployment issues. It is striking that these are the two countries that did not participate at all (Sweden) or only once (Germany) in the three wars. While the interpretation of the German constitution regarding the 'out of area' deployment of the armed forces was controversial in the early 1990s, a clarification by the Constitutional Court in 1994 ruled that the forces may be deployed outside NATO territory, but must be considered a 'parliamentary army'. All cabinet proposals to deploy German armed forces on missions abroad for other than purely humanitarian aid purposes require the prior approval of a simple majority in parliament. Parliament approves or rejects a mission's mandate, duration and general operational issues (Wagner 2006: 42–3). In Sweden, the government is empowered to decide on the deployment of up to 3,000 troops without consulting parliament if these troops operate within the framework of a peacekeeping mission under the auspices of the UN or the OSCE; deployment in peace-enforcement missions, however, must be authorised by parliament. In practice, the Swedish government has usually sought the approval of parliament, even in cases where this is not legally required (Wagner 2006: 53–4). The Swedish parliament is allowed to decide on the mission's mandate and its duration (Born and Urscheler 2004: 63).

As stated above, the Canadian, British and Australian governments each decided on one occasion to participate in wars against the majority popular will. It is plausible that this phenomenon, which questions the core argument of democratic peace, can be partly explained by the substantial lack of parliamentary co-decision powers in these countries.[5] It is noteworthy that the parliamentarians were also divided over these decisions and that considerable opposition was voiced in parliament. The British Prime Minister Blair even faced the largest-ever parliamentary rebellion against the Iraq War within his own Labour Party, but could count on support from the Conservatives. The prime ministers of these three countries do not have to ask for formal permission to deploy troops, but are well advised to notify and consult their parliaments. In practice, these governments often submit specific motions related to deployment to a parliamentary vote, which is non-binding but of symbolic value and allows for public debate.

In sum, apart from the three aforementioned highly controversial decisions, all other governmental decisions to go to war were either supported by majorities in parliament or were not submitted to a (symbolic) vote before the fighting began.[6] DP research thus has to take into account

---

[5] For an elaboration of this argument, but with regard to different countries in the run-up to the Iraq War, see Eberl and Fischer-Lescano (2005) and Dieterich *et al.* (2009).

[6] See here also the overview of military conflicts prior to 1990 provided by Rousseau (2005: 342–3); Rousseau's table shows that democratic publics and parliaments have often (strongly) supported the initiation of the use of force by their governments.

the great variety of parliamentary oversight powers that restrain governments to very different degrees (Rousseau 2005: 140–8). But what is
perhaps even more important is that political elites and citizens alike can
also develop preferences favouring the use of force in a given conflict,
i.e. there are some justifications that are accepted as legitimate reasons
for war. In such cases, wars fought by democracies are not *necessarily*
indications of democratic deficits, as, for example, Ernst-Otto Czempiel
(1996) has argued. The next section will therefore present data from
our comparative content analysis of national parliamentary debates that
give more detailed information on the argumentative patterns justifying
(non-)participation in wars. Notwithstanding differing oversight powers
in deployment issues, most parliaments staged debates on the matter
prior to the beginning of the war.[7]

3   Justifying (non-)participation in 'democratic wars': results of a comparative content analysis of parliamentary debates

We have made some qualifying statements on classic DP assumptions in
Section 2.2. This, however, is not to say that democracy has no impact
on the crucial foreign policy decision on war/no war. Across our country sample, we have discerned such an impact in the strongly perceived
need for governments to make a case for their policies that resonates
with the public. This finding seems to contradict the limited effect of
unpopular policies on election success, but obviously political leaders
are to some extent averse to risks. While they may think that they have
a chance of remaining unscathed at the ballot, they do not know for
sure and thus try their best to minimise the risk of an unpopular policy
(Rousseau 2005: 20–2). In addition, they may often actually believe
what they say. As a consequence, governments and their affiliated parliamentarians try to shape their arguments in a way that is acceptable
to majority opinion. They play to norms and values that are popular
because they are part and parcel of national identities and foreign policy role conceptions (see Chapter 2). These norms constitute an overall
normative structure that provides a reservoir of arguments that can
be employed either to legitimise the use of force or to denounce it
as inappropriate for the own country (Duffield 1999; Harnisch and
Maull 2001).

---

[7] For methodological issues on this content analysis, see Chapter 2.

3.1   National debates on war participation: some striking findings

The data of our content analyses of parliamentary discourses show that these debates are quite controversial but that most speakers present only their own point of view and hardly consider the alternative positions. Only 41.7 per cent of all 408 war proponents and only 38.1 per cent of all 373 war opponents take up at least one of the other group's arguments, and this rather selectively. These findings suggest that parliamentary debates on the most fundamental issue, that of peace and war, follow ideological lines and formal procedures. This observation notwithstanding, the aggregate data show a number of striking results relevant for DP theory that warrant a closer look and indicate neglected fields of DP research.

The two most frequent arguments against war that war *proponents* deemed worth considering were, first, the claim that peaceful means had not yet been exhausted (15.7 per cent of speakers). They thus display a stronger preference for peaceful solutions than their associates who plead for earlier military action, but accept the legitimacy of using force for the given purpose once peaceful means have failed. The second counter-argument accepted as valid by war advocates was the fear of own casualties (15 per cent). The intensely debated issue of 'casualty aversion' of democratic publics plays a crucial role for the micro-foundations of democratic peace (see below, Section 3.1.3). The third and fourth most frequent counter-arguments accepted by war proponents as being worth debating are concern about civilian casualties, raised by only a tiny fraction of 6.1 per cent of speakers, and the lack of a UN mandate, addressed by 4.4 per cent of the proponents. Such speakers often conceded in their argumentation that these counter-arguments were important but then pointed to even more compelling arguments in support of war.

Of those *opposing* a military engagement, 15.5 per cent also subscribe to the strong enemy image of the war opponent that war supporters invoke (see below, Section 3.1.4); 8.3 per cent embrace the concept of a 'diplomacy backed by force' (see below, Section 3.1.1) and 6.4 per cent accept that a humanitarian catastrophe is a potentially legitimate argument for war. Finally, 5.4 per cent concede that the crises have resulted in a worrying regional instability (in the Middle East, in Europe) that needs to be addressed. Like the war proponents, war opponents admit that these arguments are essentially valid but that there are even more serious reasons that lead the speaker to reject military action.

3.1.1   Self-entrapment: the show of force as a slippery slope

On the 'democratic road to war' (Elman 1997), a surprisingly large number of parliamentarians accept the necessity of a show of military force to back 'coercive diplomacy' (George 1991; Schultz 2001; Art and Cronin 2007) and to enforce compliance by military means. At a first glance, this argument does not necessarily imply military conflict: it is the aim of coercive diplomacy to impose compliance by demonstrating – but not actually using – one's military capabilities, i.e. to send credible signals to the adversary and demonstrate unified resolve (Schultz 2001: 23–116). But deploying troops in a crisis theatre is a risky business and can be understood as the first step on a slippery slope to war: once the troops are on site, a countdown starts since they cannot be deployed abroad indefinitely due to complex logistics and high costs. Simultaneously, pressure mounts to accept only full compliance as the face-saving solution. Withdrawal without compliance is the least acceptable option, raising the likelihood of the actual use of force. Empirically, coercive diplomacy has failed in most cases, and has led to war in the majority of cases (Art and Cronin 2007). In conclusion, deciding in favour of threatening force often means actually choosing the war option in the long run. While many parliamentarians accept this connection, some – especially very early in a conflict – do not see (or refuse to see) that they are stepping onto a slippery slope.

The democracies in our sample did not simply rush into war from one day to the next, but spent some months publicly deliberating the potential use of force. The argument 'we need to show force' was employed frequently in the public debates in all countries and by most speakers. Of all parliamentary speeches coded in all countries and wars, 57.4 per cent of those supporting a military mission referred to this particular argument, while at least 8.3 per cent of the opponents accepted 'diplomacy backed by force' as a legitimate use of one's own military.

3.1.2   The salience of international law

The path to war is not only paved with military build-ups in the theatre of conflict but also accompanied by the efforts of the democracies involved to establish the legality of a potential use of force. While this insight is quite common for international lawyers, the issue of the international legitimation of a military action has been virtually completely ignored by mainstream US DP research to date:[8] our case studies show

---

[8] A number of German researchers have problematised this blind spot; for constructive proposals on how to integrate international law issues into DP research see, for example, Brock (2007) and Liste (2012). See also Eberl (2008).

the high salience of international law, in particular the legitimating role of a UNSC mandate. Each democratic government feels compelled to justify its behaviour 'somehow' with reference to international law – or, more precisely, with what the government takes to be the current position of international law or international state practice.

For some democracies, an orderly mandate from the UN is an absolute prerequisite. For some, it can be replaced by a common legal interpretation by the Western Alliance. For a few, it suffices that a nationally accepted interpretation proves the case to be lawful. The need to make a strong legal case if the issue is disputed (such as in 1999 or 2003) is felt much more strongly by everybody else – Britain and Australia included – than by the US. The latter's role conception of world leadership with the consequence of special responsibility, combined with exceptionalism, empowers the US government to make the case that it stands above international law. Legal arguments are still used occasionally, but with much less emphasis than by other countries. The legality of going to war is thus a very important aspect in all democratic publics. What that means, however, is disputed among them.

This contestedness of international legal norms (Wiener 2008) is evident in the national parliamentary debates, which witnessed intense disputes between proponents and opponents of a war. For those supporting a military mission, international law was a crucial source for legitimating their position: in the case of the 1991 Gulf War (which is the least controversial instance as regards legitimation and a clear UN mandate), almost half of all advocates (46.4 per cent) referred to the fact that the troop deployment was covered by international law, while more than two-thirds (70.6 per cent) understood the deployment as a means of actually enforcing international law. Although the situation was much more controversial in 2003, a quarter (25.4 per cent) of all advocates declared a potential war against Iraq to be covered by international law, and even more (41.5 per cent) claimed it would enforce international law. Even in the Kosovo War of 1999, where NATO had no UN mandate to use force, one in five proponents (19.7 per cent) claimed to be acting within the boundaries of international law and 16.1 per cent understood NATO action as enforcing international law. As regards war opponents, arguments related to international law played an important role here too: in 1991, a quarter (26.6 per cent) questioned the legality of a potential war against Iraq, and in both 1999 and 2003, almost half the speakers did so (46.6 per cent and 48.1 per cent respectively).

These findings suggest that the legitimacy provided by international law and the UN resonates highly within Western publics and forces both proponents and opponents of a military mission to address the issue of legality. But as the analysis shows (and as is known from constructivist research on norms in general), systems of norms such as the UN Charter can be interpreted in quite different, sometimes even opposite, ways (Finnemore and Toope 2001: 747; MacMillan 2005: 8). In addition, even if proponents understand that the given legal text as such prohibits their actions, they switch to an 'auxiliary norm' and argue that the action is enforcing the 'spirit' of the law that otherwise could not be enforced due to procedural obstructions in the UNSC. Alternatively, they claim, as in the Kosovo War, that international law as it currently stands is not adapted to new challenges and that a 'creative development' of law is thus required.

3.1.3   Casualty aversion

As described above, most parliamentary speakers do not deliberate on potential arguments challenging their position. The most striking exception for war proponents is the issue of *casualty aversion*. Of all proponents, 15 per cent accept the fear of one's own losses as a relevant argument worth considering, while only 6.1 per cent are concerned about the civilian casualties of the adversary. Normative variants of DP theory assume that Western democracies value the life of every individual highly due to their normative principles originating in the Enlightenment (Schörnig 2007: 96–7). Our data, however, suggests a norm hierarchy, putting one's own soldiers above foreign civilians (Mandel 2004: 11; Shaw 2005: 79–83; Watts 2008: 54–5). This hierarchy could be grounded in rationalist considerations (soldiers as assets of national power; they are costly to train, and when they are wounded or killed in action, the state has to compensate the soldier or his or her relatives) or in communitarian feelings (soldiers as members of one's own community to whom one owes more concern than to strangers with whom the solidary bonds are looser).

Recent empirical research suggests that the effects of this hierarchy can be seen on the battlefields: civilian casualties will be minimised as long as the safety of the Western soldiers is more or less guaranteed. But when facing a trade-off situation, most military commanders as well as political decision-makers will ensure the safety of their own personnel at the expense of the civilian population (Downes 2008: 246; Levy 2010: 401–3). Interestingly, however, war opponents did not resort to this line of reasoning in our parliamentary discourses. Not only did they consider own and foreign casualties as equally relevant, they also voiced their concern about potential civilian casualties of the adversary more frequently (31.4 per cent) than about potential own fatalities (25.2 per cent). One can only speculate why war opponents do not resort to the powerful argument of potential friendly losses more frequently in order to change the proponents' opinions. One reason could be that proponents of a war tend to frame potential casualties from a rationalist or a communitarian perspective (as noted above), whereas opponents tend to accentuate universalist-moral perspectives. Another reason might be that focusing on the safety of one's own troops might open a debate about asymmetric means of warfare, technological superiority, strategy and tactics where it is hard to hold the moral high ground. The content analysis is unable to answer the question of whether war opponents choose such a framing out of personal conviction or due to strategic considerations (e.g. in order to 'shame' war proponents). The difference in framing is nevertheless interesting to note.

Our data suggest that war proponents resorted to a rationalist (rather than communitarian or universalist-moral) framing; they combined their references to potential own casualties significantly more frequently with references to the national interest or national security than was to be expected.[9] This finding corresponds to the argument commonly found in the debate on casualty aversion that the more the national interest is regarded as being affected, the more casualties will be accepted by the national public (e.g. Larson 1996). From this point of view, the argumentative structure can be understood as a 'hedging strategy' (Schörnig 2007: 106): by raising the casualty issue while simultaneously stressing the importance of the mission for the national interest, proponents try to hedge themselves against a potential 'tipping' of public opinion against the mission in the event of disproportionate losses.

3.1.4 *Mobilising the public through enemy images?*

If the assumptions of DP theories on the great reluctance of democratic publics towards war are correct, advocates of military actions could be expected to use particular discursive strategies to mobilise popular support. One time-tested strategy here is the demonisation of the adversary and the construction of a strong enemy image (Fiebig-von Hase and Lehmkuhl 1997). The increased use of such pejorative language could therefore be expected, at least from war proponents. The data show that in the run-up to the Gulf War in 1990–1, a moderate third (34.6 per cent) of all proponents referred to such highly negative descriptions, while in the run-up to the Kosovo War in 1998–9, only a fifth (20.4 per cent) described Milošević as a cruel enemy worth fighting. In 2003, things were different when nearly three-quarters of war proponents (72.9 per cent) used this kind of rhetoric with regard to Saddam Hussein, although very often in connection with references

---

[9] $\chi^2(1) = 18.03, p < 0.001; \phi = 0.213, p < 0.001.$

to WMD, which should not be acquired by such a ruthless dictator. The distinction between references to national security and an enemy regime blurred at this point when WMD were mentioned in relation to the person Saddam Hussein, leaving the potential consequences for the respective homeland to the imagination of the audience.

Given the rather moderate figures regarding enemy images in 1991 and 1999, it is interesting to note that the construction of a strong enemy image was much more common in newspaper editorials advocating war (see the case studies) than in parliament. This suggests, first, that members of parliament might feel restrained by an implicit code of 'civilised' conduct that prevents the use of 'untamed' rhetoric. Second, demonising the adversary forecloses peaceful solutions at the 'last minute'. Especially in the run-up to the 1991 and 1999 wars, the two dictators were still regarded as potential negotiating partners even shortly before the start of hostilities.

3.2   National differences and similarities in argumentation

There are some remarkable similarities in the way certain states in our sample justify their participation or non-participation in the three wars. In order to measure similarity, we correlate the standardised frequencies or 'relevances' of all 135 data points,[10] interpreting the correlation coefficients as a measure of the degree of structural similarity in the national use of particular arguments. Table 10.1 depicts similarities between the six countries where national parliaments debated all three wars.[11, 12]

The table shows an interesting structure. First, it reveals that even the most dissimilar countries, Sweden and the US, have a positive correlation in their respective argumentations and that the correlation coefficients in general are in most cases rather close, suggesting a basic similarity between all these Western democracies. Taking a closer look, the argumentations used in the political debates in Canada, Germany and France are especially similar to each other. Attached to this group is Sweden, which shows a remarkable similarity to Germany but is not as similar to Canada or France as these are to each other, suggesting that Canada and especially France lean towards the 'middle ground' compared to

---

[10] See Appendix, Section 1 for the formal calculation of the 'relevance' of a particular argument in a particular conflict.

[11] Australia is excluded here as there was no parliamentary debate about Australian participation in the Kosovo War, leaving Australia with only 90 data points rather than 135.

[12] The bold numbers indicate the most similar country in the column to the country depicted in the row. For example, from the perspective of France, Germany is the most similar country (but Germany is most similar to Canada).

Table 10.1 *Similarity between six countries based on Pearson's correlation, three conflicts; n = 135**

	CAN	FRA	GER	SWE	UK	USA
CAN	1.000	0.704**	**0.727****	0.606**	0.629**	0.552**
FRA	0.704**	1.000	**0.708****	0.578**	0.580**	0.494**
GER	**0.727****	0.708**	1.000	0.717**	0.628**	0.500**
SWE	0.606**	0.578**	**0.717****	1.000	0.495**	0.318**
UK	0.629**	0.580**	0.628**	0.495**	1.000	**0.767****
USA	0.552**	0.494**	0.500**	0.318**	**0.767****	1.000

** Correlation is significant at the 0.01 level (2-tailed). The highest 'similarity' of one country with another country is highlighted.

Germany and Sweden. On the other hand, the discourses in the UK and the US are most similar to each other; similarity drops – especially in the US case – with regard to the other countries. In addition, Table 10.1 shows, unsurprisingly, that both Sweden and the US are the most dissimilar countries.

Taking Australia into account by ignoring the Kosovo case (since that was not debated at all in Australia) and focusing on the two wars against Iraq only for all countries, the result remains stable as Table 10.2 (correlating 90 relevances) shows.

When dealing with the Iraq wars, Australia, the UK and the US form a rather solid cluster with sharp drops in similarity to the other four countries, which are also very similar to each other. The similarities suggested by these two tables are not surprising since the US and the UK participated in all three wars and Australia in two wars, while the other four countries abstained altogether or decided to participate selectively due to substantial objections.[13]

Given these impressions concerning the similarities and dissimilarities between the countries analysed and the bifurcation within two clusters of similar democracies, the question arises of what these states have in common apart from their similar behaviour when it comes to waging or abstaining from war. The analysis above (Section 2.1), which is based on the individual case studies, has already suggested some explanations.

---

[13] The Australian decision not to participate in the Kosovo War was of a different character (see Schörnig, Chapter 5 in this book) to the decisions of the four countries that decided on substantial grounds against participation in the respective wars. Australia did not reject NATO's war over Kosovo, nor did it object to any particular aspect of that military action as the other countries did with regard to their non-participations in the wars.

Table 10.2 *Similarity between all seven countries based on Pearson's correlation, Gulf War 1990–1 and Iraq War 2003 only; n = 90*[**]

	AUS	CAN	FRA	GER	SWE	UK	USA
AUS	1.000	0.584**	0.597**	0.507**	0.390**	**0.770****	0.728**
CAN	0.584**	1.000	0.679**	**0.801****	0.727**	0.575**	0.469**
FRA	0.597**	0.679**	1.000	**0.783****	0.526**	0.521**	0.488**
GER	0.507**	**0.801****	0.783**	1.000	0.775**	0.533**	0.398**
SWE	0.390**	0.727**	0.526**	**0.775****	1.000	0.445**	0.313**
UK	**0.770****	0.575**	0.521**	0.533**	0.445**	1.000	0.746**
USA	0.728**	0.469**	0.488**	0.398**	0.313**	**0.746****	1.000

[**] Correlation is significant at the 0.01 level (2-tailed). The highest 'similarity' of one country with another country is highlighted.

A comparison of the use of the arguments of every country in any conflict with those of every other country would allow for the most detailed impression of similarities and differences, but the picture would not be very clear given the large number of arguments. For this reason, we calculated the average relevance of a particular argument in a particular country over all three wars.[14] For reasons of space, we focus in the following analysis only on those pro and contra arguments that have proven most relevant across all seven cases, based on average expression and range, leaving us with 19 arguments. This selection offers a clear overall picture.[15] Depicting the results as 'nets' allows us to interpret them as 'argumentative maps' that convey a graphical insight into a country's peculiarities. In addition, the figures show the average expression of each argument calculated across all other countries (shown in bold), giving an impression of the relative relevance of the argument vis-à-vis the debates in the other democracies.

3.2.1   The 'average democracy'

Figure 10.1 shows the average argumentative map across all the democracies investigated except Australia for all three wars.

---

[14] See Appendix, Section 1 for the formal calculation of the average relevance of each argument. At this point, however, it is safe to say that *within each country* the *average argument based on all 45 possible arguments* would have a score of 100. Scores below 100 show that the argument was underrepresented in the debates, while scores above 100 indicate a higher-than-average use.

[15] The particular values for all 45 arguments both with and without Australia (see above) can be found in Appendix Tables A.1 and A.2.

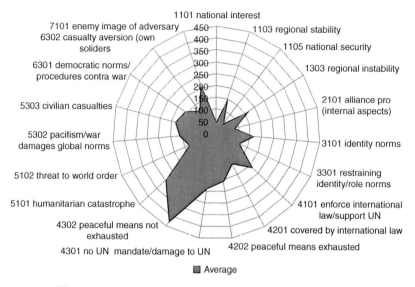

1101 national interest
7101 enemy image of adversary
6302 casualty aversion (own soliders
6301 democratic norms/ procedures contra war
5303 civilian casualties
5302 pacifism/war damages global norms
5102 threat to world order
5101 humanitarian catastrophe
4302 peaceful means not exhausted
4301 no UN mandate/damage to UN
1103 regional stability
1105 national security
1303 regional instability
2101 alliance pro (internal aspects)
3101 identity norms
3301 restraining identity/role norms
4101 enforce international law/support UN
4201 covered by international law
4202 peaceful means exhausted

■ Average

Figure 10.1 Argumentative map average democracy

The findings are interesting in the light of our initial assumptions derived from Immanuel Kant's three Definitive Articles in his essay on *Perpetual Peace* (elaborated in Chapter 1). In the following brief discussion, we emphasise those arguments among the most relevant 19 that are used with above-average frequency by the 'average democracy', with the average here being 170. The 'peaceful means not exhausted' argument excels as the one uttered by far the most frequently. It leads to two important conclusions. First, as one of the principles of international law, it shows the strength of legitimacy and legality considerations. This is in line with the interpretation of the Second Definitive Article of Kant's *Perpetual Peace*, notably if we add the utterances of 'peaceful means exhausted', 'no UN mandate' and 'enforce international law', all of which score well beyond 170. Second, as the argument most often used to postpone military action, it underlines impressively Kant's expectation that democratic citizens will show great hesitation before consenting to take up arms.

Other considerations related to this Article, such as the observation or violation of democratic norms in making the decision for war, play a minor role, and democratic regime change – which as we have seen was very much in the minds of political leaders in the warring parties of 2003 – is not even among the 19 arguments used most frequently. Casualty aversion seems surprisingly low compared to the importance attributed to it before. However, it is high in countries with actual war experience (see argumentative maps by country), suggesting that it is contingent on frequent involvement in combat.

The importance of humanitarian considerations in contrast – in line with the Third Definitive Article – is also clearly visible, reaching the 300 mark, and being strengthened by the concern about 'civilian casualties', which scores slightly above average. Cosmopolitan considerations are thus noticeably present when democracies deliberate war beyond self-defence. This is all the more remarkable as 'realist' arguments, notably 'national interest' and 'national security', are expressed with surprising infrequency. The only 'realist' concern that scores above average is 'regional stability', which is more of an 'order' than a 'national interest' consideration.

It is also in line with our initial considerations that law and humanitarian arguments are double-edged; they are used to support as well as to oppose going to war. The ambivalences of the liberal normative framework permeate the discourses that we analysed.

Finally, the 'enemy image' of the adversary scores fourth-highest on average. This tends to support our assumption that the possibility of the presence of a (non-democratic, dangerous) 'unjust enemy' works as an important catalyst pushing democracies towards using military force.

Altogether, the 'average democracy' emphasises international law when considering war, harbours grave humanitarian concerns, wants regional stability, abhors 'rogue states', is little concerned about risks to democratic norms and procedures at home and does not speak loudly about democratic regime change. Measured against this average type, national profiles can be seen in sharp relief.

3.2.2   National maps

Starting with the US (see Figure 10.2),[16] all arguments belonging to a 'realist' category (national interest, regional stability, national security; north-eastern quadrant) score higher than in the average Western democracy, indicating that power-related arguments are more accepted in the US discourses than in other Western states. The only 'realist' argument that scores below average is, in fact, an argument against intervention, i.e. fear that the intervention itself might lead to regional instability. In addition, arguments related to the UN or international law in a broader understanding (enforce international law, covered by international law and the question of whether or not all peaceful means have

---

[16] It is important to note that in the individual country maps 'average' stands for the 'average use of the particular argument across all countries under scrutiny' to allow a comparison of the particular country with the 'average democracy' described above.

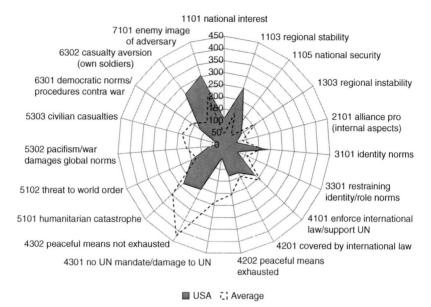

Figure 10.2 Argumentative map United States

been exhausted; southern quadrant) score below average, suggesting that international law is regarded as a less important argument by the US legislative and executive than by other Western states. Furthermore, alliance-related arguments are used less frequently than the average in other countries. An interesting issue is the fact that humanitarian arguments (humanitarian catastrophe as an argument *for*, concern about civilian casualties as an argument *against* military engagement; western quadrant) both score below average, while the fear of losing US soldiers in combat is very prominent in US debates (north-west quadrant). This focus on one's own soldiers in contrast to the civilian population of the opponent is consistent with insights from research on casualty aversion (Mandel 2004: 11; Shaw 2005: 79–83).

Besides the tendency to rely on power-related arguments, there are also strong indicators for normative considerations that become evident in frequent references to the national identity/role conception in foreign policy as well as to enemy images. It is striking that references to enemy images are used much more frequently in the US discourse than in any other democracy analysed. Both types of arguments, taken together, highlight the liberal-democratic missionary essentials as well as the Manichaean element in the US political culture and foreign policy tradition. In this context, the argument of using force in order to protect

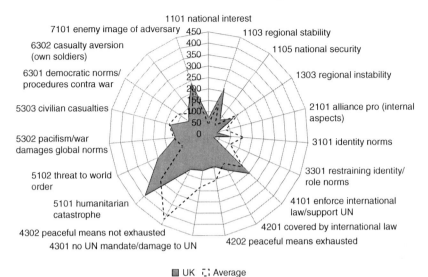

Figure 10.3 Argumentative map United Kingdom

the political and economic world order also scores slightly higher than average. In sum, 'realist' arguments mix with normative impulses in the discourses of the liberal superpower.

As Tables 10.1 and 10.2 indicated, the debates in the US are rather similar to those in the UK and Australia; a notion that is supported by the respective argumentative maps.

As in the US case, pro-war arguments that are related to power score above average while concern about causing regional instability also scores below average in the UK (see Figure 10.3). In contrast to the US case, arguments related to international law convey a mixed impression. While positive references to international law as legitimating an intervention score relatively high, the question of whether or not all diplomatic means have been exhausted or of the lack of a UN mandate as a constraining factor score considerably low. On casualties, the picture is more balanced than in the US case, but still shows similarities. While the relative importance of casualties among one's own troops compared to civilian casualties is lower in the UK than in the US, bringing both categories roughly to equal scores, fear of losing one's own soldiers still ranks higher in the UK than in other Western democracies.

As in the case of the US, British MPs tend to use pejorative language when describing the adversary as an enemy, raising this argument to a value well above average. This displays a strong normative underpinning

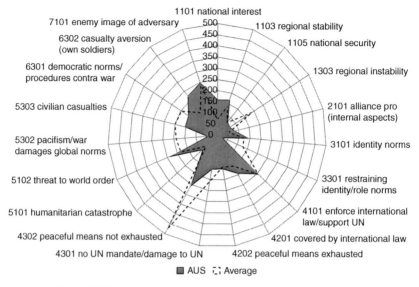

Figure 10.4 Argumentative map Australia

of the UK discourse, which is even more striking in the high salience of a humanitarian catastrophe as a potential reason for war. The latter sets the UK clearly apart from the US. While one might suspect the influence of the Kosovo War, Table A.1 in the Appendix, which focuses on the two wars against Iraq only, reveals that even in these cases humanitarian aspects were important in the British discourse. Taken together with the relatively frequent use of the argument that the political and economic world order must be defended by force, these numbers show that the British discourse is also marked by a specific mixture of normative-liberal and 'realist' arguments.

Looking at Australia (see Figure 10.4), one again sees a number of similarities, but we should take into account the fact that Australia did not have a Kosovo debate. Hence the lines represent the Gulf War and Iraq War discourses only.

As in the cases of the US and UK, arguments related to power score higher than in other Western countries, with a specific focus on national interests. In addition, Australian MPs seldom fear regional instability caused by military intervention. With respect to international law, there is a similar pattern to the UK as arguments related to law are usually understood as legitimating military engagement, and less often as a restraint. Australia is more similar to the US than the UK regarding casualties, ranking the safety of its soldiers higher than the safety of the

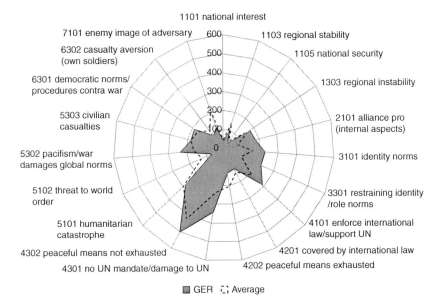

1101 national interest

7101 enemy image of adversary   600   1103 regional stability

6302 casualty aversion   500   1105 national security
(own soldiers)
                                 400
6301 democratic norms/   1303 regional instability
procedures contra war   300

5303 civilian   200   2101 alliance pro
casualties   100   (internal aspects)

5302 pacifism/war   0   3101 identity norms
damages global norms

5102 threat to world   3301 restraining identity
order   /role norms

5101 humanitarian   4101 enforce international
catastrophe   law/support UN

4302 peaceful means not exhausted   4201 covered by international law

4301 no UN mandate/damage to UN   4202 peaceful means exhausted

■ GER ⌐¦ Average

Figure 10.5 Argumentative map Germany

opponent's civilians. Although humanitarian aspects played a minor role in the run-up to both wars against Iraq (indicated by the low average score), Australian MPs referred to casualty aversion more often than their counterparts in the other countries under study. As in the US case, references to the Australian national identity/role conception are usually put forward in the context of *supporting* military engagement and almost never as a restraint. As with the US and UK, the Australian debates have a tendency towards a 'realist' line of argumentation combined with normative considerations. The normative impulses, however, are far less pronounced in the Australian argumentative map than in the two other countries.

While the three countries above have been the most 'war-prone' in our sample, we now contrast these cases with the argumentative maps of democracies that have fought selectively in the three wars. Figure 10.5 depicts the German parliamentary discourses.

In contrast to the cases just debated, all arguments related to power score below average, except for concern about intervention causing regional instability. Defending the current world order by military means also ranks below average, while most arguments related to international law score above average, especially the lack of a UN mandate and doubts about whether all diplomatic means have been exhausted.

The fear of causing death among civilians seems higher than the fear of sending German troops into dangerous missions – however, Germany only participated in the Kosovo War and only with a limited contribution to NATO's air forces; this might have defused concerns about a risky military engagement.[17] What is equally striking, compared to the other three countries, is the very infrequent recourse to a strong enemy image in German parliamentary discourses. The impression of more normatively oriented debates is strengthened by the importance of references to pacifism and concern about the damage to global norms by war. The specific actions that speakers derive from norms relating to Germany's national identity/role conception are much more disputed than in the US or Australian cases. Speakers refer to lessons learnt from the Nazi past in order to both legitimate and reject the use of force. Finally, arguments in support of joining military action because of membership commitments to the NATO Alliance are more common than in other Western states.

As stated above, the German discourses are rather similar to those of Canada, France and Sweden, with France and Canada being more different from Sweden than Germany, and France being the most dissimilar from Germany within this group. This indicates a kind of middle position for Germany within this group and a middle-ground tendency for France within the whole group of seven.

Looking at the Swedish case in Figure 10.6, the vast differences from the US (which is most dissimilar to Sweden) become even more obvious, but the peculiarly 'reduced' Swedish discourse should be judged in light of the fact that Sweden is a neutral country and did not fight in any of the three wars.

First, it is obvious that the Swedish discourse is dominated by the argument that peaceful means had not been exhausted at the time. While this argument does not rule out military participation in the future, it restrains the actor in the present, putting a premium on additional diplomatic efforts to avoid military confrontation. Of all the countries, Sweden's MPs are the most concerned that diplomacy should be given another chance. But as can clearly be seen, this argument is not an exception as almost all international law arguments score higher than average in the Swedish debates. In sharp contrast, power-related lines of argumentation are virtually absent from the Swedish debates, only the counter-argument that military intervention might cause regional

---

[17] Recently, increasing casualties among German soldiers have increasingly influenced the German debate about participation in the Afghanistan war. The low score of casualty aversion vis-à-vis civilian deaths might also be due to Germany having little experience with *Bundeswehr* combat casualties before Afghanistan. It seems plausible to assume that we would see a different picture here today. See, for example, Schörnig (2009).

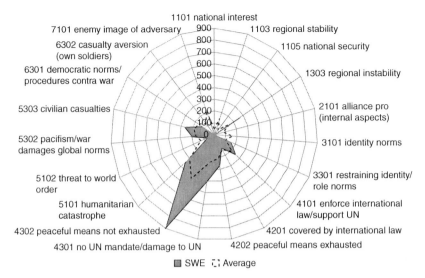

Figure 10.6 Argumentative map Sweden

instability showed up. Other normative arguments also score highly: references to a humanitarian catastrophe, to civilian casualties as well as to pacifism and the concern that war damages global norms were quite prominent. Speakers usually refer to Sweden's national identity/foreign policy role conception (e.g. neutrality, peaceful mediator) as restraining the use of force rather than deriving a legitimation for participating in military missions.

Canada, as depicted in Figure 10.7, presents a below-average use of power arguments, which in this case even applies to the counter-argument of causing instability through war. This suggests that power is not common as an underlying logic in public debates in Canada.

Canadians regard themselves as guardians of a law-based international order but, as the map in Figure 10.7 shows, most of such arguments score below average. This can be traced back to the relative strength of such arguments in some other countries, but it could also be an indication that Canadians are more concerned about legitimacy issues than about pure legality questions regarding the use of force. In addition, they frequently argue about whether or not all diplomatic means have indeed failed. Canadians adopt a strong humanitarian position: both the pro-war argument of stopping a humanitarian disaster and the contra argument of civilian casualties figure more prominently than average, while the fear of losses among Canadian troops remains slightly below average. As in the German (and to a lesser extent the Australian) case, the alliance

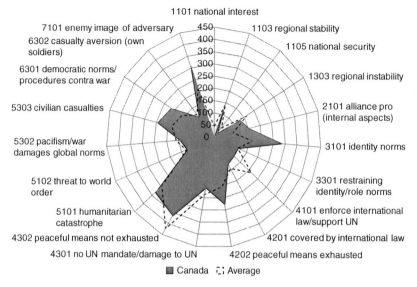

Figure 10.7 Argumentative map Canada

with the US, and in Canada's case also NATO, is rather important to Canadians.

Unlike Germans and Swedes, Canadians – who, in contrast to the former, participated in two wars – tend more often to describe the opponent in terms of an enemy. This underlines their value-laden outlook on world order issues. However, this interpretation is not as clear-cut as in the US, Australian or British cases since restraining interpretations of Canada's 'self' and its international role score significantly higher than in those three cases, and the enemy image as a reason to go to war is frequently contrasted with the moral reservations of war opponents. The argumentative map suggests that the Canadian debates are more influenced by normative than by 'realist' considerations, putting Canada in line with Germany and Sweden.

Figure 10.8 depicts the argumentative map of France, which participated in two wars.

French speakers show an average or slightly below average use of power-related arguments supporting military engagement (but significantly lower than in the US or Australian case), while the counter-argument that war might cause instability is higher than average – like in Germany and Sweden. As in these countries, arguments related to international law are frequently used and the question of whether peaceful

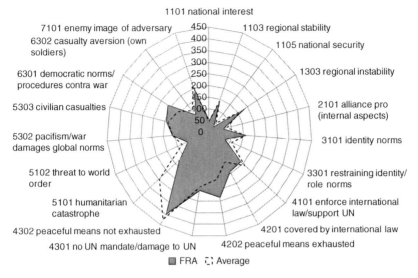

Figure 10.8 Argumentative map France

means have been exhausted is strongly debated. Also similarly to the German and Swedish discourses, protecting the political world order is not as important an argument as in the US or Australia, and potential deaths among the civilian population of the opponent arouse more concern than losses among French troops.

Remarkably for a former colonial power that has fought quite a number of wars in the past and for a nation that considers itself the European cradle and guardian of liberal values, enemy images have not been prominent in the French discourses since 1990. French delegates are not as restrained as German and Swedish MPs, but references to such strongly negative descriptions of the adversary are still below average. In general, the French debates show a (weak) mixture of 'realist' and normative argumentation and many arguments score close to average. But from the perspective of the US, Australia or the UK, the French discourses lack a clear focus on power-related arguments and rely too strongly on arguments related to international law.[18]

---

[18] As the country chapter on France shows, the French role conception as a great power with global outreach and the pursuit of national interests is often framed in normative language. In a similar vein, France's rather instrumental conception of multilateralism is often cloaked in a normative 'Europe' discourse.

4   Summary: implications for democratic peace research

To conclude the comparative analysis, we briefly summarise the major findings of this chapter that pose challenges to DP assumptions or point to neglected aspects that should be taken up in further research.[19] They suggest that the relationship between democracy, peace and war is much more contingent than causal assumptions of DP scholarship imply:

1   Citizens' preferences: most governmental decisions to engage in military action beyond self-defence were backed by majorities of the citizens. They are not necessarily averse to the use of force per se, but can accept it as legitimate under certain circumstances.

2   Those heads of government who advocated war contrary to the majority of their citizens were not punished for this decision at the ballot box.

3   Liberal democracies possess *de jure* and *de facto* differing oversight powers in military deployment issues. Some political systems such as the 'Westminster' model or (semi-)presidential systems leave much leeway for the executive. Parliamentary oversight powers were weak in the case of the three governments that decided against the majority of their citizens (Australia, Canada, UK). Further research should inquire into the relationship between executive leeway, parliamentary control and military engagements.

4   The role of parliamentary control is less important when government, parliament and the public develop similar attitudes towards a crisis. The study has shown that political elites can submit a whole range of legitimating reasons for fighting a war that seem to resonate with the public.

5   The discursive mobilising strategy of constructing strong enemy images of the adversary was less prominent in parliamentary discourses than expected. The media, however, felt less 'restrained'. While the analysis of 'othering' and enemy image construction is well established in critical security studies, it is less established in DP research. Further empirical inquiries should address the role of 'othering' in legitimating the liberal use of violence.

6   The path to war is often prepared by military build-ups and 'coercive diplomacy'. Democracies enter a potential slippery slope by advocating credible threats of force. This risk of 'self-entrapment' can enhance the war-proneness of democracies.

---

[19] We do not claim that there is absolutely no DP-related research in these fields. We have pointed in the respective sections of this chapter to studies that are pertinent. However, systematic comparisons are usually lacking.

7 The (lack of) international legitimation of a military action is highly relevant for shaping domestic perceptions of legitimacy. In particular, the role of the UN should be integrated into DP research. However, as the interpretation and application of norms are inevitably controversial, no clear-cut predictions about the effect of international law on the domestic level follow from this.

8 In the past, casualty aversion research has been conducted mainly on the US. More comparative research is desirable as the issue is important for both proponents and opponents of war. More attention should be dedicated to a hierarchy of norms: not all casualties are 'ranked' equally. The protection of one's own soldiers usually reigns supreme, given actual combat experience.

9 National collective identities have a considerable influence on shaping both argumentative structures and policy options based on these structures. This aspect will be addressed in more detail in the last chapter.

REFERENCES

Art, Robert J. and Cronin, Patrick M. 2007. 'Coercive Diplomacy', in Chester A. Crocker, Fen Osler Hampson and Pamela Aall (eds.), *Leashing the Dogs of War: Conflict Management in a Divided World*. Washington, DC: US Institute of Peace, pp. 299–318

Auerswald, David 2000. *Disarmed Democracies: Domestic Institutions and the Use of Force*. Ann Arbor, MI: University of Michigan Press

Bellamy, Alex J. 2008. *Responsibility to Protect*. New York, NY: John Wiley & Sons

Born, Hans and Urscheler, Marlene 2004. 'Parliamentary Accountability of Multinational Peace Support Operations: A Comparative Perspective', in Hans Born and Heiner Hänggi (eds.), *The 'Double Democratic Deficit': Parliamentary Accountability and the Use of Force under International Auspices*. Aldershot: Ashgate, pp. 53–72

Brock, Lothar 2007. 'Universalismus, politische Heterogenität und ungleiche Entwicklung: Internationale Kontexte der Gewaltanwendung von Demokratien gegenüber Nichtdemokratien', in Anna Geis, Harald Müller and Wolfgang Wagner (eds.), *Schattenseiten des Demokratischen Friedens: Zur Kritik einer Theorie liberaler Außen- und Sicherheitspolitik*. Frankfurt a.M.: Campus, pp. 45–67

Brock, Lothar, Geis, Anna and Müller, Harald 2006. 'The Case for a New Research Agenda: Explaining Democratic Wars', in Anna Geis, Lothar Brock and Harald Müller (eds.), *Democratic Wars: Looking at the Dark Side of Democratic Peace*. Basingstoke: Palgrave Macmillan, pp. 195–214

Bueno de Mesquita, Bruce, Morrow, James D., Siverson, Randolph M. and Smith, Alastair 1999. 'An Institutional Explanation of the Democratic Peace', *American Political Science Review* 93 (4): 791–807

Chiozza, Giacomo and Goemans, H. E. 2004. 'International Conflict and the Tenure of Leaders: Is War Still *Ex Post* Inefficient?', *American Journal of Political Science* 48 (3): 604–19

Czempiel, Ernst-Otto 1996. 'Kants Theorem: Oder – Warum sind die Demokratien (noch immer) nicht friedlich?', *Zeitschrift für Internationale Beziehungen* 3 (1): 79–101

Dieterich, Sandra, Hummel, Hartwig and Marschall, Stefan 2009. '"Kriegsspielverderber?" Europäische Parlamente und der Irakkrieg 2003', *Zeitschrift für Internationale Beziehungen* 16 (1): 5–38

Downes, Alexander B. 2008. *Targeting Civilians in War*. Ithaca, NY: Cornell University Press

Duffield, John S. 1999. 'Political Culture and State Behavior: Why Germany Confounds Neorealism', *International Organization* 53 (4): 765–803

Eberl, Oliver 2008. *Demokratie und Frieden: Kants Friedensschrift in den Kontroversen der Gegenwart*. Baden-Baden: Nomos

Eberl, Oliver and Fischer-Lescano, Andreas 2005. 'Grenzen demokratischen Rechts? Die Entsendeentscheidungen zum Irakkrieg in Großbritannien, den USA und Spanien', *HSFK-Report* No. 8/2005, Frankfurt a.M.

Elman, Miriam Fendius 1997. 'Introduction', in Miriam Fendius Elman (ed.), *Paths to Peace: Is Democracy the Answer?* Cambridge, MA: MIT Press, pp. 1–57

2000. 'Unpacking Democracy: Presidentialism, Parliamentarism, and Theories of Democratic Peace', *Security Studies* 9 (4): 91–126

Fiebig-von Hase, Ragnhild and Lehmkuhl, Ursula (eds.) 1997. *Enemy Images in American History*. Providence, RI: Berghahn

Finnemore, Martha 2003. *The Purpose of Intervention: Changing Beliefs about the Use of Force*. Ithaca, NY: Cornell University Press

Finnemore, Martha and Toope, Stephen 2001. 'Alternatives to "Legalization": Richer Views of Law and Politics', *International Organization* 55 (3): 743–58

Fisher, Louis 2004. *Presidential War Power*. Lawrence, KS: University Press of Kansas

Friedman, Gil 2008. 'Identifying the Place of Democratic Norms in Democratic Peace', *International Studies Review* 10 (3): 548–70

George, Alexander L. 1991. *Forceful Persuasion: Coercive Diplomacy as an Alternative to War*. Washington, DC: US Institute of Peace

Grimmett, Richard F. 2009. 'War Powers Resolution: Presidential Compliance', *CRS Report for Congress* RL33532, Washington, DC

Harnisch, Sebastian and Maull, Hanns W. 2001. 'Conclusion: "Learned Its Lesson Well?" Germany as a Civilian Power Ten Years after Unification', in Sebastian Harnisch and Hanns W. Maull (eds.), *Germany as a Civilian Power? The Foreign Policy of the Berlin Republic*. Manchester University Press, pp. 128–56

Hils, Jochen 2008. 'Der "demokratische Krieg" als Folge verfälschter Präferenzbildung? Eine systematische Formulierung des Manipulationsverdachts der liberalen Theorie der Internationalen Beziehungen', *Zeitschrift für Internationale Beziehungen* 15 (2): 237–71

Houben, Marc 2005. *International Crisis Management: The Approach of European States*. London: Routledge

ICISS (International Commission on Intervention and State Sovereignty) 2001. *The Responsibility to Protect: Report of the International Commission on Intervention and State Sovereignty*. Ottawa, ON: International Development Research Centre

Larson, Eric V. 1996. *Casualties and Consensus: The Historical Role of Casualties in Domestic Support for U.S. Military Operations*. Santa Monica, CA: RAND

Levy, Yagil 2010. 'The Tradeoff between Force and Casualties: Israel's Wars in Gaza, 1987–2009', *Conflict Management and Peace Science* 27 (4): 386–405

Liste, Philip 2012. *Völkerrecht-Sprechen: Die Konstruktion demokratischer Völkerrechtspolitik in den USA und der Bundesrepublik Deutschland*. Baden-Baden: Nomos

MacMillan, John 2005. 'Introduction: The Iraq War and Democratic Politics', in John MacMillan and Alex Danchev (eds.), *The Iraq War and Democratic Politics*. London: Routledge, pp. 1–19

Mandel, Robert 2004. *Security, Strategy, and the Quest for Bloodless War*. Boulder, CO: Lynne Rienner

Müller, Harald and Wolff, Jonas 2006. 'Democratic Peace: Many Data, Little Explanation?', in Anna Geis, Lothar Brock and Harald Müller (eds.), *Democratic Wars: Looking at the Dark Side of Democratic Peace*. Basingstoke: Palgrave Macmillan, pp. 41–73

Peters, Dirk and Wagner, Wolfgang 2011. 'Between Military Efficiency and Democratic Legitimacy: Mapping Parliamentary War Powers in Contemporary Democracies, 1989–2004', *Parliamentary Affairs* 64 (1): 175–92

Rosato, Sebastian 2003. 'The Flawed Logic of Democratic Peace Theory', *American Political Science Review* 97 (4): 585–602

Rousseau, David L. 2005. *Democracy and War: Institutions, Norms, and the Evolution of International Conflict*. Stanford University Press

Rummel, Rudolph J. 1979. *War, Power, Peace: Understanding Conflict and War*, vol. IV. London: Sage

Russett, Bruce 1993. *Grasping the Democratic Peace: Principles for a Post-Cold War World*. Princeton University Press

Schörnig, Niklas 2007. 'Visionen unblutiger Kriege: Hightech-Antworten zur Umgehung der Opfersensibilitätsfalle', in Anna Geis, Harald Müller and Wolfgang Wagner (eds.), *Schattenseiten des Demokratischen Friedens. Zur Kritik einer Theorie liberaler Außen- und Sicherheitspolitik*. Frankfurt a.M.: Campus, pp. 93–121

2009. 'In der Opferfalle: die Bundesregierung und die zunehmenden Gefallenen der Bundeswehr in Afghanistan', *HSFK-Standpunkt* No. 2, Frankfurt a.M.

Schultz, Kenneth A. 2001. *Democracy and Coercive Diplomacy*. Cambridge University Press

Shaw, Martin 2005. *The New Western Way of War: Risk-Transfer War and Its Crisis in Iraq*. London: Polity Press

Wagner, Wolfgang 2006. 'Parliamentary Control of Military Missions: Accounting for Pluralism', *DCAF Occasional Paper* No. 12, Geneva

Anna Geis, Harald Müller and Niklas Schörnig

Watts, Stephen 2008. 'Air War and Restraint: The Role of Public Opinion and Democracy', in Matthew Evangelista, Harald Müller and Niklas Schörnig (eds.), *Democracy and Security: Preferences, Norms and Policy-Making*. London: Routledge, pp. 53–71

Wiener, Antje 2008. *The Invisible Constitution of Politics: Contested Norms and International Encounters*. Cambridge University Press

11   The appropriateness of the liberal use of force: 'democratic wars' under US hegemony

Anna Geis and Harald Müller

1   Introduction

In the preceding chapter we put together the findings on the individual democracies from the country chapters and subjected them to a cross-country, cross-war comparison. In this last chapter, we draw on the insights from this comparison with a view to summarising the contribution of this volume to an emerging theory of democratic war. We start by deconstructing the notion of the Western 'value community'. While Western democracies no doubt do share core liberal values and norms, the meaning, hierarchy and operational application of these values and norms to specific situations is disputed between them (Section 2). As this contestation also takes place at the domestic level, each of them is in principle capable of participating in specific types of democratic wars, but also of refusing to participate in others (Section 3). Interdemocratic contestation, however, is not an incidental, but a systematic phenomenon: depending on the type of democracy that it embodies, a state is more likely to participate often, rarely or not at all. We attempt to develop a list of factors that enable each of our democracies to participate in military intervention, and then develop a heuristics based on those enabling factors (Section 4). Next, we check this briefly against two other cases, the Afghanistan and Libyan wars (Section 5). The findings lead us to modify the heuristics and to enlarge the number of enabling (or inhibiting) factors to be taken into account. From there we develop two generalised working hypotheses that may guide future research (Section 6).

Following this, we caution against too bold a generalisation by historically contextualising our findings: first, the decisive role of the US as a catalyst for military action is emphasised; given the US hegemony in military affairs, US participation and leadership is required in most military contingencies to make them possible in the first place and to open the opportunity for other democracies to participate. 'Democratic war' without the US will remain a rarity (such as the 2011 French Ivory

Coast operation). What that means for a future in which US defence budgets could shrink significantly, and other, non-democratic powers enhance their military capabilities, remains to be seen. Second, heeding Heraclitus's saying that you cannot step twice into the same river, we note that intervention decisions might be path-dependent. Democracies draw lessons in one direction or the other from what they have experienced in their last intervention, and that might impact on the development of their political cultures and influence their readiness to go to war (Section 7). Finally, we indicate what our approach might be able to contribute to a critical liberal theory that does not renounce its basic values, but adds a self-reflective and thereby self-critical layer to the traditional ethical self-confidence and self-assertiveness that are so characteristic of liberalism in our days (Section 8).

2   Unpacking the liberal 'community of values'

Our investigation into 'democratic wars' underlines that democratic peace (DP) research as it stands contains many open questions, pitfalls and blind spots. While we have not inquired into the peaceful relations between consolidated democracies, we have analysed the flipside of this democratic peace: given the assumed reluctance of democratic polities towards fighting wars, how can democratic actors legitimate military actions against non-democracies? And given the variance among democracies' participation in military actions, how can we account for these differences?

The country chapters of this volume suggest that almost all causal claims that promote the peacefulness of democracies according to DP theory could *in principle* be turned into the contrary: cost–benefit considerations, international institutions and international law, democratic and liberal norms and values not only advance peaceful action but also contribute to legitimising military actions. The overall findings are strongest with regard to the relevance of domestic and international norms, i.e. *cultural-normative* explanations of democratic peace contain the most 'productive' contradictions. Social-constructivist approaches therefore prove helpful in understanding (non-)participation in the respective war. The individual country chapters suggest that norms structuring the country's national identity and foreign policy role conception can elucidate why the state participated in or refrained from a war. The comparison of the democracies also suggests that the broad spectrum of liberal norms and the ambivalence of norms account for many of the differences between the seven democracies.

As with other complex social phenomena, we do not claim to comprehensively 'explain' the conflict behaviour of liberal democracies – different social science approaches can only illuminate certain aspects of such a phenomenon as war. As many studies within the field of DP scholarship are grounded in rationalism, our social-constructivist study helps to carve out the crucial role of norms. And as many liberal democracies claim to pursue 'universal' values in their foreign policies, it is particularly important to dissect such norms, to reflect the tensions arising from them and to differentiate appropriate policy options.

It was Tony Blair's New Labour government that accentuated an 'ethical foreign policy' in the late 1990s. Britain was portrayed as a 'force for good' in the world, which would defend its values by force, if need be (Dunne and Wheeler 2001; Fey, Chapter 4 in this book). However, as the other country chapters in this book show, all democracies have developed rather benign self-images of their foreign policies as serving a higher common good beyond narrow self-interest. The notion of an ethical foreign policy has gained ever more ground within Western and international public spheres during the last two decades and should not be dismissed from a Realist perspective as a mere disguise for 'bare' material national interests (Heins and Chandler 2007: 5–8). However, our investigation of national legitimating processes reveals important differences among democratic polities: they differ in their emphasis on certain values, and they differ in the crucial issue of under what circumstances military force is an appropriate means of foreign policy. The way a democratic public conceives of its international power position, its alliance obligations, its international 'mission', its interpretations of international law, the desirable world order and its significant 'others' can vary quite noticeably among Western democracies.

The common political parlance of the 'community of Western democracies' as a coherent community of values sharing all the same norms is deceptive. Even such a fundamental foreign policy issue as peace and war reveals a high differentiation of norms and interpretations and many differing judgements on the appropriateness of the use of force, both within democracies and between them. The next section will discuss such national standards of appropriateness in more detail.

3   No absolute barriers against the use of force

As outlined in the Introduction to this book, the concept of 'democratic wars' is related to, but not fully congruent with, that of 'liberal wars'. By 'liberal wars', Freedman (2005: 98) and Vasquez (2005: 311) mean ideal types of wars that are justified by the interveners with humanitarian or moral claims. Our conception of 'democratic wars' refers to wars that are fought for liberal purposes, i.e. wars that are justified by reasons that are compatible with liberal norms. Such norms need not be confined to a humanitarian agenda only. The country chapters in this book show that in fact a large spectrum of liberal norms is invoked in justifying military actions, and that normative-liberal motivations always mix with more 'traditional', narrow national interests – whether these are prominently debated in public or not. The selectivity of Western military actions indicates that normative goals such as protection of human rights have to be weighed against the costs and risks for one's own polity. Such risks and costs are part of the 'long recognised point that hard democratic state structures and capabilities are in certain respects and to a certain extent counter-balanced by their softer societal core – or underbelly – which limits the ability of democratic states to take full advantage of their military superiority' (MacMillan 2005: 3).

The readiness to take up arms is modified by four elements: the fear of own casualties, the 'national interest' (narrowly understood), alliance relations and the legality of the intended military action. These modifications vary across the countries, but this variance appears at two levels. First, as the content analysis of parliamentary debates shows, arguments related to these four elements appear with different relative shares in the overall panoply of arguments put forward in the public discourse. Second, as process tracing in the country chapters suggests, there are varying discrepancies between the arguments used in the public discourse and further reasons motivating the decisions of the executive leadership. To a degree, motivations of governments differ;[1] to another degree, there is a different readiness on the part of politicians to reveal such reasons frankly in public. Either variation contains interesting hints as to differences in political culture.

The fear of casualties among one's own soldiers is obviously relevant for those countries that are involved in war relatively frequently. The case of unified Germany underlines this logical connection: as long as Germany engaged in low-level military actions, the fear of own casualties was a public non-issue; it is only with the recent intensification of its Afghanistan mission and the decreasing prospects for the success of this mission that the rising number of German casualties raises concerns about the legitimacy of a continued engagement. The issue of sacrificing own citizens in military actions far beyond one's borders is salient for all publics of militarily active democracies, but explicit references to

---

[1] On the problematique of 'verifying' motivation, see Chapter 2.

a 'national interest' can mitigate such concerns. This means that either there must be good reason to believe that casualties will remain low, or some palpable 'national interest' must be claimed to be at stake (Larson 1996: 99–101).

When 'national interest' was explicitly invoked in the public discourses, this referred to traditional notions of this concept such as geopolitical considerations or security threats. It is striking that there is a clear gap between those democracies whose discourses refer noticeably to such 'realist' arguments – the US, Australia and the UK – and those where such arguments are used to a significantly lesser degree, i.e. Canada, Germany, Sweden and, rather surprisingly, France. Their participation or non-participation are framed more often in normative and idealistic terms, in accordance with the norms encapsulated in their national identity and foreign policy role conceptions. However, one argument occupies a special position within the 'realist' references across the parliaments of all countries: regional (in)stability. Speakers in the more 'bellicose' democracies refer relatively frequently to regional stability as justifying military action, while speakers in the more restrained countries use the argument of regional instability quite often to caution against military action (see Tables A.1 and A.2 in the Appendix). Although we located this argument within the 'power frame' in our coding scheme (see Table 2.2), the argumentative context of references to this argument in the individual speeches shows that it can also be understood in terms of normative order and hence should be more correctly understood as a hybrid between realist and normative outlooks on policy; at least in the speakers' argumentation, 'regional stability' takes on the air of a common good that transcends narrow national interests.

Our country chapters show that alliance relations impact heavily on the readiness to engage in a military action: 'Being a good ally' can be such an important element of one's national identity/role conception that it might even constitute a 'national interest' in itself. Interestingly, the alliance motive, which was a factor in the considerations of the executive leadership in the UK, Australia and to some degree also Canada, does not really show up in the public debates,[2] where other arguments – legal, moral and domestic – are in the foreground. Apparently, the political elite was concerned that emphasising alliance considerations would not be received well in a population that is critical of too strong a political dependency on the US. This suggests a 'democracy gap' between

---

[2] Only in Canada did the neoconservative opposition make this point during the 2003 Iraq War debate.

the political leadership and the people concerning the significance and desirability of a solidary alliance commitment. It might even point to a role/identity conception that is bifurcated between the people and the elite in this specific regard. This issue is all the more salient as contemporary 'democratic wars' are not fought by one democracy on its own, but are usually conducted as coalition warfare. In particular within the framework of international organisations such as NATO or, more recently, the European Union, executives cooperate closely on the international level and shape decisions to a large extent, often leaving it up to national parliaments to 'rubber-stamp' executive commitments (Wolf 1999). The US as the liberal hegemon plays a crucial, but ambivalent, role in Western alliance considerations and national decisions on (non-)participation in 'democratic wars'. This ambivalent role of the US will be discussed in more detail in Section 7.1.

The last factor contributing to variance is the type of legal argument justifying the military action. What constitutes an acceptable legal basis can be perceived quite differently by domestic audiences: a correct constitutional procedure for deciding in favour of a military intervention plus a legal case that counts as plausible in the legal culture of the country in question; a common decision by the alliance based on a legal argument, which is just another facet of alliance saliency; or, at the other pole of the legality continuum, a clear and unambiguous mandate from the UN Security Council for using force in the specific case.

4   'Democratic wars' and different national standards of appropriateness

Based on the findings of the country chapters, we can now inductively identify the necessary conditions that *permit*, but do not determine, the seven democracies to become involved in the various types of a 'democratic war'. As the preceding chapter has shown, their political behaviour is strongly modified by characteristics of their political cultures; hypotheses can thus be formulated for groups of democracies that are close to the same ideal type. Such conditions refer to underlying national norms and standards of appropriateness prevalent in the political culture of the individual democracy and point to potential future cases of the respective democracy's war participation. As has been widely discussed in social-constructivist research, norms enable and restrain political actions, but they do not determine specific decisions (Kowert and Legro 1996: 483–96; Müller 2007: 306). Since the concrete meaning of a norm in a given situation requires specification (Wiener 2008), norms can only circumscribe the broader spectrum of acceptable and unacceptable policy options within a community that shares these norms. Precisely how they have influenced a political decision is a matter of empirical analysis.

The sample of the seven democracies – depicted in Table 11.1 – appears to be divided into a more *legalist* and a more *national interest-/alliance-oriented* group. The only strictly legalist country is Sweden, where norms of military restraint and neutralism call for the insistence on a UN mandate. Canada, France and Germany are also fairly legalist, but very strong humanitarian concerns can override legal concerns. Of the three, Germany's political culture is closest to Sweden's because of Germany's particular historical pathway.[3] An element of military restraint still persists in the political cultures of Germany and Sweden, although their security policies have undergone considerable changes since the 1990s. These restraining norms do not take effect as being absolutely prohibitive, but as nevertheless representing a significant inhibition to participate in military action. The 'good reasons' legitimating the use of force must be strong, and the international law as well as the multilateralist conditions must be more than simply permissive; some tangible pressure must be inherent in them to overcome this barrier (such as 'alliance solidarity' in the German case). No such barrier exists in the political culture of democracies with more positive experiences of their military past and with war victories.

Despite a certain recent re-emergence of the concept of the 'Anglosphere' as a group of English-speaking states more likely to follow the US into war (Vucetic 2011: 43), our heuristics should not be read as suggesting some kind of 'Anglo-Saxon bellicose culture', which would contravene the far more complex findings of the individual country chapters. While the US is the least legalist-oriented case in our sample, the lack of a UN mandate is a much larger problem for Britain and (to a lesser degree) Australia; and Canada is as legalist as France or Germany. France, on the other hand, as a self-proclaimed 'world power' and as victor in two world wars is as ready, in principle, to take up arms for a supposedly good cause as the 'Anglo-Saxons'.

In France, legalism and a preference for strengthening the UN amalgamate with the national interest in possessing great power status, which is bolstered largely by permanent UNSC membership and the *force de frappe*. France has traditionally kept a distance from the US

---

[3] Tables 10.1 and 10.2 in Chapter 10 – which focused on the analysis of the parliamentary debates only – showed a slightly different ranking. However, pulling together the evidence from process tracing, content analysis, media analysis and opinion polls, this ranking here reflects the actual similarities in the national culture more accurately.

Table 11.1 *Heuristics: necessary enabling conditions for war participation by war type and country*

Country	Type of war		
	Order war For all states: dramatic breach of international legal rules such as war of aggression + ...	Humanitarian intervention For all states: perception of extraordinary human rights violations + ...	War for regime change For all states: confrontation with a dictatorship whose actions at home and abroad set it apart from the average authoritarian regime + ...
United States	National interest + low casualty expectations	National interest + low casualty expectations	National interest + low casualty expectations
United Kingdom	Legal case + alliance/US support	Legal case + alliance/ US support	Legal case + alliance/ US support
Australia	UN mandate or US alliance support + national interest + low casualty expectations	UN mandate or US alliance support + national interest + low casualty expectations	UN mandate or US alliance support + national interest + low casualty expectations
Canada	UN mandate	UN mandate or legal case + alliance support	UN mandate (?)*
France	UN mandate	UN mandate or [European] alliance support	UN mandate (?)*
Germany	UN mandate (?)**	UN mandate or alliance support (?)***	No
Sweden	UN mandate	UN mandate	No (?)****

* Our cases provide no clear evidence of this assessment. The Canadian and French discourses, however, leave the possibility open that, with a UN mandate, these two countries might also consider participation in this war type. While regime change as a reason to go to war was rejected in the Canadian debate and only embraced by the Canadian neoconservative opposition, the high importance of a UN mandate might induce the Canadians to consider participation in a UN-mandated war. However, this is purely hypothetical, as China and Russia are unlikely to support a regime change war in the UN Security Council. This showed clearly in the recent Libyan case: China and Russia acquiesced in a mandate that aimed at the protection of the threatened civilian population, but protested strongly when NATO transformed the operation into one of air support for the rebels' offensive with a view to deposing Colonel Gaddafi.

and NATO, but 'alliance' support – here understood rather in terms of European solidarity – is occasionally (in the Kosovo War) considered a sufficiently good multilateral legitimiser for overcoming legalistic considerations.[4] The notion of alliance consensus or working with the US as a quasi-substitute for a UN mandate is more widespread in the UK and Australia. It appears that the 'legalist group' has a certain conception of international law that cannot be circumvented, whereas the UK government regards international law more as being subject to its lawyers' own framing. The lawyers are to provide the people and the parliamentarians with a sophisticated justification for the government's preferred policy.

The US stands out as a nation willing to put its (perceived) own national interest above concerns of international law; war support was lowest when the national interest in fighting was most disputed (Kosovo). The US is also most inclined to frame the pertinent conflict in Manichaean terms as a fight against an evil enemy. In the US and Australia, however, this low barrier to taking up arms is somehow mitigated by strong concerns about potential casualties. Nevertheless, in none of our cases was this concern strong enough to block the path to war.

5   Considering two other cases: Afghanistan and Libya

How does this heuristics of Table 11.1 stand if we apply it, in a tentative way, to two other cases of wars fought by democracies, namely in

Notes to Table 11.1 (*cont.*)

** The empirical case of 1991 does not support this assessment, but the Gulf War took place before an altered interpretation of the German constitution was declared by Germany's highest court (as *permitting* participation in certain missions, 1994). It is not implausible that Germany would participate in another UN-mandated order war.

*** The Kosovo case supports this assessment. However, the German government argued afterwards that this was an absolute exception.

**** Our 2003 Iraq case supports 'no', but a (purely hypothetical) UN mandate for a regime change war would pose the 1991 dilemma for the UN-loyal Swedish anew. It is uncertain how the dilemma would be solved in a future case.

[4] As Martha Finnemore (2003: 82) has observed on this phenomenon: 'Multilateralism legitimizes action by signaling broad support for the actor's goals. Intervenors use it to demonstrate that their purpose in intervening is not merely self-serving and particularistic but is joined in some way to community interests that other states share. Making this demonstration is often vital in mustering international support for an intervention ... and can be crucial in generating domestic support as well.'

Afghanistan and Libya? We would expect the current Afghanistan War to be the first case where *all seven* countries participate. The Afghanistan War is, scientifically speaking, overdetermined: it represents simultaneously all three war types, and for the US even also self-defence. Since this is a military action to contain transnational terrorism (and to prevent the resurgence of state support for it), the war clearly has both a security and an order perspective: security, because it aims at containing and reducing the terrorist threat to the international society of states; order, because it strives to restore a state monopoly of force on the territory of Afghanistan, curbing the freedom of action of non-state actors and thereby restoring an important element of the interstate order based on international law. Because it is meant to protect the Afghans against the return of a merciless, fanatical, inhumane dictatorship, it also has a humanitarian element. And because there is (or *was* initially, at least) the ambition to make Afghanistan a democracy, it also has the character of regime change. The operations are covered by both a UN mandate and a NATO decision.

The conditions for participation by all seven countries are thus fulfilled, and indeed they all participate, neutral Sweden included. In 2001/2, Sweden deployed 300 soldiers in the Northern Provinces and later enlarged this contingent to 450 troops. The conservative government announced in 2007 that it would not only reinforce the ground troops further, but would also have the Swedish Air Force participate in air operations. This latter component led to considerable public disputes because it blurred the distinction between a humanitarian mission and pure war-fighting. The same contradiction is also visible in the German debate. Thus, in Sweden and Germany, one sees both aspects: the predicted participation because the necessary conditions do obtain, and the continued effect of the norms of pacifist or military restraint in national identity, which inhibit participation in 'too much' war. Once the necessary conditions are fulfilled, these norms no longer impact on the question of participation per se, but on the *degree* of participation.

Five out of our seven countries participated in the 2011 Libyan War – mandated by the UN under the principle of the 'responsibility to protect' and organised by NATO – while Australia and Germany abstained. Once again, for the five participants the following conditions obtained: an impending humanitarian catastrophe and an orderly UNSC mandate (the fact that NATO changed the mandate to defend the Libyan civilian population in order to provide air support for the rebels in their effort to depose Gaddafi, transforming the character of the war from humanitarian intervention to regime change, does not impact on the initial decision to join). Australia's abstention, once more, is plausible

Table 11.2 *Approval of Libyan intervention*

Country	Approve (%)	Disapprove (%)
United States	59	35
United Kingdom	53	42
France	58	39
Sweden	69	28
Germany	37	60

Source: GMF (2011: 81).

as the Mediterranean is far beyond Australia's geopolitical scope. Germany, however, is a clear outlier. Germany's participation could be expected as the Libya case invoked all the necessary conditions: the humanitarian motive, the UN mandate and Alliance solidarity. Yet the German government decided to abstain in the Security Council decision (being a non-permanent member at the time) and consequently did not participate in the military operations.

How can we explain this deviation? The most plausible explanation is that the military 'culture of restraint' of the Federal Republic of Germany, which has been challenged by the increasing military missions of unified Germany, was strongly reinforced by the perception of the failure of the Afghanistan campaign paired with the experience of more than 50 German soldiers killed in action (as of December 2011). Pacifist attitudes have regained ground in Western Europe's most populous state as a result of this experience. Recent poll data by the German Marshall Fund (GMF 2011) covering five out of our seven countries (US, UK, France, Sweden and Germany) lend some support to this interpretation. Asked about the future prospects of stabilising Afghanistan, Germany has the highest share of pessimists (79 per cent) and the lowest share of optimists (19 per cent) among all the nations polled (GMF 2011: 37). Generally, 71 per cent of Germans reject the proposition that war might sometimes be necessary to obtain justice (for Sweden, 57 per cent), and 80 per cent refuse to send troops abroad to instal democracy (compared with 50 per cent of Swedes who approve) (GMF 2011: 69, 80). Table 11.2 shows approval and disapproval rates for Libyan intervention for all five states.

The table indicates that, under the right conditions and without the experience of significant own casualties in Afghanistan,[5] Swedes can

[5] According to icasualties.org, Sweden has suffered five casualties in Afghanistan so far.

	Factors facilitating decision for war $\longrightarrow$		
Opportunity structure level			
War for what?	Regime change	Order	Humanitarian intervention
War against whom?	Autocracy	Cruel autocracy	Cruel, threatening autocracy
War by which authority?	Coalition of the willing	Alliance	UN Security Council
War by which democratic consent?	Elite	Public opinion	Parliament
War at what cost?	Moderate expectation of casualties	Uncertainty	Low expectation of casualties
Actor type level			
War by whom?	Great power/national interest- or alliance-oriented middle power	+ legalist good international citizen	+ historically traumatised legalist civilian power

Figure 11.1 Opportunity structure constellations and actor types

become militant democratic interventionists.[6] Germans, on the other hand, apparently feel stronger inhibitions at the end of almost two decades of military operations abroad than they did initially. Even so, future participation is not to be precluded.

6   Refining our tools: working hypotheses for the future

On the basis of our own research, and drawing in addition on the brief discussion of the Afghanistan and Libya cases, we can draft a chart (Figure 11.1) depicting constellations of variables that provide opportunity structures that facilitate the decision to go to war, increasing from left to right. The figure harks back to the introductory chapter and enhances the discussion of democratic wars by two further aspects: democratic legitimisation and the problem of war costs (notably casualties).

---

[6] Sweden, while a small country, can field capable fighting forces, relying on a strong domestic arms industry; indeed, Sweden has adopted the 'Revolution in Military Affairs' more extensively than some of the larger countries in our sample.

Democracies are more prone to fight a 'humanitarian intervention' than a war for regime change, with 'order wars' sitting at the centre. Autocracies that are seen as both dangerous and cruel towards their own population are a more popular target than simple non-democracies. A Security Council mandate makes it much easier to mobilise support for an intervention than the legal position of a small group of states. Alliances stand in the middle of this continuum. Parliamentary support is most conducive, followed by majority public opinion. Deciding in favour of war is very difficult if the war is expected to claim many casualties, while overwhelming superiority promising low casualties facilitates a decision in favour of war immensely. The last line ('actor type level') does not refer to circumstances, but to state actors and their political cultures: great powers and middle powers with views strongly oriented towards national or alliance interests are more likely to enter war, while 'civilian powers' with a strong legalist attitude are much less war-prone. As the Libyan discussion reveals, a trauma-induced pacifism like the one found in Germany might add another layer of aversion to taking up arms.

The figure enables us to formulate two general hypotheses. These hypotheses could be applied in further research: the more the opportunity structure tends to the right of the figure, the easier it is for an individual democracy to decide in favour of military action, and the more democracies are likely to do so. The more the individual democracy is positioned to the right of the actor type continuum, the easier it is for its government to decide in favour of war even if some of the opportunity structure variables have values towards the left of the figure.

Democracies, in conclusion, are war-capable on liberal grounds, but under distinctly different necessary enabling conditions. More research is required to specify these conditions beyond the preceding, still tentative considerations.

7 Contextualising 'democratic wars': a phenomenon of a passing liberal age?

In a similar vein to Chapter 10, where we made some qualifying statements about democratic peace assumptions, we will now discuss some potential limitations and caveats of 'democratic war'. The country chapters in this volume show that, with differing accentuations, all these liberal democracies consider themselves as being 'forces for good', as orienting their foreign policies towards universally good causes beyond a narrowly understood national interest. Under what circumstances and for what 'good causes' individual democracies are willing to use force, however, is controversial both among the democracies and within their publics. The heuristics depicted in Table 11.1 suggests that even democracies with a political 'culture of restraint' or pacifist elements such as Germany and Sweden are prepared (Germany) or can be increasingly expected (Sweden) to join major military actions.

However, as the heuristics reflects three wars of the past, it does not anticipate potential future dynamics. In the same way as democratic peace, which is not an eternal 'fact' of international relations that will remain unchallenged by whatever historical changes the future might bring, democratic war appears to be a phenomenon that is closely connected to specific historical and political contexts. We have investigated a particular and rather short period of time following the end of the Cold War, which marked a liberal heyday and gave rise to an unchallenged global hegemony on the part of the US. The following sections discuss the ambivalent role of the liberal hegemon (Section 7.1) and the potential consequences of 'learning processes' within democratic publics (Section 7.2). The decision to participate in or to abstain from a war is not usually an isolated, singular event for democratic leaderships, but is discursively embedded within a much longer chain of events, where one's past experiences with the use of force are evaluated in the light of the challenges and risks of a pending crisis.

7.1   The role of the liberal hegemon, the United States

Importantly, our findings suggest that the conditions for 'democratic wars' might obtain only under US liberal hegemony. The US appears to have the lowest barrier to taking up arms; casualty aversion is most pronounced there, but the capabilities to keep casualties low are also the best, given the high-tech weapons systems and proficiency of the US military (Shaw 2005). In a normative respect, the *relative* ease with which a US president can decide in favour of war is troubling since such a decision by the US is a limiting *conditio sine qua non* for the other democracies to participate in any major military operation: without the US, 'democratic wars' would remain impossible under most conceivable circumstances. In that sense, America is still the 'indispensable nation', as the former US Secretary of State Madeleine Albright once put it: 'But if we have to use force, it is because we are America; we are the indispensable nation. We stand tall and we see further than other countries into the future, and we see the danger here to all of us.'[7]

---

[7] Albright in an interview on NBC TV, 19 February 1998. Online: http://secretary.state. gov/www/statements/1998/980219a.html.

As long as smaller democracies fight under the protective shield of the overwhelming military power of the US, they bear a comparatively moderate share of the overall burden, a factor that presumably has a deep impact on the national discourses.[8] The liberal superpower is clearly expected to contribute far more to providing the public good 'security' (broadly understood) that all the other democracies also wish to benefit from. All public discourses investigated in this book were staged in the expectation that the US would lead the war effort; democracies contributing a rather limited share to this effort might therefore lean to more normative and idealistic justifications since intolerable costs are not anticipated. However false such expectations might turn out to be given the inherent dynamics of military conflicts – the allies did not anticipate the protracted violence in Iraq and Afghanistan, for example – the liberal hegemon and its allies certainly do not start from the same basis.

There are two consequences that open up intriguing new questions: first, the ways in which the US' political determination to take up arms reverberates in other democracies. The effect is by no means clear beyond the necessary opportunity structure for war participation that the employment of US military force accords. On the one hand, there is the driving force of solidarity (or bandwagoning) with the liberal hegemon, which appears to be strongest in the elites of the UK and Australia. The country chapters suggest that this inclination is somehow stronger on the political right than on the left, but this is a nuanced, not a fixed bifurcation. On the other hand, distancing oneself from the US can motivate leaders to reject war participation (and they may score domestic points with such a position). This tendency appears to be stronger on the political left than on the right, but, again, these are no absolutes. This points to the more general question of whether there is a pattern regarding political camps and war participation: of the altogether 13 governments that decided in favour of war participation across the three wars, seven were centre-left and six were centre-right. Among those abstaining, five governments were centre-left and three were centre-right. In all three wars, the pattern was mixed (though the

---

[8] An interesting case in point was the German discourse on the deployment of German armed forces to the temporary EU force 'EUFOR RD Congo', which was to support the UN mission MONUC during the period encompassing the elections in the DR Congo in summer 2006. Since Germany was supposed to lead the EU mission, the national discourse, usually marked by normative argumentation, acquired exactly the 'realist' ring that 'bellicose' nations display: whether the mission was in the German 'national interest', whether the armed forces were adequately equipped at all and whether the mission would not be too dangerous. We thank Stephen Watts for suggesting this point to us.

'humanitarian intervention' in Kosovo attracted the greatest centre-left majority with four out of five centre-left governments participating, and the two conservative governments divided, one participating and one abstaining). There is thus no clear distribution pattern that would allow a prediction of participation along party political lines.

Second, internal decision-making within the US becomes a decisive determinant for almost all 'democratic wars'. The domestic decision-making process and the distribution of war support and aversion within the US thus play a crucial role for the frequency of democracies going to war. While one might intuitively ascribe a higher readiness to initiate military intervention to (neo)conservatives, the country chapter on the US does not support this hypothesis. War readiness appears to depend on the capability of the executive to frame a cause in terms of both values *and* national interests, and is often influenced by partisan politicking. It is the overall mood among the public and in the political class that seems to be the major influence on US war readiness. The crucial role of US leadership, contingent on US military hegemony, is a factor that deserves increased attention from those studying 'democratic wars'.

7.2   Democracies' potential for learning processes

Apart from the significance of the liberal hegemony of the US, which might be a passing historical phenomenon, a second aspect calls for contextualising the heuristics of 'democratic wars' in Table 11.1: it cannot anticipate learning processes like the 'Vietnam syndrome' that might occur in democratic publics following foreign policy disasters such as the Iraq War or the Afghanistan War. Among all regime types, liberal democracies possess the comparative advantage that policy failures can, in principle, be detected and debated publicly (Schmidt 2008: 458–61), which might motivate major policy changes in the future. The very term 'learning processes' carries strong normative assumptions, but should in our view be understood from the subjective perspective of the affected polity: as a discursive process in which 'failures' or 'wrong-doings' as well as responsibilities (for example, of one's political and/or military leadership) are recognised, debated and addressed.

Remarkably in this regard and typical for democracies only, the Netherlands reviewed their parliamentary powers in deployment issues following the war in Bosnia, the UK and Spain did so following the Iraq War (Eberl and Fischer-Lescano 2005; Houben 2005: 119–84) and France in the context of its Afghanistan mission. In a similar vein, numerous parliamentary inquiries following years after a government's decision to participate in a military action are a specifically democratic way of reviewing a problematic past event.[9] Undeniably, such efforts can yield several results: they might be confined to a critical debate with no palpable consequences; they might have short-term consequences, such as the indictment of individuals; or they might trigger long-term learning processes that entail institutional responses such as increasing parliamentary oversight power or juridical review competencies. Whatever the practical consequences are in specific cases, this democratic practice of retrospection and introspection could, in principle, influence the standards of appropriateness in a national polity.

The 2002 resignation of the entire Dutch government led by Wim Kok represents a singular response to an inquiry report – albeit by the Netherlands Institute for War Documentation, not parliament. This report on the massacre in Srebrenica in 1995 found that the Dutch soldiers responsible for the protection of the UN 'safe area' Srebrenica had failed completely to prevent the massacre, which was the worst single atrocity in Europe since the end of the Second World War. The report harshly criticised the government for sending its soldiers into a danger zone without a proper mandate or the weapons needed to defend the tens of thousands of refugees who had fled to the Dutch base seeking protection.

Although governmental decisions on war (non-)participations are often analysed independently of each other, such decisions are usually embedded in longer histories and narratives on the use of force and experiences with violence. Such narratives can be attached to a specific polity such as the 'never again war' narrative of post-Second World War Germany or the 'Vietnam trauma' of the US. But given that more recent military actions are often conducted jointly by coalitions, experiences of 'success' or 'failure', guilt or shame, can also be invoked as common narratives of several nations. It must be emphasised that specific experiences by themselves do not prescribe specific policy options for the future. Learning from past events might suggest intervening in future cases or refraining from costly involvements: for example, 'lessons learnt from the Bosnian War' was one important argument in the Western Kosovo discourse. Both Europeans and the US conceded that they had completely failed to deal adequately with the Bosnian conflict (1992–5), which claimed about a hundred thousand casualties in the midst of Europe, and recognised the necessity not to repeat that mistake in the Kosovo crisis. On the other hand, experiences with highly

---

[9] The Iraq War as the most disputed war among the three wars examined here led to quite a number of inquiries in the United States and the United Kingdom.

problematic and protracted military missions such as the more recent Iraq War and the Afghanistan War, which have involved Western troops in massive violent conflicts on the ground for years now, may trigger public debates on the limits to the material and human costs that a democratic public is willing to bear. Such dynamics are not anticipated in our heuristics since they are difficult to calculate. The German attitude towards the Libyan intervention discussed above is most probably an example of such an experience-driven reinforcement of an already considerable aversion to use force.

The Afghanistan case in particular might caution against further Western 'adventurism': public pressure on the governments to pull out sooner rather than later has been increasing in almost all the Western countries that participate in the Afghanistan mission, which has been continuing for more than a decade now, as casualties among their own troops rise and the impression of a lack of progress prevails. As the comparison in Chapter 10 shows, one's own casualties are the most relevant argument against military participation for those who otherwise advocate using military force in foreign policy. The experience of high losses for no viable cause might erect a new hurdle against future military missions (Gelpi *et al.* 2006). In other words: a withdrawal from Afghanistan without having achieved a clear victory might herald a new phase of restraint similar to the post-Vietnam era. Path-dependent shifts of attitudes towards military intervention thus present another important field for future inquiry.

8   A critical liberalism: normative ambivalence and historical contingency

In concluding this volume, we turn once again to liberalism – conceived both as the variety of International Relations (IR) theories of that brand and the dominant ideological fabric of Western democracies. Our investigation of 'democratic wars' shows that 'liberal reasons' for war, which Michael Doyle has highlighted in his interpretation of the Kantian legacy (Doyle 1983: 230), are not uniformly compelling. They are framed differently in the public discourses of different democracies, and they lead democratic actors to different conclusions. History, identities and role conceptions play a major role in these different outcomes. The foreign policies of liberal democracies are highly ambivalent in that they can foster peaceful relations as well as violent conflict and raise numerous dilemmas. While the ambivalence and contestedness of norms is an important topic in constructivist IR studies (Müller 2004; Wiener 2008), this has not been addressed adequately in DP research that focuses on the *peace promoting* effects of norms. Our study is intended to demonstrate the importance of normative ambivalence in democratic foreign policies.

Research on a 'democratic distinctiveness' in international politics (Owen 2004) has expanded enormously over the last decades (Geis and Wagner 2011), with 'democratic peace' remaining the nucleus of this theorising. Given the comprehensive literature on democracy and conflict behaviour, this cannot any longer be united under one common strand of liberal IR theory, but individual studies may draw on rationalist liberal theories, combinations with constructivist approaches, normative liberal internationalism, or even integrate realist variables.[10] Notwithstanding such diverse (meta)theoretical underpinnings of studies, the ambivalence of norms so far has no systematic place in research on democratic distinctiveness. One reason might be that such a conception of normative 'fuzziness' impedes the kind of parsimonious and coherent theorising on the domestic level of international politics, as, for example, Andrew Moravcsik (1997) has developed in his preference-based liberal theory. Another reason might be that normative ambivalence also disturbs the optimist narrative of liberal internationalism that envisions 'all good things going together', i.e. that connects democracy, international organisations, economic interdependence and peace in a virtuous cycle (Czempiel 1986; Russett and Oneal 2001).

Our study on 'democratic wars' combines elements of liberal theory (focusing on the domestic level and opening up the 'black box' of the nation-state) with constructivist approaches (conceiving of actors' preferences as malleable, of norms as crucial in understanding policy choices and of (normative) structures as enabling as well as restraining actors' choices). The national standards of appropriateness enshrined in collective identities and role conceptions are relatively stable but at the same time subject to change (Müller 2007). The contestation and interpretation of norms is path-dependent, but situated in a broader historical constellation that itself can change. As Tarak Barkawi and Mark Laffey (2001) rightly point out, mainstream DP research lacks a historical contextualisation of the main subjects of its studies, namely democracy, peace and war. In line with such an argument, we propose to study both democratic peace and war as historically contingent phenomena and not as 'facts'. Our approach of regarding democratic wars

---

[10] A comprehensive study in this regard is Russett and Oneal (2001), which draws on a number of theoretical strands. For overviews on the combination of liberal-constructivist and rationalist theories in the field of DP research, see Müller and Wolff (2006) and Panke and Risse (2007).

as the flipside of democratic peace does not confirm either highly optimist or completely bleak outlooks on the future.

We discussed in Section 7 above that 'democratic wars' might be a transient historical phenomenon of the liberal hegemony of the US. The inclination to fight 'democratic wars' is very much contingent upon the existence of a liberal superpower that leads other liberals into such wars and bears the brunt of the costs. Twenty years after the end of the Cold War, the global power constellations are more ambivalent (Müller 2009). Current debates on the world order deal with the consequences of the 'rise of authoritarian powers' such as China and Russia: will they be accommodated by the liberal powers? Will they turn themselves into liberal states in the long run? Or is liberal hegemony finally coming to an end, being replaced by a multipolar world (e.g. Gat 2007; Deudney and Ikenberry 2009; Mahbubani 2009)?

The unresolved debates on the future of the world order refer us back to the DP theory itself: the remarkable success of DP research in the US after the end of the Cold War can to a large extent be explained by an ideological alignment between liberal theory and practice (Hobson 2011) – DP research provided good news about democracy, legitimated the US foreign policy of 'democratic enlargement' and bolstered the prospect for a new peaceful (liberal) world order after the collapse of the Soviet Union. After more than two decades of extensive research, the mainstream research programme has passed its zenith. The historical and political setting has been changing significantly since 1990. Phases of democratic triumphalism in the earlier 1990s have been followed by disenchantment and scepticism regarding the further spread of democracy in the wake of the Iraq and Afghanistan Wars. Recently, the so-called 'Arab Spring' and the regime change war in Libya have seemed to reanimate democratic optimism. But narratives of the 'decline' of the West suggest that the global setting is quite different from the early 1990s (Cox 2011).

Given the indissoluble link between political theories and political practice (Ish-Shalom 2006; Geis 2011; Hobson 2011), one might conclude that the time is now also ripe for a more ambivalent scholarly narrative on democratic peace. Our findings underline that a 'triumphalist' and self-certain liberalism is unwarranted (Smith 2011). Instead, the return to the critical legacy of the Enlightenment is a good antidote: the practice of self-criticism and self-reflection (*Selbstaufklärung*) as an emancipatory exercise of the self as well as the acknowledgement of ambivalence should caution against liberal hubris. In this vein, our study is intended to contribute to a critical liberalism. The self-image of morally superior 'forces for good' held within liberal democracies is a soft-focus effect; a more accurate self-portrayal would reveal its Janus face.

REFERENCES

Barkawi, Tarak and Laffey, Mark 2001. 'Introduction: The International Relations of Democracy, Liberalism, and War', in Tarak Barkawi and Mark Laffey (eds.), *Democracy, Liberalism, and War: Rethinking the Democratic Peace Debate*. Boulder, CO: Lynne Rienner, pp. 1–24

Cox, Michael 2011. 'Power Shift and the Death of the West? Not Yet!', *European Political Science* 10 (3): 416–24

Czempiel, Ernst-Otto 1986. *Friedensstrategien. Systemwandel durch internationale Organisationen, Demokratisierung und Wirtschaft*. Paderborn: Schöningh

Deudney, Daniel and Ikenberry, G. John 2009. 'The Myth of the Autocratic Revival', *Foreign Affairs* 88 (1): 77–93

Doyle, Michael W. 1983. 'Kant, Liberal Legacies, and Foreign Affairs', *Philosophy and Public Affairs* 12 (3): 205–35

Dunne, Tim and Wheeler, Nicholas J. 2001. 'Blair's Britain: A Force For Good in the World?', in Karen E. Smith and Margot Light (eds.), *Ethics and Foreign Policy*. Cambridge University Press, pp. 167–84

Eberl, Oliver and Fischer-Lescano, Andreas 2005. 'Grenzen demokratischen Rechts? Die Entsendeentscheidungen zum Irakkrieg in Großbritannien, den USA und Spanien', *HSFK-Report* No. 8/2005, Frankfurt a.M.

Finnemore, Martha 2003. *The Purpose of Intervention: Changing Beliefs about the Use of Force*. Ithaca, NY: Cornell University Press

Freedman, Lawrence 2005. 'The Age of Liberal Wars', in David Armstrong, Theo Farrell and Bice Maiguashca (eds.), *Force and Legitimacy in World Politics*. Cambridge University Press, pp. 93–107

Gat, Azar 2007. 'The Return of Authoritarian Great Powers', *Foreign Affairs* 86 (4): 59–69

Geis, Anna 2011. 'Of Bright Sides and Dark Sides: Democratic Peace beyond Triumphalism', *International Relations* 25 (2): 18–24

Geis, Anna and Wagner, Wolfgang 2011. 'How Far Is It from Königsberg to Kandahar? Democratic Peace and Democratic Violence in International Relations', *Review of International Studies* 37 (4): 1555–77

Gelpi, Christopher, Feaver, Peter D. and Reifler, Jason 2006. 'Success Matters: Casualty Sensitivity and the War in Iraq', *International Security* 30 (3): 7–46

GMF (The German Marshall Fund of the United States) 2011. *Transatlantic Trends 2011: Topline Data July 2011*. Online: http://trends.gmfus.org/transatlantic-trends/topline-data

Heins, Volker and Chandler, David 2007. 'Ethics and Foreign Policy: New Perspectives on an Old Problem', in David Chandler and Volker Heins (eds.), *Rethinking Ethical Foreign Policy: Pitfalls, Possibilities and Paradoxes*. London: Routledge, pp. 3–21

Hobson, Christopher 2011. 'Introduction: Roundtable – Between the Theory and Practice of Democratic Peace', *International Relations* 25 (2): 147–50

Houben, Marc 2005. *International Crisis Management: The Approach of European States*. London: Routledge

Ish-Shalom, Piki 2006. 'Theory as a Hermeneutical Mechanism: The Democratic-Peace Thesis and the Politics of Democratization', *European Journal of International Relations* 12 (4): 565–98

Kowert, Paul and Legro, Jeffrey 1996. 'Norms, Identity, and Their Limits: A Theoretical Reprise', in Peter J. Katzenstein (ed.), *The Culture of National Security: Norms and Identity in World Politics*. New York, NY: Columbia University Press, pp. 451–97

Larson, Eric V. 1996. *Casualties and Consensus: The Historical Role of Casualties in Domestic Support for U.S. Military Operations*. Santa Monica, CA: RAND

MacMillan, John 2005. 'Introduction: The Iraq War and Democratic Politics', in John MacMillan and Alex Danchev (eds.), *The Iraq War and Democratic Politics*. London: Routledge, pp. 1–19

Mahbubani, Kishore 2009. 'The Dangers of Democratic Delusions', *Ethics & International Affairs* 23 (1): 19–25

Moravcsik, Andrew 1997. 'Taking Preferences Seriously: A Liberal Theory of International Politics', *International Organization* 51 (4): 513–53

Müller, Harald 2004. 'Arguing, Bargaining and All That: Communicative Action, Rationalist Theory and the Logic of Appropriateness in International Relations', *European Journal of International Relations* 10 (3): 395–435

   2007. 'Vorüberlegungen zu einer Theorie der Ambivalenz liberal-demokratischer Außen- und Sicherheitspolitik', in Anna Geis, Harald Müller and Wolfgang Wagner (eds.), *Schattenseiten des Demokratischen Friedens: Zur Kritik einer Theorie liberaler Außen- und Sicherheitspolitik*. Frankfurt a.M.: Campus, pp. 287–312

   2009. *Building a New World Order: Sustainable Policies for the Future*. London: Haus

Müller, Harald and Wolff, Jonas 2006. 'Democratic Peace: Many Data, Little Explanation?', in Anna Geis, Lothar Brock and Harald Müller (eds.), *Democratic Wars: Looking at the Dark Side of Democratic Peace*. Basingstoke: Palgrave Macmillan, pp. 41–73

Owen, John M. 2004. 'Democratic Peace Research: Whence and Whither?', *International Politics* 41 (4): 605–17

Panke, Diana and Risse, Thomas 2007. 'Liberalism', in Tim Dunne, Milja Kurki and Steve Smith (eds.), *International Relations Theories: Discipline and Diversity*. Oxford University Press, pp. 89–108

Russett, Bruce and Oneal, John 2001. *Triangulating Peace: Democracy, Interdependence, and International Organizations*. New York, NY: W. W. Norton

Schmidt, Manfred G. 2008. *Demokratietheorien: Eine Einführung*. Wiesbaden: VS Verlag für Sozialwissenschaften

Shaw, Martin 2005. *The New Western Way of War: Risk-Transfer War and Its Crisis in Iraq*. London: Polity Press

Smith, Tony 2011. 'Democratic Peace Theory: From Promising Theory to Dangerous Practice', *International Relations* 25 (2): 151–7

Vasquez, John A. 2005. 'Ethics, Foreign Policy, and Liberal Wars: The Role of Restraint in Moral Decision Making', *International Studies Perspective* 6 (3): 307–15

Vucetic, Srdjan 2011. 'Bound to Follow? The Anglosphere and US-led Coalitions of the Willing, 1950–2001', *European Journal of International Relations* 17 (1): 27–49

Wiener, Antje 2008. *The Invisible Constitution of Politics. Contested Norms and International Encounters.* Cambridge University Press

Wolf, Klaus Dieter 1999. 'The New Raison d'État as a Problem for Democracy in World Society', *European Journal of International Relations* 5 (3): 333–63

Appendix: methodology

1 Annex to the content analysis: calculation of the relevance and average relevance of a particular argument

In order to compare the argumentative structures of the different countries in Chapter 10, we did not refer to the simple frequency of the individual arguments, as cultures in parliamentary debate differed tremendously. While in some countries (e.g. the United States) members of the parliament used many arguments to make a case, MPs in other countries (e.g. Sweden) only referred to a few arguments. As a consequence, the figure of, for example, 30 per cent for a particular argument could mean that the argument was used either below or above average. To account for these differences, the frequencies of the arguments were standardised, thus stating the relative relevance of the arguments in relation to the average use of the arguments (the 'average argument'). The 'relevance' (or standardised frequency) is defined as the relation between the frequency (in per cent) of a particular argument and the frequency (in per cent) of the 'average argument' in a particular country and conflict. It shows whether or not a particular argument was used above or below average. Given three conflicts with 45 arguments coded in the content analysis, the calculation results in 135 data points.

Given A_{ikl} (frequency of argument i in per cent during conflict k in country l), the 'relevance' of each argument in the individual debate is calculated as follows:

$REL_{ikl} = \dfrac{A_{ikl}}{\left(\sum\limits_{i=1}^{45} A_{ikl}\right)/45} \times 100$. Consequently, the average relevance of an argument of a specific country in all three conflicts is: $RELAV_{il} = \left(\sum\limits_{k=1}^{3} REL_{ikl}\right)/3$.

The average relevance of particular arguments in all three conflicts and all countries – except Australia – is depicted in Table A.1. The average relevance of individual arguments in all seven countries in the Gulf War 1990–1 and the Iraq War 2003 (including all countries) is shown in Table A.2.

Table A.1 *Average relevances of individual arguments; six countries, three conflicts*

Argument	Country						Average (three conflicts)
	CAN	FRA	GER	SWE	UK	USA	
1101 national interest	0	51	39	0	75	111	46
1102 keep/improve power position	0	21	0	0	87	41	25
1103 regional stability	117	137	103	29	215	252	142
1104 show of force	376	270	283	386	353	252	320
1105 national security	24	31	36	0	83	127	50
1201 military superiority	69	54	29	0	43	54	41
1202 clear military/ exit strategy	0	64	16	0	0	29	18
1301 national interest contra	6	21	47	30	32	113	41
1302 loss of power	6	19	9	0	137	93	44
1303 regional instability	129	182	172	265	130	86	161
1304 increasing insecurity	24	73	60	0	54	79	48
1305 lacking power capabilities	52	10	9	0	32	16	20
1306 lacking military/exit strategy	0	41	76	94	59	121	65
1307 national security not concerned	8	0	9	0	54	93	27
2101 alliance pro (internal aspects)	151	63	180	0	39	54	81
2102 alliance pro (external aspects)	6	11	56	0	76	36	31
2201 alliance consensus	28	131	45	0	54	57	52
2301 alliance contra (internal aspects)	24	72	9	0	6	16	21
2302 alliance contra (external aspects)	0	42	36	0	0	5	14

Table A.1 (*cont.*)

Argument	Country						Average (three conflicts)
	CAN	FRA	GER	SWE	UK	USA	
3101 identity norms	287	160	227	0	103	188	161
3102 role conception	41	21	33	10	0	42	24
3201 identity/role compatibility	81	9	29	10	0	0	21
3301 restraining identity/role norms	110	75	222	156	23	62	108
3302 rejection of role ascription	0	0	0	0	11	47	10
3303 restraining expectations by others	29	36	0	59	0	39	27
4101 enforce international law/ support UN	112	186	286	250	253	181	211
4201 covered by international law	122	191	123	127	178	127	145
4202 peaceful means exhausted	276	283	132	266	142	128	204
4301 no UN mandate/damage to UN	209	252	342	402	160	52	236
4302 peaceful means not exhausted	363	399	502	897	173	205	423
5101 humanitarian catastrophe	333	178	280	350	394	232	294
5102 threat to world order	125	103	68	68	252	151	128
5201 multilateral consensus pro	92	109	47	104	88	132	95
5301 world order not threatened	49	18	9	20	24	51	28
5302 pacifism/war damages global norms	144	161	235	196	153	66	159
5303 civilian casualties	245	194	183	270	181	27	183
5304 multilateral war rejection	38	146	83	58	45	47	69
6101 regime change/ democratisation	24	11	0	113	106	70	54
6201 democratic norms/procedures respected	15	23	33	0	72	64	34

Table A.1 (*cont.*)

Argument	Country						Average (three conflicts)
	CAN	FRA	GER	SWE	UK	USA	
6202 cost reduction by swift action	41	10	0	0	58	84	32
6301 democratic norms/procedures contra war	217	216	189	127	109	121	163
6302 casualty aversion (own soldiers)	105	96	87	0	150	268	118
6303 prohibitive material costs	26	10	9	59	5	120	38
7101 enemy image of adversary	309	194	120	107	242	307	213
7301 enemy image questioned	86	129	45	49	52	51	69

Table A.2 *Average relevances of individual arguments; seven countries, Gulf War 1990–1 and Iraq War 2003 only*

Argument	Country							Average (Gulf War and Iraq War only)
	AUS	CAN	FRA	GER	SWE	UK	USA	
1101 national interest	159	0	77	48	0	96	112	70
1102 keep/improve power position	105	0	31	0	0	131	62	47
1103 regional stability	167	176	120	78	44	193	199	140
1104 show of force	306	272	181	206	439	221	192	260
1105 national security	75	36	46	55	0	125	176	73
1201 military superiority	72	20	46	0	0	65	81	40
1202 clear military/exit strategy	63	0	62	13	0	0	29	24
1301 national interest contra	90	10	31	71	44	48	92	55
1302 loss of power	23	10	29	13	0	92	94	37

Table A.2 (*cont.*)

Argument	Country							Average (Gulf War and Iraq War only)
	AUS	CAN	FRA	GER	SWE	UK	USA	
1303 regional instability	67	193	222	193	397	146	114	190
1304 increasing insecurity	69	36	110	89	0	81	111	71
1305 lacking power capabilities	55	36	15	13	0	15	0	19
1306 lacking military/exit strategy	57	0	27	71	0	8	81	35
1307 national security not concerned	6	12	0	13	0	81	100	30
2101 alliance pro (internal aspects)	82	61	77	106	0	42	11	54
2102 alliance pro (external aspects)	7	10	0	29	0	0	0	7
2201 alliance consensus	0	0	93	13	0	0	0	15
2301 alliance contra (internal aspects)	55	36	73	13	0	9	0	27
2302 alliance contra (external aspects)	6	0	29	0	0	0	0	5
3101 identity norms	143	138	120	198	0	105	150	122
3102 role conception	42	20	31	16	15	0	40	23
3201 identity/role compatibility	0	79	13	32	15	0	0	20
3301 restraining identity/role norms	23	165	112	279	234	18	70	129
3302 rejection of role ascription	13	0	0	0	0	0	40	8
3303 restraining expectations by others	48	44	54	0	89	0	36	39
4101 enforce international law/ support UN	252	168	245	363	234	331	194	255
4201 covered by international law	191	100	166	108	190	202	136	156
4202 peaceful means exhausted	151	81	166	165	118	164	161	144

Table A.2 (*cont.*)

Argument	Country							Average (Gulf War and Iraq War only)
	AUS	CAN	FRA	GER	SWE	UK	USA	
4301 no UN mandate/damage to UN	152	271	275	240	322	126	70	208
4302 peaceful means not exhausted	255	544	478	622	924	227	269	474
5101 humanitarian catastrophe	93	0	27	81	102	137	62	72
5102 threat to world order	232	145	137	81	102	378	211	184
5201 multilateral consensus pro	187	96	77	60	15	131	182	107
5301 world order not threatened	71	73	27	13	29	36	69	45
5302 pacifism/war damages global norms	45	216	207	309	293	181	76	190
5303 civilian casualties	153	367	170	252	264	158	41	201
5304 multilateral war rejection	75	56	219	125	88	68	70	100
6101 regime change/ democratisation	52	36	0	0	29	78	89	41
6201 democratic norms/procedures respected	71	22	0	16	0	92	80	40
6202 cost reduction by swift action	94	20	15	0	0	87	95	45
6301 democratic norms/procedures contra war	159	325	238	240	191	131	104	198
6302 casualty aversion (own soldiers)	222	157	93	44	0	128	255	128
6303 prohibitive material costs	6	40	15	13	88	8	126	42
7101 enemy image of adversary	248	298	170	147	160	283	352	237
7301 enemy image questioned	61	129	176	68	73	78	69	94

2   Annex to the analysis of newspaper editorials

For the analysis of newspaper commentaries and editorials, a maximum of 25 articles each were taken from a left-liberal and from a conservative newspaper of a country. In cases where the universe of pertinent articles exceeded this number, the researcher drew a random sample. Only when a particular newspaper was not available for a certain year, were additional newspapers taken into account. Since many editorials had no clear-cut position on the question of whether or not their country should or should not participate in war, it was decided to abstain from submitting the editorials to a systematic content analysis (as the content analysis rested upon a coding scheme that was tailored for discernible yes/no positions on a participation with own troops).

Country	*Newspaper (left-liberal; right of centre or conservative)*
Australia	*Sydney Morning Herald; The Australian*
Canada	*Toronto Star; Globe and Mail*
France	*Le Monde; Le Figaro*
Germany	*Süddeutsche Zeitung; Frankfurter Allgemeine Zeitung*
Sweden	*Aftonbladet; Svenska Dagbladet*
UK	*The Guardian; The Times*
US	*New York Times; Washington Times*

Index